Syrene Soundes

Syrene Soundes

False Relations in the English Renaissance

ELEANOR CHAN

OXFORD
UNIVERSITY PRESS

Oxford University Press is a department of the University of Oxford.
It furthers the University's objective of excellence in research, scholarship,
and education by publishing worldwide. Oxford is a registered trade mark of
Oxford University Press in the UK and in certain other countries.

Published in the United States of America by Oxford University Press
198 Madison Avenue, New York, NY 10016, United States of America.

© Oxford University Press 2024

All rights reserved. No part of this publication may be reproduced, stored in
a retrieval system, or transmitted, in any form or by any means, without the prior
permission in writing of Oxford University Press, or as expressly permitted
by law, by license or under terms agreed with the appropriate reprographics
rights organization. Inquiries concerning reproduction outside the scope of the
above should be sent to the Rights Department, Oxford University Press, at the
address above.

You must not circulate this work in any other form
and you must impose this same condition on any acquirer.

Library of Congress Cataloging-in-Publication Data
Names: Chan, Eleanor (Professor of history of musical culture), author.
Title: Syrene soundes : false relations in the English Renaissance / Eleanor Chan.
Other titles: Serene sounds
Description: [1.] | New York : Oxford University Press, 2024. |
Includes bibliographical references and index.
Identifiers: LCCN 2024022856 (print) | LCCN 2024022857 (ebook) |
ISBN 9780197748176 (hardback) | ISBN 9780197748190 (epub)
Subjects: LCSH: Music—England—16th century—History and criticism. |
Music—England—17th century—History and criticism. | Music—Social
aspects—England—History—16th century. | Music—Social
aspects—England—History—17th century. | Dissonance
(Music)—History—16th century. | Dissonance (Music)—History—
17th century. | Renaissance—England—History.
Classification: LCC ML286.2 .C43 2024 (print) | LCC ML286.2 (ebook) |
DDC 781.2/390942—dc23/eng/20240719
LC record available at https://lccn.loc.gov/2024022856
LC ebook record available at https://lccn.loc.gov/2024022857

DOI: 10.1093/9780197748206.001.0001

Printed by Integrated Books International, United States of America

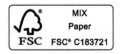

For my 阿媽 Meiling, ninety years young and always the first on and last off the dance floor.

Contents

Acknowledgements   ix
Preface   xiii

1. Introduction: The False Note, Descant, String: A History of a Foundling   1
   Thou Hast Some Crotchets in Thy Head Now   1
   How Soft Is Your Hexachord   14
   Picturing the Hexachord   23
   False Relations and the Myth of the Musical Golden Age   35
   Plan of the Book   45

SECTION I THINKING

2. The Rhetoric of Falseness or, How to Talk about a Discord   53
   Of Discords She Maketh the Sweetest Harmony   60
   Varieties of Sweetness   82
   Voicing Sweetness   95
   Conclusion: False Sweetness   109

3. Painting with Falseness: Wording Your Discord   112
   Sing to Song to Sing: In Defence of Melisma   112
   Repeat Repeat   121
   A Point   131

4. Visualizing Falseness: Or, How to Look at a Discord   137
   Discord: A Study in Silverpoint   137
   Picturing the 'Substance of Musicke'   150
   Picturing Discord   164

SECTION II PERFORMING

5. How to Train Your Discord: Performing Falseness   183
   Miscellaneity, Mélange, Melée   183
   Learning the Notes   185
   (P)laying the Table: 'O salutaris hostia'   192
   Reading Miscellaneity   207

6. *Una nota supra La/Semper est canendum Fa*: A Tale
   of Two Semitones — 212
   Exit La, pursued by Pha — 212
   A Cadence by Any Other Name Would Smell as Sweet — 221
   'Deformitie hidden by Flurish' — 235
   A Leading Note: Enter Weelkes, Aloft — 245

Afterword: 'The Bitter-Sweetest Achromaticke' — 250

Appendix I — 267
Appendix II — 287
Appendix III — 297
Bibliography — 385
Index — 405

Acknowledgements

This is a pandemic book. This is a lockdown book. This is a book written under the shadow of chronic illness. This is a book written by a full-time carer. All these conditions have influenced its shape and generation; and it is all the better for it. It might seem strange to acknowledge the working conditions under which a book was written, but I realize that such things are so often little talked about, and that as a result we allow narratives of only one type of academic working—holed away, isolated, intense, and deep-focussed periods of writing—to perpetuate. These models work for some, but not for all. I mention this on the off chance that someone someday will read this and that it might bring them solidarity, strength, and remind them they are not alone and that they, too, can do this book-writing thing. There are so, so many different ways to do academia.

And so thank you:

To the cheerleaders, who have supported this book in its most embryonic of forms (idea, rant, discussion-over-pint-or-cup-of-tea, extremely patchy drafts, for the briefest of snatched incidental moments and chats in library corridors or for the long haul): Richard Wistreich (who has witnessed this project's slow evolution over almost a decade, and whose kindness truly knows no bounds), Rebecca Herissone (the most excellent, endlessly patient, generous of mentors), Katie Bank (my road trip companion, my avatar, and my all-seeing eyes), Jenny Richards, Tim Shephard, Christine Griffiths, Katherine Butler, Samatha Bassler, Matthew Champion, Esther Osorio-Whewell, Hester Lees-Jeffries, Roddy Hawkins, Magnus Williamson, David Skinner (who first gave me the idea for this project), Kat Carson, Alan Howard, Edward Wickham, Nicolo Ferrari, Raphael Lyne, Joe Ortiz, Samantha Arten, Paddy Fumerton, Liam Hynes-Tawa, and Hannah Yip.

To the marvellous Edward Tambling for his beautiful, meticulous editions and typesetting of the Bennet, Morley, Tomkins, Byrd, and longer Weelkes; and to Bonnie Blackburn for the shorter examples of Morley, Tallis, and Weelkes in Chapter 6.

To the receptive audiences at RSA 2021 and MedRen 2020 and 2021 who heard extremely early forms of Chapters 2 and 6.

ACKNOWLEDGEMENTS

To my students, particularly Ndego, Tabi, Josh, George, Tristan, Miluka, Romano, and Alfie, whose intensely perceptive questions provided some of the most significant building blocks of this book whilst I was deeply mired in the writing process.

To Ketty Gottardo and Rachel Sloan at the Witt Collection at the Courtauld; to the kind people at National Trust Images, and everyone at Hardwick Hall, particularly Peter Randle for allowing me over the rope!

To everyone at OUP, for their infectious enthusiasm; particularly Norm Hirschy, Rachel Ruisard, and Steve Rings. A version of Chapter 6 appeared as 'The Etymology of the English Cadence', in *Music & Letters* 104: 3 (August 2023); thanks also to OUP for allowing reproduction of the material.

To the Leverhulme Trust and the Paul Mellon Centre for Studies in British Art, for generously funding this research.

To the ones who just wanted to sing early music and got disappointed whenever anything later than Bach was brought out (unless, of course, it was Cascada): James Dougal, Alex Coplan, Oli Franks, Dan Hurst, Sarah Hess, Gemma Cooper, Marcus Fantham, Mary Price, Sam Niblett, Esther (again), Conrad Watt, Laurence Price, Dan Leung, Rob Pellow, Kasia Ruskowski, Amber Reeves-Piggott, Frey Kalus, Emma Wroth, Eli Bond, Will Barnes-McCallum. Choir love is true love.

To the many, many long-suffering choirs I have sung in, with both conspicuously emphasized and conspicuously avoided false relations. In particular, to Derek: you really, *really* should have kept them in. To Sandy, Richard, Chris, Andrew, Elizabeth, Jamie, Alex, Alex, Will, Alex, and Henry, thank you for doing so.

To Cynthia Patterson, who taught three generations of Brightonian children music, and who believed it was worth teaching five-year-olds to read, sight-read, solmize, and perform music in professional contexts. Rock on.

To the sanity-maintaining ride-or-dies, thirty years and going steady, an homage to the music we made together right at the very beginning when we were still in single figures: Alice Williams, Emma Skinner, Emily Winstanley, Sarah Beard, Prash Navaratnam, Ali Hawkins, Elly Humphrey, Danny Glebocki. For the relative newbies: Rich Brown, Christian and Sarah Gray-Stephens-(Martin), Alice Robinson, Jenna Pearce, Ellen Taplin, Joe Beecham, Lulu Walmesley-Browne, Anna Delves, Emma Close-Brooks, Pete and Becky Bullock, Jack Williams, Josh Bleakley, Tariq Kwaja, Taj Deluca, Jack Taylor, Zoe Greenslade.

Once again to the tireless efforts of my feline research assistants, Opaltinaturnersoldierspy alias 'the Catan Bandit' (rest in peace, my darling), the Lady Ivington 'the Ives of March', and Juniper 'Juniboppers', 'Junitunes', 'The Murder Pancake', who gave and continue to give their unparalleled efforts and expertise whenever and however possible. 'er4', nmjk,,,,l;'lk67b n?""""""JBN'.

And finally thank you to Richard Lewis, my first reader and constant, calming companion during the writing of this book, who possesses an uncanny and unfailing capacity to make Radio 3 play atonal, discordant, or experimental music whenever he walks into a room. Still waiting on that champagne cocktail.

This book is also brought to you by Kate Bush's excellent album *Hounds of Love* (before it was cool, obviously); Wet Leg; Beyoncé; as ever, the marvellous Cher; and *The Lord of the Rings* complete soundtrack.

Preface

The Tritone Game

Once upon a time I was in a choir that loved three things above all else: early music, complaining about and yet secretly relishing experimental atonality, and games (Articulate!, Botticelli, the Magnificat Game, 'Darling Ball'—their own particularly brutal variation on water polo—you name it). In this crucible of filthy sonic transgression, the 'Tritone Game' was born. The rules were simple: you find a willing friend (or enemy) and sing a tritone (a diminished fifth or augmented fourth) apart. For those not so nerdily inclined, that's 'Mar-i-(a)' from Leonard Bernstein's *West Side Story*, or the opening two notes from the theme tune from *The Simpsons*. On the count of three, you choose to move a semitone (or, if you like, a *Jaws* theme tune) upwards or downwards (without prior agreement from said opponent/accomplice). If you both resolve in opposite directions (onto a minor sixth or major sixth or third), you 'win'. If you both resolve upwards or downwards, onto a parallel tritone, you 'lose'. It is incredibly simple, costs little time or effort, and can be played ad infinitum as you sit waiting on a train, plane, bus, or for said train, plane, or bus to arrive, from a vaporetto cruising up a Venetian canal on a sultry evening or huddling in an uncannily abandoned and disintegrating Serbian water park in freezing fog in −4 degrees centigrade, or indeed in the green room between rehearsal and concert, much to the chagrin of your fellow choristers after the first fifteen minutes or so. Incredibly simple, and the spectral, fragmentary remnant of almost a thousand years' worth of musical history and a way of reading music that has embedded itself in the substructure of our imaginations when we encounter any piece of music today.

The rules that once governed the way that the music of the English Renaissance was composed, performed, and read have long since fallen out of use. However, as the 'Tritone Game' demonstrates, they certainly had not fallen out of relevance. As this book seeks to demonstrate, these performance and composition rules had relevance that extended far beyond the sphere of technical musicology, too. Musical rules, in terms not just of their expectations but also of their physical and material deployment on the page and stage, can aid understanding of English Renaissance attitudes towards print, textualities, performance, visual culture, concepts of native English tradition, and metaphors of harmony that will be of use to scholars from across the gamut of disciplines, from book history, material culture, art history, and literary studies to historians of religion. These ways of reading music evolved during the great boom in literacy brought about by the arrival of print technologies, and during a great period of political, religious, social, and cultural turbulence. False relations—one key by-product of these performance and composition rules—are thus, amongst other things, matters of reading. They are inscribed with the anxieties of the period, and an intense need to render discord and dissonance musically beautiful and meaningful. Tritones and their fellow false relations can give insight into developing discourses of textualities, the blending of the visual and the verbal, fascination with the visual appearance of print, and the manifold ways that the people of the English Renaissance related to printed and written objects under the aspect of reading. Engagement with a text (like a piece of music notation) was a far more intricate and dynamic process during this period, and negotiating its visual complexities and parameters was frequently inherent in the way it generated meaning. Literacy was not assumed to be in a binary state of 'can/cannot'; partial literacy was far more common and, fuelled by the development of how-to books from the mid-sixteenth century onwards, music was no exception. As Katherine Hunt recently observed:

> What is being taught in [didactic how-to] texts is not only the recipe for posset or the best way to graft a plant, but also how to enter into a community of people who have the same aspirations, imperfect understanding, and varieties of curiosity as you. Further, because these are written texts, what is also being taught—if obliquely—is an understanding of reading and writing, and their limits.[1]

Reading was typically done aloud, not silently. It was often communal, rather than individual. It was, as a result, likely not continuous but a lively collage of interruptions, repetitions, participation. False relations dramatized the trials and tribulations of this style of reading, and the visual delight of

---

[1] Katherine Hunt, 'What Did Didactic Literature Teach? Change-ringing Manuals, Printed Miscellanies and Forms of Active Reading', in *Renaissance Studies*, 36: 5 (November 2022), 686–704, at 689.

negotiating between a sign as text (or 'meaningful') and as image (or 'meaningless'). Even in the sixteenth century they were a nostalgic throwback to an older way of music-making; they were thus adopted for their capacity to bring sheer sonic joy, and for religious and political ends as the long English Reformation ground onwards, imperial ambitions seeped throughout the developing concept of nationhood, and the desire for a mythologized tradition of 'English' music-making grew.

Music is a particularly enlightening case study when thinking about the dynamic nature of reading in the English Renaissance, because it relied intensely upon its graphic visuality. The shape of the hexachord system inherited from forms such as the Guidonian Hand—and the rules ordaining when and where to mutate from one to the other, how to solmize (read) its shapes and how to treat pitch—all linger behind the modern stave and its orthochronic notation. Chief amongst these traces is the positioning of the semitone interval (that *Jaws* moment again). As we shall discover throughout the course of this book, the hexachordal system permits a semitone only between *mi* and *fa* (the third and fourth degree of the hexachord) and *la* and *pha* (the sixth, and seventh degree if permitted in certain harmonic contexts). Tritones are the original false relation, as ordained by the rule '*Mi contra Fa diabolus est in Musica*' or '*Mi* against *Fa* is the devil in music'. In the period directly before the turn to tonality across the seventeenth century, *mi* against *fa* provided a gateway into a tantalizing realm of tonal possibility, possibilities that were explored, exploited, and relished by Thomas Tallis, John Sheppard, William Byrd, Thomas Weelkes, Martin Peerson, and Thomas Tomkins, and many other characters who will feature in this book.

This exploration of tonal possibility, and the delight that it brought, is what is rehearsed hundreds of years later in the Tritone Game. Over repeated matches, certain things reveal themselves. It is almost always easier to 'win' a game if you are playing with someone with whom you have previously sung a voice part, because sharing a voice part with someone seemingly acquaints you with the finely shaded gradations of their voices and the minute differences in the sound they produce when they are about to move up or down a semitone. It reinforces your sense of pitch. It is incredibly intimate. It is visual: it works perfectly well as a spectator sport. And, finally, there is a delicious, transgressive pleasure in both singing and listening to a parallel tritone. The Tritone Game is from a tiny microcosm, but examples of its lessons can be found in the day-to-day occurrences in choirs of the English choral tradition from elite to amateur.

When a singer unused to early music repertoire is presented with their first slab of sumptuous sixteenth-century polyphony, one of the questions they often ask is: 'how did you know when to flatten/sharpen that note?' And for many experienced performers of early music, the answer is simply that they do not know: they did it subconsciously. In other words, they solmized it; their bodies and their sonic imaginations know what the music should sound like, even if their minds were not able to articulate how or why. Likewise, when a certain sort of choir director opts to bowdlerize the false relations from a piece from the much-abused *Oxford Book of Tudor Anthems* in the belief that Tallis, Farrant, and so forth should be performed like a work of the High Victorian composer Charles Villiers Stanford—an experience I sincerely hope few of you will have had to endure—the effect is frequently of disrupting the tonal core of the music, rather than reinforcing it by doing away with pesky chromaticisms. False relations stand as an enigmatic monument to a past musical culture, seemingly simple, frivolous musical ornaments to the proper musical meat, and yet at the same time an invaluable lens into the pitch structures of the time. Solmization is alive and well. Long after its heyday, its structures, rules, and regulations continue to influence the way that music is learned, read, and sonically choreographed by an ensemble in performance.

This book tells the story of false relations in the English Renaissance. It does not seek to supersede meticulous preexisting technical studies of the subject (such as Karol Berger's 1987 *Musica Ficta* or Peter Urquhart's 2021 *Sharps, Flats and the Problem of Musica Ficta*) but rather to flesh out the ways that false relations, as a musical theoretical concept, complemented textual, visual, and material concerns from the broader English culture. Such context is vital for understanding the popularity, potency, and significance of false relations in England during this period. The turbulent early years of the Church of England—between Henry VIII's break from Rome in 1533, and the rise of William Laud as Archbishop of Canterbury in the 1630s—were in many ways the golden age of the false relation; they appeared in music in both elite and popular contexts, in elaborate, expensive manuscript collections and in printed broadsides, in sacred and later secular repertoire. On the way, they left their traces upon musical objects, and those we would not traditionally recognize as musical (the furnishings and interiors that surrounded musical recreation, the plays, poems, and sermons that used music as analogy, metaphor, and context). These traces can tell us much about the shifting political, religious, and cultural climates of the sixteenth and early seventeenth centuries, as well as the move towards tonality as a governing pitch structure, and the preference for harmonic over melodic musical form.

False relations shed light on a huge number of concepts that were in flux during this period. The metaphor of harmony, for example, means something very different when we consider that it typically entailed a carefully mannered use of dissonance to enhance a piece's harmonic quality. The question of how people visualized music, likewise, changed greatly during this period, shifting as a greater proportion of the population became familiar with what musical notation looked like. As a topic, false relations are of huge importance beyond the realms of academic music. For those interested in the literature, religious, political, and visual cultures of the English Renaissance, they can offer a crucial lens into the way that thought around music and its metaphors were being constructed. False relations are thus meaningful on both a superficial and on a deeper level. What follows is an exploration of ways that we can approach their enigmatic meanings, allowing them to speak their own, contemporary language, and demonstrate their own eloquence unburdened by subsequent concepts of tonality, form, and expression.

1
Introduction

The False Note, Descant, String: A History of a Foundling

Thou Hast Some Crotchets in Thy Head Now

Here Prospero uncovers Ferdinand and Miranda playing at chess.

MIRANDA *(to Ferdinand)* Sweet lord, you play me false.
FERDINAND No, my dearest love,
  I would not for the world.
MIRANDA Yes, for a score of kingdoms you should wrangle,
  And I would call it fair play.[1]

The '*solemn and strange music*', neither 'o'the air or the earth', has ended. The disarming shimmer of sonic fog has dissipated. The 'charm' is done, leaving silence and reality. And yet, as Prospero lifts the enchantment that has enabled him to reap his revenge upon Alonso (the man who had ousted him as Duke of Milan and inadvertently left him to be stranded on an enchanted island), perhaps the most magical scene of the play occurs. With a theatrical flourish, Prospero reveals his daughter, Miranda, and Alonso's son Ferdinand (missing, presumed dead), freshly in love and playing chess. Their conversation highlights somewhat more than lovers' banter and Miranda's playful revelation that the unworldliness that Prospero has fought to preserve is already crumbling. Amidst this web of false, dissembling relations (brothers, fathers, daughters, sons) lurks the shadow of a playful musical pun:[2] the falseness of music and its ability to play, mislead, and/or reveal, and the chromatic figure

---

[1] William Shakespeare, *The Tempest*, in *Mr William Shakespeares comedies, histories and tragedies*, 5.1, 175–179.

[2] Examining the cognates of word histories has become an increasingly important approach in historical analysis for those phenomena that are little documented in contemporary sources. See, e.g., Alexander Marr, Raphaele Garrod, Jose Ramon Marcaida, and Richard Oosterhoff (eds.), *Logodaedalus: Word Histories of Ingenuity in Early Modern Europe* (Pittsburgh: University of Pittsburgh Press, 2018); Ita MacCarthy, *Renaissance Keywords* (London: Legenda, 2013); Neil

of accidental inflection[3] that would become known, 300 years later, as a 'false relation'.[4] There is no explicit mention of music in this briefest of scenes, but it echoes throughout in the broader context of the thoroughly musical and music-driven plot of *The Tempest*, and in the language that Miranda adopts. To 'wrangle' was to conduct an angry dispute or noisy quarrel; it could also be a controversy, or a disputatious answer or argument.[5] Like music, it is sonic, aural, and oral. It is to altercate, contend, or bicker; to engage in controversy. Later, it was used to describe the act of influencing or persuading a person by wrangling or contention; to argue out of possession. All these meanings—the persuasion, the rhetoric, the noise, the controversy—are present in Miranda's riposte.

Foregrounding the sonic context and reading this scene through a musical lens raises exciting possibilities. What happens when we explore the far, murky reaches of a musical culture? What happens when we take seriously what those far reaches suggest about a musical culture? What happens when we approach an unassuming musical feature like a false relation through

---

Kenny, *Curiosity in Early Modern Europe: Word Histories* (Wiesbaden: Harassowitz, 1998). For more on the connection between music and play in this period, see Katie Bank, '(Re)creating the Eglantine Table', in *Early Music*, 48: 3 (2020), 359–376; and Patrick Ball, 'The Playing Cards and Gaming Boards', in Michael Fleming and Christopher Page (eds.), *Music and Instruments of the Elizabethan Age: The Eglantine Table* (Suffolk: Boydell & Brewer, 2021), 47–56.

[3] Karol Berger, *Musica Ficta: Theories of Accidental Inflection in Vocal Polyphony from Marchetto da Padova to Gioseffi Zarlino* (Cambridge: Cambridge University Press, 1987).

[4] These are the *Oxford English Dictionary*'s citations for the 'false relation' prior to its entry into common parlance in the twentieth century, none of which directly corresponds to the meaning of false relation, but all of which give a sense that the concept had latent linguistic significance during the period. Thomas Morley talks about 'false' and 'true' notes in his *Plaine and Easie Introduction to Practicall Musicke* (1597, at 92); his contemporary, John Davies, of 'false accords from her false strings be sent' (*Nosce Tepisum*, 1599, at 91). Later, Francis Bacon would state of the lute string that 'if it be unequall in his parts [. . .] we call False' (*Sylva Sylvarum*, 1626, at 171), and John Playford's edition of Thomas Campion's *Art of Composing Musick in Parts* (1655) would describe 'false fourths' and 'false fifths', 38; see https://www.oed.com/view/Entry/67884?redirectedFrom=false+relation#eid4705417 (accessed 5 November 2021). These are far from describing the same entities and epitomize the obfuscation of the false relation from its very origins. Contemporary use of the term tends to bear the connotation of a thing that does not correlate to its context, as we might expect. See, e.g., Cyril Tourneur, *The Atheist's tragedie, or The honest man's revenge* (London: Thomas Snodham, 1611), 3.1.
CHARLEMONT: O! here's the fatall monument of my [/] Dead father first presented to mine eye. [/] What's here? In memory of Charlemont? [/] Some false relation has abus'd beliefe. [/] I am deluded. But I thanke thee Heaven. [/] For ever let me be deluded thus.

[5] The Oxford English Dictionary Online (accessed 5 November 2021). By contrast, 'falseness' where it appears in early modern dictionaries does not tend to have sonic or musical connotations. Compare to Randle Cotgrave's 1611 account of 'discord'; a 'discord' is 'jarring, repugnancie, disagreement, variance, debate, altercation, strife; dissension, contention', and 'without any order or harmonie' whilst 'discordant' is 'most harsh, most untuneable'. Randle Cotgrave, *A Dictionarie of the French and English Tongues* (London: Adam Islip, 1611), fol. Ddijv.

the hinterlands of musical culture, where it intersects with the visual, the literary, the political, the religious, the intellectual? What can such an approach do to help us understand, or begin to understand a phenomenon so little documented at the time, and yet littered throughout the surviving musical works of the period, both sacred and secular? In seeking to answer these questions, *Syrene Soundes: False Relations in the English Renaissance* concerns itself not just with the notes on the page, but with the way that they influenced the broader culture of the time as the performable music they represented, as the idea of music, and as the visual, inky marks they are made of: simultaneously music, Music, and 'music', performance, notation, and the bridging between them, all of which serve as evidence for musical investigation.[6]

False (or 'cross') relations manifest as all three forms of musical evidence. In this way, they are pertinent not just to technical studies of music theory but also to those interested in the idea of music in the English Renaissance, and in their ramifications for their contemporary visual culture. They are a key stylistic feature in the polyphony of the Renaissance, and despite (or perhaps because of) this, they are curiously undocumented. We could do worse than following Peter Urquhart's 1993 definition as 'the succession of a pitch in one voice by the chromatic alteration of that pitch (or its equivalent in another octave) in another voice'; as he observes, 'the "cross" aspect of the relationship refers to the use of two different voices, and does not have anything to do with their temporal relationship. For that reason, the definition may include the "simultaneous cross-relation", that is, the simultaneous sounding of a pitch and its alteration. [...] Simultaneous cross-relations arise under the same circumstances that create non-simultaneous ones';[7] in other words, what Kian-Seng Teo referred to as 'alternate degree inflection'.[8] Today they are graphically marked as notes with the appearance of the same letter-name in different parts of the same or proximate chords, one inflected with a sharp ♯ or flat ♭ symbol, and the other uninflected or marked ♮ (see Ex. 1.1, taken from Thomas Tallis' 'O nata lux'). In the sixteenth century, they were

---

[6] In this I aim to follow Cristle Collins Judd with her assertion that 'it is worth emphasizing that the notation in which earlier music survives is only a trace of musical practice'. See Cristle Collins Judd, 'Introduction: Analyzing Early Music', in Cristle Collins Judd (ed.), *Tonal Structures in Early Music* (New York: Garland, 2000), at 5.

[7] Peter Urquhart, 'Cross Relations by Franco-Flemish Composers after Josquin', in *Tijdschrift van de Vereniging voor Nederlandse Muziekgeschiedenis*, 43: 1 (1993), 3 and 3–4. See also Peter Urquhart, *Sound and Sense in Franco-Flemish Music of the Renaissance: Sharps, Flats and the Problem of 'Musica Ficta'* (Leuven: Peeters, 2021), 1–4.

[8] Kian-Seng Teo, *Chromaticism in the English Madrigal* (London: Garland, 1989).

Ex 1.1 Example of a false relation (F♮ versus F♯); Thomas Tallis, 'O nata lux', from *Cantiones sacrae* (London: Thomas Vautrollier, 1575).

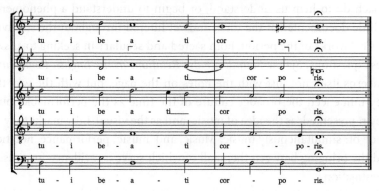

sometimes written but sometimes implied by the framework of the notation in hexachords (as we shall explore later in this Introduction) and, strictly speaking, *in*visible, extra-notational: they are thus issues of textuality and literacy just as much as issues of composition and performance, and in this way they expose the fundamental tension between orality and notation that underlies the musical culture of the English Renaissance. They are a vital aspect of the concept of harmony in the Western classic art music of the period, and yet beyond the field of musicology they are little known; despite the prevalence of the metaphor of harmony in the visual and literary cultures of the period, they have garnered little critical interdisciplinary attention.[9] It is a simple musicological fact that false relations, and related tropes of dissonance, are part and parcel of sixteenth- and seventeenth-century approaches towards harmony to the extent that to state as such is almost unforgivably banal. Nevertheless, such connotations rarely if ever percolate out into general understanding of what harmony meant in this period; our collective cross-disciplinary understanding of this most commonplace of musical metaphors risks being greatly impoverished by omitting false relations from the narrative.

False relations arose, according to Thomas Morley in his 1597 musical theoretical treatise *A Plaine and Easie Introduction to Practicall Musicke* 'a newe fashion [...] admitted for the raritie [...] onely devised to bee foisted in at a

---

[9] A notable exception is Simon Jackson, *George Herbert and Early Modern Musical Culture* (Cambridge: Cambridge University Press, 2022), 167–170.

close amongst many parts, for lack of other shift',[10] to maintain adherence to other compositional rules. Morley's example is of a simultaneous false relation; he stated that 'now a daies it is growne in such common use as divers will make no scruple to use it in fewe partes where as it might as well enough be left out' and 'it is an unpleasant and harshe musicke [...] the meeting of the flat and sharp octave hath much pleased divers of our descanters in times past and been received as current amongst others of later time' but in the same breath attempts to discredit them, claiming (incorrectly) that they had 'ever been condemned of the most skilful here in England'.[11] His ambiguous description follows the accordingly somewhat ambiguous origins of the false relation. Largely false relations were the by-product of voice-leading and the counterpoint styles of the sixteenth and early seventeenth centuries; in turn these styles were inherited from the fifteenth-century Franco-Flemish polyphonic musical style epitomized by Guillaume Dufay (1397–1474), Johannes Ockeghem (c. 1410–1497), Josquin des Prez (c. 1450–1521), and Nicolas Gombert (c. 1495–1560). Theorists appeared to believe that they were so well established that their treatment could be assumed. They were also often avoidable, by dint of the musical system of solmization which will be explored in greater detail below. As such, it is somewhat of a mystery why they rose to such stylistic prominence in the music of the English Renaissance in the sixteenth and early seventeenth centuries, by which point they were strikingly old-fashioned.[12] They had a profoundly different life in theory and in practice (both composition and performance); their documentary existence in sources beyond the music-theoretical is frustratingly vague and mercurial, with contemporary terms such as 'dissonan[t/ce]', 'discord', 'chromatical', and 'false music' all serving as potential iterations but covering a vast number of other musical devices, tropes, and figures. Composers such as Thomas Tallis (c. 1505–1585), John Sheppard (c. 1515–1558), Robert Parsons (c. 1535–1572), William Byrd (c. 1540–1623), Thomas Tomkins (1572–1656), and Thomas Weelkes (1576–1623) all, at some point in their careers, composed works which utilized audacious (and avoidable) false relations. As matters of performance they were evidently very popular 'to diverse of our descanters' and (despite Morley's statement to the contrary) 'the most skilful here in

---

[10] Thomas Morley, *A Plaine and Easie Introduction to Practicall Musicke* (London: Peter Short, 1597), 154.
[11] Morley, *Plaine and Easie Introduction*, 154 and 177. See also Rebecca Herissone, *Music Theory in Seventeenth-Century England* (Oxford: Oxford University Press, 2000), 153.
[12] Kerry McCarthy, *Byrd* (Oxford: Oxford University Press, 2013), 146.

England'. Nevertheless, amongst the other discords that were permitted in certain contexts by English (and continental) music theory of the time, false relations remain curiously unelucidated.[13] James Haar, writing of the use of false relations in mainly Italian and madrigal sources, observes

> the acceptance of, and in some composers even a somewhat exaggerated preference for, false relations created through use of written accidentals. [...] there is often no melodic need—*fa super la* or anything else—satisfied by this chromaticism. It seems clear that such accidentals were regarded as salutary condiment to the blandly diatonic modal framework within which sixteenth-century musicians worked.[14]

Whilst Haar comments briefly on 'the oft-mentioned delight in false relations taken by English musicians', he does not explore why this might be the case, and indeed why such 'delight' can be found in sacred as well as secular sources. False relations as both *res* (object, uttered note, performance) and *verba* (sign, written note, theory) are a mystery that remains broadly unsolved and unquestioned in scholarship on the musical culture of the English Renaissance,[15] a so-called golden age that witnessed enormous developments towards the establishment of the tonal system that the Western classical tradition still uses to this day.[16]

---

[13] See, e.g., Herissone, *Music Theory*, 154–170; Morley, *Plaine and Easie Introduction*, 158. It is worth observing that whilst false relations are the only form of discord that were quite so vaguely accounted for, suspension and cadence were not untroubled by jumbled accounts of causation. Herissone notes the gap between how suspended discords were used in practice, rather than the theory behind their application, and the way that this obfuscated theoretical accounts of how they should be used. This in turn led to a confusion between suspension and syncopation, such that the non-discordant 6–5 and 5–6 progressions were frequently included in discussions of suspension (e.g., in Morley).

[14] James Haar, 'False Relations and Chromaticism in Sixteenth Century Music', in *Journal of the American Musicological Society*, 30: 3 (Autumn 1977), 391–418, at 416.

[15] False relations have, however, received some attention, although not in recent decades. See Peter Urquhart, 'Cross Relations by Franco-Flemish Composers after Josquin', in *Tijdschrift van de Vereniging voor Nederlandse Muziekgeschiedenis*, 43: 1 (1993), 3–41; Haar, 'False Relations and Chromaticism', 391–418.

[16] As Megan Kaes Long argues, the structures that regulate pitch content are just as vital to the shaping of tonality as that pitch content in and of itself. See Megan Kaes Long, 'Cadential Syntax and Tonal Expectation in Late Sixteenth-Century Homophony', in *Music Theory Spectrum*, 40: 1 (2018), 52–83, at 52, and *Hearing Homophony: Tonal Expectation at the Turn of the Seventeenth Century* (Oxford: Oxford University Press, 2020). For the historiographical context see also Brian Hyer, 'Tonality', in Thomas Christensen (ed.), *The Cambridge Companion to Western Music Theory* (Cambridge: Cambridge University Press, 2002); and Harold Powers, 'From Psalmody to Tonality', in Cristle Collins Judd (ed.), *Tonal Structures in Early Music* (New York: Garland, 2000).

Thus, false relations are a vital clue into the development of tonality and discordance as a harmonic (rather than melodic) phenomenon; to leave them unacknowledged and unowned is to sacrifice a nuanced understanding of how the Western musical system evolved from the rapidly transforming musical languages of the sixteenth and seventeenth centuries. This volume seeks to untangle this clue, by situating false relations within the contemporary visual, literary, political, and religious contemplations of musical falseness, and ways that it could produce meaning. It adopts a deliberately broad definition of false relations, in keeping with the profoundly inconsistent contemporary approach towards them; for whilst Morley defined false relations in their simultaneous form, Thomas Campion and later Charles Simpson illustrated the rule only in proximate form, contrary to its origins.[17] In so doing, this book embraces the fundamental muddiness surrounding the concept of the false relation, and the way that it chimes with, alludes to, masquerades as, and evokes general forms of musical discord and indeed its non-discordant cousin, diatonic chromaticism. If we embrace the semantic capaciousness, radical ambiguity and lack of consensus (What makes music false? When does discordance become too much discordance? Are linear instances permitted? Are simultaneous instances allowed? Are proximate?) at the heart of the false relation, we reach towards a different, and enriched, understanding of English Renaissance musical culture. Beneath the sedimentary layers of association that false relations have accumulated over the course of five centuries, the false relation offers the potential for a rich insight into aspects of musical culture that have as yet gone unexplored.

From amongst many other more explicit instances of musical falseness in the literature of this period, and indeed in the work of Shakespeare himself, I deliberately chose the brief conversation between Miranda and Ferdinand as an evocative, tantalizing, and only partial mention to open this introductory chapter. It is the perfect illustration of the conceptual seepage of musical notation and its conundrums in the English Renaissance, and the way that they leaked off the page and into the collective consciousness of everyday

---

[17] Herissone, *Music Theory*, 153. James Haar likewise did not draw a hard and fast distinction between the simultaneous and proximate false relation. Indeed, his arguments suggest that he leans towards a definition of the false relation as proximate. 'In a few cases, the cross relations are not only direct but simultaneous, making one wonder whether they can or should be interpreted literally. No theory of "cautionary" accidentals would seem to account for these spots. If they are not mistakes—the left-hand partbook not knowing what the right is doing—they are further evidence of the deliberate indulgence in cross relations characteristic of this music'; see Haar, 'False Relations and Chromaticism', 411.

life, appearing in fleeting, suggestive glimpses in visual, material and textual objects. Is it a reference to musical falseness? Is it not? As a metaphor and as a mode of writing, musical falseness is one of the most powerfully provocative things that we have inherited from a rich and diverse episode in history. The literature of the period demonstrates that readers and audiences were fascinated by the concept of musical falseness, broadly defined as the idea that music *could* be false. The role of music on the Jacobean stage has already received critical attention from Ross Duffin, Katherine Larson, and Simon Smith, amongst others.[18] However, yet to be explored is the way that the concept of false music diffused throughout the culture of the English Renaissance; nor how it can help us understand the rampant rise of the musical style of the false relation, contrary to its nominal prohibition in contemporary music theoretical treatises.

Throughout *The Tempest*, music functions as a key signifier of enchantment, and in turn of veracity. It is the lodestar by which the audience is guided through what is 'real' (a true part of the fiction of the play) and 'false' (a trick by one of the characters, either by sneakiness or through magic):[19] '*solemn and strange music*' is queued where Ariel conjures a banquet to spook the shipwrecked Alonso, Sebastian and company; to persuade Ferdinand through the 'sweet air' that Alonso is dead and at a depth of 'full fathom five', transformed into something 'rich and strange'; and '*soft music*' where Prospero stages an enchanted masque to celebrate the impending marriage of Miranda and Ferdinand. Ariel, Prospero's fairy, describes how the audience 'smelt music: so I charm'd their ears' as they watched the masque. Music signals the moral status of the characters; Caliban hears 'sounds and sweet airs that give delight [/] and hurt not', where Sebastian and Alonso hear 'nothing'. Such an approach is not unique to *The Tempest*; the 'musical discord',[20] and the search for the 'concord of this discord', runs throughout

---

[18] Katherine R. Larson, *The Matter of Song in Early Modern England: Texts in and of the Air* (Oxford: Oxford University Press, 2019); Scott Trudell, *Unwritten Poetry: Song, Performance and Media in Early Modern England* (Oxford: Oxford University Press, 2019); Simon Smith, *Musical Response in the Early Modern Playhouse, 1603–1625*, (Cambridge: Cambridge University Press, 2017); F. W. Sternfeld, *Music in Shakespearean Tragedy* (London: Routledge and Kegan Paul, 1963).

[19] Across this period the role of music as an aid to epistemological investigation was becoming increasingly important, as thinkers laid the groundwork for the later 'scientific' approaches of the mid-seventeenth century onwards. See Katherine Butler, 'Myth, Science, and the Power of Music in the Early Decades of the Royal Society', in *Journal of the History of Ideas* 76: 1 (2015), 50–55; Penelope Gouk, *Music, Science and Natural Magic in Seventeenth-Century England* (New Haven, CT: Yale University Press, 1999).

[20] For a detailed and nuanced account of 'harmony' in Shakespeare and the debate over whether music's benefits outweighed its dangers in its privileged role as direct conduit to the heart and soul, see Linda Phyllis Austern, *Both from the Ears and Mind: Thinking about Music in Early Modern*

Midsummer Night's Dream, whilst the 'discord' at the heart of Ulysses' degree speech in *Troilus in Cressida* is the infamous emblem of the defeat of the Trojans. Elsewhere we find Shakespeare playing with the concept of false music, in the casket scene of *The Merchant of Venice*, as Lorenzo woos Jessica:

> LORENZO The man that hath no music in himself,
> Nor is not moved with concord of sweet sounds,
> Is fit for treasons, stratagems and spoils;
> The motions of his spirit are dull as night,
> And his affections dark as Erebus.
> Let no such man be trusted. Mark the music.[21]

Richard II, dethroned and imprisoned, finds in his 'generation of still-breeding thoughts' interrupted by a musical episode whose falseness (in this instance in terms of rhythm and meter) leads him to reflections upon his mortality:

> *Music*
> RICHARD Ha, ha! Keep time: how sour sweet music is,
> When time is broke and no proportion kept!
> So is it in the music of men's lives.
> And here have I the daintiness of ear
> To cheque time broke in a disorder'd string;
> But for the concord of my state and time
> Had not an ear to hear my true time broke.
> I wasted time, and now doth time waste me.[22]

And in perhaps the most famous example, Romeo and Juliet playfully discuss Romeo's departure through the musical metaphor of the lark and the nightingale, and the falseness of their song.

England (Chicago: University of Chicago Press, 2020), 89–154. For an example of the early modern doubt over the status of music see Stephen Gosson, *The Schoole of Abuse* (London: Thomas Woodcocke, 1579), fol. 8r–v.

[21] William Shakespeare, *The Merchant of Venice*, in *Mr William Shakespeares comedies, histories, & tragedies Published according to the true originally copies*, 5.1.
[22] William Shakespeare, *Richard II*, in *Mr William Shakespeares comedies, histories, & tragedies Published according to the true originally copies*, 5.3.

> JULIET   It is, it is. Hie hence! Be gone, away!
> It is the lark that sings so out of tune,
> Straining harsh discords and unpleasing sharps.
> Some say the lark makes sweet division.
> This doth not so, for she divideth us.[23]

Musical falseness was not limited to Shakespeare's lexicon. John Marston's *The Malcontent* opens with the stage direction '*the vilest out of tune Music being heard*', and music (or music that is heard by some, doubted by others) pervades the plot:

> PIETRO   Where breathes that Music?
> BILIOSO   The discord rather than the Music is heard from the Malcontent *Malevoles* chamber.[24]

Such cursory mentions suggest that these metaphors were common currency to their audiences.[25] Much has been made of the importance of harmony as a musical metaphor, but little as to the specific implications of non-harmonious music, of discord, of the contemporary prevalence of musical figures and tropes that indulged in thwarting the developing tonal expectations entailed in the rise of harmony over melody.

One approach of use to the present investigation is that of Joseph M. Ortiz's exploration of the 'radical promiscuity' of musical meaning in his 2011 monograph, *Broken Harmony*. Ortiz unpacks Shakespeare's frequent exploitation of the gap between the *logos* of meaningful language and the *materia* of musical sound.[26] In insisting upon the 'rhetorical advantage gained by eliding the difference between ['actual' music and musical metaphors...], a careful bait-and-switch game between musical sound and visual allegory [which] can often help illustrate a philosophical or political point, while making that point seem grounded in the real, observable workings of the physical world', Ortiz insists that the 'sight of music shapes our listening'.[27] This dynamic is palpable in perhaps the most striking instance of musical falseness of the

---

[23] William Shakespeare, *An excellent conceited tragedie of Romeo and Juliet as it hath been often (with great applause) plaid publiquely* (London: John Danter, 1597), 3.5, 26–30.
[24] John Marston, *The Malcontent* (London: Valentine Simmes for William Aspley, 1604), 1.2.
[25] Austern, *Both from the Ears and Mind*, 90.
[26] Joseph M. Ortiz, *Broken Harmony: Shakespeare and the Politics of Music* (Ithaca, NY: Cornell University Press, 2011), 3.
[27] Ibid., 8.

period, found in a close contemporary of *The Tempest*: Thomas Middleton and Thomas Dekker's *The Roaring Girl* (c. 1607–1610, first printed 1611), which fictionalizes the real-life and notorious cross-dressing thief Mary Frith (alias Moll Cutpurse). The false potential of music implicitly pervades the language of how Moll Cutpurse (the titular 'roaring girl whose notes till now never were heard') describes herself and her ability to dissimulate to her would-be suitor Sebastian,[28] and her ability trick Sebastian's father Alexander into hiring her as Sebastian's music tutor.

> MOLL   He that can take me for a male musician,
> I cannot choose but make him my instrument,
> And play upon him.[29]

The plot of *The Roaring Girl* is driven by deception; Sebastian pretends to woo Moll, in order to persuade Alexander that Mary Fitz-Allard, Sebastian's true sweetheart, is an acceptable wife despite her small dowry, whilst Moll's interview for the position of Sebastian's music tutor is, in turn, a trap laid by Alexander to reveal the plot. At the centre of these multiple and overlapping layers of falseness is Moll herself, 'false' because of her preference for masculine clothing and behaviours that eschew her femininity (hence her 'roaring' epithet, roaring meaning in the contemporary lexicon to brawl and carouse), her noisiness, and her frequent masquerading as a viol-toting musician who even, at one point, serenades the audience with a ballad.[30] Throughout, she moves through the noisy landscape of London: from the 'wrangling street' of Holborn, via the 'jingling of golden bells' of the disreputable morris dance in 1.2 to the 'gruntling of five hundred hogs coming from Romford market'. She is, Sir Alexander claims in 1.2 (215–216), 'a mermaid/[which] Has tolled my son to shipwreck': her slippage between noise and music, through her falseness, epitomizes her dangerous appeal. As Jennie Votava notes, 'in the theatre of Thomas Dekker and Thomas Middleton, the polyvalent concept

---

[28] For more on the role of noise in *The Roaring Girl*, see Jennie Votava, '"The Voice that will Drown All the City": Un-Gendering Noise in *The Roaring Girl*', in *Renaissance Drama*, 39: 1 (2011), 69–95; see also Mary Beth Rose, 'Women in Men's Clothing: Apparel and Social Stability in *The Roaring Girl*', in *English Literary Renaissance*, 14 (1984), 367–91; Valerie Forman, 'Marked Angels: Counterfeits, Commodities, and *The Roaring Girl*', in *Renaissance Quarterly*, 54 (2001), 1531–1560; Matthew Kendrick, '"So strange in Quality": Perception, Realism and Commodification in *The Roaring Girl*', in *Criticism*, 60: 1 (2018), 99–121.
[29] Thomas Dekker and Thomas Middleton, *The Roaring Girl* (London: Nicholas Okes for Thomas Archer, 1611), 4.1.
[30] Votava, 'The Voice that will Drown All the City', 79.

of noise, emerging from the already unfixed, labile, ephemeral realm of sound, becomes a privileged locus of staging radical ambiguity. The voice of the "Roaring Girl" constitutes noise, broadly construed, precisely on account of its tendency to interfere with dominant Renaissance codes defining gender, acts of speech, and even noise itself. Like the noise at Babel, Moll's interference has ultimate expression in the sound of "nothing".[31] At no point do Dekker and Middleton mention musical falseness, but arguably they do not need to: the plot and the interaction between characters, one of them frequently toting a viol, do it for them.

We ignore such covert manifestations of musical metaphor at our peril. These literary instances can tell us much about false relations in the English Renaissance. Due to the absence of documentary evidence regarding contemporary attitudes towards false relations, our understanding of their reception and role will always be fragmentary; however, by exploring beyond the comfortable realm of what is notated (an exploration that false relations in their very material manifestation encourage us to undertake, as we shall see below), we can move towards an appreciation of how those fragments might have interacted, intersected, and fitted together. To modern ears the false relation can appear more or less innocuous. The sounding of major and minor inflections of a note either simultaneously or in proximity, across two different voice parts, it fits well within the twenty-first-century model of tonality that we have inherited from hundreds of years of Western musical theory. It did not gain its name until the nineteenth century, but it has many contemporary forebears. The *Oxford English Dictionary* lists a number: the false string, the false note, the false descant. None of these instances correlates directly in terms of specific meaning, but all of them demonstrate that falseness was a thing, attribute, conundrum often associated with music. The false relation itself was of vital importance for the musical culture of the English Renaissance, as David Nott observes:

> A genuine interest in English Renaissance music must incorporate an investigation of available treatises (including discussions of *musica ficta* and ornamentation), an understanding of the importance of Elizabethan dissonance, and an extensive experience with principles of sixteenth-century voice-leading acquired by *singing* vast quantities of this literature. This exposure to the contrapuntal techniques of the Tudor composers will

---

[31] Ibid., 91.

introduce the artist to certain idiomatic features of Elizabethan polyphony. One important feature of this encounter will involve a familiarity with the 'cross-relation' phenomenon, its distinctive characteristics, and a 'feel' for appropriate stylistic utilisation.[32]

What are we to make of this phenomenon, hitherto unelucidated in critical literature on the music of the English Renaissance, and largely left to speak for itself (as merely a 'feel' for appropriate stylistic utilization) in the surviving notational evidence?

This book seeks to investigate the possibilities suggested by the fragmentary evidence surrounding false relations, rather than avenues of concrete causation. In this way, it hopes to excavate beneath the historiography and mythologies that have grown up around the musical culture of the English Renaissance to how it might originally have been experienced. First, however, it is important to survey the historiographical ideas that have contributed to the way we have hitherto understood the false relation. This Introduction is divided into three parts. The first situates the false relation within its musical-theoretical context, with a particular view to rendering this technical information accessible to those from outside of the field of musicology in order to galvanize their understandings of the metaphor of harmony, and what it could mean during the English Renaissance. The second unpacks the visual connotations of this technical musical-theoretical context, in light of the representational expectations and compositional strategies of the visual culture of the period; it will be of particular interest to those who work on visual and material culture, and to musicologists unfamiliar with the artistic conventions of the period. Finally, this Introduction concludes with a general exploration of the context within which we have received the false relation today, in the twenty-first century. Shedding light on the baggage that the false relation has accumulated over the centuries since it first rose to stylistic prominence, it focuses on the Victorian revival of English Renaissance music and the role that the false relation played in nineteenth- and twentieth-century conceptualizations of the English choral tradition. In this way, it seeks to demonstrate that the false relation is of critical and conceptual use far beyond the specific realms of academic musicology, and that its paradoxes and appeal can galvanize understanding of the English

---

[32] David Nott, 'The Cross Relation in English Choral Music from Tallis through Purcell' (unpublished PhD Dissertation, University of Cincinnati, 1976), 11–12.

Renaissance from a multitude of disciplinary angles, as a visual, material and textual phenomenon, as well as musical.

How Soft Is Your Hexachord

The false relation of the English Renaissance cannot be fully appreciated or indeed comprehended without contextualization within the musical cultures of the time. Chief amongst these is solmization, the tool by which generations of students of music were taught to sight-read. False relations are first and foremost a matter of musical literacy, and of musical writing. Without approaching them as such (in other words, as a Saussurian issue of the relationship between sign and signified, the note as material mark and the note as performed), we cannot hope to begin to understand the manner in which they once operated, were apprehended, and were appreciated (or, indeed, *not* appreciated). Regardless of how musically literate one is in modern terms, solmization offers an invaluable route into this sonic architecture. In particular, it is vital that we recognize the different ways that musical literacy was achieved and the different concept of pitch space that it required. It was not, as it is today in the twenty-first century, visualized as a closed and continuous circle of pitches, but instead as a series of segments 'tackt' together, and possible to bind only at certain key points. From the eleventh century onwards, most musical theoretical treatises in Western Europe introduced would-be musicians to notation via the didactic tools apocryphally believed to be passed down by Guido d'Arezzo amongst others: the Guidonian 'hand' mnemonic and the hexachord.[33] Hexachords were six-note scales, constructed around what we would now call a major sixth on the pitch or solmization syllables *ut re mi fa sol la*. Each of the hexachords, likewise, C 'the natural' hexachord, G the 'hard', and F and the 'soft', had the same melodic structure, proceeding tone tone semitone tone tone upwards, or in Guido's terminology, *ut re mi fa sol la* (hence the process of reading music in this manner became known as to solmize and solmization, after the syllables *sol mi*). These hexachords overlapped to form the full gamut of permissible notes. As a result, as Anne Smith notes:

---

[33] For more on the role of learning music, see Thomas Christensen, 'Music Theory & Pedagogy', in Iain Fenlon and Richard Wistreich (eds.), *The Cambridge History of Sixteenth Century Music* (Cambridge: Cambridge University Press, 2019), 414–438.

One was always aware of the intervallic content of the melody being sung. Thus the solmization syllable of an individual note depends not only on its absolute pitch, but is also a function of the hexachord in which one is currently singing.[34]

Three were officially authorized or *recta*: those starting on C, F, and G. Together they were generally diatonic, corresponding to the white notes on a modern piano, with the addition of B-flat. Hexachords that did not start on C, F, or G were *ficta* hexachords, classified variously as 'false', 'invented', 'hooked on', and so on, because they are outside the gamut or contrary to the solmization logic of the Guidonian hand (see Fig. 1.1).[35]

The system largely developed for monophonic song cultures of earlier centuries but continued to be used well into and beyond the period with which this book concerns itself.[36] By the sixteenth century, there was less concern over which note the hexachord began on and whether it could be considered *recta* or *ficta*, and the position of the flat could be shifted (most commonly to E). Nevertheless, the ghost of this practice, and its nominal prohibition, continued to exercise its influence over the musical practice of the English Renaissance.[37] Not least was this important to the process by which an aspiring musician could produce *ficta*. Contemporary English musical theoretical treatises by and large assumed a considerable amount of prior knowledge in their accounts of the rules of solmization. This was compounded by the fact that theorists and pedagogues tended to layer various teaching tools of the past one upon the other, rather than throw out older tools in favour of new ones.[38] Thus in the interest of clarity, and for those unfamiliar with early modern music theory, a full overview of the guidance for producing *ficta* is best obtained by turning to a modern, synoptic account. We should, however, do so with a degree of caution; as Peter Urquhart notes, modern misunderstandings of '*musica ficta*' as editorial or performance accidentals rather than the medieval (and more authentic sense) of *musica*

---

[34] Anne Smith, *The Performance of Sixteenth Century Music* (Oxford: Oxford University Press, 2011), 20–21.
[35] Thomas Brothers, *Chromatic Beauty in the Late Medieval Chanson: An Interpretation of Manuscript Accidentals* (Cambridge: Cambridge University Press, 2006), 1.
[36] For more on the continuation of solmization into the eighteenth century, see Nicholas Baragwanath, *The Solfeggio Tradition: The Forgotten Art of Melody in the Long Eighteenth Century* (Oxford: Oxford University Press, 2020).
[37] Lionel Pike, *Hexachords in Late Renaissance Music* (first published Farnham: Ashgate, 1998; this edition New York: Routledge, 2018), 2–3.
[38] Urquhart, *Sound and Sense in Franco-Flemish Music of the Renaissance*, 70.

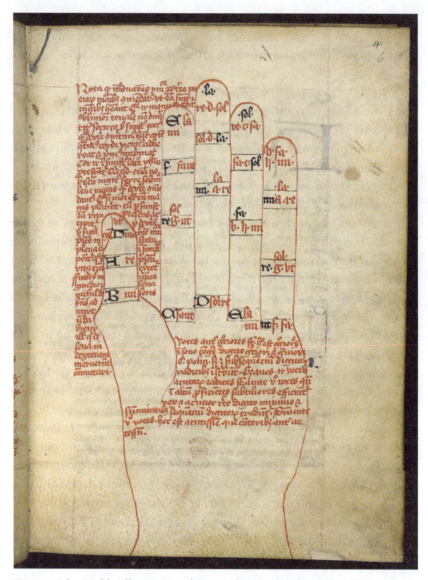

Fig. 1.1 John Wylde, illustration of the Guidonian Hand in red and blue or brown foliate penwork, c. 1460, from the prologue of *Musica Manualis cum Totale*, in Lansdowne MS 763, owned by Thomas Morley and likely taken by Thomas Tallis out of Waltham Abbey following its dissolution, fol. 6. London, British Library. Reproduced by kind permission of the British Library under CC-BY.

ficta as solmization outside of the parameters of the Guidonian hand can obfuscate how accidentals were deployed.[39] A sensitive account can be found in Rebecca Herissone's description:

> If a composer wished to make use of notes which were not included in the gamut at all, either because they fell outside its range, or because they did not belong in one of the three real or *recta* hexachords, he had to create false or *ficta* hexachords on other scale degrees. A *ficta* hexachord on D, for example, would allow him to use the note F-sharp, and one on B-flat would allow E-flat. Where this was the case, signs were generally used to warn a singer that the music was on the point of moving outside its normal territory. The most convenient notes to which to attach such signs were *mi* and *fa*, since the *mi–fa* interval was the only semitone within each hexachord. A singer could be alerted that the music had moved into an unexpected hexachord (either *recta* or *ficta*) by the presence in the stave of the sign 'natural' (which became 'sharp')—indicating that the next note on that line or space as *mi*—or 'flat', which denoted it was *fa*. Importantly, such symbols were only used when it was felt that the singer would be unable to perceive the mutation from context, and were frequently absent in common mutations into the F hexachord. Over time, it became considered acceptable for a *ficta* hexachord to be given artificial *recta* status for the duration of a piece, so that, for instance, the three main hexachords in operation might be C, F, and B-flat, rather than G, C, and F.[40]

In the hexachord the semitone between *mi* and *fa* was the 'most easily identifiable and expressive interval of the system […] an indicator of the hexachord in use: *mi fa* is like the pole star in navigation'.[41] Herissone is writing specifically of the English musical tradition; Jessie Ann Owens observes on the other hand that, broadly speaking, there were two approaches towards the understanding of the gamut that are superficially similar, but

---

[39] For a nuanced discussion of the difference between *ficta* as it is defined in the original music treatises, and *ficta* as it is understood (anachronously) today, see ibid., 17–19.

[40] Herissone, *Music Theory*, 75. See also Gregory Barnett, 'Tonal Organization in Seventeenth-Century Music Theory', in Thomas Christensen (ed.), *The Cambridge History of Western Music Theory* (Cambridge: Cambridge University Press, 2002), 408–410.

[41] Pike, *Hexachords in Late Renaissance Music*, 52. Pike also observes that 'The semitone—which, as we have seen, was the most characteristic interval of the hexachord, and the one most often invoked for expressive purposes—occurs in the very centre of each hexachord, between *mi* and *fa*. It is this very interval (or rather, its position) that does most to determine which hexachord is in use: the importance of the semitone for this purpose is paramount.' Pike, *Hexachords*, 13.

in terms of application and crucially in the use of *mi* and *fa* solmization symbols, different: the approach used on the continent, and the approach used in England.[42] By and large this shift away from continental understanding occurred across the reign of Elizabeth.[43] In England, the process of solmizing was the key factor (rather than the C, F, or G hexachord and the temporary institution of artificial *recta* hexachords, as argued by Herissone), meaning that the governance of pitch space can more helpfully be thought of as three scales distinguished by their number of flats (or *fa* solmization symbols).

> In contrast to continental practices, which gives rules for mutating between hexachords (for example, notes are sung differently depending on whether or not the line is ascending or descending), in England the key signature usually determines the solmization, and in fact affixes particular syllables to particular pitches. The decision about how many syllables to use—only four, usually four but with the occasional additions of a fifth and six syllable, six, or seven—occurs within the context of the near-universal adoption of a system employing three scales (no flat, one flat, two flats) in practice if not in theory.[44]

Under the aegis of key, *fa* (and, by extension, *mi*) had a subtly different semantic inflection in an English context than in a continental one: their capacity to alter the meaning of the fabric of a piece of music was greater for its ability to inform the positioning of the visual pitch pattern. In contemporary terms, the false relation arose from the application of *mi* and *fa* in different iterations in different parts: the solmization of a given note, for example E, as *mi* in the Altus part and as *fa* in the Medius part. This chromatic *mi–fa* (between parts) was also likely implicated in the diatonic *mi–fa* (within a single part). Thus they capitalize on the radical ambiguity at the heart of the solmization system. This ambiguity, we should note, is strikingly similar to the provocative gap between music as *logos* and music as *materia* observed by Ortiz, above.

As previous musicological scholarship has discussed, the ambiguity of the hexachord was complemented by attendant ambiguities in the contemporary

---

[42] Jessie Ann Owens, 'Concepts of Pitch in English Music Theory c. 1540–1640', in Cristle Collins Judd (ed.), *Tonal Structures in Early Music* (New York: Garland, 1998), 191–192.
[43] Ibid., 232.
[44] Ibid., 192.

musical theoretical literature of the English Renaissance. Herissone notes that 'there is ample evidence to suggest that, even in the late sixteenth century, English theorists were rather poorly informed about the hexachordal system. Terminology was, at best, confused.'[45] The term 'hexachord' is broadly speaking a modern one and does not appear in the majority of musical theoretical treatises, either English or continental.[46] Accordingly, there were a variety of terms to describe their *recta* forms that roughly followed the continental terminology of *deduction* and *proprietas*, with Thomas Morley's 1597 *Plaine and Easie Introduction to Practicall Musicke* (and then later Thomas Ravenscroft's *Treatise of Music*) referring to them as 'properties' that can be either 'B *quarre*', 'Properchant', or 'b *molle*', the anonymous *Pathway to Musicke* in 1587 as 'songs' that can be either 'sharp', 'natural', or 'flat', and John Dowland's translation of Ornithoparcus listing them as 'deductions', for example.[47] Whilst there were plenty of descriptions of solmization available in the works of William Bathe, William Barley, and Thomas Campion (to name merely the printed examples), Morley was the only theorist to explain the medieval pitch concept in its entirety during the English Renaissance.[48] There was moreover a fundamental tension at play in the act of sight singing: the music was simultaneously the note in and of itself as notated on the page, and the visual pattern by which it was being read. It was both the abstract concept of the music, and the ephemeral performance of music. As Nicholas Baragwanath observes:

> The technique is analogous to that used by modern jazz musicians. Taking a chord progression as a conceptual framework, they are able to create music of astonishing complexity and variety by applying a few rules such as associated modes, chord substitutions, and guide tones. The essence of the method is to keep in mind a simple framework while subjecting it to conventional transformations that do not alter its substance. The mental image of the chord progression remains unaffected by changes to its musical realization.[49]

---

[45] Herissone, *Music Theory*, 78.
[46] Cooper, 'Englische Musiktheorie', 184.
[47] Morley, *Plaine and Easie Introduction*, 14; Ravenscroft, *Treatise of Musicke*, fol. 2r; *Pathway to Musicke*, 4; Dowland, *Andreas Ornithoparcus*, 26; see also Owens, 'Concepts of Pitch', 193; and Herissone, *Music Theory*, 78.
[48] Morley, *Plaine and Easie Introduction*, 10–18.
[49] Baragwanath, *The Solfeggio Tradition*, 9.

Insisting upon this dual identity might appear to be nothing more than a tiny, pedantic quibble but, as we shall see throughout this book, it was a vital undercurrent to the rise of the stylistic of the false relation. Stefano Mengozzi's recent study of Renaissance reception of medieval music theory epitomizes the dilemma by framing it as a collision (and fundamental incompatibility) between the octave series of pitch letters A–G (or *litterae*) that had 'long been in place as the foundation of the diatonic system' and the 'virtual system of the *ut–la* segment' of the hexachord (the *voces*), which amounted to two different and competing representations of musical space.[50] For Mengozzi, the hexachord should always be interpreted as *verba*, sign, never *res*, object.[51] In turn, this serves as his proof that the hexachord was never as widely applied as musicologists had previously argued, and that it served more as an ideological symbol that ultimately contributed to the authority and infallibility of the church.[52] What Mengozzi does not entertain is the idea that this tension might have been a source of delight to practitioners and students of music in the English Renaissance. Their apparent visual difference, 'sets of *ut–la* syllables [that] pointed to a model of pitch organization set up into overlapping segments, [whilst] the series of pitch letters from A–G established a competing model that was continuous, linear and cyclical, in the Middle Ages as it is today' would not have been troubling to a culture raised with the 'cognitive style'[53] of England in the sixteenth and early seventeenth centuries. This will be discussed in greater detail in the next section of this Introduction, but for the present it is worth observing that regardless of how one approaches solmization of the hexachord (as sight-singing tool, as ideology, as immutable, or as a flexible guideline that contradicted a coexisting pitch-space model), its parameters are in many ways the key to understanding many of the contradictions behind the false relation. In the process of pushing against the limits of these

---

[50] Stefano Mengozzi, *The Renaissance Reform of Medieval Music Theory* (Cambridge: Cambridge University Press, 2010), 110–111. The concept of a 'soft', contextual hexachord had been raised before, as in Margaret Bent's argument for the 'function of anticipation as aural cues for responsive intervallic adjustments'; see Margaret Bent, *Counterpoint, Composition and Musica Ficta* (London: Routledge, 2002), 2. For another perspective on this, see Powers, 'From Psalmody to Tonality', 276.

[51] Mengozzi, *Renaissance Reform*, 111. Compare this approach to, e.g., that of Gregory Barnett; see Gregory Barnett, 'Tonal Organization in Seventeenth-century Music Theory', in Thomas Christensen (ed.), *The Cambridge History of Western Music Theory* (Cambridge: Cambridge University Press, 2002), at 408.

[52] Mengozzi, *Renaissance Reform*, 14.

[53] Michael Baxandall, *Painting and Experience in Fifteenth-Century Italy* (Oxford: Oxford University Press, 1972), 40.

old-fashioned but surprisingly eloquent pitch divisions, the musicians of the English Renaissance created an avant-garde sonic style that left its distinctive stamp upon the way written, imagined, and conceptualized music evolved into the forms we know today.

Early modern false relations, in turn, should strictly be considered the result of the medieval attitude towards chromaticism, as recently explored by Thomas Brothers. Brothers notes that between the thirteenth and sixteenth centuries there are commonly two justifications for the use of *musica ficta*, and the false relations that it entails: necessity and beauty (or *pulchritudo*, 'for the sake of beauty').[54] *Ficta* were permissible where they rendered the intervals of fifths, fourths, and octaves perfect, where they would otherwise not be by the virtue of the voice-leading of the separate melodic lines of each part. A perfect fifth below B-flat (belonging to the gamut in the F *molle* or soft hexachord) requires an E to be inflected *fa* (not belonging to the gamut).[55] Because the rules of solmization had developed for monophonic music, there was little to no guidance as to whether preservation of harmonic relations should be prioritized over other factors such as imitation, counterpoint, and so on. Moreover, *ficta* could be beautiful for the way in which it enhanced the delight of *musica recta*, of its consonance and regularity, enhancing the sense of systematic, diatonic order by its brief diversion into disorder. In this way it interacts tantalizingly with the virtues of the rhetorical trope *varietas*, as Mary Carruthers notes, the 'word of many colours'.[56] *Varietas* was the pleasingly balanced variation that aided the beautiful *ductus* of eye (or ear) through a thing (a passage of music, a picture). Thus, the presence of *ficta* contributed to the overall consonance of a piece of music by its variation on the regularity of *musica recta*. This may appear a statement of the blindingly obvious, but it is important in conducting this investigation into false relations that such things *are* stated, such that we might begin to reflect upon why they are so very obvious to us. In turn, it is vital that we unpack the implications of these reasons.

Solmization is thus perhaps best approached as a form of musical pirate's code: more like guidelines, anyway. Brothers concludes that the key to approaching how *musica ficta* functions is 'syntactic flexibility'.[57] Certainly

---

[54] Brothers, *Chromatic Beauty*, 3–4.
[55] Ibid., 3.
[56] Mary J. Carruthers, 'Varietas: A Word of Many Colours', in *Poetica*, 41: 1 and 2 (2009), 11–32.
[57] Brothers, *Chromatic Beauty*, 12.

its application in terms of the non-harmonic, false relation appears to have been patchy in practice, as Herissone notes:

> English writers do not seem to have been wary of movement between perfect and imperfect intervals in principle, although some specific progressions were discouraged. Rather, their failure openly to advocate such progressions seems to have been due to their eagerness to promote the use of parallel imperfect consonances.[58]

English theorists follow Zarlino in his prohibition of non-harmonic relations such as parallel major thirds, but continued to use them in their own compositions; indeed, Morley, though he states that false relations had 'ever been condemned of the most skilful here in England', uses false relations in his own compositions, and indeed without comment in his own examples elsewhere in the *Introduction*.[59] As the seventeenth century progressed and something closer to our own concept of tonality began to come into play, the inconsistencies of musical theoretical accounts of acceptable false relations continued. We heard above that Thomas Campion and later Charles Simpson illustrated the rule forbidding *mi* against *fa* in proximate form, contrary to the origins of the rule, which had prohibited only simultaneous use of *mi* against *fa*.[60] This fundamental ambiguity in application, consistent from the beginnings of the solmization system until the point at which it became outmoded in the later seventeenth century, is key to understanding the false relation. The hexachord's provocative pattern offered a framework to fill, manipulate, overlook, and toy with the gamut and the idea of pitch. This provocation particularly appealed to composers and musicians of the English Renaissance, precisely because of the cultural tropes, approaches, and parameters within which they operated beyond a specifically musical context. Indeed, as this section has demonstrated, the very terminology used to describe the solmization system does not fit into any of the patterns by which English composers construct a tonality, as Owens observed over twenty years ago: 'freeing the investigation from concepts associated with mode or key will make it possible to look more closely at how composers realize a particular tonality, and may eventually help us to understand the distinctive sounds of

---

[58] Herissone, *Music Theory*, 152.
[59] Morley, *Plaine and Easie Introduction*, 177; Herissone, *Music Theory*, 153. Morley's own false relations can be found at 54 and 278 and are discussed by Barry Cooper; see Cooper, 'Englische Musiktheorie', 220.
[60] Herissone, *Music Theory*, 153.

English music from this period'.[61] Such considerations extend beyond the verbal and the words used to describe the system to the methods of visualization that would have fed into the way the solmization system would have initially been read, as well as the visual associations and expectations it would have been bolstered by. In the next section, we will briefly explore the visual idiom of the English Renaissance, and the impact it would likely have had on the way that music was 'read' as a material, physical, printed, or written object. In turn, we shall see that this different visual idiom is vital for understanding the false relation and its evident appeal to composers, performers, and listeners.

Picturing the Hexachord

In turning to the visual ramifications of the hexachord it is important, first, to highlight the fact that English Renaissance art objects are often a far cry from what nonspecialists expect from a work of the high renaissance. Indeed, the visual culture of the English Renaissance has historically been derided as inferior to that of its Italianate (specifically, Tuscan) equivalent due to its refusal to play by the rules of perspective, form, harmony, and design enshrined by the latter tradition: its art objects are, for example, fundamentally disinterested in capturing fixed-point perspective and proportion, as we shall see throughout this book. However, this old-fashioned interpretation has largely been debunked in recent years by studies that have demonstrated the great subtlety and skill that can be discerned in examples of English visual culture when they are approached and analysed on their own terms, rather than forced into categories that they simply do not fit.[62] Its cognitive style—its 'stock of patterns, categories and methods of inference; training in a range of representational conventions; and experience, drawn from the environment, in what are plausible ways of visualizing what we have incomplete information about'[63]—is fundamentally different from that of its continental contemporaries. Sixteenth-century English did not have a term for 'design', because artists and artisans had no conceptual use for it. When they did what we would now call 'designing', they were undertaking a process that had little to do with sketching an idea out on a piece of paper. The Italian equivalent term that would come to dominate

---

[61] Owens, 'Concepts of Pitch', 232.
[62] For a recent example, see Christina J. Faraday, *Tudor Liveliness: Vivid Art in Post-Reformation England* (London & New Haven, CT: Yale University Press for the Paul Mellon Center for Studies in British Art, 2023).
[63] Baxandall, *Painting and Experience*, 32.

art theory and ideas about renaissance art forms was '*disegno*'. In Italian, '*disegno*' connoted two things: the intention, purpose, or plan of a thing, and the graphic representation of that thing, a sketch composed of lines and tones. Only the first sense—of the intention, purpose, plan or 'pattern'—entered Elizabethan English as 'design'.[64] Far from being a pedantic etymological quibble, such a difference is vital when approaching musical notation via its visual manifestation. The English approach elided the difference between the mental image and the material image: conjuring a pattern or plan (like a hexachord) within the mind was the same as elucidating it in the materiality of ink, breath, or sound. Michael Baxandall concluded that the word that most accurately translated the concept of *disegno* was, in fact, 'draft': the preliminary version that is ultimately superseded by a more perfect copy, by dint of draft's early modern cognates 'extended, stretched, pulled' from the mind.[65] Here, for example, is Franciscus Junius' definition from his treatise *The Painting of the Ancients* (first published in Latin in 1637, and English in 1638):

> Lineall picture therefore as it is the ground of all Imitation, so doth it represent unto us the first draught onely of what is further to be garnished with pleasant and lively colours. Whence it is that many who have a deeper insight in these Arts, delight themselves as much in the contemplation of the first, second, and third draughts which great Masters made of their workes, as in the workes themselves: neither is it any marvell that they should be so much ravished with this contemplation, seeing they do not onely perceive in these naked and undisguised lineaments what beautie and force there is in a good and proportionable designe, but they doe likewise see in them the very thoughts of the studious Artificer, and how he did bestirre his judgment before he could resolve what to like and what to dislike.[66]

---

[64] Michael Baxandall, 'English *Disegno*', in Edward Chaney and Peter Mack (eds.), *England and the Continental Renaissance* (Woodbridge: Boydell Press, 1990), 205; Eleanor Chan, *Mathematics and the Craft of Thought in the Anglo-Dutch Renaissance* (London: Routledge, 2021), 103–104. For other examples of this principle being applied, see Gloria Kury, '"Glancing Surfaces": Hilliard, Armour and the Italian Model', in Lucy Gent (ed.), *Albion's Classicism: The Visual Arts in Britain 1550–1660* (London: Paul Mellon Center, 1995); and Tara Hamling, *Decorating the Godly Household: Religious Art in Post-Reformation Britain* (London & New Haven, CT: Paul Mellon Center, 2010).

[65] For exploration of the musical draft in a slightly later context, see Rebecca Herissone, *Musical Creativity in Restoration England* (Cambridge: Cambridge University Press, 2015), 196–204.

[66] Franciscus Junius, *The Painting of the Ancients* (London: Richard Hodgkinsonne, 1638), 270–271.

By the late 1630s, 'lineall pictures' or drafts had become desirable art objects to certain members of the elite such as Charles I, Junius, and his employer Thomas Howard, 14th Earl of Arundel. Nevertheless, in this very early discussion of the attractions of drawings and sketches the trace of that elision between intention and graphic representation endures: 'lineall picture[s]' preserve 'the very thoughts of the studious Artificer'.

'Lineall pictures' or drafts are important to the way we think about music notation in an English Renaissance context. Applied to the concept of the hexachord and solmization (visual tools used in *learning* to read, but ultimately superseded by an internalized visual pattern), 'draft' takes on a special resonance: the hexachord reverses the dynamic from preliminary (material) version into finalized (immaterial) version, but it also demonstrates the fundamental visuality at play in the very idea of music notation as it was understood in the English Renaissance. Established as a visual form from the very moment of a musical reader's first encounter (as printed or manuscript diagram or indeed the physical hand of a music master), the hexachord and the solmization process retain their visuality well after they have been internalized and immaterialized. Sense perception and cognition were understood as thoroughly entwined during this period: sense impressions or *phantasmata* were processed through the imagination or *phantasia* and cognition or *cogitatio* where they were impressed like molten wax and then fixed or set for future reference in the memory or *memoria*, still bearing the imprint of the *phantasmata*.[67] Thus for reader-performers in the English Renaissance the retention of material, visuo-sensory form would have been entirely expected and familiar, and integral to the way that the hexachord and solmization were recalled: a preservation of the 'very thoughts' of the performer/composer.

Acknowledging the difference between English Renaissance and modern Western attitudes towards visual apprehension is vital when thinking about a system of signification like the hexachord, within which the tension between *verba* and *res* (visual, theoretical), sign and ephemeral, performed utterance, is so palpable. It can be tempting to skim over the question of what happened when a person encountered and read a piece of printed or written musical notation. How much can the act of reading musical notation have changed over four centuries? Of course, as we have seen above in the discussion of

---

[67] E. Ruth Harvey, *The Inward Wits: Psychological Theory in the Middle Ages and the Renaissance* (London: Warburg Institute, 1975).

the hexachord and the collision between *voces* (the solmized notes *ut, re, mi*, etc.) and *litterae* (the notes A, B, C, etc.), it has changed a great deal. In this book I would like to emphasize that the change was not simply in the structure of pitch space and the way that notational conventions were marked on the page, but also in the expectation of what those visual marks were *for*, the kind of visual engagement they invited, and what they meant for the shape of the music that would be performed. Mengozzi argues that 'all hexachords are soft', and that previous interpretations of the solmization system have insisted too emphatically on their rigid application where in fact they served as a 'soft superstructure overlaid on a hard heptachordal layer that had long been in place as the foundation of the diatonic system'.[68] However, analysed through the lens of the visual culture of the English Renaissance, all musical notation is 'soft'. The act of looking at any visual object (be it narrative, diagrammatic, emblematic, or so on) was not passive in the English Renaissance. Any viewer was actively involved in the construction of the meaning of a visual object, exercising what E. H. Gombrich referred to as the 'beholder's share', the 'creative imagination by projection'.[69] The 'beholder's share' is a part of visual experience in most cultures, but it is particularly pressing in English visual culture in this period, due to the lack of conceptual separation between the 'pattern' and the 'draft', and due to the common compositional strategies of its art objects which did not preordain a viewing position or direction for visual interpretation (as is the case in art objects designed around fixed-point perspective). This way of seeing has an impact, in turn, upon visual conceptual forms like hexachords and how one can solmize them. It is highly likely that this greater degree of visual pliability enabled English composers and musicians to sculpt and warp hexachordal solmization into the form needed for their distinctive tonality. Looking is making, is creating.[70] To 'read' the inky marks of printed or written musical notation was always to manipulate its soft, malleable form (both as hexachords and *litterae*) to construct music, 'music', and Music.

For evidence of the perceptible delight that the people of the English Renaissance experienced at such malleability, rather than the fixed, governed,

---

[68] Mengozzi, *Renaissance Reform*, 111.

[69] E. H. Gombrich, *The Sense of Order: A Study in the Psychology of Decorative Art* (London: Phaidon, 1979), 155 and 161.

[70] Another version of this theory can be found in Tara Hamling's 'synoptic image', which exploited the 'potent appearance and associations' of traditional religious imagery to 'manipul[ate] visual memory, as an enduring form of Protestant propaganda', incrementally shedding 'contextual composition' which enhanced 'not only its mnemonic quality but also its polychronic temporality, allowing it to speak to the Protestant cause across time and place'. See Tara Hamling, 'Memorable Motifs: The Role of "Synoptic" Imagery in Remembering the English Reformation', in Alexandra Walsham, Bronwyn Wallace, Ceri Law, and Brian Cummings (eds.), *Memory and the English Reformation* (Cambridge: Cambridge University Press, 2020), 185–206, at 191 and 206.

directed viewing of its Tuscan counterpart, we need look no further than the many surviving examples of its visual culture. A classic feature is the skewed, queasy perspective that reads as fundamentally wrong to us, trained as we are to interpret fixed-point perspective as the accurate or 'realistic' mode of depiction. Artists and artisans in England were simply not interested in capturing an image from a single viewing position, and from a single moment. Instead, they sought to capture an ambient impression, from multiple viewing points and multiple moments in time, polychronic and synoptic.[71] This sort of composition can be found in the anonymous *Life of Sir Henry Unton* (c. 1596), which aims quite literally to synoptically depict its protagonist's life from cradle to grave in a manner that can appear chaotic to modern eyes. Other images that we will explore in this book include the Elizabethan wall painting at Thame (c. 1570) and the so-called *Great Picture* attributed to Jan Van BelCamp (1646), which depicts the life of Lady Anne Clifford. These visual art objects use skewed perspective to allow the viewer to read them in any direction and manner that they choose, rather than directing the eye to a specific focal point. We can read Henry Unton's life from birth to death, from death to birth, from the masque to his casual music-making around the table at the centre of the painting; this variety of directions is inbuilt in the very composition of the image and the expectations of its artist(s) as to how it would be visually approached and interpreted.

The visual logic of this way of seeing extends to the graphic forms and structures of musical notation, and the pitch space they evoke within the minds of would-be readers of that notation. The system of musical notation may resemble that of the modern orthochronic system in a way that the so-called fine art objects of the English Renaissance do not, due to the fundamental shift in representational conventions and ideas around what constitutes a realistic depiction. Nevertheless, a stave read through eyes accustomed to such visual conventions would inevitably mean an array of subtly but radically different things when compared to a stave read through eyes trained in the way of seeing we are accustomed to today, in the twenty-first century. We will explore ideas about the visual acuity required to solmize further below, in Chapter 4, but for the present it is worth noting that through this earlier way of seeing, it did not matter that there was a tension between a six-note pitch segment and the seven-letter, eight-note octave. Likewise, it would not necessarily have mattered whether or not the inflection of *mi* or *fa* that enables semitone intervals, and with them false relations, were

---

[71] Hamling, 'Memorable Motifs', 206.

graphically signified or not. To be musically literate within this visual culture was to be able to read *through* the shape of notation, not *along*: to recognize it as a penetrable surface beneath which other patterns existed in palimpsest. As a student of music learned the patterns, inferences, and conventions of the solmization system and gradually committed them to memory, they would have become comfortable with seeing the ghost of the note inflected with *fa* where they opted to inflect it *mi*, and with the logic of the six-note segment superimposed over the seven-letter segment, and vice versa. This was a visual culture that was still developing conventions of abstract diagrammatics in mapping, surveying, and other geometrical operations.[72] All three were crucial to the growing middle classes, the developing colonial expansionist project, and the embryonic scientific interest in causation that were sweeping across England in the latter half of the sixteenth century. All three, as systems, very nearly resemble those that we use today. Nevertheless, they are all marked by the same fundamental difference in visual apprehension. English geometrical treatises from the second half of the sixteenth century, for example, list 'twiste', 'twyne', 'spirail', and 'worme' lines as acceptable forms of the second of Euclid's geometrical elements.[73] Precisely because of the lack of directional expectation in the visual conventions of the period, this would not have been jarring or indeed incompatible with the geometrical lessons these works aimed to impart. A far more active way of looking embedded within the visual conventions of a culture enables the reconciliation of orthogonal geometrical element with 'twiste' or 'twyne'. A similar logic applies to the 'competing' models of pitch space of the *voces* and the *litterae* that infused the hexachord: the friction between the two would have been part and parcel of the visual experience of music in the English Renaissance.

Further evidence that this is an appropriate and enlightening way of thinking about musical notation can be found in the prevalence of notation itself within surviving examples of visual culture. *Four Children Making Music* by the Master of the Countess of Warwick (c. 1565; Fig. 1.2)

---

[72] For more on the development of the surveying system, see Henry S. Turner, *The English Renaissance Stage: Geometry, Poetics, and the Practical Spatial Arts* (Oxford: Oxford University Press, 2006); see also Katherine Hunt and Rebecca Tomlin (eds.), *Numbers in Early Modern* Writing (special issue), *Journal of the Northern Renaissance*, 6 (2014); Yelda Nasifoglu, 'The Changing Nature of Mathematical Diagrams in Seventeenth Century England' in Philip Beeley, Yelda Nasifoglu, and Benjamin Wardhaugh (eds.), *Reading Mathematics in Early Modern Europe: Studies in the Production, Collection and Use of Mathematical Books* (London: Routledge, 2021), 61–101.

[73] Robert Recorde, *The Pathway to Knowledge, Containing the First Principles of Geometry* (London: Reynold Wolfe, 1551); Leonard Digges, *A Geometrical Practice, named Pantometria* (London: Henrie Bynneman, 1571).

Fig. 1.2 Master of the Countess of Warwick, *Four Children Making Music*, oil on panel, c. 1565. Private Collection: by kind permission of the Weiss Gallery.

features two prominently displayed partbooks, one of which is entirely legible as the four-part motet Josquin *Domine ne in furore / Turbatus est*.[74] The other masquerades very feasibly as legible but in fact only features a pattern of shapes resembling notes on a stave (albeit with casual and hurried round script where the legible partbook has carefully formed diamond-shaped noteheads). The presence of the legible partbook serves as what Kerry McCarthy refers to as an 'attractive prop' which may have been in the Master's studio,[75] or perhaps added to enhance the veracity of the virginals; it was not necessarily the prized possession of the subjects that it appears to be, although this is also a feasible reading of the painting. In any case, the presence of musical notation both legible and illegible suggests that it is the attractive appearance of the notation as ink on page, a visually appealing surface pattern both meaningful and meaning*less*, that resulted in their inclusion in the painting. *Four Children Making Music* is not the only example of music being prominently displayed as part of the visual interest of an art object. An anonymous appliqué furnishing panel from a series depicting the liberal arts at Hardwick Hall shows the figure of Music (MVSIQUES) holding a book of music with another open at her feet (Fig. 1.3); the tiny silk pages of the latter are painted in yet more minuscule, and legible musical notation.[76] An anonymous embroidered furnishing panel (probably a bed valance) of c. 1570–1599 features a black servant boy objectified into the role of decorative music stand or table and holding a music book with leger lines but no clefs as the centrepiece of its music-making group (see Fig. 1.4). *The Great Picture* likewise shows Anne Clifford as a young girl in the left-hand panel, clutching an open music book (Fig. 1.5), whilst Lady Grace Talbot's 1591 portrait depicts her standing beside a virginals and a French prayer book open at the notation for Psalm 16 'Preserve me O God, for in thee do I put my trust' (Fig. 1.6). The visual appearance of musical notation held great appeal for the people of the English Renaissance and their general preference for the compositional influence over pattern, rather than hierarchical order.

---

[74] Kerry McCarthy recently identified the music in the painting, previously believed to be by Byrd. Kerry McCarthy, 'Josquin in England', in *Early Music*, 43: 3 (2015), 449–454.
[75] McCarthy, 'Josquin in England', 450.
[76] I am grateful to Katie Bank for pointing out to me that music at Hardwick Hall is frequently depicted as books—in other words, something to be read.

Fig. 1.3 Anonymous, 'MVSIQVES' furnishing panel depicting the figure of Music with a music book, appliqué silk, and velvet scraps with embroidery in couched gilt and silver-gilt thread and spangles in candelabrum and scrolling stem patterns over a linen base, second half of the sixteenth century. National Trust: Hardwick Hall, Derbyshire. Object No. 1129552.

Fig. 1.4 Anonymous, bed valance, silks, and wools in tent stitch, stem stitch, and couched work on linen, c. 1570–1599, Dundee: Victoria & Albert Museum, Accession Number T.136-1991. By kind permission of the Victoria & Albert Museum.

I stated above that the false relation epitomized the ambiguities of the solmization system. In contemplating the system through the lens of the contemporary visual culture, we can begin to move towards an understanding of why that ambiguity might have brough such delight to listeners, performers, and lovers of music in the English Renaissance. The aspects of visual culture that they so enjoyed were reflected and magnified in their musical culture, compounded by its ephemerality, its dual identity as printed or written music and uttered or performed music in voice. The act of reading was a far more physical, materially involved one in the sixteenth century, because reading was so frequently performed aloud 'within the paradigm of vocality'.[77] As a result, it was heavily collaborative and indeed heavily involved; again, not the passive reception of text that we take the process to be in the present day. The notes on the page are far more mercurial than our current mode of reading allows. Alive to the possibilities of this protean, dynamic, and intricate concept of reading, the experience of approaching a musical text in the English Renaissance would likely have made the opportunity to choose between a *mi* and *fa* inflection exciting and pleasing. This excitement and pleasure

---

[77] Jennifer Richards and Richard Wistreich, 'Introduction: Voicing Text 1500–1700', in *Huntington Library Quarterly*, 82: 1 (Spring 2019), 3–16, at 9; Jennifer Richards, *Voices and Books in the English Renaissance* (Oxford: Oxford University Press, 2019).

Fig. 1.5 Attributed to Jan van Belcamp, *The Great Picture*, 1646, oil on panel triptych, 254 cm × 500 cm, Kendal: Abbott Hall Art Gallery. Public Domain.

Fig. 1.6 Anonymous, *Portrait of Lady Grace Talbot*, 1591, oil on panel, 112 cm × 90 cm, National Trust: Hardwick Hall, Object No. NT1129101. By kind permission of the National Trust.

likewise would not have been limited to the performers themselves: they were available to any listeners who knew the music being performed, and the frisson of anticipation and surprise involved in not knowing whether the performer would inflect *mi* or *fa*, but that both were possible.[78] Hearing the

---

[78] See Bent, *Musica Ficta*, 2–5.

unuttered along with the uttered, the note actually performed, draught with pattern rather than either/or, was part and parcel of this musical experience.

It is hard to overestimate the importance that a difference in visual culture would have held for the act of reading. Prior to this book, little attention has been paid to these tiny yet crucial differences, for the effect they have on the status of the inked marks on the page and the pitches they represent (or imply, by their pattern structure). Objections such as those proposed by Mengozzi would have been incomprehensible to a musician, aspiring or realized, professional or amateur, trained in the cultural conventions of the English Renaissance simply by virtue of what a visual object like a musical text could mean, represent, and be interpreted as within the parameters of that culture. Such considerations have been obscured by successive decades (and indeed, centuries) of mythology surrounding the Guidonian hand, solmization, and the false relation. As we shall see in the following section, the mythology surrounding the false relation has been instrumental in the cultivation of the concept of an English musical tradition and style.

False Relations and the Myth of the Musical Golden Age

We have explored aspects of broader English Renaissance culture that would likely have fed into an appreciation of the false relation and all that it offered, sonically, tonally, visually, and conceptually. In this section, we turn to the discourses of mythology that have contributed to our present-day understanding of the false relation, and the burdens that they place upon English Renaissance musical style and what it has been said to represent.[79] In order to do so, it is necessary to briefly step away from the sixteenth and seventeenth centuries, to examine how their musical culture was received and understood by subsequent performers, theorists, and listeners. Beneath the sediment of meaning that false relations have accumulated over the centuries, a different interpretation is accessible, and one that moves us closer towards the way they were once understood by their original performers and listeners. This section aims to excavate beneath some of these layers of sedimented meaning, to demonstrate the value of probing the association between the false relation and Englishness. Chief amongst these ideas was that of the 'natural' harmony of English Renaissance choral music. The

---

[79] Meirion Hughes and Richard Stradling, *The English Musical Renaissance 1840–1940: Constructing a National Music* (Manchester: Manchester University Press, 2001), 76.

concept was one promoted by nineteenth-century interpretations of the works of Tallis, Byrd, and their contemporaries. Suzanne Cole's exploration of Tallis and Victorian England unpacks the belief promoted by Victorian musicologists that 'the English possessed a "natural" taste for harmony [. . . that the] role of music in th[e] Reformation [. . .] was to make the liturgy particularly amenable to English taste. [. . .] Hence the music to which the English liturgy was set must be quintessentially English; it must contain within it that which is most sympathetic to what he perceives to be a distinct English national character.'[80] By and large this was inspired by the now-infamous passage from Gerald of Wales' thirteenth-century *Descriptio Cambriae* which argues for the inherent tendency towards song in the 'Britons':

> The Britons [the Welsh] do not sing in unison, like the inhabitants of other countries; but in many different parts. So that when a company of singers among the common people meet to sing, as is usual in this country, as many different parts are heard as there are performers, who all at length unite in consonance, with organic sweetness. In northern parts of Great Britain, beyond the Humber, on the borders of Yorkshire, the inhabitants use the same kind of symphonious harmony except that they only sing in two parts, the one murmuring in the base, and the other warbling in the acute or treble. Nor do these two nations practice this kind of singing so much by art as habit, which has rendered it so natural to them, that neither in Wales, where they sing in many parts, nor in the North of England, where they sing in two parts, is a simple melody ever well sung. [. . .] But as not all the English sing in this manner, but those only of the North, I believe they had this art at first, like their language, from the Danes and Norwegians, who sued frequently to invade and so occupy, for a long time together, those parts of the island.[81]

This passage inspired much scholarship based on the concept of the English predilection for harmony, but little in the way of analysis as to what this meant for the music of continental Europe that so clearly inspired much

---

[80] Suzanne Cole, *Thomas Tallis and His Music in Victorian England* (Woodbridge: Boydell & Brewer, 2008), 172.

[81] Quoted in ibid., 177. For a much later example of this concept's continuing influence, see Edward J. Dent, 'On the Composition of English Songs', in *Music & Letters*, 6: 3 (1925). These ideas were still being promoted in the 1940s, with assertions such as that of J. A. Westrup: 'Song still lives, because we are a singing nation. From Dowland to the present day the line, though sometimes thin, is scarcely broken.' J. A. Westrup, 'Music', in Ernest Baker (ed.), *The Character of England* (Oxford: Clarendon Press, 1947), 406.

of the English choral music that nineteenth-century musicologists admired. The Reverend J. Powell Metcalfe, for example, distinguished the 'natural' harmony with which chant was 'enriched' from the *arithmetical* harmony' that preceded the Reformation.[82] Whether or not Metcalfe's distinction between 'natural' and 'arithmetical' harmony is the result of a misunderstanding of the musical rules discussed above is somewhat of a moot point: the supposed superiority of the English choral style over the continent is of more use to the present investigation. We will already note the paradox of describing the style as defined by a 'natural harmony' when the fundamentally non-harmonic false relation was such a definitive feature of its acoustic. Such a paradox is crucial to the obfuscation surrounding the false relation (not least the fables of the 'forbidden' *diabolo in musica*, the tritone) that inflects our understanding to this day.

Interpretations of the English Reformation from the nineteenth century are heavily influenced by the rhetoric of the newly established Church of England and the ideas that it promoted from the very moment of its inception in Henry VIII's break from Rome. Geoffrey of Monmouth's twelfth-century *Historia Regum Britanniae* established the origins of British kingship in Brutus the Trojan, grandson of Aeneas (of Virgil's *Aeneid*), who arrived in Britain in 1170 BC; the accession of Henry VII and the foundation of the Tudor dynasty had been spun as the fulfilment of Merlin's prophecy that the Britons would one day overcome the Saxons, who had driven them into Cornwall and Wales after the death of King Arthur, the great hope of Brutus' line.[83] Following the break from Rome, religious myths were interwoven into this propagandistic interpretation of British history and its connection to antiquity: recycling, repurposing, and 'remembering' one concept of past, as a way of forgetting.[84] The Church of England was firmly believed to have apostolic foundations, most commonly thought to have been established by Joseph of Arimathea (the apocryphal founder of the first English church in Glastonbury), but also variously associated with St Paul and

---

[82] Cole, *Thomas Tallis*, 173.

[83] Ibid., 175; see also Sydney Anglo, 'The *British History* in Early Tudor Propaganda', in *Bulletin of the John Rylands Library*, 44 (1961), 17–48.

[84] By and large, we should approach this process as 'like manuscript palimpsests that bear traces of the texts that have been erased [. . .] only partially successful in banishing the memory of the Catholic past'. For more on this process, see Alexandra Walsham, Brian Cummings, and Ceri Law, 'Introduction: Memory and the English Reformation', in Alexandra Walsham, Bronwen Wallace, Ceri Law, and Brian Cummings (ed.), *Memory and the English Reformation* (Cambridge: Cambridge University Press, 2020), 1–47, at 25.

St James.[85] English Christianity, as practiced by the Britons, continued uncorrupted until the arrival of Augustine and his influence from Rome; the Reformation was thus nothing but a return to the pure expression of Christianity intended by God when Joseph of Arimathea, St Paul, or St James arrived on British soil.[86] These interpretations were vastly at odds with the evident trauma caused by the Reformation and the uprooting of devotional traditions that had continued unbroken for many hundreds of years; nevertheless, the seduction of this mythology of Englishness, especially as aspirations towards empire and colonialism began to take on new urgency with so-called discovered new worlds, was evidently powerful. We will explore the connotations of these developments below in Chapter 6.

The role of the 'non-harmonic' false relation within this understanding of English musical identity is a complex one. The false relation came into existence in polyphonic repertoire, often composed for a devotional purpose; whilst it soon spread to secular forms such as the chanson, the madrigal, and the ballett, it continued to appear in sacred contexts well into the late seventeenth century even where it had fallen out of fashion in other genres.[87] The religious context is thus particularly important to any interpretation of false relations and their role in the broader musical culture of the English Renaissance. We will never know what Tallis, Byrd, Weelkes, Tomkins, or Gibbons thought about the mythology of English episcopacy, but we can be relatively certain that they knew of these theories and their propagandistic importance to the Tudor dynasty. In turn, though it is rather a stretch to imagine that they envisioned their own music as built around a 'natural' opposed to 'arithmetical' harmony (a dichotomy that simply did not exist in the Tudor conception of mathematics, mathematics then being understood principally as a signature of the divine influence upon the cosmos), it is likely that their knowledge of these theories about the apostolic origins of the Church of England influenced the music they composed (for Tudor monarchs, their Stuart successors, and their courts), and that stylistic use of false relations could have been a result of knowledge of those theories. The conjecture that false relations could be an expression of or refutation of the belief in the superiority of English Christianity is fundamentally unprovable.

---

[85] This was a project actively promoted by Matthew Parker, Archbishop of Canterbury, from 1559 to 1575. See Harry Spillane, '"A Matter Newly Seene": The Bishops' Bible, Matthew Parker, and Elizabethan Antiquarianism', in *Reformation*, 27: 2 (2022), 107–124.

[86] See, e.g., John Foxe, *Actes and Monuments* (London: 1563), Vol. 1, 516.

[87] See Thomas Tomkins' audacious *O Sing unto the Lord a New Song*, with its false relation laden 'alleluia' section, first published 1630 but likely performed earlier, or Martin Peerson's *Laboravi in Gemitu*. This approach was still being used (albeit in more restrained form) by the late seventeenth century, with the setting of 'I Was Glad' variously attributed to John Blow and Henry Purcell.

Nevertheless, in investigating the cultural role of false relations and this form of musical writing it is important that we keep such potential readings in mind. The value of investigating beyond the notes on the page to the broader culture that influenced the original reception of false relations is that these possibilities can be entertained, and can allow us to situate the musical style they evoke within the full range of cultural influences they originally developed out of (however preposterous some of them now appear).

We are now able to recognize the ideas surrounding the mythical foundation of the Church of England for what they are: rhetoric developed by a small nation faced with a rapidly expanding world, few political allies, and the need to rationalize the exploitation that the colonized empire they desired to construct (in order to bolster their position against this expanding world and their relative lack of political allies) would require.[88] Fictions these myths may be, but they were nevertheless powerful in shaping the fortunes of the Tudor dynasty and the lives of all those who lived under Tudor rule. In turn, ideas about the mythical origins of the Britons as the chosen Christian nation have heavily influenced the development of musical style in England, at the very least as an ideal to which to aspire. As composers such as Ralph Vaughan Williams, Gustav Holst, Frederick Delius, Edward Elgar, and later Benjamin Britten and Herbert Howells sought to build upon the 'English' (Briton-ish, or Welsh) tradition of music, they reached back to the music produced during and immediately after the Reformation, through the 'father' of English choral music, Thomas Tallis.[89] In 1989, Wilfrid Mellers was still able to state of Elgar's music that

> The unconscious intrusion of inflexions derived not only from the English language but also from English folk song, and from the modal reflections of those melodies in Tudor polyphony.[90]

---

[88] Intriguingly, these myths echo those established by the political class in the English Renaissance itself; see Hall, *Things of Darkness*.
[89] Cole, *Thomas Tallis*, 55; see also Heather Weibe, '"Now and England": Britten's *Gloriana* and the "New Elizabethans"', in *Cambridge Opera Journal*, 17: 2 (2005), 141–172, and *Britten's Unquiet Pasts: Sound and Memory in Postwar Reconstruction* (Cambridge: Cambridge University Press, 2012); Paul Hopwood, 'Polite Patriotism: The Edwardian Gentleman in English Music, 1904 to 1914', in *Nineteenth-century Music Review*, 16: 3 (2019), 383–416; Ceri Owen, 'Making an English Voice: Performing National Identity during the English Musical Renaissance', in *Twentieth-century music*, 13: 1 (2016), 77–107; Alain Frogley, 'Constructing Englishness in Music: National Character and the Reception of Vaughan Williams', in Alain Frogley (ed.), *Vaughan Williams Studies* (Cambridge: Cambridge University Press, 1996), 1–22; Wilfrid Mellers, *Vaughan Williams and the Vision of Albion* (London: Barrie & Jenkins, 1989); Paul Harrington, 'Holst and Vaughan Williams: Radical Pastoral', in Christopher Norris (ed.), *Music and the Politics of Culture* (London: Lawrence & Wishart, 1989), 106–127; Frank Howes, *The English Musical Renaissance* (New York: Stein & Day, 1966).
[90] Mellers, *Vision of Albion*, 9.

Mellers's interpretation does not elide the English language with the 'modal reflections of [folk song] melodies in Tudor polyphony', but the way he connects the two draws striking similarities with Metcalfe's interpretation of over a century earlier. The 'natural' English harmony remained a guiding light of the English musical tradition throughout what Frank Howes, Meirion Hughes, and Robert Stradling referred to as the 'English musical renaissance'.[91] Indeed, we might surmise that the choice of this term was in fact an explicit move to ally the musical tradition of the latter half of the nineteenth and first half of the twentieth century with that of the Renaissance (broadly, the fifteenth to early seventeenth centuries) itself. This is the context within which, for example, Ralph Vaughan Williams composed his *Fantasia on a Theme by Thomas Tallis* (1909) and Benjamin Britten his masque-opera *Gloriana* (1953), to celebrate the coronation of Elizabeth II and draw direct continuities with Elizabeth I and the 'golden age' that she had come to represent by utilizing devices from Edmund Spenser's *Faerie Queene* (1590); almost fifty years might separate the two pieces, but they are both manifestations of the 'nationalistic movement in which musicians staged particular narratives and performances of cultural renewal, negotiating questions of national identity and modernity by appealing to distant (and often fictitious) national pasts, in search of "authentic" sounds and experiences of musical Englishness that had supposedly been lost in an increasingly industrialized and urbanized society'.[92] The memory of the music of the English Renaissance, distant and often fictitious or idealized, has had a powerful impact upon English national identity.

Neither Vaughan Williams's *Fantasia on a Theme* nor Britten's *Gloriana* features false relations as a particularly brazen stylistic feature. A better example can perhaps be found in that of Herbert Howells, whose attendance (aged eight) at the premiere of Vaughan Williams's *Fantasia on a Theme* at the Gloucester Three Choirs Festival in 1910 shaped his compositional approach (and his taste for polyphony) throughout his life;[93] Howells would later claim to consider himself belonging to the Tudor period 'not only

---

[91] Howes, *English Musical Renaissance*; Meirion Hughes and Richard Stradling, *The English Musical Renaissance 1840–1940: Constructing a National Music* (Manchester: Manchester University Press, 2001); see also Michael Trend, *The Music Makers: Heirs and Rebels of the English Musical Renaissance, Edward Elgar to Benjamin Britten* (London: Weidenfeld & Nicholson, 1985).

[92] Owen, 'Making an English Voice', 78. See also Meirion Hughes and Richard Stradling, *Constructing a National Music*.

[93] Paul Spicer, *Herbert Howells* (Bridgend: Seren, 1998), 22.

musically but in every way'.[94] Nowhere is this more palpable than in his *Gloucester Service* (1946). Philip Cooke notes the 'schizophrenic quality' epitomized by his use of harmony:

> On a purely musical level his harmony can be reduced to a series of added chords, false relations and piquant 'blue' notes, but this goes no way to explaining the expressive qualities behind the music. For it is in the harmony that we find ecstasy and agony often transmuted into a series of 'pleasure/pain' chords that are strewn throughout the canticles. These take many different shapes, though Howells repeatedly returns to two favoured chords: a bitonal interlocking of seemingly unrelated triads, and the simultaneous false relation in inner parts for purely dramatic effect. [. . .] A lot of the dissonances in these works result from the highly contrapuntal, polyphonic nature of Howells' vocal music: the linear flow of the music, and the highly melismatic word-setting (especially in the Gloucester Service) and the ambiguous dissonances created by the collision of these polyphonic lines help to enhance in the quality of 'otherness': it is challenging music (aurally and practically) but it somehow manages to be both traditional and yet progressive—there is plenty of dissonant music, but it is never *too* dissonant to disrupt the continuum of tradition to which Howells felt very much connected.[95]

There is a lot going on in Cooke's analysis, not simply pertaining to the place of the *Gloucester Service* amongst Howells's corpus of works, but also of how the music of Howells fits into the English choral tradition in general. For the purposes of an investigation into false relations and their afterlives, we should note two things: that Cooke associates the 'dissonant' 'collision' of polyphonic lines and 'strident use of the minor second' with 'otherness' and yet also with 'the continuum of tradition', and that he highlights them as hallmarks of the desire to express 'ecstasy' and 'agony', as 'pleasure/pain' chords. Cooke appears unaware that the way that he writes of the 'ambiguous dissonances' of Howells feeds into an overall ambivalent interpretation of

---

[94] Lionel Pike, 'Howells and Counterpoint', in Philip A. Cooke and David Maw (eds.), *The Music of Herbert Howells* (Woodbridge: Boydell & Brewer, 2008), 22.

[95] Philip A. Cooke, 'A "Wholly New Chapter" in Service Music: Collegium Regale and the Gloucester Service', in Philip A. Cooke and David Maw (eds.), *The Music of Herbert Howells* (Woodbridge: Boydell & Brewer, 2008), 86–99, at 95 and 96–97. Note also Jeremy Summerly's contention that the *Gloucester Service* is an ode to the English Renaissance trope of the 'English' cadence; Jeremy Summerly, 'The English Cadence', in *Leading Notes*, 6: 1 (1996), 7–9.

how Howells fits into the English choral tradition: is it the quality of 'otherness' in his use of false relations that allies him to the continuum of tradition, or is it the way that he plays with the paradoxes of polyphony (and its inherent linearity) used alongside harmony? The slippage in his analysis and blurring of two discrete issues into one (an 'otherness' of dissonant collision that had been inherent in the choral tradition at its very foundation in the sixteenth century) encapsulates the way that false relations have come to be packaged. They are glossed over, their fascinating complexities, connotations, and paradoxes reduced to a series of anecdotes that insist on their 'otherness'.

This is the context within which we have received false relations as a historical musicological phenomenon. There is an uneasy resemblance between the anxieties over origins that spawned the so-called English musical renaissance, and the ideas discussed above surrounding the mythical origins of the Church of England: both eras were overwhelmingly concerned with establishing a narrative around collective English history, and the concept of an English (largely white) race.[96] False relations therefore served a crucial role in the fashioning of Englishness in a manner that we are only just beginning to appreciate. The sixteenth and early seventeenth centuries (that first heyday of the false relation) witnessed a burgeoning project to establish a mythology of the origins of first the Tudor dynasty, then the English aristocracy, and finally as the concept percolated down throughout society, the English in general. Texts such as William Camden's *Britannia* (1610)[97] are the most obvious surviving remnant of this way of conceptualizing a coherent, exceptional, and lauded collective English past, but such thought can be found in, for example, Edmund Spenser's epic romance *The Faerie Queene* (1590) and Thomas Tallis and William Byrd's explicit proclamation at the beginning of their *Cantiones sacrae* (1575) that their intention is to bring the 'Englysh metre' to the continent. Rising to prominence during two crucial periods in the evolution of the British Empire as a celebrated stylistic of English musical tradition, the false relation is thus both witness and vital tool in the formation of what Matthieu Chapman refers to as 'a world made

---

[96] See Dennis Britton, *Becoming Christian: Race, Reformation, and Early Modern English Romance* (New York: Fordham University Press, 2014), for the way that English theologians appropriated the forms of romance to transform Christians into a race and argue that salvation could be ensured by race, particularly 35–58.

[97] William Camden, *Britain, or a Chorographicall Description of the most flourishing Kingdomes, England, Scotland, and Ireland, and the lands adjoining, out of the depth of Antiquitie* (London, 1610).

in the image of whiteness' (not simply in terms of complexion and corporeality, but spreading outwards to the whiteness of certain traits and tastes, such as reason, objectivity, and civility, and, as Noémie Ndiaye observes, 'remind[ing us] that whiteness is an unstable conceptual assemblage drawing on various categories such as phenotype, religion, class, nationality, sexual manners [and] modes of civility among others').[98] We will explore this phenomenon later, in the concluding two chapters of this book; for the present, however, it is important to observe that the fact that false relations gained musical capital during these two time periods is not a coincidence and part of a broader pattern to be found in diverse other cultural products that spoke to the formation of English identity.

The resemblance between Victorian and Tudor approaches to the formation of English identity can be found not only in the turn towards music and a musical tradition of 'natural' harmony: it can be found, too, in the literature that enjoyed a boom in popularity over the late nineteenth and early twentieth and late sixteenth and early seventeenth centuries. During both periods, pastoral and romance (especially Arthurian romance) were immensely popular and came to represent 'nativeness' opposed to continental (and corrupting) 'otherness'. As Margo Hendricks notes, the interest in nativeness was inherent in the romance genre from the very beginning, tied to the genre's aspiration (albeit imaginative) to the practice of historiography and interest in the social and cultural value of heritage represented by the romantic culmination of 'happy ever after', such that 'when we look at early modern English romances, regardless of form, there is a pervasive engagement with race-making, whether it is tied to nation, ethnicity, or colourism—and sometimes all three'.[99] Dennis Britton and Tiffany Werth argue that this manifested particularly in a reappropriation of Catholicism: 'the attributes of

---

[98] For more on the 'assumption that whiteness and Englishness are inextricably linked at the first ontological instance' and the fact that 'with the dissolution of the monasteries, emerging imperialist missions, colonization, and the discovery of the black slave (Slave?), the boundaries of "English" identity and their relation to whiteness, were in constant flux, shifting and permeable and expanding and contracting with each new encounter', see Matthieu Chapman, 'Whitewashing White Permanence: The (Dis)/(re)membering of White Corporeality in Early Modern England', in *Literature Compass* (5 Dec 2022), 1–14, at 5 and 8. Crucially, Chapman notes that Englishness and whiteness were not conceptually linked in any stable sense in the English Renaissance: whiteness was associated to dismemberment, sickness, and death. For more on this see Ian Smith, *Black Shakespeare: Reading and Misreading Race* (Cambridge: Cambridge University Press, 2022), especially 1–30 and 40–48; and Noémie Ndiaye, 'Read It for Restoratives: *Pericles* and the Romance of Whiteness', in *Early Theatre*, 26: 1 (2023), 11–27, at 17.

[99] Margo Hendricks, *Race and Romance: Coloring the Past* (Chicago: University of Chicago Press, 2022), Chapter 1 (unpaginated).

romance are interleaved with English religious identity [...] the fascination with romance lay precisely in its contested use of successful motifs drawn from a discredited Catholic heritage'.[100] This rise in popularity was not least for the way that the forms of the romance and pastoral genres, constructed out of 'memes', rendered them particularly flexible tools for mythologizing and 'superimposing new layers of meaning over pre-existing ones',[101] as Helen Cooper explores:

> [A meme is] an idea that behaves like a gene in its ability to replicate faithfully and abundantly, but also on occasion to adapt, mutate, and therefore survive in different forms and cultures. [...] The 'far away and long ago' that is almost a defining feature of the genre, the freeing of romances from familiar place or chronology, makes it especially easy for them to be appropriated for interpretations that fit the immediate historical or cultural moment of subsequent readers. [...] The community of Tudor England looked to romance as the site where its values could be questioned and tested but ultimately reaffirmed.[102]

The romance genre was borne out of medieval forms of narrative and survived the advent of humanism and the classical revival, much loved until the end of the seventeenth century and beyond. In an English Renaissance context, it lies behind the trend for the pastoral forms and tropes typical of the madrigal and ballett that rose to prominence at the turn of the seventeenth century and found curious blended manifestations in pieces such as Thomas Weelkes's 'Hark All Ye Lovely Saints Above' (a blending of both pastoral and devotional imagery that melds romance with 'discredited Catholic heritage' in the way described by Werth above). By and large the fundamental appeal of the romance genre is in its archaism, and its pretensions towards historiography.[103] Its 'memes' and tropes were familiar from tales learned in childhood; their repetition and reinvention created a sense of

---

[100] Tiffany Jo Werth, *The Fabulous Dark Cloister: Romance in England after the Reformation* (Baltimore: Johns Hopkins University Press, 2011), 3–4. For more on this see Britton, *Becoming Christian*; and Emily Griffiths Jones, *Right Romance: Heroic Subjectivity and Elect Community in Seventeenth-Century England* (Philadelphia: University of Pennsylvania Press, 2019).
[101] Walsham, Cummings, and Law, 'Introduction', 25.
[102] Helen Cooper, *The English Romance in Time: Transforming Motifs from Geoffrey of Monmouth to the Death of Shakespeare* (Oxford: Oxford University Press, 2004), 2–6. See also Werth, *Dark Cloister*, 1–18.
[103] Hendricks, *Race and Romance*.

continuity and ultimately of tradition. False relations can be read as one of these memes, 'able to replicate faithfully and abundantly, but also on occasion to adapt, mutate, and survive in different cultures'. Like whitewashed wall-paintings and broken rood screens, they can be considered another of the many 'palimpsestic remnants of England's religious past':[104] remembered both as the relic of a prior, lost devotional practice, and as a pernicious influence from the Catholic continent. As we saw above, with Cooke's analysis but also with Morley's own contemporary comments on false relations, they were (and continue to be) perceived as both native (but archaic) and as 'other' or 'strange'. We shall discuss this in greater detail below, in Chapter 6, but for the present it is worth noting that the traditional/other dichotomy has inflected understanding of the false relation from the very moment that they became hallmarks of the English Renaissance choral style. As we shall see throughout this book, their origins as a stylistic feature of sacred repertoire are key to understanding this dichotomy of significance and palimpsestic identity.

Such ways of seeing, thinking, and knowing are not incidental to the way that the false relation operated in the English Renaissance: they are, on the contrary, inherent in their very warp and weft. The subsequent range of meanings and associations they have gained, however fragmentarily, bear the trace of these different approaches to apprehending music as a seen, thought, and known entity. This book seeks to give space to these approaches and their ramifications upon our understanding of false relations in two predominant ways: as a thought phenomenon, imagined within the minds of musicians and listeners, and as a performed phenomenon, brought to life by professional and amateur practitioners. In the absence of a full elucidated documentation, it is necessary to look elsewhere for our fragmentary evidence.

Plan of the Book

This book is divided into two main sections: Thinking and Performing. The first seeks to situate the false relation within the broader milieu of the English Renaissance, focusing in on the literary, rhetorical, material, and visual cultures of the period. In so doing, its aims are twofold. First, to render

---

[104] Werth, *Dark Cloister*, 2.

the familiar musical theoretical topics of the hexachord and solmization unfamiliar by approaching them from angles that have not previously been deemed of relevance to this technical musical material: considerations such as the collision (rather than complements) between textual and musical form and the poetics of their appearance upon the page, approaches towards literacy, and visuality, as briefly touched upon above. Second, to provide an avenue into understanding the hexachord, solmization, and false relation from those not from a musical theoretical background, in a manner that will render such material accessible and relevant to the cultural developments of the English Renaissance. Doing so will reveal the benefits of recognizing that the false relation chimes with a number of the visual and textual concerns that characterize English culture in the sixteenth and early seventeenth centuries.

Chapter 2 investigates possible routes towards understanding the murkier corners of understanding of the false relation and of discord, dissonance, and the chromatic (all words that potentially signify false relation or the experience of hearing/performing false relation) in general by entertaining metaphor and the power of suggestion as a tool of musicological analysis, and the importance of the evocative trace as evidence alongside the concrete, documented connection. It investigates the literature of the period, both explicitly and implicitly musical, to shine a light on the lexicon of falseness through its unexpected synonym, 'sweet', and all that sweetness (as sugar, as persuasion, and as artifice) came to represent as the sixteenth century turned to the seventeenth. In so doing, it will demonstrate some of the ways in which the *mi–fa* interval continued to exercise its spectral influence over the musical culture of the English Renaissance, even as fixed-scale solmization began gradually to replace the mutable solmization system.

Turning from possible words used to describe musical falseness and the false relation, Chapter 3 looks (as far as is possible) at the texts that can be allied to false relations. It explores the false relation and its relationship to ideas about word painting, chromaticism, and expression, both contemporary and those still adopted in the twenty-first century. It argues that, rather than focusing on individual word groups and types (noun, proper noun, adjective, verb), a more productive reading can be gained by focussing in on phrasing patterns, the structure and semantics of rhetorical tropes, and on the burgeoning forms of punctuation ('distinction' or 'pointing', in contemporary terminology). The false relations of the English Renaissance rose to prominence during the great push to establish a vernacular liturgy.

As this chapter demonstrates, the syntax of the *Book of Common Prayer* (1549) and *Whole Booke of Psalmes* (1562) hold the key to reaching towards an understanding of the semantic, expressive role of the false relation. Complementing the preceding chapter, it will demonstrate that by allying analysis of the music to poetic rhetorical tropes, we can move towards more detailed understanding of chromatic expressiveness.

Continuing our focus on the broader culture surrounding the false relation, Chapter 4 seeks to explore the responses, contemplations, and analogies of discord in the visual culture of the English Renaissance. In many places, these can be seen to offer evocative insight directly into the culture of false relation, through their suggestive inferences and through their metaphorical and allegorical import. This chapter argues that solmization should be considered a matter of visual culture alongside musical culture, both in the context within which it was learnt, and in the visuo-spatial demands it places upon a student learning to read music. It explores ideas about the 'substance' of music as defined by Thomas Wright and by Campion, and the visual culture parallels to be found in thinking about what music was made of. Finally, returning to the pitch-space diagrams of William Bathe, Thomas Morley, and Thomas Campion, it will explore the visual implications of the practice of solmization and the *mi–fa* interval through the lens of the rise of the table format and the developing graphic, diagrammatic forms of visual culture.

Returning to more solid musicological ground in section two, Performing, the book will then consider the way in which they were taught and disseminated amongst choristers and the general public, and finally examine the development of one of its classic tropes, the 'English' cadence and its utilization of the *una nota supra la, semper est canendum fa* (one note above *la* should be solmized as *fa*) rule inherited from Guido d'Arezzo. Looking at two musical manuscripts which have been demonstrated to be explicitly didactic, the Hamond Partbooks and *A Booke of In nomines & other solfainge songes* alias Add. MS 31390, Chapter 5 examines how young choristers and amateurs learnt how to perform false relations. Building outwards from the core of its two main exemplars, it examines the visual traces of the ways that this notational culture inferred false relation by dint of the way it utilized the hexachord structure as pattern to assist in navigating the visual rhetoric of musical space. Elsewhere, it will be seen that the visual acuity demanded by the solmizing system was strongly related to those of the broader visual culture of the English Renaissance, solidifying the claims of the preceding chapter.

Finally, Chapter 6 looks at '*fa*' and '*la*', and the rule that ordained the inferring of *la* as flattened in the solmization system. It will consider their relationship to the split seventh and the split fourth, as they are now known, and the cadential figures which developed out of these practices. Not least of these are the so-called English cadence. Using this musical trope as its lodestar, this chapter examines the dual accusations of archaism and strangeness levelled at false relations by Thomas Morley in his *Plaine and Easie Introduction*. The 'English' cadence shines a light upon the movement towards tonality, the twilight period of solmization, and understanding of false relation. This chapter will conduct an etymology of the cadence, making use of etymology's older, more playful, punning role as the rhetorical trope *etymologia*, in order to demonstrate that (English or not), the cadence has much to tell us about this poignant period of English history. Using the methodological approaches elucidated in Chapters 2 and 4, it will argue that the delight in false relations and their semantic capacity was well established and appreciated in contemporary sources beyond the explicitly musical.

Ultimately, this book seeks to demonstrate the value of attempting an overview of English Renaissance culture through the lens of the tiny and generally unremarked trope of the false relation. In so doing, it does not aim to deal in certainties but rather the possibilities offered by approaching the fragmentary traces of a musical trope little documented, full of contradiction, and frequently not even visibly present on the page, and the way that it reflects, refracts, and interacts with the broader concerns of English Renaissance culture. It attempts to imagine the experience of listening and performing music that was available to professionals and amateurs, as a process that could be successful and could often be fraught with potential error. The appearance of printed musical theoretical treatises around the end of the sixteenth century indicates that there was a growing (and broadening) market for musical knowledge, beyond the professional. There is ample evidence that we should take the aspiring amateur musician and the trials and tribulations that faced them in attempting to learn to read and perform (as epitomized in Thomas Morley's Philomathes) seriously. Techniques like solmization could be opaque and abstruse to such readers, much as they can be to those trained in the Western musical tradition today. The barriers that faced these musical readers and the connotations that assisted them in their understanding are as important as those faced by the boy choristers who went on to be professional musicians.

Likewise, this book does not seek to provide a comprehensive list of all iterations of false relation during the period, but rather to push the boundaries of what can be counted as documentary evidence by looking at a series of episodes where the false relation appears only as a fleeting phantasm of the musical cultures of the English Renaissance. It leans into the uncertainty and the twin poles of the semantic bagginess and fogginess of the false relation, recognizing that the way it was documented invites a different way of reading musical evidence than has hitherto been attempted.[105] Whilst words like 'discord', 'chromatic', and 'dissonant' did not always mean the technical figure that we now know as the false relation, they contain the possibility of those meanings to subsequent readers throughout the sixteenth and seventeenth centuries: any instance of these words must be approached as a possible reverberation unless specifically defined otherwise by its author. It is hoped that this reading of false relations will broaden the horizons of what can and cannot be considered a musical object, piece of evidence or topic in the English Renaissance, and to invite revision of familiar figures, material and musical terrain. The visual, the textual, the political, and the intellectual are always important to the musical. The false relation provokes us to think seriously about what it suggests about the *mise-en-page*, about reading habits, about performance habits, about literacy both visual and textual. What follows is an experiment in meeting it on its own terms.

---

[105] Amanda Eubanks Winkler, 'Musicologists, often methodologically aligned with historians, have generally been uncomfortable with uncertainty. We seek evidence—librettos, musical scores—to support our claims.' Amanda Eubanks Winkler, *Music, Dance and Drama in Early Modern English Schools* (Cambridge: Cambridge University Press, 2020), 3.

SECTION I
THINKING

2
The Rhetoric of Falseness or, How to Talk about a Discord

By them the formes of outward things she learnes,
For they returne into the fantasie,
What ever each of them abroad discernes,
And there inrole it for the Minde to see.

But when she sits to iudge the good and ill,
And to discerne betwixt the false and true;
She is not guided by the *Senses*' skill,
But doth each thing in her owne mirrour view.

Then she the *Senses* checks, which oft do erre,
And even against their false reports decrees;
And oft she doth condemne what they preferred,
For with a power above the *Sense*, she sees.

Therefore no *Sense* the precious ioyes conceives,
Which in her private contemplations bee;
For then the ravish't spirit the *Senses* leaves,
Hath her owne powers, and proper actions free.

Her harmonies are sweet, and full of skill,
When on the Bodie's instrument she playes;
But the proportions of the wit and will,
Those sweet accords, are even the angels layes.

These Tunes of *Reason* are *Amphion*'s Lyre,
Wherewith he did the *Thebane* City found:

> These are the Notes wherewith the Heavenly *Choir*,
> The Praise of him which made the Heav'n, doth sound.[1]
>
> [...]
>
> So, though the Clouds eclipse the *Sun*'s fair Light,
> Yet from his Face they do not take one Beam;
> So have our Eyes their perfect Pow'r of Sight,
> Ev'n when they look into a troubled Stream.
>
> Then these Defects in *Sense's* Organs be;
> Not in the *Soul*, or in her working Might:
> She cannot lose her perfect Pow'r to see,
> Though Mists and Clouds do choak her Window-Light.
>
> These Imperfections then we must impute,
> Not to the Agent, but the Instrument:
> We must not blame *Apollo*, but his Lute,
> If false Accords from her false Strings be sent.[2]

Musical falseness runs like the warp through the weft of John Davies's description of human perception in his *Nosce Teipsum* (1599). It coruscates through his cross-rhymed quatrains, hinting towards the cultural norms, knowledge, and associations that he anticipates in his readership. The 'false[ness]' and 'false reports' that are discerned by the mind's 'owne mirrour view' intertwine with the metaphor of her 'sweet' and 'skil[ful]' harmonies, the 'Bodies instrument' which she manipulates to play 'sweet accords' and the 'notes' of the 'Heavenly choir', weaving the imagery together into a coherent concept of the 'Mists', 'Clouds', and 'Imperfections of the 'false Accords from [...] false Strings' that can obscure the 'mirrour view'. 'Sweet' and 'false accords' shimmer between opposites and, unexpectedly, tantalizingly, manifestations of each other. The casual presence of this trope as assumed knowledge in a treatise about perception provides the reader a vital suggestive clue as to the nature of the false relation and what people might have thought of them in

---

[1] John Davies, *Nosce Teipsum* (London: Richard Field for John Standish, 1599), 'Of the Soule of Man', verses 46–51.
[2] Ibid., 95.

the English Renaissance. There is very little in the way of explicit reference to false relations in contemporary writing about music, and even less that offers a clue as to how they were conceptualized as positive entities that were enjoyable to listen to and to perform. In this chapter, I suggest that one potential and provocative trace of this lost way of thinking can be found in one of Davies's keywords: 'sweet'.

'Sweet' is by far the most common descriptor of pleasant sound or music in early modern English.[3] 'Sweete musicke/s',[4] 'sweete harmonie', 'sweet notes', 'sweet strayes', 'sweet delightes',[5] 'sweet aires',[6] '[musical] workes with ayre so sweet perfumed',[7] 'sweet noise', 'sweet in the eare' are all phrases used in the late sixteenth or early seventeenth century to describe an enjoyable musical experience, or of sound so pleasant that it could be musical. Such phrases often appear in non-musical texts, in plays, poems, and rhetorical treatises, but they also appear in the paratextual, in ephemera of printed collections of music, and in musical theoretical texts. Sweetness is from the language of medieval music theory, inherited by and still in use in the English Renaissance. The F hexachord was known as the *molle*, the soft, the sweet; flatness in general (as a result of the F hexachord's key distinguishing feature, B-flat) was often associated with sweetness. As this chapter will explore the possibilities across the sixteenth and early seventeenth centuries, these connotations had seeped into the collective consciousness and diffused from the idea of flatness into the idea of sharpness, of fictive hexachords and the concept of false relation (both simultaneous and proximate) in general. We cannot reactivate the cognitive architecture of the period, and to aim to do so would be foolish. We can, however, explore the suggestive traces of how people once thought about false relations as a way of musical knowing. As we shall see, the concept of 'sweet' offers a potentially illuminating lens into how false relations might once have been understood.

---

[3] Jessie Ann Owens (ed.), *Noyses, Sounds and Sweet Aires: Music in Early Modern England* (Seattle: University of Washington Press, 2007); Christopher Marsh, *Music and Society in Early Modern England* (Cambridge: Cambridge University Press, 2010); Simon Smith, *Musical Response in the Early Modern Playhouse 1603–1625* (Cambridge: Cambridge University Press, 2017); Katherine Hunt, 'The Art of Changes: Bell-Ringing, Anagrams, and the Culture of Combination in Seventeenth-Century England', in *Journal of Medieval and Early Modern Studies*, 48 :2, 387–412.

[4] John Wilbye, 'I Live, and Yet Methinks I do Not Breathe', in *The Second Set of Madrigals for 3–6 Voices* (London: Thomas East, 1598); Thomas Dekker, *Old Fortunatus* (London: S. Stafford, 1600).

[5] Thomas Morley, 'Now is the Month of Maying'; Thomas Weelkes, 'Ha ha! Ha ha! This world Doth Merrily Pass' (1608).

[6] Shakespeare, *The Tempest*, 3.2.

[7] 'I. W. in Commendation to the Author', in Thomas Morley, *A Plaine and Easie Introduction to Practicall Musicke* (London, 1597).

Although the cliché of sweet music was typically used to describe a pleasant musical experience, it cannot be denied that it also held some pejorative connotations, particularly when allied to false relations (or what we should approach as possible descriptions of false relations in mentions of 'dissonance' and 'chromatic'). Charles Butler, for example, condemned the 'effeminate' effect of accidentals.[8] In his *Histrio-Matrix* (1633), William Prynne goes further, denouncing 'the various sorceries of effeminate songs' and the way such music 'tickle[s] or effeminate[s] our eyes or eares, bewaring pleasure'. On the other hand,

> Modest and chaste harmonies are to be admitted, by removing as farre as may be all soft effeminate musicke from our strong and valiant cogitation, which using a dishonest art of warbling the voyce, doe leade to a delicate and slothfull kinde of life. Therefore Chromaticall harmonies are to be left to impudent malapartnesse in wine, to whorish musicke crowned with flowers.[9]

Both of these texts were printed in the 1630s and are coloured by the religio-political context of the rise of William Laud, but there is ample evidence that such attitudes were consistent across the English Renaissance. Here is the Schoolmaster Richard Mulcaster defending the use of music, in his *Positions* (1581):

> *Musick* moueth great misliking to some men that waye, as to great a prouoker to vaine delites, still laying baite, to draw on pleasure: still opening the minde, to the entrie of lightnesse. And in matters of religion also, to some it seemes offensiue, bycause it carieth awaye the eare, with the sweetnesse of the melodie, and bewitcheth the minde with a *Syrenes* sounde, pulling it from that delite, wherin of duetie it ought to dwell, vnto harmonicall fantasies, and withdrawing it, from the best meditations, and most vertuous thoughtes to forreine conceites, and wandring deuises.[10]

---

[8] Charles Butler, *Principles of Musik* (London: John Haviland, 1636), 96.
[9] William Prynne, *Histrio-Matrix* (London: Edward Allde and William Jones, 1633), 275. See also Prynne's description of church music: 'As for the Divine Service and Common prayer, it is so chaunted and minsed, and mangled, of our costly hired, curious, and nice Musitions (not to instruct the audience withall, nor to stirre up mens mindes unto devotion, but with a whorish harmony to tickle their eares:) that it may iustly seeme, not to be a noyse made of men, but rather a bleating of bruite beasts', 285.
[10] Richard Mulcaster, *Positions* (London: Thomas Vautrollier for Thomas Chard, 1581), 38–39.

For the reasons explored above, the fact that this passage does not explicitly mention false relations should not prevent us from entertaining the possibility that Mulcaster had them (amongst other musical stylistic features) in mind as he wrote of the 'sweetnesse of the melodie' that 'carieth away the eare' and 'bewitcheth the minde with a Syrenes sounde'.

This chapter investigates possible routes towards understanding the murkier corners of the false relation by entertaining metaphor and the power of suggestion as a tool of musicological analysis, and the importance of the evocative trace as evidence alongside the concrete, documented connection. It does not seek to find a definitive answer to the question of musical sweetness, but rather to explore the possibilities of what 'lingers'[11] behind its façade as a musical experience that is 'pleasant, pleasing to the senses'. In so doing it entertains methods of inference that allow insight into the 'ways in which certain words rose to prominence, changed shape, and retreated from view; inflated and deflated semantically; sedimented into settled uses or veered off in unexpected directions'.[12] Without allowing for the inevitable leakage between different semantic branches, some of them 'deflated' or 'sedimented', some of them seemingly irrelevant or superficial, we cannot hope to appreciate the fascinating conceptual sleight of hand that produced the rich context and concept of false relation we explored above in the Introduction. This chapter investigates the literature of the period, both explicitly and implicitly musical, to shine a light on the idea of false relation through the cliché of musical sweetness. In so doing, it will demonstrate some of the ways in which the *mi–fa* interval continued to exercise its spectral influence over the musical culture of the English Renaissance, as fixed-scale solmization came to replace the mutable hexachord system.

'Sweet' music is one of the most fascinating yet seeming innocuous 'syrupy'[13] clichés to have left its mark on the Western history of music. Indeed, the adjective 'sweet' itself is so mundane that it does not make an appearance in any of the dictionaries of the period; Randle Cotgrave's 1611 *Dictionary of French and English Tongues* completely omits it, as does Henry Cockeram's

---

[11] Jeffrey Masten, *Queer Philologies: Sex, Language, and Affect in Shakespeare's Time* (Philadelphia: University of Pennsylvania Press, 2016), 8–9.

[12] Alexander Marr, Raphaele Garrod, José Ramón Marcaida, and Richard Oosterhoff, *Logodaedalus: Word Histories of Ingenuity in Early Modern Europe* (Pittsburgh: University of Pittsburgh Press, 2018), 2.

[13] Masten, *Queer Philologies*, 3.

English Dictionarie, or An Interpreter of Harde Wordes of 1623.[14] Cockeram instead lists the word cloud around 'dulced' (or dulcet), 'dulcitude, dulcidity' ('sweetnesse'), and 'dulciloquy' ('sweet speaking'), evidently in the belief that the more Latinate term would class as 'Hard Wordes' where the Germanic/Old English term would not.[15] Nevertheless in that final term 'dulciloquy' we begin to see a key facet of what the early modern English identified as notable about the 'sweet': it is to do with voice, utterance, eloquence, the ability to convey meaning. Already in this connotation we begin to gain a sense of the turbulence beneath the hackneyed surface of the musically 'sweet'; as Joseph M. Ortiz has demonstrated, frequently there is a problematically gaping chasm between music and wordy eloquence due to 'the radical promiscuity of musical meaning in early modern England', such that the use of 'sweet' as a musical adjective takes on the sense of a knowing smirk towards this fundamental rift.[16] *Eliotes Dictionary*, as compiled by Thomas Elyot and edited by Thomas Cooper in 1559, likewise does include the Latin '*dulce*' and its cognates but does so in a frustratingly circumspect manner. '*Dulce*' and '*dulcimer*' are 'sweetly, genteelly', '*dulcedo, dulcitas etc.*' are 'sweetnesse', '*dulciarius*' 'perteynynge to sweet things', and '*dulciarus*' is a 'marchpane made with almondes and sugar'.[17] Eliot via Cooper lists things 'flowing sweetly', 'he that speaketh sweetly' and '*dulcis*' as 'sweet, pleasant, contrary to sharp and vehement'. The cognates of '*suavis*' are likewise 'sweet or pleasant' in speech, kisses 'as in joy' or 'sweet' in odour or taste, of a person having pleasant taste. The innocuous sweetness listed by early modern English lexicographers is undercut only by John Palsgrave's 1530 *Lesclarcissement de la langue francoyse*: Palsgrave lists 'swetetunying' as 'modulation', an apparent reference to the trope of *varietas* as well as the connotations of voice and utterance we see in Cockeram and Elyot, and the only explicitly musical sense in the dictionaries of Renaissance English.[18] This single blip in over a hundred years of lexicographical endeavour is the only moment that chimes with the richness of what 'sweet' music offered to musicians, composers, and writers about music. We all know that 'sweet' as an adjective can mean 'pleasant'. In the guise of its sheer obviousness, to assert as

---

[14] Henry Cockeram, *The English Dictionarie, or, An Interpreter of Hard Wordes* (London: Nathaniel Butter, 1623).
[15] Ibid., fol. E3r.
[16] Joseph M. Ortiz, *Broken Harmony: Shakespeare and the Politics of Music* (Ithaca, NY: Cornell University Press, 2011), 11.
[17] Thomas Elyot, *Eliotes Dictionarie by Thomas Cooper the third tyme corrected* (London: Tho. Bertheleti, 1559), unpaginated.
[18] John Palsgrave, *Lesclarcissement de la langue francoyse* (London: J. Hakuyns, 1530), unpaginated.

such can appear utterly, unforgivably bland. However, in this chapter, we shall see that this guise in fact masks a dynamic web of meshed meanings. Beneath the cliché of sweet music as a descriptor of 'pleasant' experience are clues to the cultivation of taste and the epistemological, moral role played by music in early modern culture and experience.

The role of the term 'sweet' in medieval music theory has been previously explored by Bonnie Blackburn, Gregor Herzman, and Rob Wegman; the ongoing impacts of their arguments will be explored below. Most important to the present investigation is Wegman's discussion of Tinctoris and his allowance of 'dissonance' for 'the sake of ornament and necessity', in other words because 'acquired taste' allows for perception of dissonance as a form of sweetness.[19] It is not a surprise to find sweetness being applied to musical dissonance; this is a manifestation of what Rosalie L. Colie has referred to as the epidemic of paradox in learned Renaissance circles, whereby through rhetorical flourish university-educated gentlemen used the paradox to 'dazzle by its mental gymnastics, by its manipulation, even prestidigitation, of ideas, true or *false*' (my italics).[20] Indeed, Linda Phyllis Austern has explored this very context with relation to the musically 'sweet' and musical irony.[21] However, it is clear that in the context of the English Renaissance something rather different is at play, as Henry Peacham's wondering observation epitomizes: 'how doth Musicke amaze us, when assures [sic] of discords she maketh the sweetest Harmony?'[22] In other words, rather than relying upon the *sprezzatura* sleight of hand that Colie describes, Peacham directly draws attention to the paradox rather than 'frustrat[ing...] satisfaction in the ordinary sense' as 'the paradox can only satisfy by surprise, by its twist, its gimmick'.[23] A similar sentiment can be found in the *Pathway to Musicke*, which defines concord as 'unlike voyces within themselves, tackt together, sweetly sounding unto the eare'.[24] The shifting political climate (propelled not simply by global expansionism, aspirations towards empire across Europe in the sixteenth century, and the associated boom in

---

[19] See Rob Wegman, 'Sense and Sensibility in Late-Medieval Music: Thoughts on Aesthetics and "Authenticity"', in *Early Music*, 23: 2 (1995), 298–314.
[20] Rosalie L. Colie, *Paradoxia Epidemica* (Princeton, NJ: Princeton University Press, 1966), at 22; see also 5–8, 34–35.
[21] Linda Phyllis Austern, '"Sweet Music with Sour Sauce": The Genesis of Musical Irony in English Drama after 1600', in *Journal of Musicology*, 4: 4 (1986), 472–490.
[22] Henry Peacham, *The Compleat Gentleman* (London: Francis Constable, 1622), Chapter 11.
[23] Colie, *Paradoxia*, 35.
[24] Attributed to John Case, *The Praise of Musicke* (Oxford: Joseph Barnes, 1586); for more on this see Linda Phyllis Austern, *Both from the Ears and Mind: Thinking about Music in Early Modern England* (Chicago: University of Chicago Press, 2020), 100.

commodification),[25] but also by anxieties over nationhood which would ultimately result in James I and VI's coining of the term 'Great Britain' combined together to produce a very different understanding of the concept of 'sweetness' in the sixteenth and early seventeenth centuries. Coupled to this, the rise of the stylistic trend for false relation specifically and chromaticism more generally invites a different mode of reading sweetness. As we shall see in the first case study of this book, John Bennet's madrigal pairing 'O Sweete Griefe'/'Rest Now, Amphion' as a cliché can be productively allied to the guilty, paradoxical pleasure of the false relation in the face of its nominal prohibition by contemporary music theorists.

False relations began in sacred repertoire, and by and large it is in music for devotional purposes that they can be found throughout the English Renaissance. This tendency is bound up in the Reformation context of England throughout the period, as we shall explore throughout this book. In this chapter, however, we will briefly turn from the sacred music of the period towards its secular cousins: the madrigals, consort songs, and balletts that explore the concept of musical sweetness and its intriguing (albeit fragmented) connection to thinking about chromaticism more broadly, and the solmization ramifications of the false relation. Drawing a strict distinction between sacred and secular music in this period is in many ways anachronistic, given the vital role that *The Whole Booke of Psalmes*, for example, played in domestic recreational music-making across the second half of the sixteenth century. However, doing so enables us to focus directly upon vernacular handling of the musically 'sweet' in a period in which native words, metre, and music were becoming increasingly more important to the English. As we turn away from the technical form of the false relation to the general musical style it was part of, the term 'sweet' reveals itself to be of vital importance to understanding of chromaticism and the delight that a ductile, elastic approach to solmization provided to listeners and performers in the English Renaissance.

Of Discords She Maketh the Sweetest Harmony

In 1599, John Bennet (c. 1575–1615) published his one and only solo-authored collection, *Madrigals to Foure Voyces*. Little is known of Bennet's life. We do not know whether he served as a musician in the entourage of a court favourite or if he was attached to a church, chapel, or cathedral. His

---

[25] Patricia Fumerton, *Cultural Aesthetics: Renaissance Literature and the Practice of Social Ornament* (Chicago: University of Chicago Press, 1991).

earlier life is a little clearer; he appears to have studied at Abingdon School (then Roysses' School) under John Roysse (c. 1500–1571) and that he had been a chorister either there, elsewhere in Abingdon, or nearby. He was certainly closely connected to the court and likely to the Chapel Royal; his consort song 'Eliza, Her Name Gives Honour' was written as a paean to Elizabeth I and likely performed as part of a royal entertainment in the 1590s,[26] he contributed a madrigal ('All Cre'tures Now') to Thomas Morley's *Triumphs of Oriana* (1601), and his madrigal collection was printed under Morley and William Barley's music-printing monopoly. Four of his psalm settings appear in William Barley's psalter of 1599, and six of his songs were published in Thomas Ravenscroft's *A Briefe Discourse of the True (But Neglected) Charact'ring of the Degrees* (1614). In terms of style, David Brown notes that his work resembles that of Morley's most closely but with distinctive features from Weelkes, Wilbye, and Gibbons.[27] This is the case in the final two madrigals in his 1599 collection: 'O Sweete Griefe' (Madrigal XVI) and 'Rest Now Amphion' (Madrigal XVII):

> O sweet griefe, O sweet sighes, O sweet disdaining:
> O sweet repulses. Sweet wrongs, sweet wrongs, sweet lamenting.
> Words sharply sweet, and sweetly sharp consenting,
> O sweet unkindness, sweet feares, sweet complaining.
> Grieve then no more (my soule) those deepe grones strayning,
> Your bitter anguish now shall have re-lenting
> And sharpe disdaines receaue their full contenting.
>
> Rest now Amphion, rest
> Rest thy charming lier
> For Daphnes love (sweet love) makes melody
> Her loves concord with mine doth well conspire
> No discord jars in our loves simpathie,
> Our concords have some discords mixt among,
> Discording concords makes the sweetest song.[28]

---

[26] Katherine Butler, *Music in Elizabethan Court Politics* (Woodbridge: Boydell & Brewer, 2015), 29 and 41.
[27] David Brown, 'John Bennet', *Grove Music Online* (accessed 24 May 2022). See also I. Godt, 'John Bennet and the Directional Convention: An Introduction to Madrigalism', in Paul R. Laird (ed.), *Words and Music* (Binghamton, NY: Binghamton University, 1990), 121–146.
[28] John Bennet (c. 1575–1615), *Madrigals to Foure Voyces* (London: Printed in little Sainte Hellens by H. Ballard for William Barley, the assigne of Thomas Morley, 1599).

Brown notes the manner in which 'O Sweete Griefe' adopts 'the measured manner, amorphous imitation, long-drawn lines, and textural consistency reminiscent of a pre-madrigalian, English tradition' or 'older native root'. We might argue that this is a result of Bennet's deliberate reaction to the text he was setting, and the ideas he was encapsulating. In many ways these madrigals form a pairing: 'Rest Now, Amphion' responds to the concerns of 'O Sweete Griefe' both stylistically and in theme. 'O Sweete Griefe' features an almost excessive *epizeuxis* of 'sweet', breaking its first three lines into a sugary glut of poignant sweetness; *epizeuxis* seems to have been one of Bennet's favourite text-setting approaches, as *All cre'tures now* likewise features emphatic repetition of the word 'merry'. The 'griefe' of 'O Sweete Griefe', conceptualized as 'sweet sighes', 'sweet repulses', 'sweet unkindness', 'sweet feares', 'words sharply sweet, and sweetly sharp consenting', and 'sharpe disdaines' becomes resolved in the 'rest' of 'discording concords [that] make the sweetest song'.

Bennet was not the only composer to dramatize sweet sharpness; John Wilbye's 'Sweet Honey-Sucking Bees/ Yet, Sweet, Take Heed' from his *Second Set of Madrigals for 3–6 Voices* (1598) likewise explores these themes in conceptualizing the sharpness of the beloved's 'flaming' eye dart with the bee's sting (e.g., between Altus and Cantus at bars 46 and 86).[29] Thomas Morley's 'O grief e'en on the bud that fairly flowered' (from his 1597 collection *Canzonets or Litle Short Aers*, Ex. 2.2) provides the most interesting counterpoint in terms of sharpness, without sweetness. Like Bennet's madrigal pair, in 'O Sweete Griefe' Morley adopts a marked sharpness evident between the Tenor 2 and Soprano parts at bar 15, with a more conventional play between B♭ and B♮, and a more surprising false relation between the Tenor 1 C♯ and Tenor 2 C♮ at bar 20. However, Bennet was the only composer to paint sharpness, and literal chromatic sharpness, as 'sweet'. Sharpness might appear an unusual choice for exploring the concept of false relation; it is well established that they typically appeared as a play between B♮ and B♭ (or B-*fa*), as can be found for example in William Byrd's 'Awake Mine Eyes' (1611),[30] his 'As I Beheld a Herdman Wild' (1589),[31] and Thomas Weelkes's 'Ha! Ha! This World Doth Pass', illustrating the 'many an Indian ass' that 'goes for an Unicorn', and 'Tan Ta Ra Cries Mars' (1608),[32] illustrating the death of the

---

[29] John Wilbye, *Second Set of Madrigals for 3–6 Voices* (London: Thomas East, 1598).
[30] William Byrd, *Psalmes, Songs and Sonnets: Some Solemne, Others Ioyfull, Framed to the Life of the Words* (London: Thomas Snodham, 1611).
[31] William Byrd, *Psalms, Sonets and Songs and Sadnes and Piete, Made into Musicke of Five Parts* (London: Thomas East, 1588).
[32] Thomas Weelkes, *Ayeres or Phantasticke Spirites* (London: William Barley, 1608).

Ex. 2.1 John Bennet, 'O Sweete Griefe', from *Madrigalls to foure voyces* (London: William Barley, 1599).

O sweet grief

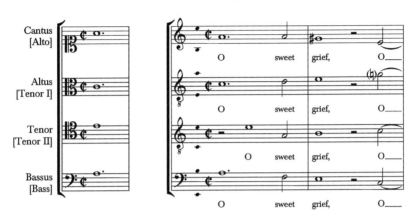

64 SYRENE SOUNDES

Ex. 2.1 Continued

Ex. 2.1 Continued

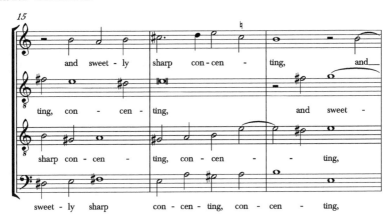

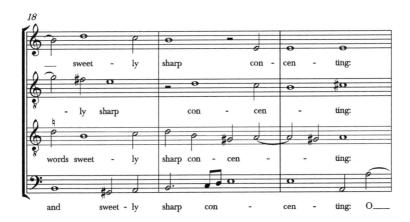

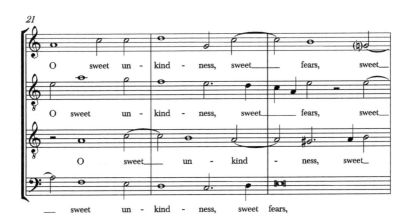

66 SYRENE SOUNDES

Ex. 2.1 Continued

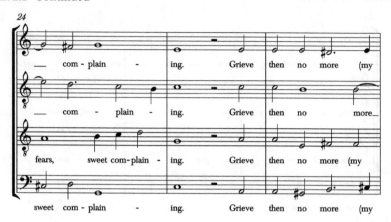
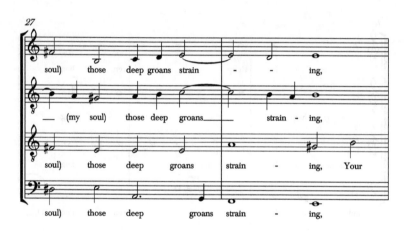

Ex. 2.1 Continued

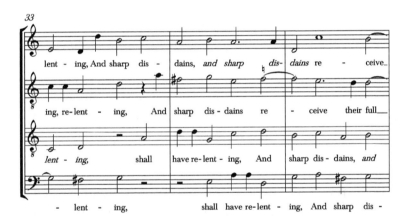

speaker's 'sweeting'. Sharpness, however, was also crucial in enabling composer/performers to stretch the potential of solmization to its very limits and to play with tonal instability in their word-painting. Graphically marking a note as sharp inevitably affects the way that it is solmized within the context of the piece, because it alters the solmization syllables of its surrounding pitches. Increasingly towards the turn of the seventeenth century, solmization provided a framework which composer/performers could manipulate and subvert to amplify the expressive capacities of its style. Crucially, it allowed them to interrogate and problematize its lyrics and trite terms such as 'sweet', as Bennet demonstrates. His two-part madrigal is illustrated throughout with instances of sharp sweetness which, were they a rhythmic sliver closer, would register as proximate false relations. 'O Sweete Griefe' features the vast majority, and the discord passes between parts (see Ex. 2.1); at bar 3, between the Cantus and Tenor parts, and illustrating the phrase 'sweet sighs, oh', between the Cantus G♮ and Tenor G♯ at 'O sweet unkindness' at bar 23, and finally at 'and sharp disdaines receive their full contenting' between the Altus and Bassus at bars 34–35. The sinuous melodic lines, alluding to the compositional styles of the early sixteenth century, allow the performer space to elegantly execute each of these near misses with insouciance. Each instance is marked and explicitly graphically signified. Bennet thus dramatizes the sweetness of grief, sighs, disdaining, sighs, fears not only with literal sharpness but also with a knowing, redolent allusion to the logic of solmization.

The energy of 'O Sweete Griefe' dissipates and stills in 'Rest Now, Amphion' (see Ex. 2.3). The madrigal is constructed around alternating homophonic duos and full polyphonic contrapuntal phrasings that hark back to the structure of 'O Sweete Griefe', and its nostalgic style. False relations are far fewer, but their presence is nevertheless enlightening. There is an instance between the Soprano and the Tenor parts at bar 12, amplifying the word 'melody' with a clash between G♮ and G♯. Melody is another important cognate of 'sweet', as Robert Cawdrey defined it in his *Table Alphabeticall* in 1604: melody was 'sweet sounding, or sweete musick'.[33] This was the first period in which melody could connote a 'tune', as a discrete entity. It was verbal as well as nominal in this period, and also closely associated with lyric and the beauty of sound in the arrangement of words, to make them

---

[33] Robert Cawdrey, *A table alphabeticall conteyning and teaching the true writing, and understanding of hard usuall English words* (London: I. Roberts for Edmund Weaver, 1604), unpaginated.

THE RHETORIC OF FALSENESS 69

Ex. 2.2 Thomas Morley, 'O Grief, E'en on the Bud', from *Canzonets, or little short aers to five and six voices* (London: Thomas Short, 1597).

O grief, e'en on the bud

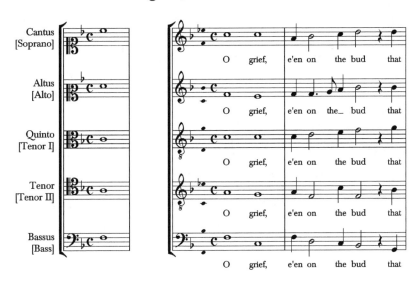

Ex. 2.2 Continued

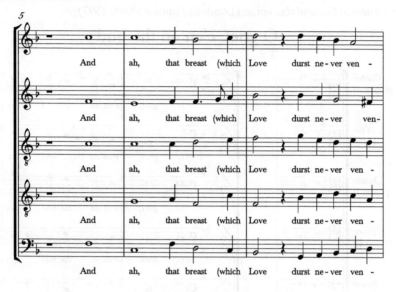

Ex. 2.2 Continued

Ex. 2.2 Continued

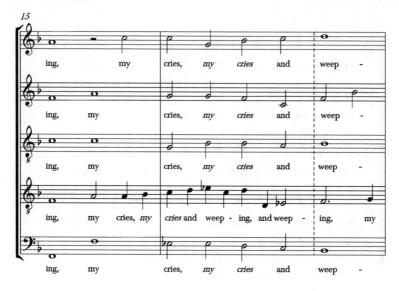

THE RHETORIC OF FALSENESS 73

Ex. 2.3 John Bennet, 'Rest Now, Amphion', from *Madrigalls to foure voyces* (London: William Barley, 1599).

Rest now, Amphion

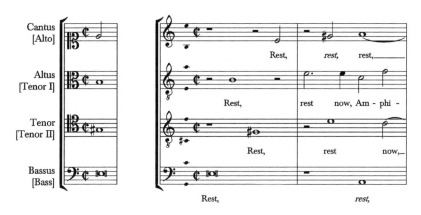

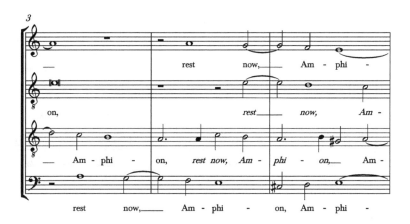

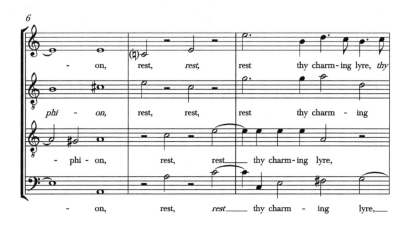

Ex. 2.3 Continued

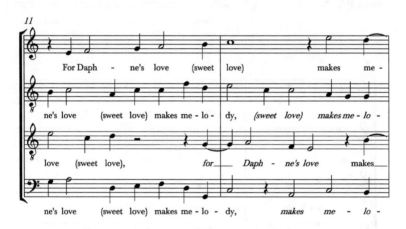
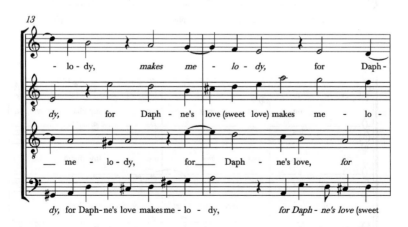

Ex. 2.3 Continued

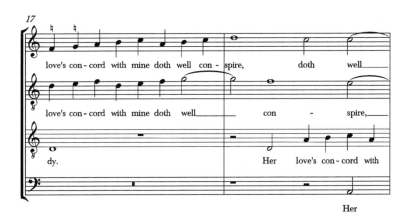

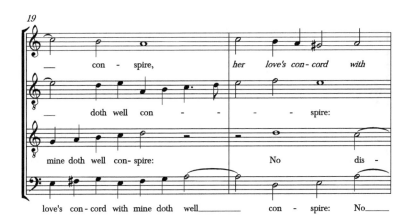

Ex. 2.3 Continued

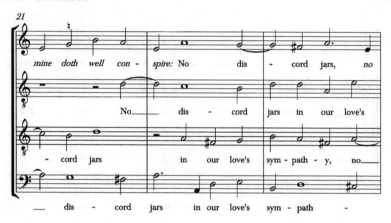

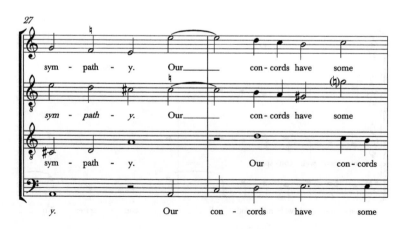

THE RHETORIC OF FALSENESS 77

Ex. 2.3 Continued

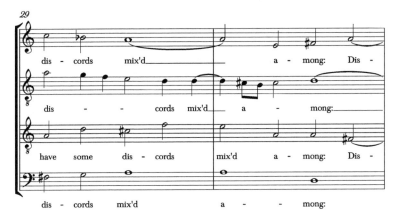
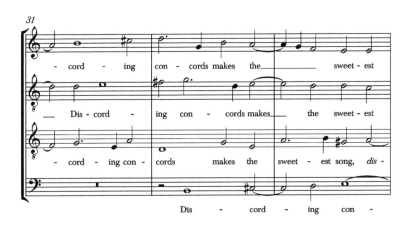

Ex. 2.3 Continued

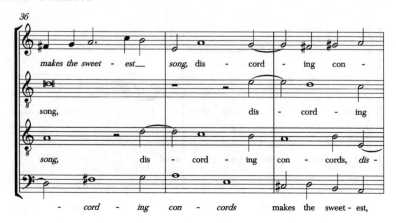

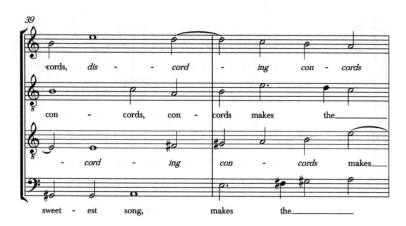

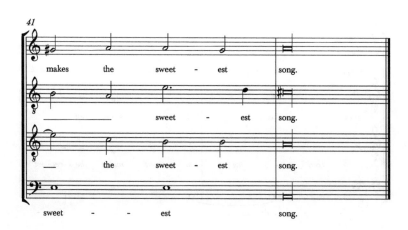

sound musical; writers such as George Puttenham aspired to 'further [. . .] the pleasant melody of our English meeter',[34] for example. The sonic texture established at this point continues in the middle section: the phrase 'discord jars' is embellished throughout the madrigal with an F♯ in all parts from the Bassus entry at bar 19 to bar 43, with a handful of choice exceptions at key moments in the Cantus and Altus. Finally, with the Cantus B♮ at bar 57, at the words 'discords mixed', the madrigal moves slowly towards its conclusion of 'discording concords [that] make the sweetest song'.

By the tail end of the sixteenth century, false relations were far more often proximate rather than simultaneous (as testified in the examples from Bennet's madrigal pairing); as a practice it would receive a brief resurgence in the compositions of composers such as Thomas Weelkes and Thomas Tomkins, but by and large the tendency was to leave the execution of false relation to the discretion of the performers, who could lean as heavily or indeed as lightly as they wished upon the discordance. Nevertheless, Bennet's madrigal pairing suggests something rather exciting at play beneath the surface of musical sweetness: the 'sweet' B-*fa* of the *molle* F hexachord could permeate beyond its soft, lascivious flatness into the English Renaissance's language of false relation. In other words, it could productively be approached as a way of talking about false relation, about enjoyment of it, and the experience of performing and listening to it. The musical metaphor 'sweet' offers a potential and tantalizing avenue into a way of hearing, knowing, and musicking that contemporary musical theoretical treatises simply do not offer.

Bennet's interpretation of musical sweetness as relevant for the topic of solmization and the false relations it produces is unique as an explicit elucidation. He does not use the term in his prefatory material, and the prefatory material of Ravenscroft's *A Briefe Discourse of the True (But Neglected) Charact'ring of the Degrees* (1614), within which Bennet had six songs, features a typical take on musical sweetness. This is John Davies's letter in praise of the treatise, included in the preface:

> If *Musicke* then, moue all that *All* doth moue;
> That's not compriz'd in *ALL* that spights her State:
> If not in *ALL*, it's nought; which who doth loue
> is worse then nought, to loue what Heau'n doth hate:

---

[34] George Puttenham, *The Arte of English Poesie* (London: Richard Field, 1589), 107.

> For, *NOUGHT* is nothing; sith it was not made
> By that great *WORD*, without which made was nought:
> Then, if that nought but *NOUGHT* doe her inuade,
> Like God, her goodnesse is surmounting *THOUGHT!*
> But no man is so ill that hath no good;
> So, no man in the *Abstract* can be nought:
> Then 'tis no man that hates sweete *Musickes* moode,
> But Some-thing worse then all that can be thought.
> A *Beast?* O no: A *Monster?* Neither. Then
> Is it a *Deuill?* Nothing lesse: for, these
> Haue *Beings* with an *Angell*, or a *Man*;
> But that exists not, that sweete *Notes* displease.[35]

Nevertheless, 'sweete' is one of the load-bearing words in Davies's argument for the universal importance of music. In this way it is possible to suggest that 'sweetness' was a vital way of managing the threshold between the musical and the non-musical, priming readers, listeners, and performers (professional and amateur) for appreciation of dulcet sound: the inclusion of the word 'sweet' within a musical text, either lyrics to a song or within prefatory material, alerted people to the fact that the piece was 'harmonious and well-proportioned'.[36] Bennet's usage might be a unique attitude towards what made music 'harmonious'. However, there is contemporary evidence that his approach towards what made something 'harmonicall' or 'harmonious' was not so very idiosyncratic. E.K. (alias Edmund Spenser)'s dedication of *The Shepheardes Calendar* to Gabriel Harvey frames musical experience in a similar manner:

> [But] All as in most exquisite pictures they use to blaze and portraict not onely the daintie lineaments of beautye, but also rounde about it to shadow the rude thickets and craggy clifts, that, by the basenesse of such parts, more excellency may accrew to the principall (for oftimes we fynde our selves, I knowe not how, singularly delighted with the shewe of such ftenti rudenesse, and take great pleasure in that disorderly order) even so doe those rough and harsh termes enlumine [sic] and make more clearly to

---

[35] John Davies, to TR, in Thomas Ravenscroft, *A Briefe Discourse of the True (But Neglected) Charact'ring of the Degrees* (London: Edward Allde, 1614).
[36] Katherine R. Larson, *The Matter of Song in Early Modern England: Texts in and of the Air* (Oxford: Oxford University Press, 2019), 35.

appeare the brightnesse of brave and glorious words. *So ftentimes [sic] a dischorde in musick maketh a comely concordaunce*: so great delight tooke the worthy poete Alceus to behold a blemish in the joynt of a wel shaped body (my italics).[37]

In E.K.'s (and Peacham's) imagination, sweet harmonies were made out of 'dischorde'. As explored briefly above, this was a concept directly taken from medieval music theory and thus is not an English Renaissance innovation. A cursory glance over the works of figures like John Sheppard, Thomas Tallis, William Byrd, and Thomas Weelkes demonstrates that the specific dissonance of false relations was often used to signal impending cadences (or, to use Morley's term, 'close[s]') in English Renaissance Music; Tallis's use at 'corporis' in 'O nata lux' is perhaps one of the most famous examples, but such instances can also be found in the secular music of the period, as in Byrd's 'Penelope That Longed for Sight' (1589). Another intriguing instance can be found in Byrd's fascinating partsong 'O Sweet Deceit' (before 1611),[38] where the false relation is alluded to within single voices rather than across separate parts and appears to announce the beginning of new textual passages and the development of the idea of the 'false disembl'd thoughts'.

> O sweet deceit in speech contained;
> O sugar'd cup, wherein we drink our poison;
> O false disembl'd thoughts of most disdained;
> O subtle seas, that none can sound with reason!
> What Circe can with all her craft and witches,
> More mischief work than men with flatt'ring speeches?
> Like Harpias vile, which poets' feigning graces
> To make the world the more at them to wonder,
> They say these people have fair women's faces
> And claws that tear men's hearts asunder;
> In court they dwell and make their occupation
> To cozen simple folk with adulation.[39]

---

[37] 'E.K.', Dedicatory Epistle to Edmund Spenser, *The Shepheardes Calender* (London: Hugh Singleton, 1579).
[38] For an extended musical analysis of 'O Sweet Deceit' see Richard Turbet, 'Two Invisible Songs by Byrd', in *The Musical Times*, 158: 1938 (Spring 2017), 57–62.
[39] British Library Add. MS 29247, the 'Paston Manuscript' (after 1611), fols. 77r–v.

Such instances do not illustrate the words 'O sugar'd cup' but the increasing effect of its sweet 'poison' throughout the madrigal, for example the play between B♮ and B♭ on the Alto line 'What Circe can with all her craft' (bars 35–37) and F♯ and F♮ in the second Alto line 'More mischief work' at bar 42. Watching the Mechanicals in the closing scene of Shakespeare's *Midsummer Night's Dream*, Theseus ponders 'how shall we find the concord [/] Of this discord' (5.1, 60), providing a tantalizing hint that this was a commonly understood practice beyond musical circles. However, the example of Bennet's 'O Sweete Griefe'/'Rest Now, Amphion' demonstrates that it is important that we recognize that these late sixteenth-century statements of fourteenth- and early fifteenth-century ideas about discord treatment are concepts grounded in a fascination for the archaic, like Bennet's sinuous long-drawn lines and consistent harmonic texture. The persistence or revival of this concept is worth lingering over: much had changed over the intervening century in ideas to do with what extent of discordance was acceptable, but also in terms of what 'sweetness' could connote. In the following section, we will step briefly away from our musical examples to look at the abstract idea of sweetness had developed across the sixteenth century. There is clearly more to the cliché of 'sweet music' than meets the ear.

Varieties of Sweetness

Scholarship on the metaphor of 'sweetness' has revealed a diverse range of important associations, both inherited from medieval understandings and as embryonic forms presaging the arrival of Barbadian sugar in England, in the later seventeenth century.[40] Prior to the sixteenth century, 'sweet' was typically associated with honey; aspirations towards empire gradually shifted towards the taste, instead, of sugar. In the English Renaissance, via what Gitanjali Shahani defines as the 'attitude' of sugar,[41] 'sweet' things carried echoes of prestige, the exotic, and the ornamental: 'sugar effectively comes to be prized for its decorative value, its artifice, which itself is tied to its status as exotic and foreign. [...] Sugar in these instances is sweet precisely for

---

[40] Sidney W. Mintz, *Sweetness and Power: The Place of Sugar in Modern History* (New York: Viking, 1985), 155; Gitanjali Shahani, *Tasting Difference: Food, Race, and Cultural Encounters in Early Modern Literature* (Ithaca, NY: Cornell University Press, 2020), 60.

[41] Shahani, *Tasting Difference*, 58.

its ability to perform luxury, by placing the home in relation to the world'.[42] Contemporary texts demonstrate the active role imagined for sugar in this period, as John Gerard's 1597 description demonstrates. Gerard notes that

> the Sugar Cane is a pleasant and profitable reede [. . .] it drieth and cleanseth the stomacke, maketh smooth the roughnesse of the brest and lungs, cleareth the voice, and putteth away hoarsenesse, the cough and all sourenesse and bitternesse [. . .] of the juice of this reede is made the most pleasant and profitable sweete, called Sugar, whereof is made infinite confections, confetures, sirupes, and such like, as also preserving and conserving sundrie fruits, herbes and flowres; as Roses, Violets, Rosemary, flowres, and such like, which still retained them the name of Sugar, as Sugar Roses, Sugar Violet, &c.[43]

Sugar is 'sweet' as noun, a premodifying prefix that signifies its costly (indeed, bloody)[44] opulence and artifice. Connotations relating to honey still endured throughout the sixteenth century and evolved into the metaphor of gustatory or culinary appreciation, as it relates to the 'consumption' of books; Elizabeth L. Swann and Wendy Wall have explored the striking 'use of the language of taste to describe processes of readerly and editorial discrimination, extraction and collation'.[45] Taste did not enter English vernacular usage as an aesthetic term until the mid-seventeenth century, but Swann argues that this was not the point. Rather, 'in its earliest incarnations, taste defined as literary discrimination was understood not simply as a figurative application

---

[42] Ibid., 60.

[43] John Gerard, *The Herball or Generall Historie of Plantes* (London: John Norton, 1597), 39. Gerard also explicitly links enslaved labour to the product and prestige of sugar: 'In some places they use a great wheele, wherein slaves do tread and walke as dogs do in turning the spit: and some others do feed as it were the bottome of the said wheele, wherein are some sharpe of hard things which do cut and crush the Canes into powder. [. . .] The Canes being thus brought into dust or powder, they put them into great cauldrons with a little water, where they boyle until there be no more sweetnesse left in the crushed reeds [. . .] and so afterwards it is carried into all parts of Europe, where it is by the Sugar Bakers artificially purged and refined to that whitenesse as we see'.

[44] Shahani, *Tasting Difference*, 57.

[45] Ibid., 52–79; Elizabeth L. Swann, '"To dream to eat Books": Bibliophagy, Bees and Literary Taste in Early Modern Commonplace Culture', in Jason Scott-Warren and Andrew Zurcher (eds.), *Text, Food and the Early Modern Reader: Eating Words* (London: Routledge, 2018), 69–88, at 74; Elizabeth L. Swann, '"Sweet above compare"? Disputing about Taste in *Venus and Adonis*, *Love's Labours Lost*, *Othello* and *Troilus and Cressida*', in Simon Smith (ed.), *Shakespeare/Sense* (London: Bloomsbury, 2020), and *Taste and Knowledge in Early Modern England* (Cambridge: Cambridge University Press, 2020); Wendy Wall, *Recipes for Thought: Taste and Knowledge in the Early Modern Kitchen* (Philadelphia: University of Pennsylvania Press, 2015). See also Louise Stewart, 'Social Status and Classicism in the Visual and Material Culture of the Sweet Banquet in Early Modern England', in *The Historical Journal*, 61: 4 (2018), 913–942; and Mintz, *Sweetness and Power*.

of a term that had previously been used only to describe physical sensation, but as rooted in the phenomenal reality of reading and writing as it engaged the senses'.[46] This latter definition is influenced by Mary Carruthers's exploration of 'sweetness' as an aesthetic descriptor in medieval literature, through the terms *dulcis* and *suavis*, to 'charm' and to 'persuade'.[47] *Suavis* in modern English became cognate with 'suaded' and 'persuaded';[48] it was cognate with the Old English *swete* through the same Indo-European root, meaning that persuasion quite literally is 'to sweeten' speech. *Dulcis*, as we encountered above with Cockeram and Elyot, translated the Greek word *charis*, which in modern English became 'charm'; on the other side of its etymological ancestry, 'charm' was related to the Latin *carmen*, meaning 'song, verse or incantation'.[49] Both became closely associated with the idea of healing medicine. Thus the origins of the cliché of 'sweetness' at play in sixteenth-century English understood it as a form of appreciation that 'heals and restores', returns balance to the humours, and that is wholesome, pleasing, and beneficial.[50] In reading sweetness in early modern English, readers were invited into a heightened consciousness of their ability to infer, invoke, and associate meaning through allusive delectation.[51]

Something rather different is at play when it comes to 'sweet' as a metaphor in a musical context, although some instances inevitably carried these connotations. As we saw above, English Renaissance music had inherited a technical musical 'sweetness' from medieval theory, from Ciceronian rhetoric, from Pythagorean/Platonic understanding of music, and (crucially for the present investigation) in the form of the note B♭ or B-*fa*.[52] The technical

---

[46] Swann, '"To dream to eat books"', 83.

[47] Mary Carruthers, 'Sweetness', in *Speculum*, 81: 4 (2006), 999–1013, and *The Experience of Beauty in the Middle Ages* (Oxford: Oxford University Press, 2013). For more on the classical roots of the terms, see A. H. Mamoojee, 'Suavis and Dulcis: A Study of Ciceronian Usage', in *Phoenix*, 35: 3 (1981), 220–236.

[48] It is worth noting Robert Toft's contention that 'by the early sixteenth-century, "moving" the audience had become the "principal object" of music'; Robert Toft, *With Passionate Voice: Re-Creative Singing in 16th Century England and Italy* (Oxford: Oxford University Press, 2015), 4.

[49] Ibid.

[50] Ibid., 89 and 104.

[51] There is a strong tradition of eliding eating with consumption of music. See Kate van Orden, 'Domestic Music', in Iain Fenlon and Richard Wistreich (eds.), *The Cambridge History of Sixteenth Century Music* (Cambridge: Cambridge University Press, 2019), 335–378, at 351–359; Flora Dennis, 'Scattered Knives and Dismembered Song: Cutlery, Music and the Rituals of Dining', in *Renaissance Studies* 24: 1 (2010), 156–184.

[52] Bonnie J. Blackburn, 'The Lascivious Career of B-flat', in Laurie Stras and Bonnie J. Blackburn (eds.), *Eroticism in Early Modern Music* (London: Routledge, 2017), 19–42. See also Gregor Herzfeld, 'Süße: Eine Metapher der mittelalterlichen Musiktheorie', in *Archiv für Musikwissenschaft*, 69: 1 (2012), 1–12; and Wegman, 'Sense and Sensibility'.

context, encountered above in the Introduction, is worth briefly revisiting. The three main hexachords C, F, and G constituted the white notes of a modern piano, with the addition of the note B♭, B-*molle*, or B-*fa*. Thus two iterations of which were permissible: B-*fa* and B-*mi*, B-*fa/molle* (from the soft, sweet F hexachord) and B-*mi/durum* (from the hard, bitter G hexachord). This dichotomy created the technical possibility of accidentals, which in turn resulted in the innovation of what became known as *ficta* hexachords that began on other, non-authorized notes to allow for the *mi–fa* semitone between different pitches. Moreover, the necessity of mutation to *ficta* hexachords was often not written down or signified within the fabric, but had to be achieved mentally, through the imagination. In other words, 'sweet' music was a matter of dissonance, and the matter of the provocative *mi–fa* semitone interval at the heart of the hexachord pattern. For many, but not all, the sweetness of B♭ was viewed as dangerous; however, this did not stop the trope continuing into the sixteenth century in the secular form of the madrigal, in which the word *dolce* was frequently signalled with an unexpected turn to B♭.[53] To a considerable extent this appears to have been fuelled by the feminine and 'lascivious' associations held by the note, and the fact that its characterization as 'soft' and 'sweet' as opposed to the 'hard' or 'bitter' B♮ or B-*mi*/B-*durum* rendered it 'unstable [and] liable to change' or rather, in the terms we have explored above, liable to unbalance.[54] This concept of sweetness, whilst not applicable to all instances of 'sweet' as musical metaphor, cast a long shadow across the musical culture of the English Renaissance. 'Sweet' music had the potential to be problematically elastic, bound as it was to the unpredictable practice of *musica ficta* which could 'drown' the senses, as Aemilia Lanier put it. We will note, too, that the connotations of artifice and ornament as explored by Shahani, and of good taste or appropriate style, as explored by Swann, have distant but distinct resonances in this version of 'sweetness'.

It is vital that this sense of sweetness be taken into account when approaching the question of 'sweet' music in explicitly musical texts, and in writing about music where it can be reasonably assumed that the writers knew the principles of solmization (as in the case of Lanyer and Spenser). The issue of the *mi–fa* interval was at the heart of the false relation style that gripped the musical

[53] Blackburn, 'Lascivious B-flat', 26.
[54] Ibid.

culture of the later sixteenth century;[55] its afterlife continued well into the abandonment of hexachord mutation and the practice of fixed-scale solmization.[56] The way in which it was conceptualized and alluded to in contemporary texts can offer a crucial insight into the understanding of harmony and its role within an act of music-making. Across the late sixteenth and early seventeenth centuries the innovations of composers and performers in the English culture of music-making laid what is now recognized as the groundwork for the new understanding of tonal structure that is still in use today, in the twenty-first century. At the epicentre of this developing discourse was the seemingly innocuous cliché of musical sweetness. Every mutation between hexachords to place the *mi–fa* interval between a different set of pitches could activate the spectre of B-*mi* and B-*fa* within the imagination of the reader/performers, and the tantalizing sweetness of the latter. It is tempting to read the note B♭ as 'sweet' purely for the capacity for greater tonal movement it triggered.

It is possible to detect something of the way the idea of false, discordant sweetness percolated beyond the musical sphere by turning, again, to some of the non-musical texts of the period. The theory of faculty psychology meant that the senses in the early modern period were not viewed as distinct modes of perception, but rather as intricately related, often blurred; one need look no further for evidence of this than Thomas Tomkis's riotous university play *Lingua* (c. 1607), in which the five senses debate the inclusion of Lingua or Voice 'apparelled in a Crimson Satten gowne, a Dressing of white Roses, a little Skeane tyed in a purple Skarfe, a paire of red Buskins drawne with white Ribband, silke garters gloues, &c.,'[57] as one of their number among the senses, and then compete for the 'coronet' of the best sense.[58] The coronet, in case of doubt, is inscribed 'He of the five who prove himself best/Shall have his temple with this coronet blest'. It is worth observing that much critical ink has been spilled on the fact that Lingua is female whilst the senses, contrary to medieval precedent, are male.[59] However, for the present investigation it

---

[55] James Haar, 'False Relations and Chromaticism in Sixteenth-Century Music', in *Journal of the American Musicological Society*, 30: 3 (1977), 391–418.

[56] For more on this, see Samantha Arten, 'The Origin of Fixed-Scale Solmization in *The Whole Booke of Psalmes*', in *Early Music* 46: 1 (2018), 149–165.

[57] N.B. the symbolism of crimson here. 'A maid yet rosed over with the virgin crimson of modesty' appears in William Shakespeare, *Henry V*, in *Mr William Shakespeares comedies, histories and tragedies Published according to the true originall copies* (London: Isaac Iaggard, and Ed. Blount, 1623), 5.2, line 294. Or the Geneva Bible (1560): 'Thogh your sinnes were as crimsin, they shalbe made white as snowe', Isaiah 1:18. The King James Version has it as 'Though your sins be as scarlet, they shal be made white as snow/though they be red like crimson, they shall be as wool.'

[58] Thomas Tomkis, *Lingua, or Combat of the Tongue* (London: G. Eld, 1607). 1:1 l. 1–2

[59] Jennifer Richards, 'The Voice of Anne Askew', in *Journal of the Northern Renaissance*, 9 (2017).

is notable that the play opens with Lingua and Auditus, the 'musical' senses, sparring on strikingly musical terms:

> LINGUA
> Nay good *Auditus* doe but heare me speake.
> AUDITUS
> *Lingua* thou strik'st too much vpon one string,
> Thy tedious plaine-song grates my tender eares.
> LINGUA
> 'Tis plaine indeed, for Truth no descant needs,
> *Vna's* her name, she cannot be diuided.
> AUDITUS
> O but the ground it selfe is nought, from whence
> Thou canst not relish out a good diuision:
> Therefore at length sur-cease, prooue not starke madde,
> Hopelesse to prosecute a haplesse sute:
> For though (perchance) thy first straines pleasing are,
> I dare ingage mine eares, the cloze will jarre.[60]

'One string', 'plaine-song', 'descant', '*Vna*' (*una corda*, one string), 'ground', 'straines', 'the cloze will jarre': these are all direct from the language of contemporary musical treatises, as we shall explore below. As the scene progresses, however, the metaphorical terms of reference subtly shift. Auditus' passing shot at Lingua as he departs at the end of the scene is pitched through the language of taste, through an objection to Lingua's 'sharpe vinigar' words:

> AUDITUS
> Heauens looke on my distresse,
> Desend me from this rayling viperess:
> For if I stay her words sharpe vinigar,
> Will feet me through, *Lingua* I must be gone:
> I heare one cal me more then earnestly.
> *Exit Auditus*[61]

---

[60] Tomkis, *Lingua*, 1:1 l. 3–13.
[61] Ibid., 1:1.

Lingua responds by adopting the metaphor and expanding upon it, to startling effect:

> LINGUA
> Fie *Lingua* wilt thou now degenerate:
> Art not a woman, doost not loue reuenge,
> *Delightfull speeches, sweet perswasions*
> I haue this long time vsd to get my right,
> My right that is to make the Senses sixe;
> And haue both name and power with the rest.
> *Oft haue I seasoned sauorie periods,*
> *With sugred words, to delude Gustus taste,*
> *And oft embelisht my entreatiue phrase*
> *With smelling flowres of vernant Rhetorique,*
> Limming and flashing it with various Dyes,
> To draw proud *Visus* to me by the eyes:
> And oft perfum'd my petitory stile,
> With Ciuet-speach, t'entrap *Olfactus* Nose,
> And clad my selfe in Silken Eloquence,
> To allure the nicer touch of *Tactus* hand,
> But all's become lost labour, and my cause
> Is still procrastinated.[62] (my italics)

In Lingua's soliloquy we witness sweetness in action. Swann's 'phenomenal reality of reading and writing as it engaged the senses'[63] is undeniably present in the 'seasoned savourie periods [/] With sugred words', but the shift from 'reading and writing' to 'voicing' introduces another aspect to 'sweetness' via Shahani's concept of the 'attitude of sugar'.[64] Lingua transforms her 'sharpe vinigar' into 'sweet perswasions' that include 'savourie periods [...] with sugared words', 'smelling flowers of vernant Rhetorique', 'Limming and flashing with various Dyes', 'perfum'd [...] petitory stile with Civet-speach' and 'silken Eloquence'. Such imagery echoes that of the above quote from Spenser's 'Dedicatory Epistle' and his analogy of the 'blaze and portraict'. This sweetness, musical in the way it is debated between Auditus/Hearing

---

[62] Ibid.
[63] Swann, '"To dream to eat books"', 83.
[64] Jennifer Richards, *Voices and Books in the English Renaissance: A New History of Reading* (Oxford: Oxford University Press, 2019); Larson, *Matter of Song*.

and Lingua/Voice has only partly to do with taste. More tantalizing is the way in which it 'perswa[des]' with an embellishment appropriate to each sense 'savourie periods' between 'sugared words', limned, civited, silken.[65]

Sweetness as it relates to both Lingua and Auditus (and indeed to a lesser extent Gustus/Taste and Olfactus/Smell) becomes complicated throughout the course of the play. Lingua, frustrated with the Five Senses and their refusal to allow her to be numbered amongst them, drugs their wine at a banquet. Auditus' response is particularly interesting; as a result of Lingua's drugged wine he is made to hear 'sweetness' where previously he heard only 'sharpe vinigar':

AVD.
Hearke, hearke, hearke, hearke, peace, peace, O peace: O sweete, admirable, Swanlike heauenly, hearke, O most mellifuous straine, O what a pleasant cloase was there, O full, most delicate.
COM. SEN.
How now *Phantastes*, is *Auditus* mad?
PHAN.
Let him alone, his musicall head is alwaies full of od crotchets.
AVD.
Did you marke the dainty dryuing of the last pointe, an excellent maintayning of the songe, by the choise timpan of mine eare, I neuer heard a better, hist, st, st, hearke, why theres a cadence able to rauish the dullest Stoicke.
COM. SEN.
I know not, what to thinke on him.
AVD.
There how sweetly the plane-song was dissolued into descant, and how easily they came of with the last rest, hearke, hearken the bitter sweetest Achromaticke.
COM. SEN.
Audatus.
AVD.

---

[65] Holly Dugan, *The Ephemeral History of Perfume: Scent and Sense in Early Modern England* (Baltimore: Johns Hopkins University Press, 2011), 5. The language of smell was far more nuanced in early modern English than it is today: 'Objects ambered, civited, expired, fetored, halited, resented and smeeked; they were described as breathful, embathed, endulced, gracious, halited, incensial, odorant, pulvil, redolent and suffite.'

90 SYRENE SOUNDES

Thankes good *Apollo* for this timely grace, neuer could'st thou in fitter: O more then most musicall harmony, O most admirable consort, haue you no eares? doe you not heare this musicke?
PHAN.
It may bee good, but in my opinion, they rest too long in the beginning.
AVD.
Are you then deafe? do you not yet perceiue the wondrous sound the heauenly orbes do make with their continuall motion, hearke, hearke, O hony sweete.
COM. SEN.
What tune do they play?
AVD.
Why such a tune as neuer was, nor euer shalbe heard, marke now, now marke, now, now.
PHAN.
List, list, list.
AVD.
Hearke O, sweete, sweete sweete.[66]

Music should be sweet; as Davies noted, "tis no man that hates sweete *Musickes* moode".[67] However, the excessive 'sweete, sweete, sweete' sweetness Auditus hears in his hallucinated music, 'such a tune as never was, nor ever shalbe heard', causes Communis Sensus (Common Sense, the viceregent of Queen Psyche) and Phantastes (Imagination) to doubt Auditus' sanity. The message is clear. The problem is only partially the hallucinatory aspect of the failure of Auditus' hearing. Sweetness is only 'sweet' in moderation, or where appropriate. A 'musicall head [...] alwaies ful of od crotchets' is acceptable, but the cloying, sickliness of the 'sweete admirable [...] mellifluous straine [...] sweetly the plane-songe was dissolved in [...] bitter sweetest Achromaticke [...] hony sweete [...] O, sweete, sweete, sweete' is extreme.[68]

[66] Tomkis, *Lingua*, 3.7. 'Swanlike' is often seen in close proximity to sweet; see prefatory material to Joshua Sylvester. It was likely a well-accepted trope, rather than an allusion to Orlando Gibbons's five-part madrigal 'The Silver Swan', which was first published in his *First Set of Madrigals and Motets of Five Parts* (London, 1612), although it could have been given that Gibbons's patron Sir Christopher Hatton (and the likely composer of the lyrics) and Gibbons himself were both at Cambridge at approximately the same time, Hatton graduating in 1599 and Gibbons in 1606.
[67] Davies, to TR, in Ravenscroft, *A Briefe Discourse of the True (But Neglected) Charact'ring of the Degrees*.
[68] For a comparison, think of Ophelia's description of Hamlet's madness as 'sweet bells jangled out of time'; William Shakespeare, *Hamlet*, in *Mr William Shakespeares comedies, histories and tragedies*

THE RHETORIC OF FALSENESS 91

The final important facet of the metaphor of the musical 'sweet' is another tasting concept that was frequently found in the company of the 'sweet': the 'spice' or 'spiced'. 'Sweet spices' are a biblical trope and they infused their way into the literature of the English Renaissance, both explicitly and implicitly musical (the most notable of which is the Chaucerian phrase 'sweet spiced conscience', which still held enough linguistic currency to make an appearance in Ben Jonson's *Bartholomew Fair* in 1614). Spicy sweetness, for example, makes an appearance in the titular poem of Aemilia Lanier's *Salve Deus Rex Judaeorum* following the Resurrection, with Christ the Eternal 'Bridegroome that appears so faire':

[...]

His lips like skarlet threeds, yet much more sweet
Than is the sweetest hony dropping dew,
Or hony combes, where all the Bees doe meet;
Yea, he is constant, and his words are true,
His cheekes are beds of spices, flowers sweet;
His lips like Lillies, dropping downe pure mirrhe,
Whose loue, before all worlds we doe preferre.[69]

This stanza appears to be a gloss on the biblical occurrences of 'sweetness'. Psalm 19 has God's judgement as 'sweeter also than honey, and the honey comb'; Psalm 55 has companionship with God as 'sweet counsel'. In Psalm 119 we hear the psalmist declare 'How sweet are thy words unto my taste! Yea, sweeter than honey to my mouth', and in Psalm 141, 'When their judges are overthrown in stony places, they shall hear my words; for they are sweet'; the passage 'His cheekes are beds of spices, flowers sweet' itself is from the Song of Solomon 5:13. The final phrase is somewhat of an enigma, but can be unpacked to an extent by exploring the etymology of the word 'spice'. 'Spice' derives from Latin *species*, in the sixteenth and early seventeenth centuries meaning outward form, appearance; the visible form of the Eucharist, an image, a phantom, and imagined thing and *speces*, a part, portion, category, trace, or touch. Anatomically, species were the things that enabled

Published according to the true originall copies (London: Isaac Iaggard, and Ed. Blount, 1623), 3.1, lines 154–159.

[69] Aemilia Lanyer, *Salve Deus Rex Judaeorum*, Fol. Fv.

human interaction with the world, through the competing extromissive and intromissive theories of sense perception. Closely related to the species was *pneuma*, spirit or breath,[70] emitted by God, the Cosmos, and humanity and connecting all in the great chain of being.[71] To write of Christ's cheeks as 'spiced' was to activate this rich collection of meanings, signifying at once his mortality and his divinity, through his vital breath.

Spice may appear an odd choice for an investigation into early modern words about music. Nevertheless, a brief survey of the common denominator between the varied early modern meanings reveals that spice, spiced, spicy is indeed germane to ideas about music and its sweetness. Each of these meanings pertain to alteration: the addition of something (that which spices) to ornament or embellish our reading of the existing experience. In this way it assists the eloquence or persuasion. Spice did not gain an explicit musical usage until the later seventeenth century, and at that in Italian, rather than English. However, its usage is pertinent. The composer and violinist Giovanni Maria Bononcini, writing about the semitone in his *Musico Prattico* in 1673, described it as the 'condimento della musica', the 'spice of music':

> The semitone is the spice of music, in that every melody would be bitter and unendurable to the ear without it, and it is the origin of the diversity of all the intervals of music, since the differences between the intervals [*gl'intervalli Musicali*] originate in the variety of the positions it occupies within them.[72]

Bononcini reveals an interesting dynamic at the heart of the idea of music and taste, and with it the concept of musical sweetness. It was allied to the practice of solmization and the audacious *mi–fa* interval. The kind of 'spice' that Bononcini writes about towards the latter end of the early modern period is, therefore, dangerous. It leans towards discord. However, it also provides

---

[70] See Larson, *Matter of Song*, 65–72.

[71] See Christine Göttler, 'Vapours and Veils: The Edge of the Unseen', in Christine Göttler and Wolfgang Neuber (eds.), *Spirits Unseen: The Representation of Subtle Bodies in Early Modern European Culture* (Leiden: Brill, 2008); Sven Dupre, 'Images in the Air: Optical Games, Magic and Imagination', in Göttler and Neuber (eds.,), *Spirits Unseen*; and David Summers, *The Judgment of Sense: Renaissance Naturalism and the Rise of Aesthetics* (Cambridge: Cambridge University Press, 1987).

[72] Giovanni Maria Bononcini, *Musico Prattico che brevemente dimostra il modo di giungere alla perfetta cognizione di tutte quelle cose, che concorrono alla composizione de i canti, e di ciò ch'all'arte del contrapunto si ricerca* (Bologna, 1673). See Geoffrey Chew, 'The Spice of Music: Towards a Theory of the Leading Note', in *Music Analysis*, 2: 1 (March 1983), 38.

precisely the discord that creates E.K.'s 'comely concordaunce': it is the foil to sweetness. The example of *Musico Prattico* is admittedly far removed from the others explored in this chapter, in terms not only of time but also of language. Nevertheless, it is arguable that it hints towards an understanding of the figurative meanings of spice that has left its traces in sources closer to the turn of the seventeenth century.

Through its etymological origins, the 'spice[/d]' has a tantalizing musical resonance. The enunciation of music is the activation of *musica mundi* through *musica humana* and *musica instrumentalis* via the medium of aural/oral species as breath.[73] The spice, *spiritus*, breath, voice, is an important reverberating harmonic to the concept of 'sweet' music. This may sound outlandish, but it is important to take into account the manner in which dead metaphors and the histories of words can accumulate to provide stratified meaning.[74] 'Spice' rarely appears as a descriptor or metaphor of music, but it frequently appears in, or in proximity to, musical contexts. Take the 'discord' and 'musical confusion' at the heart of the plot of Shakespeare's musical metaphor-laden *Midsummer Night's Dream* (c. 1594): 'the invisible yet ever-present Indian boy in the *Dream*—the root cause of all discord in fairyland, the 'absent centre' of fairyland, [in Shankar Raman's words]'.[75] Crucially, the Indian boy is 'never so sweet a changeling'. He was also conceived by Titania's votaress and seemingly the 'spicéd Indian air' ('air', another musical term)[76] that enables sails to grow 'big bellied': one of his mother's 'trifles' (trifle, crucially, derived from the Old French *trufler*, to mock or deceive, another falsehood).[77] Oberon's contribution is also a musical spice: the way he describes the location of the 'flower, herb', 'love-in-idleness' to Puck is framed in sonic terms, where the mermaid's 'dulcet and harmonious breath' causes 'certain stars [to] sho[ot] madly from their spheres' (2.1 133–138). Elsewhere in the literature of the period, spice and music are proximate. The anonymous

---

[73] Jennifer Richards has recently argued for the importance of recognizing voice and vocal enunciation as a reading practice. See Richards, *Voices and Books*.
[74] Marr et al., *Ingenuity*, 2.
[75] Shahani, *Tasting Difference*, 42.
[76] Larson, *Matter of Song*, 65–72.
[77] William Shakespeare, *Midsummer Night's Dream, Mr William Shakespeares comedies, histories and tragedies Published according to the true originall copies* (London: Isaac Iaggard, and Ed. Blount, 1623), 2.1 109–118. See also Margo Hendricks, '"Obscured by dreams": Race, Empire, and Shakespeare's *A Midsummer Night's Dream*', in *Shakespeare Quarterly*, 47: 1 (Spring 1996), 37–60; and Lubaaba Al-Azami, '"In the Spiced Indian Air": Trading Coin and Cloth in the Empire of the Great Mughal', https://memorients.com/articles/in-the-spiced-indian-air-trading-coin-and-cloth-in-the-empire-of-the-great-mughal (accessed 26 April 2021).

Bel-Vedere, or The Garden of Muses (1600) uses music and 'spices' as two similes in its chapter 'Of Vertue':

> As Musicke profits nothing but by sound,
> So vertue helpes not if it saile in life.
> Like as the Sunne obscures all lesser lights,
> So vertues lustre damps all enuies sleights.
> As spices in their bruising sauor most,
> So vertue in affliction best is seene.[78]

Music and spice are separated into a stanza together, and by the rocking repetition of 'As...', 'So...' are knitted together as ballast for virtue. Julia rejects Delio's gold in John Webster's *Duchess of Malfi* with reference to a specific spice, stating that 'a lute-string far exceeds it. [/] It hath no smell, like cassia or civet',[79] and Fitzgrave dismisses his turn of speech as a 'spice of poetrie' in Middleton's *Your Five Gallants* (1608).[80] This is to say nothing of the many instances of 'spice' in sermon literature and in recipe books.[81] As a variety of sweetness, the spiced has a lot to teach us about the metaphor of sweet music.

The metaphor of sweet music carries the traces (indeed, the 'spice') of all these diverse meanings. It indicated a pleasant musical experience, but not necessarily one that was unproblematic or unambiguously morally sound. It was intricately entwined into the musical culture of the period, in the way it was made and read through hexachords, and in the limitations and transgressions entailed in translating the *mi–fa* interval, and the 'lascivious' rule-breaker B♭/B-*fa*, into different pitch spaces. It connoted artifice; this could be both positive, as in Lanyer's description of Pembroke's style, or it could be negative, 'false', a dissimulation. 'Sweet' music thus encapsulated the subtleties and nuances of a way of knowing and hearing that enshrined discords like false relations in the English Renaissance.

---

[78] Anonymous, *Bel-vedere, or The Garden of the Muses* (London: F.K. for Hugh Astley, 1600), 20. (Of Vertue).

[79] See also Thomas Middleton, *The Roaring Girle* (London: Nicholas Okes for Thomas Archer, 1611), in which Mistress Openworke describes her faculty for language in the following terms: 'I had my Lattine tongue, and a spice of the French.'

[80] Thomas Middleton, *Your Five Gallants* (London: George Eld for Richard Bonlan, 1608).

[81] See, e.g., Hugh Plat, 'Introductory Poem' to *Delightes for Ladies to Adorne their Persons, Tables, Closets and Distillatories with Beauties, Perfumes and Waters* (London: Peter Short, 1602), unpaginated; Gervase Markham, *Countrey Contentments, or the English Huswife* (London: John Beale, 1623); Margaret Yelverton, *Booke of Phisicke Surgery Preserves and Cookery with Sundrie Other Excellent Receites*, Wellcome Library MS 182, fol. 186.

Voicing Sweetness

So much for the metaphorical understanding of sweet music in the broader culture of the English Renaissance: what was happening in the musical texts? The traces of the conceptual connection between sweetness and false, dissonant chromaticism are palpable in the musical theoretical texts of the English Renaissance. The anonymous *Praise of Musicke* (1586), sometimes attributed to John Case, has the most to say on the subject, but this is largely in terms of anchoring the concept of music within its classical precedents and emphasizing its role in Humanist endeavour. We can, however, infer the writer's defence against the problematic connotations of 'sweetness' entailed within earlier groups of meaning. The writer styles music as 'so sweete, so good, so vertuous, so comely a matrone among other artes',[82] combatting the troublesome feminine associations listed above through the respectable 'matrone', and states that its tendency to tantalize the imagination is not of concern because '[the sweetness of music] neither in it self needeth the colour & shadowes of imaginations, being aboue all conceiptes: nor in the pleasure thereof any externall ornament: being sweeter than canne be counterfeited by fictions, or expressed by fantasies.'[83] In his *A New Way of Making Foure Parts in Counterpoint* (1610), Thomas Campion uses 'sweet' music in rather more technical terms:

> Of all things that belong to the making up of a Musition, the most necessary and useful for him is the true knowledge of the Key or Moode, or Tone, for all signifie the same thing, with the closes belonging unto it, for there is no tune that can have any grace or sweetnesse, unlesse it be bounded within a proper key, without running into strange keyes which have no affinity with the aire of the song.[84]

Both demonstrate that 'sweetness' was an integral facet of musical experience. There is some disagreement between the two as to what the musically 'sweet' actually entails; Campion is evidently more concerned about how to avoid the 'strange keyes' offered by excessive use of *ficta* hexachords

---

[82] Attributed to John Case, *The Praise of Musicke* (Oxford: Joseph Barnes, 1586), unpaginated.
[83] Ibid., 40.
[84] Thomas Campion, *A New Way of Making Fowre Parts in Counter-Point by a most familiar, and infallible rule* (London: T. Snodham for John Browne, 1610), fol. D4r.

(as demonstrated by his discussion on appropriate observation of the 'half note' or *mi–fa* interval, see Fig. 2.1) and thus rehabilitating sweetness as a purely positive feature of music, whereas the anonymous author of the *Pathway* is more concerned to emphasize the gentility of the 'sweetness' of

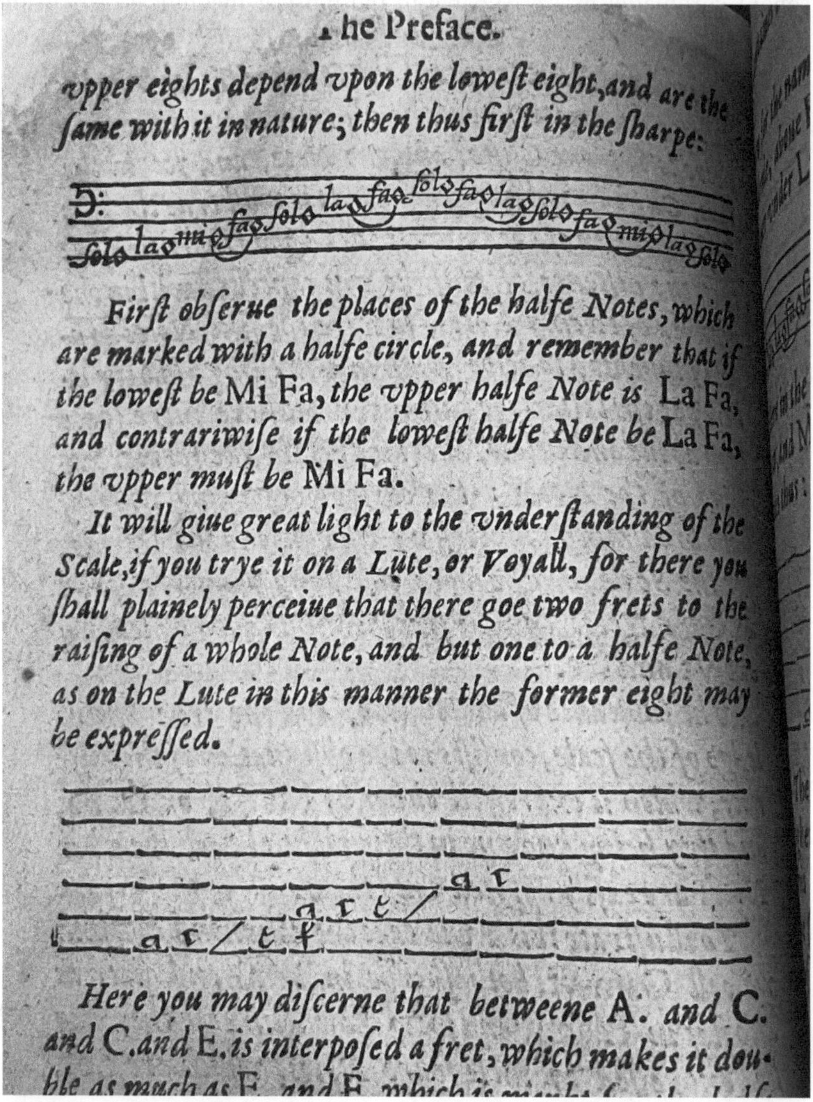
The Preface.

vpper eights depend vpon the loweſt eight, and are the ſame with it in nature; then thus firſt in the ſharpe:

Firſt obſerue the places of the halfe Notes, which are marked with a halfe circle, and remember that if the loweſt be Mi Fa, the vpper halfe Note is La Fa, and contrariwiſe if the loweſt halfe Note be La Fa, the vpper muſt be Mi Fa.

It will giue great light to the vnderſtanding of the Scale, if you trye it on a Lute, or Voyall, for there you ſhall plainely perceiue that there goe two frets to the raiſing of a whole Note, and but one to a halfe Note, as on the Lute in this manner the former eight may be expreſſed.

Here you may diſcerne that betweene A. and C. and C. and E. is interpoſed a fret, which makes it double as much as E. and F. which is ...

Fig. 2.1 Thomas Campion, explanation of the 'halfe note', in Thomas Campion, *A New Way of Making Fowre Parts in Counter-Point* (London: T. Snodham for John Browne, 1610), fol. B4r. London, British Library, Catalogue No. 1042.d.33(3.). Photograph author's own.

music. However, both enshrine 'sweetness' as a keyword in musical ways of knowing and listening.

The most technical[85] instance of musical sweetness can likewise be found in a discussion of meticulous ways to manage discord and concord, in Thomas Morley's *A Plaine and Easie Introduction to Practicall Musicke* (1597).[86] The *Introduction* is composed in dialogic format as a conversation between Master Gnorimus and his Pupil, Philomathes.[87] Philomathes is ashamed that, at a banquet, 'supper being ended, and Musicke bookes, according to the custome being brought to the table: the mistresse of the house presented mee with a part, earnestly requesting mee to sing. But when after manie excuses, I protested unfainedly that I could not: euerie one began to wonder. Yea, some whispered to others, demaunding how I was brought up.'[88] He seeks out Master Gnorimus, who begins to improve his musical knowledge. Accompanied by a diagram of concords and discords illustrating the relations (see Fig. 2.2),[89] Morley's Master introduces Philomathes to the rules of musical composition. He states that 'when a discord is taken, it is to cause the note following be the more pleasing to the eare' and that 'discords mingled with concordes not onelie are tollerable, but make the descant more pleasing if they be well taken,'[90] echoing E.K. in *The Shepheardes Calendar*, twenty years earlier, and a concept that had been prevalent in music theory texts for hundreds of years.

It is important to note here that Morley fashions Master Gnorimus as a man explicitly averse to false relations; as we shall discover below in Chapter 6, he describes them as 'both naught and stale like unto a garment of a strange fashion, which being new put on for a day or two will please because of the noveltie, but being worne thread beare, wil growe in contempt [. . . it has been] robde out of the capcase of some olde Organist, but that close though it fit the finger as that the deformitie whereof may be hidden by flurrish, yet is it not sufferable in compositions for voices, seeing there be such hard discordes taken as are flat against the rules of musicke'.[91] We should

---

[85] See Wegman, 'Sense and Sensibility', 300–301.
[86] Morley, *Plaine and Easie Introduction*.
[87] Ibid.
[88] Ibid., 1.
[89] Ibid., 71.
[90] Ibid., 74 and 73.
[91] Ibid., 154.

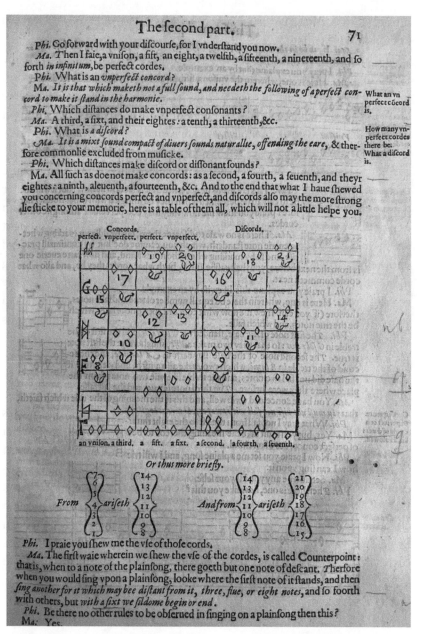

Fig. 2.2 Thomas Morley, diagram of concords and discords, in Thomas Morley, *A Plaine and Easie Introduction to Practicall Musicke set downe in forme of a dialogue* (London: Peter Short dwelling on Breedstreet Hill at the signe of the Starre, 1597). Photograph author's own.

not, therefore, expect any explicit conditions by which the specific discord of false relations are permitted within the *Introduction*; however, given the semantic bagginess of terms such as 'discord' and 'dissonance' in this period it is important that we entertain the possibility that some of these instances are applicable to false relations. Following this overview, Master Gnorimus proceeds to rehearse Philomathes through acceptable 'mingl[ings]' of discords and concords in lavishly, carefully illustrated examples. There are sweeter intervals in polyphonic composition, of which Master Gnorimus claims the sixth (or the *ut–la* interval) is the 'sweetest'. However, the Master condemns Philomathes' composition for the overuse of the sixth 'standing [...] a whole brief [breve] together in the third bar in the counter and tenor parts' where it would be better to be 'lightlie touched'. Sweetness in Morley's account is again about balance, about moderation. Sixths are concordant, but their power to 'express [...] those passions' is greatly compromised by being accentuated or intensified by excessive duration and doubling in parts.

Elsewhere in the *Introduction* the use of 'sweet' is more obviously related to voice and text:

> You may also vpon this plainesong make a way wherein the descant may sing euerie note of the ground twise, which though it shew some sight and maistry, yet will not be so sweet in the eare as others.[92]

> Likewise marke in what maner any part beginneth and you shal see some other reply vpon it in the same point, either in shorter or longer notes also in the 22. barre when the Tenor expresseth the point, the base reuerteth it, and at a worde I can compare it to nothing but to a wel garnished garden of most sweete flowers, which the more it is searched the more variety it yeldeth.[93]

> Likewise take a voice being neuer so good, and cause it sing aboue the naturall reach it will make an unpleasing and unsweete noise, displeasing both the singer because of the straining, and the hearer because of the wildenes of the sound.[94]

The first and third examples hark back to the idea of sweetness as balance, moderation, wholesomeness, lack of excess; interestingly, the third example

---

[92] Ibid., 124.
[93] Ibid., 162.
[94] Ibid., 167.

was misprinted as 'sweete' and identified in the errata published at the end of the treatise, demonstrating that 'sweete' was an expected premodifier of 'musicke'. The second example is the contribution of Polymathes (Philomathes' erstwhile brother, whom we encounter at the beginning of the *Introduction* seeking to improve his mathematical knowledge, and who encourages Philomathes to seek Master Gnorimus). All other instances of 'sweet' as a descriptor of music are uttered by the Master, or in the prefatory material: the Master is quite literally the arbiter of musical taste. However, Polymathes' comment is the only moment in the text in which the *suavis* kind of sweetness, the persuasiveness, of music is fully elucidated. He identifies what would be referred to in modern musical terms as the antecedent and consequent, '[when] any part beginneth and you shal see some other reply vpon it in the same point [. . .] when the Tenor expresseth the point, the base reverteth it' as 'sweete' due to the 'variety it y[i]eldeth' and the way that it is 'wel garnished'. 'Garnish' crucially connoted 'furnishing, equipment' in early modern English, as well as 'adornment'. It is the shaping of the music, the way that it is well supplied, that drives its sweetness.

Morley's use of the concept of 'sweete musicke', through the personae of Master Gnorimus and Polymathes, is not simply about 'harmonicall relation'. It often relates to harmony but only in the sense of specific features that will enhance the overall impression of musical order. This has much to do with the persuasiveness, or indeed aptness, of the 'express[ion]', and little to do with harmonic regularity. Polymathes' comment on the composition carries irresistible overtones of the 'sweet' flowers of rhetoric trope, and in this way encapsulates Morley's use of the term 'sweet'. 'Sweet' music for Morley lies in the pithy, suitable communication or demonstration of a musical idea, be that through the entwining of parts, through properly mannered repetition and reiteration, or through the deployment of a singer with an appropriate range to prevent 'straining' and the 'wildenes of [. . .] sound'. Morley is not alone in this interpretation; two decades later, we find Thomas Ravenscroft using the 'sweet' in a similar manner in 1614:

> [Music's] *Composure* I dare warrant, 'tis not onely of *Ayre*, made for some small tickling of the outward Sence alone, but a great deale more solide, and sweetly vnited to *Number*, *Measures*, and *Nature* of the *Ditty*. The earnest affections which a man hath, in the vse of such *Recreations* as they are made for, are so fully exprest in them, for *Tact*, *Prolation*, and *Diminution*, that not onely the *Ignorant* Eare must needs be pleased with them, for their

Variety of *sweet Strayes*, and the *Humorous Fantastick* eare satisfied, in the *Iocundity* of their many *Changes*, but also the *Iudicious* hearer will finde that in them, which passes the *Outward* sence, & strikes a *rare delight of Passion* vpon the *Mind* it selfe, that attends them.[95]

The musically 'sweet' had much to do with expression, and the way of knowing that it encouraged through hearing.

This is an important distinction, and one that can be found throughout the musical texts and paratexts of the early modern period. Individual features, the minutiae of eloquent expression, are that which renders something 'sweet'; these are the things that snag a performer/listener's attention.[96] Such an understanding of the term drives Thomas Weelkes's dedicatory letter to George Philpott at the beginning of his *Madrigals to 3, 4, 5 & 6 Voyces* (1597), composed just before he was appointed organist at Winchester College.[97] Weelkes's literary flair is unusual amongst his fellow composers of the late sixteenth and early seventeenth centuries, and so the letter makes for a particularly entertaining read:

> Compelled me to present before you, these six dishes full of divers Madrigalls, the first fruicts of my barren ground, unripe, in regard of time, unsavourie, in respect of others; not much delightsome, onely once to looke on, for at first mens eyes are not matches: not sweet, onely once to tast off, for presently the pallet cannot gieve passage to his savourie sentence. Therefore tast, and againe I pray you, if they lyke your appetite, spare not my Orchard: if they offend your Stomack, laye them by to ripen, and you shall prove of my latter Vintage.[98]

Musical sweetness permeates the intricate twists and turns of this extended metaphor of taste. Weelkes's statement that his madrigals are 'not sweet, onely once to tast off' flirts with the trope of *aposiopesis*, the figure of breaking off suddenly in speech. In this formulation the 'breaking off'

---

[95] Thomas Ravenscroft, Preface, *A Briefe Discourse of the true (but neglected) use of Charactring the Degrees, by Perfection, Imperfection and Diminution in Mesurable Musicke, Against the Common Practise and Custome of These Times* (London, Edward Allde for Tho. Adams, 1614), unpaginated.

[96] Raphael Lyne, *Shakespeare, Rhetoric and Cognition* (Cambridge: Cambridge University Press, 2011).

[97] David Brown, *Thomas Weelkes: A Biographical and Critical Study* (London: Faber & Faber, 1969), 47–49.

[98] Thomas Weelkes, 'To the Right Worshipfull George Philpott Esquire', in *Madrigals to 3, 4, 5 & 6 Voyces* (London: Thomas East, 1597), 129 fol. Ai.

is alluded to by the caesurae that cleaves the 'sweet' and the 'tast[e]', before bringing the clause to a neat conclusion, 'for presently the pallet cannot gieve passage to his savourie sentence': it is not digestible without repeated sampling. The sweet and savoury, rather than serving as antonyms as they would in modern English, are fulfilling the same signifying function in this clause. 'Savoury' entered English in the thirteenth century from the Old French, Anglo-Norman term *savouré*, meaning sweet, pleasant, pleasant to the taste, fragrant, seasoned, and *spiced*. It is a term that is also allied to a spiritual connotation, but more in the sense of a thing that is pleasing to the spirit than providing balance. It gradually came to signify a salt, piquant, or umami taste across the sixteenth century;[99] however, Weelkes's usage suggests that he wishes his reader/performer/listener to interpret the 'sweet' and the 'savourie' as general terms of delectation, rather than specific flavours. They are arguments for the eloquence of his musical style.

Weelkes is a particularly flamboyant rhetorician. Nevertheless, the dedicatory letter to his first book of madrigals provides an insight into the general contemporary understanding of the musically sweet, and how a piece or performance of music could be made sweet. In glossing Weelkes's dedication, Simon Smith notes that the allusion appears to be towards the sense of smell, rather than the sense of taste.[100] It is of course anachronous to draw a hard and fast distinction between the senses in early modern England, as demonstrated only too well by Lingua's reference to her 'perfum'd [...] stile' and 'Silken Eloquence'. However, the interpretation raises the possibility of an interesting allusion. Psalm 141, in Archbishop Parker's 1567 translation, features the following tantalizing imagery: 'O let my sute: in syght so ryse, [/] as doth incense to thee: My rayse of handes: as sacrifice, [/] of might, Lord let it bee'.[101] Mary Sidney Herbert's later translation of circa 1599 unpacks the allusion and renders the sweetness of the incense explicit:

---

[99] Thomas Elyot, *Pasquil the Playne* (1533):
Pas. I praye the Harpocrates teache me howe thou doest season thy sylence, doest thou hit with salte or with spyces?
 Harpocrat. Naye, with sugar, for I vse lyttell salte.
 Pas. And that maketh your counsayl more swete than sauery. (sig. B8).
[100] Simon Smith, *Musical Response in the Early Modern Playhouse 1603–1625* (Cambridge: Cambridge University Press, 2017), 71–72.
[101] Matthew Parker and Thomas Tallis, *The Whole Psalter translated into English metre* (London: John Day, 1567), 405. For comparison see later translations such as the King James Bible (1611), 'let my prayer be set before thee as incense: and the lifting up of my hands as evening sacrifice'; *The Bible: Authorized King James Version* (Oxford: Oxford University Press, 2008). See also the *Praise of Musicke* (attributed to John Case: 'so no doubt but the songes of the faithful may be as a sweete odor of incense vnto him, and most gratefull in his sight', 147.

THE RHETORIC OF FALSENESS   103

> As sweet perfume to skies let what I pray ascend:
> Let these uplifted hands, which praying I extend,
> As evening sacrifice unto thee directed.[102]

In this way sweetness-as-smell stands in synecdochically for the words of the 'pray[er]' or 'sute'; the petitions are imagined reaching God in the way that perfume or scent on the air reaches our noses, in a metaphor that emphatically insists on the invisibility and immateriality of voice, words, song, prayer.[103] The psalm itself alludes to the phrase 'sweet savour unto the Lord', which appears throughout the Old Testament with regards to sacrifice of thanks. It is a phrase that appears numerous times, directly or as a frame of reference, in Exodus, Leviticus, Numbers, and Chronicles, with one iteration in Ezra (6:10) and one in Philippians (4:18).[104] These repeated petitions, weighing the 'sweet', the 'savour', would have been familiar in early modern devotional frameworks, both to Weelkes and to his readership whom he urges to 'tast, and againe', in order to appreciate his 'sweet' madrigals and their 'savourie sentence'. Weelkes summons a host of broader cultural allusions in constructing his concept of musical sweetness and musical appreciation. Thus he frames musical appreciation in figurative terms, as the appreciation of perfume 'savourie', echoing the fragrant, pleasant, crucially spiced *savouré*, and as the appreciation of taste, as well as wholesomeness and persuasion.

The conception of pleasant 'sweete musicke' at play in the early modern English vernacular is, in this way, rather more complex than it may first appear. Weelkes provides the most elucidated example of 'sweete' as musical term, but he is certainly not the only composer to use it in a complicated manner. However, 'sweete musicke' is surprisingly rare in the paratextual, prefatory material of collections of music, written or purporting to be written by the composer.[105] Another rare example is William Byrd's use in his *Psalmes, Sonets and Songes of Sadnes and Pietie* (1599). Dedicating his

---

[102] Mary Sidney Herbert, *The Sidney Psalter: The Psalms of Sir Philip and Mary Sidney* (Oxford: Oxford World's Classics, 2009), Psalm 141, ll. 4–6, 271.
[103] For more on this see Dugan, *Ephemeral History*.
[104] *The Authorized King James Bible* (2008), Exodus 29:18, 29:25, 29:41, 30:7; Leviticus 1:9, 1:13, 1:17, 2:2, 2:9, 2:12, 3:5, 3:16, 4:7, 4:31, 6:15, 6:21, 8:21, 8.28, 17:6, 23:18; Numbers 15:3, 15:7, 15:10, 15:13, 15:14, 15:24, 18:17, 28:2, 28:6, 28:8, 28:13, 28:24, 28:27, 29:2, 29:36; 1 Chronicles 29:21; 2 Chronicles 2:4, 13:11, 16:14.
[105] This is likely due to the unstable concept of musical authorship in this period. See Rob Wegman, 'From Maker to Composer: Improvisation and Musical Authorship in the Low Countries, 1450–1500', in *Journal of the American Musicological Society*, 49: 3 (Autumn 1996), 409–479; M. Everist, *Discovering Medieval Song: Latin Poetry and Music in the Conductus* (Cambridge: Cambridge University Press, 2018), 151–180.

collection to Sir Christopher Hatton, he states his hope that 'these poore songs of mine might happely yeeld some sweetnesse, repose, and recreation vnto your Lordships mind, after your dayly paines & cares taken in the high affaires of the Common Wealth', which plays upon the connotations of wholesomeness and healing in the 'sweet' etymological ancestry.[106] John Farmer's letter to Edward de Vere, Earl of Oxford, prefacing his *First Set of English Madrigals* (1599) is another interesting variation on the theme. He does not pitch his letter in direct terms of sweetness but appears instead to respond to, or pastiche, that of Weelkes published two years previously:

> In this I shall be most encouraged, if your Lordship vouchsafe the protection of my *first fruites*, for that both for your greatnes you best can, and for your iudgement in Musicke best may: for without flattrie be it spoken, those that know your Lordship know this, that vsing this science as a recreation, your Lordship haue ouergone most of them that make it a profession. Right Honorable Lord, I hope it shall not be *distastfull* to number you heere amongst the fauourers of Musicke, and the practisers, no more then Kings and Emperours that haue beene desirous to be in the roll of Astronomers, that being but a starre faire, the other an Angels Quire. (my italics)[107]

Gustatory language became a commonplace in the secular song collections of the late sixteenth and into the seventeenth century, as a means of priming the reader, performer, or listener for the appropriate way to receive the music. John Dowland's 1610 collection *A Musicall Banquet furnished with a varietie of delicious ayres* represents perhaps the pinnacle of the genre, with his analogy of the musical collection to 'a carefull Confectionary, as neere as might be I have fitted my Banquet for all tastes.'[108] The word 'confectionary' was a very recent coinage, appearing only around 1599 out of the root word 'confection' and its developing connotations of 'prepared, composed, mixed together' (a sense which it had held since the late fourteenth century) into its verbal form, which presupposed preparation with sugar or syrup. In each sense the connotation of curation, of the care that has gone into the melange,

---

[106] William Byrd, 'To the Right Honorable Sir Christopher Hatton', in *Psalmes, Sonets and Songes of Sadnes and Pietie* (London: Thomas East, 1599).

[107] John Farmer, 'To the Right Honorable my Very Good Lord and Maister, Edward DeVere Earle of Oxenforde', in *The First Set of English Madrigals: To Foure Voices* (London: William Barley, 1599), unpaginated.

[108] John Davies, *A Musicall Banquet Furnished with a varietie of delicious ayres, collected out of the best authors* (London: Printed by Thomas Snodham for Thomas Adams, 1610), unpaginated.

is key. The sweet 'confection' of music can be seen in shadowy embryonic form in Farmer's gustatory language in his note 'To the Reader', which appears on the page following his letter to de Vere:

> I could aduise the studious in Musicke so to imploy themselues, that they might seeme to be rightly borne vnder the sweete aspect of *Venus*, which, as the Astronomers witnesse, is the Dominatrix in Musitians natiuities: it is the onely grace in a Musitian to follow this course, so to fitte both note and number as if like Twinnes of one mother, they may seeme to be all one which yeeldeth great abundance of variety.[109]

Farmer parodies Weelkes's 'sweet [. . .] dishes ful of divers Madrigalls' by extending the metaphor to include the cosmic music of the spheres, the *musica mundi* and the 'sweete aspect of Venus'. It is a playful homage, and one that demonstrates that the discourse surrounding musical sweetness was lively amongst musicians themselves.

All three of these examples of paratextual 'musical sweetness' are from secular collections of songs from the late sixteenth century. This is not coincidental. 'Sweet' appears in high volumes in the lyrics of the secular songs around the turn of the seventeenth century.[110] The authorship of lyrics is often uncertain in early modern song collections, but the volume of instances is worth lingering over. By way of a brief survey, the word appears 80 times in Byrd's 1589 *Songs of Sundrie Natures of Some Gravitie*,[111] 137 times in Thomas Watson's *The First Set of Italian Madrigals Englished* (1590),[112] 113 times in Morley's *Madrigralls to Foure Voyces* (1594),[113] 61 times in George Kirbye's *The First Set of English Madrigals to 4, 5 and 6 Voyces* (1597),[114] 139 times in John Wilbye's *First Set of English Madrigals to 3, 4, 5 and 6 Voices* (1598),[115] 118 times in Michael Cavendish's *Fourteen*

---

[109] John Farmer, 'To the Reader', in *The First Set of English Madrigals: To Foure Voices*, (London: William Barley, 1599), unpaginated.

[110] This is an important corpus of works in terms of technical musical development, as recently demonstrated by Megan Kaes Long, *Hearing Homophony: Tonal Expectation at the Turn of the Seventeenth Century* (Oxford: Oxford University Press, 2020).

[111] William Byrd, *Songs of Sundrie Natures, Some of Gravitie, and Others of Myrth* (London: Thomas East, 1589).

[112] Thomas Watson, *The First Set of Italian Madrigals Englished* (London: Thomas East, 1590).

[113] Thomas Morley, *Madrigalls to Foure Voyces* (London: Thomas East, 1594).

[114] George Kirbye, *The First Set of English Madrigals to 4, 5 and 6 Voyces* (London: Thomas East, 1597).

[115] John Wilbye, *First Set of English Madrigals to 3, 4 and 5 Voices* (London: Tho. Este alias Snodham, 1598).

Ayres in Tabletorie to the Lute Expressed with Two Voyces (1598),[116] 123 times in John Bennet's *Madrigalls to Four Voices* (1599),[117] 122 times in Weelkes's *Balletts and Madrigals to 5 Voyces* (1608),[118] 52 times in Gibbons's *First Set of Madrigals and Motets* (1612),[119] 57 times in Tomkins's 1622 collection *Songs of 3, 4, 5 and 6 Partes* (1622),[120] and 336 times in the original madrigal collection *Musica Transalpina* (1588). It appears to have had a strong connection to the madrigal genre that arrived in England through the final printed collection listed above, and which made secular music widely available for the first time.[121] It is not within the scope of this chapter to investigate this striking fashion; likewise, the influence of the biblical, devotional 'sweet' briefly explored above is not to be underestimated. Nevertheless, it is worth observing that the professional or amateur musician would have been hard pressed to avoid the 'sweet[ness]' of music in early modern England.

Nor would the professional or amateur musician have been easily able to avoid the striking variety of its manifestations, and its fundamental 'semantic instability'. Byrd's 1589 collection *Songs of Sundrie Natures* features 'Compell the Hawke', a fascinating partsong that flirts with chromaticism through lyrics by Thomas Churchyard, which play on the metaphorical relations between the hunt of the hound and hawke, and the pursuit of love:

> Compell the Hawke to sitt that is unmand,
> or make the Hound untaught, to draw the Deere,
> or bring the free against his will in band,
> or move the sad a pleasant tale to heare,
> your time is lost, and you are neare the neere:
> So Love ne learnes by force the knot to knit,
> he serves but those that feele sweete fancyes fit.[122]

---

[116] George Cavendish, *Fourteen Ayres in Tabletorie to the Lute Expressed with Two Voyces and the Base Violl or the Voice and Lute and Only 6 More to Four Voyces and in Tabletorie, And 8 Madrigalles to 5 Voyces* (London: Peter Short, 1598).

[117] John Bennett, *Madrigalls to Four Voices* (London: H. Ballard for William Barley, 1599).

[118] Thomas Weelkes, *Balletts and Madrigals to 5 Voyces* (London: Thomas Este, 1608).

[119] Orlando Gibbons, To the Right Worthy Sir Christopher Hatton, *First Set of Madrigals and Motets of 5 Parts: apt for Viols and Voyces* (London: Thomas Snodham, 1612).

[120] Thomas Tomkins, *Songs of 3, 4, 5 and 6 Partes* (London: Thomas Snodham, 1622).

[121] It is important to note that the madrigal form was far more engaged with the intellectual culture of the period than has previously been acknowledged, so the presence of 'sweet' in these collections is likely to do with their role in 'knowledge building'. See Katie Bank, *Knowledge Building in Early Modern Music* (London: Routledge, 2020).

[122] William Byrd, *Songs of Sundrie Natures*, fol. F1v; Thomas Churchyard, from Richard Tottel and Nicholas Grimauld, *Songes and Sonnets* (London: 1577).

The false relation crucially appears nowhere near the final couplet and its 'sweete fancyes fit'. Instead, it is used to illustrate the 'hawke to sit that is unmand', the 'draw[ing of the] Deere', and the 'bring[ing of] the free against his will in band'. It is contained within single lines, passing from the Tenor to the Superius, and is delicately restrained although consistently threatened through repetition of the chromatically sharpened F–G stepwise motif. The pinnacle of its eloquence lies in the laying of the false relation far from the expected lyrics, illustrating the force that 'knit[s]' the 'knot' instead in the containment of the hawk, hound, and free. It is a dynamic also at play in the collection's 'See those sweet eyes', and in the blazon song 'Of Gold All Burnished/Her Breath Is More Sweet'.[123] The full lyrics of the latter are as follows:

> Of gold all burnished, brighter than sunbeams,
> Were those curled locks upon her noble head
> Whose deep conceits my true deserving fled.
> Wherefore mine eyes such store of tears outstreams.
> Her eyes, fair stars; her red, like damask rose;
> White, silver shine of moon on crystal stream;
> Her beauty perfect, whereon fancies dream.
> Her lips are rubies; teeth, of pearls two rows.
> Her breath more sweet than perfect amber is;
> Her years in prime; and nothing doth she want
> That might draw gods from heaven to further bliss.
> Of all things perfect this I most complain,
> Her heart is rock, made all of adamant.
> Gifts all delight, this last doth only pain.[124]

Proximate false relations build from the 'curled locks upon her *noble* head', 'her beauty perfect', 'her lips are rubies' to 'her breath is more sweet than perfect Amber is'. These are simply a cross-section of instances from one of the better-known collections by one of the better-known composers of the English Renaissance, but the reader will note that many of the instances

---

[123] Ibid., fol. G2r.
[124] Kim F. Hall notes the importance of commodification/objectification in the rise of the blazon form, which is a crucial undercurrent to Byrd's madrigal. See Kim F. Hall, *Things of Darkness: Economies of Race and Gender in Early Modern England* (Ithaca, NY: Cornell University Press, 1995), 62–116.

of sweetness discussed above make an appearance in *Songs of Sundrie Natures*.

Elsewhere the false relation also appears in 'sweet' contexts. In Weelkes's 1608 collection of *Balletts and Madrigals* we find his madrigal 'Sweet Love, I will no more abuse thee' spiced with the ignominious 'lascivious' B♭/B-*fa* on the 'abuse' that the 'sweet love' is being detached from, both in Cantus and Altus and accompanied by an F♯ in Altus and Tenor. As a chromatic move it manipulates the spectre of the F hexachord and its B-*fa*, a self-conscious move pointing directly to its thwarting of the rules of musical theoretical decorum. This befits its equally self-conscious, self-referential lyrics:

> Sweet love, I will no more abuse thee
> Nor with my voice accuse thee
> But tune my notes unto thy praise
> And tell the world love ne're decaies
> Sweet love, doth concord ever cherish
> What wanteth concord some doth perish.[125]

Accordingly, the phrase 'my voice accuse' and 'tune my notes' also features false relation between Cantus, Bassus, and Altus. The madrigal returns to a restrained passage over the phrase 'sweet love, doth concord ever cherish' before concluding with a swashbucklingly assured false relation-laden sequence for the final line 'what wanteth concord some doth perish'. Simultaneously this final passage signals the close of the madrigal (the fact that it 'wants concord' and so will perish) and also cheekily thwarts the concept of concord itself. In Weelkes's assured hands, it is possible to watch the 'concord' being found out of the 'discord', the 'dischorde that maketh a comely concordaunce', knowingly laid before the performer/listener. Weelkes's propinquity for chromaticism is well established;[126] however, it is fascinating to see it played out through the concept of the 'sweetness' of his music, and how protean and fluid it could be.

Byrd and Weelkes provide merely two examples of many, separated by two decades. Their approaches naturally differ stylistically. Nevertheless, both suggest the centrality of sweetness to the idea of the musically 'false',

---

[125] Weelkes, *Balletts and Madrigals*, fol. B2r.
[126] Dennis M. Arnold, 'Thomas Weelkes and the Madrigal', in *Music and Letters*, 30: 1 (January 1950), 1–12.

discordant. It was a foil with which composers could play, thwarting and conforming to expectations and exposing the fundamental ambiguity of the metaphor of music. Perhaps the most audacious example can be found in John Farmer's 1599 madrigal 'Sweet Lord, Your Flame Still Burning', which melds the devotional sense of 'sweetness' with the romantic connotations used by Byrd and Weelkes. The fact that it was used within a church setting is demonstrated by the fact that it was preserved in the late sixteenth-century organ book Add. MS 29996, now in the British Library and once owned by Thomas Tomkins (fol. 40v).[127] The paradoxes of sweetness evidently caused great inspiration and delight for the composers of the English Renaissance and served as a highly apposite text setting for the chromatic experiments that enshrined the false relation within the English Renaissance stylistic. Such instances are sparse traces of what was once so widely accepted it was not deemed worthy of comment or explanation; however, their frequency demonstrates that such traces are worth taking seriously. It is vital that our approaches to that music take the inspiration and delight it fuelled into account.

Conclusion: False Sweetness

Both the explicitly and implicitly musical texts of the English Renaissance provide a fascinatingly varied use pattern for the concept of the musically 'sweet'. As Gregor Herzfeld noted with regards to the use of 'sweet' in medieval music theory, it never became semantically stable.[128] However, with the musical, economic, and political developments of the English Renaissance, this instability generated a wealth of new or developing meanings that shimmered around the trend for musical dissonance, discord, 'falseness', dissimulation. The arrival of Shahani's 'attitude' of sugar as a rival form of sweetness to honey epitomized this dynamic, as demonstrated by the Duchess's dismissal of her suitor in John Webster's heavily musical *Duchess of Malfi* (1614): he is 'a Mere Stick of Sugar Candy. You may quite look through him'.[129] We might compare the 'mere stick of sugar candy' to Morley's

---

[127] Farmer, *The First Set of English Madrigals*.
[128] Herzfeld, 'Süße', 1.
[129] John Webster, *The Duchess of Malfi* (1614; first published London: Nicholas Ores, 1623), 3.1 42–43.

objection to 'false notes', and his claims that such devices are 'robbed out of the capcase of an old organist', 'garment[s] of strange fashion' and 'deformitie [...] hidden by flurish'.[130] Sweet music was bound to such musical features as the 'discord that maketh a comely concordaunce', the breath or species which by being 'bruis'd' can be most savoured. Briefly, fuelled by its competing semantic forebears and new cultural inferences, it came to refer to the ways that one relished dissonances like false relations as a way of knowing.

In this sense, 'sweet' music captures something important at the heart of the concept of musical falseness and the false relation in the English Renaissance, as composers of the period strove to cultivate a distinctively English musical tradition, constructed out of an English musical past. It is an undercurrent in the other examples of the lexicon, in the expectation that concord will follow discord and that the listener/performer's role in the piece of music is to find that 'discord', as Theseus states in *Midsummer Night's Dream*. It is present in the 'crosse' relation that recalls the Crucifixion, as sacrifice, suffering, and as ultimate achievement of redemption, in the sweet spices that by 'bruising' provide the most savour. These metaphors all provide tantalizing evidence that twenty-first-century enjoyment and appreciation of false relations was felt far more explicitly as a virtue in the English Renaissance. The concept is familiar, and of course logical. However, the preceding exploration of a single word cloud of dissimulation, the artificial, ornamental, sugary 'sweet' has demonstrated how far the accidental false relation, born 'for lack of other shift', became a source of delight in the musical culture of the English Renaissance. It is a sense that is found throughout the literature of the period, as in, for example, John Florio's 1603 translation of the *Essais* of Michel de Montaigne. In Montaigne's essay 'That our Desires are Encreased by Difficulty', he notes that difficulties are 'the things that give relish and tartness to the sawce. [...] It is much sweeter when it itcheth, and endeared when it gauleth.'[131]

This chapter has explored the manifold suggestive ways that 'sweetness' was used as a modifying adjective for music, musical experience, and the musically related. It has unpacked the possible ways that the sweet can illuminate aspects of English Renaissance hearing, knowing, and auditory

---

[130] Morley, *Plaine and Easie Introduction*, 164; the 'capcase' was a small chest for carrying items of apparel such as 'laces, pinnes, needles'; Thomas Dekker, *The Belman of London* (London: 1608), sig. D4v.
[131] John Florio, *Essays written in French by Michael Lord of Montaigne* (London: Melchior Bradwood, 1613), 346.

imagination that cannot be accessed through more specific musical terminology; at the same time it has embraced the semantic capaciousness and contradictions inherent in the cliché of sweet music, traits that can often swamp 'sweet' music in a glut of meaning that can verge on the meaning*less*. Through the example of John Bennet's madrigal pair 'O Sweete Griefe'/'Rest Now, Amphion', it has considered a tantalizing clue as to the way that medieval concepts of sweet flatness percolated, in the English Renaissance, into ideas of sweet sharpness and solmization *ficta* as an enjoyable, delectable phenomenon. The wholesome, the persuasive, and the godly good or 'natural' all exercised a semantic pull on the musically sweet and entwined it firmly within a broader understanding of where music came from, how it functioned, and what it was for. Music was pleasant for its sugary artifice, for its charming persuasiveness, and for the opportunities it offered listeners and performers to assay themselves against these 'syrene soundes' and 'whorish sorceries', expose themselves to the seductively lascivious dangers of false relations in 'chromaticall harmonies' whilst remaining good English Protestants, untouched by its potential Romish bewitchments. With this recognition, it is possible to move towards a deeper understanding of ways of knowing through hearing and performing used by early modern listeners, performers, and readers of music, all of which will be vital as we explore how false relations were learned and used.

3
Painting with Falseness
Wording Your Discord

Sing to Song to Sing: In Defence of Melisma

In 1668 Nathaniel Tomkins published the *Musica Deo Sacra & ecclesiae Anglicanae, or, Musick dedicated to the honour and service of God, and to the use of the cathedral and other churches of England, especially of the Chappel-Royal of King Charles the First*, a complete and sumptuous collection of sacred works by his father Thomas Tomkins (1572–1656).[1] Amongst its settings of five services, five psalm tunes, the Preces, and two proper psalms and ninety-four anthems there is an exquisite if unassuming seven-part setting of Psalm 149 (itself a ritornello of sorts of Psalm 96), with an elegant run of false relations in its 'alleluia' section:

> O Sing unto the Lord a new Song
> Let the congregation of saints sing praise unto him.
> Let Israel rejoice in him that made him:
> Let the children of Sion for ever sing:
> Alleluia.

In the previous chapter we explored what happened when we focussed in on a single word and its cognates when thinking about the use of false relations both in technical musical texts, and in writing about music more generally; unsurprisingly and despite the ambiguity of how they were written about in extant music theory, we saw that they were considered in a positive light for the manner in which they enhanced the sweetness of the harmony. Continuing our textual literary theme, the next chapter will examine

---

My sincerest thanks to Edward Wickham, whose research on the intelligibility of words in music between 2009 and 2014 first sowed the seeds of the thoughts about text-setting and comprehension that led to the arguments in this chapter.

[1] Thomas Tomkins, *Musica Deo Sacra & ecclesiae Anglicanae, or, Musick dedicated to the honour and service of God, and to the use of the cathedral and other churches of England, especially of the Chappel-Royal of King Charles the First* (London: William Godbid, 1668).

the relationship between expression and chromaticism, word painting, and false relations. Far from being a matter that concerns only these two discrete elements (single semantic unit, single harmonic interaction), I argue that an investigation that avoids anachronism can only be conducted when taking into light the meeting, friction, and collision between textual and musical form.[2] Patricia Fumerton has recently noted the intricate interplay of attempting to match poetic stress and musical stress together as one that pulls on a variety of influences both contained on the musical page and beyond its bounds: '[Form] is a process; it is not an end. Putting ballad parts together created (and still creates today) new possibilities, orientations, and imaginations. Any piece that snaps satisfyingly into another piece (or not) triggers improvisational alterations and reconceptualizations to the players' guiding, imagined whole. Assembling ballad parts, like playing with Lego blocks, is full of satisfaction, frustration, and surprises.'[3] False relations are one of Fumerton's Lego blocks, one of many constituent elements that can be combined to signal the phrasings of the English Renaissance. In this chapter, through the lens of Tomkins's 'O Sing unto the Lord', we will see that false relations were frequently adopted to aid comprehension of the texts that they set, by playing with the interplay between literary and musical form. Such an assertion, much like the claims regarding sweetness and falseness explored above, is not unexpected and certainly not radical. However, the obviousness of these connections and associations still needs unpacking and elucidating; without clarifying the connection that we—inheritors of the English choral system and in an age where its sixteenth-century tropes and operations still make sense and are reasonably accessible—perceive as obvious, we risk losing the opportunities to cement these relationships for future generations, for whom they will not necessarily be inevitable. Writing of the rather different but comparable repertory of homophonic secular partsong, Megan Long notes that 'schematic text-setting establishes a robust metrical skeleton upon which composers could hang all kinds of rhetorical, formal, harmonic, and tonal materials.'[4] As we shall see throughout our case

---

[2] For more on the new formalism and connection to song, see Katherine M. Larson, *The Matter of Song in Early Modern England* (Oxford: Oxford University Press, 2019), 42–63. For a more general exploration of form in early modern England, see Ben Barton and Elizabeth Scott-Baumann (eds.), *The Work of Form: Poetics and Materiality in Early Modern Culture* (Oxford: Oxford University Press, 2014).

[3] Patricia Fumerton, *The Broadside Ballad in Early Modern England: Moving Media, Tactical Publics* (Philadelphia: University of Pennsylvania, 2020), 13.

[4] Megan Kaes Long, *Hearing Homophony: Tonal Expectation at the Turn of the Seventeenth Century* (Oxford: Oxford University Press, 2020), 83.

study, Tomkins's setting of 'O Sing unto the Lord', such an approach rewards us with unexpected insight into the intricate symbiosis between textualities and musical literacy in the English Renaissance, precisely by how it aids the phenomenon Long describes.

'O Sing unto the Lord' was, of course, far older than its publication date (see Appendix I).[5] Worcester Cathedral (where Tomkins had been organist since 1596) was likely the original place of composition and the intended choir, rather than 'the Chapel-Royal of King Charles the First'; the claim to the contrary appears to be a symptom of Restoration zeal on the part of Nathaniel Tomkins and/or his publisher, William Godbid. 'O Sing' had been in existence since at least 1617, when it appears in the orphan partbook now known as the Southwell Tenor Book and held in the Bodleian Library in Oxford.[6] The partbook's preface is meticulous in documenting its origins and purpose:

> Be it remembered that these eight anthem books with an organ book unto them belonging, having pricked into them threescore and eight [sic] anthems, were bestowed on the quire of the Collegiate Church of Southwell of the bountiful and friendly gift of Mr Jarvas Jones of Oxford one of the sons of Walter Jones sometimes Prebend Resident[r]y of the Prebend of Normanton within the said Church. Anno D[omi]ni 1617.[7]

Despite the explicitly stated date, John Morehen speculates that certain clues (such as the absence of any compositions by Orlando Gibbons) indicate that the partbook was planned rather earlier, possibly as early as 1612, the date of Tomkins's 'Know You Not', the second anthem in the partbook and composed for the funeral of Prince Henry.[8] 'O Sing unto the Lord' appears with a large number of compositions by Tomkins, including perhaps its closest stylistic cousin, 'Almighty God, the Fountain of All Wisdom', a setting of the fifth

---

[5] Thomas Tomkins, *Musica Deo Sacra: VI*, ed. and transcribed by Bernard Rose (London: Stainer and Bell for the British Academy, 1992).

[6] The Southwell Tenor Book, alias MS Tenbury 1382, fol. 65v–66. For more on the partbook see John Morehen, 'The Southwell Minster Tenor Part-book in the Library of St Michael's College, Tenbury (MS. 1382)', in *Music & Letters*, 50: 3 (1969), 352–364. Indeed, Morehen notes that the partbook may in fact have been intended for secular use and have been inspired by Tomkins's secular output; the book refers to each part with the mainly secular terms, *cantus, altus, tenor, bassus, quintus,* and *sextus*. See Morehen, 'The Southwell Minster Tenor Part-book', 363.

[7] Morehen, 'The Southwell Minster Tenor Part-book', 354.

[8] Ibid., 356.

collect after communion as listed in the 1559 *Book of Common Prayer*;[9] other composers who feature prominently in the partbook include William Byrd, Thomas Morley, John Bull, and Thomas Weelkes. Tomkins was acquainted with the majority of these men either through his association with Thomas Morley,[10] as Gentleman Extraordinary of the Chapel Royal (a position he held from around 1603), and as Gentleman Ordinary of the Chapel Royal under Gibbons (a position he held from 1621). Morehen concludes that it is likely he was closely connected to the compilation of the partbook, either in an advisory capacity, or as the mentor to the person who advised the contents, possibly John Fido whose works also feature in the partbook, and who served as assistant organist under Thomas Tomkins at Worcester Cathedral.[11] Tomkins had lived and worked across an enormously broad and eventful episode in England's musical history, from the height of Elizabeth's reign to the execution of Charles I and the interregnum, such that Anthony Boden has referred to him as 'the last Elizabethan'.[12] 'O Sing unto the Lord' arguably contains the traces of each layer of musical style, trend, and development; it reverberates the slow but steady rise of tonality.

Nowhere is this truer than in his intricate choreographing of the interplay between word and music. It is clear that words mattered especially to Tomkins. The lyrics are slightly altered from that of the Psalm to be found in the King James Version, and that of the *Book of Common Prayer*, which allows division of the motet into three discrete parts gathered around the reiteration of the verb 'Let', nominal 'him', and the almost-homophone shift from nominal to verbal 'song' and 'sing' where the original texts used 'King' and the connective 'and'.

Authorized King James Version (1611)

Praise ye the Lord. Sing unto the Lord a new song,
and his praise in the congregation of saints.
Let Israel rejoice in him that made him:
let the children of Zion be joyful in their King.[13]

---

[9] Oxford: Bodleian Library, the 'Southwell Tenor Book', MS Tenbury 1382, fol. 32–32v.
[10] See Dennis Collins, 'Thomas Tomkins' Canonic Additions to Thomas Morley's *A Plaine and Easie Introduction to Practicall Musicke*', in *Music & Letters*, 76: 3 (1995), 345–355.
[11] Morehen, 'The Southwell Minster Tenor Part-book', 358.
[12] Anthony Boden (ed.), *Thomas Tomkins: The Last Elizabethan* (London: Routledge, 2005).
[13] *The Authorized King James Bible* (Oxford: Oxford University Press, 1997; this ed. 2008), 722.

1662 Book of Common Prayer Version

O sing unto the Lord a new song:
let the congregation of saints praise him.
Let Israel rejoice in him that made him:
and let the children of Sion be joyful in their King.[14]

Tomkins's Version (1617)

O Sing unto the Lord a new Song
Let the congregation of saints sing praise unto him.
Let Israel rejoice in him that made him:
Let the children of Sion for ever sing:
Alleluia.

This may appear a pedantic quibble to modern eyes and ears, but for an audience, performer, or congregation of the early seventeenth century, raised in the Protestant tradition of the Word, it would have been a marked alteration. Each minute variation would have snagged the ears and subtly shifted the apprehension of the text's meaning, just as surely as the substitution of 'Ghost' and 'Spirit' registers in the ears of churchgoers in the twenty-first century. Tomkins's structure is largely polyphonic, built around the repetition and inversion of discrete phrases formed around each text segment. Imitative duos and trios overlap, constantly shifting imitative allegiance, creating a densely woven texture not often found in music of the early seventeenth century;[15] indeed, this style breaks only for one homophonic passage at 'let the congregation of saints' (bars 21–27). Nevertheless, 'O Sing unto the Lord' is evidently heavily influenced by Tomkins's earlier madrigal compositions and his experiments with the madrigal style. The reiterations of 'let' and 'him' serve as way-markers, signifying to listener and performer the beginning and end of phrases; likewise, the shift from 'song' to 'sing' delineates the edges of the textual concept (we are invited to join the song, and the singing becomes continuous and eternal, 'for ever', illustrating the skilful and seamless interweaving of phrase to phrase. The motive of the rising fourth (e.g., in the opening phrase 'O sing' in all parts, the Medius 'rejoice' at bar 43) unifies

---

[14] *The Book of Common Prayer: The Texts of 1549, 1559 and 1662*, ed. Brian Cumming (Oxford: Oxford University Press, 2013), 610–611.

[15] Dennis Collins observes that, despite the fact that Tomkins rarely used canonic imitation in either his vocal or his keyboard works, his strict imitative technique was masterful, as demonstrated by his canonic addition to the *Introduction*. See Collins, 'Thomas Tomkins' Canonic Additions', 345.

the harmonic texture throughout, despite the flirtatious pastiche of melodic, horizontal compositional techniques to be found in the interlocking lines of the first, third, fourth, and fifth textual segments.

What, then, can Tomkins's setting of Psalm 149 tell us about false relations in the English Renaissance? There are some (non-simultaneous) false relations in the body of the anthem, for example between the Medius parts and Decani Contratenor at bars 17–19 announcing 'a new song', again at bars 30–31 and finally between Medius Decani and Medius Cantoris at bar 32, both illustrating the words 'sing *praise* unto him' (my italics). However, the real fireworks occur during the 'Alleluia' section (see Appendix I). In following this technique, Tomkins is adhering to a conventional stylistic approach that permitted false relations and exuberant counterpoint in 'Amen', 'world without end, amen', and/or 'alleluia' sections. The music of the English Renaissance is riddled with settings of these lyrics that threaten to empty them of their semantic import, transforming them into nonsense syllables like the madrigalian 'fa la'. The 'fa la' refrain had a formal role, signifying the boundary between verse and refrain but at the same time allowing 'flashier counterpoint'.[16] The 'alleluia'/'amen' refrain functions in a similar manner, but with a crucial difference: its formal role is one of gathering together, rather than marking a boundary. Typically placed at the end of a piece or section, the 'alleluia'/'amen' signifies a conclusion, but in a manner that emphasizes the hand of the composer/performers in shaping the form of the piece and bringing it to that carefully crafted conclusion. Lacing these passages with false relations emphasizes the skill and order it takes to perform the music. Masquerading as 'near-misses', they are fleeting, insouciant reminders of the potential for chaos that lurks beneath the surface of the music. This dynamic can be found at play in, for example, Gibbons's 'O Clap Your Hands' (likely composed for his admission as Doctor of Music at Oxford in 1622), 'Lord for thy Tender Mercy's Sake' (before 1580) variously attributed to John Hilton and Richard Farrant, and Thomas Weelkes's 'Alleluia I Heard a Voice' (before 1613). However, if simply for the sheer volume of false relations used, Tomkins's is arguably one of the most ebullient examples and an excellent case study for the phenomenon in general. The rising fourth motive returns in the exchanges between Medius and Contratenor parts, impelling the dissonance with its insistence on the tritone interval. The result is a dizzying

---

[16] Megan Kaes Long, *Hearing Homophony: Tonal Expectation at the Turn of the Seventeenth Century* (Oxford: Oxford University Press, 2020), 144.

and sophisticated cascade of false relations. In one sense they illustrate 'the children of Sion for ever sing[ing]' with the torrent of overlapping 'alleluias', a classic example of word painting albeit one that insouciantly pulls against the advice of Thomas Morley that 'for as it will be thought a great absurditie to talke of heaven and point downward to the earth: do it will be counted a great incongruitie if a musician upon the words hee ascended into heaven shoulde cause his musicke to descende'.[17] In another sense, they allow us a rather different insight into early seventeenth-century attitudes towards setting text to music. Erasmus' infamous statement on the state of the English choral scene in 1515 is well known, but worth reproducing:

> Those who are more doltish than really learned in music are not content on feast days unless they use a certain distorted kind of music called *Fauburdum* [sic]. This neither gives forth the pre-existing melody nor observes the harmonies of the art. In addition, when temperate music is used in church in this way, so that the meaning of the words may come more easily to the listener, it also seems a fine thing to some if one or other part, intermingled with the rest, produces a tremendous tonal clamour, so that not a single word is understood. Thus the whims of the foolish are indulged and their baser appetites are satisfied.[18]

Narratives surrounding the English Reformation have typically focused on the idea that its trajectory by and large was built around the idea of rendering text legible, both in music and in liturgy more generally, such that every single word is understood.[19] 'O Sing unto the Lord' suggests something subtly different. If we take Nathaniel Tomkins and William Godbid's claims that the anthems of *Musica Deo Sacra* were composed for Charles I's Chapel Royal at face value, this is unsurprising; Charles I greatly favoured the more elaborate devotional approaches associated with Catholicism, a factor that

---

[17] Thomas Morley, *A Plaine and Easie Introduction to Practicall Musicke* (London: Peter Short, 1597), 178.

[18] Desiderius Erasmus, *Opera Omnia*, ed. J. Clericus (Leiden, 1703–1706), Vol. VI, 731C–732C. Quoted in Clement A. Miller, 'Erasmus on Music', in *The Musical Quarterly*, 52: 3 (1966), 338–339; see also Kerry McCarthy, *Tallis*, 6; and Rob Wegman, *The Crisis of Music in Early Modern Europe, 1470–1530* (London: Routledge, 2005), 164.

[19] Daniel Swift, *Shakespeare's Common Prayers: The Book of Common Prayer and the Elizabethan Age* (Oxford: Oxford University Press, 2012). For more on this approach, see Peter Stallybrass and Roger Chartier, 'Hamlet's Tables and the Technologies of Writing in Renaissance England', in *Shakespeare Quarterly*, 55: 4 (2004); and Patrick Collinson, *The Birthpangs of Protestant England: Religious and Cultural Change in the Sixteenth and Seventeenth Centuries* (Basingstoke: Macmillan, 1988).

ultimately led to the Civil War and his deposition and execution. However, the more feasibly Jacobean date of composition for 'O Sing unto the Lord' offers a more radical possibility. Listening to its alleluia section, our ears are not drawn to each and every of the reiteration of the word, but rather given the impression of a choppy melismatic sea of each delineated phoneme of its anatomy. 'Al-le-lu-i-a' dissolves, before our very ears, into nonsense syllables that showcase the delights and dangers of an older style of composition: it subverts the concept of lyric and words set to music, pulling their comprehensibility to their very limits, threatening to empty them of meaning and yet never quite expunging their semantic import. Tomkins's anthem culminates in a turbulent overwhelming slab of sound that parodies and emphasizes the semantic perils of polyphonic counterpoint and the hexachord system. 'O Sing unto the Lord' paints, rather than its words, its polyphonic imitation, with false relation.

Chromaticism is expressive. This is a platitude that, despite the ambiguity of the adjective 'expressive', seeps into twenty-first-century Western classical music curricula the world over.[20] It is one of the building blocks of how budding musicians are, today, taught about harmony, tonality, and the relationship between note and word.[21] The music of the English Renaissance offers many textbook examples useful in teaching this dictum, both in the vernacular and in Latin; 'such things', to be found in Thomas Mudd's pithy anthem, 'Let thy Merciful Ears'; 'miserere mei' in Byrd's 'Ave Verum Corpus', and 'desolatus est' in 'Civitas sancti tui'; 'corporis' in Tallis's 'O Nata Lux' and 'mercy' in 'Hear the Voice and Prayer'; Orlando Gibbons's '*sound* of the trumpets' in 'O Clap Your Hands Together'; constantly threatened in Weelkes's 'When David Heard' and William Mundy's 'O Lord the Maker of All Things' (within lines, but never quite simultaneous across parts). However, the ambiguous term 'expression' belies the far more complex relationship at play between textualities and musicalities, both in how we interpret the connection today in the twenty-first century, and in how the connection seems to have functioned in the sixteenth. By focussing in on false relations, one specific subcategory of chromaticism, the knottiness of this relationship becomes clear. The presence of chromaticism in sacred

---

[20] See, e.g., James Haar, 'False Relations and Chromaticism in Sixteenth-Century Music', in *Journal of the American Musicological Society*, 30: 3 (Autumn 1977), 391–418, at 404; Pierre Boulez, *Orientations* (London: Routledge, 1986), 254.

[21] The ambiguity of the term 'expression' appears to go hand in hand with the similarly ambiguous term 'clarity'. See Megan Kaes Long, *Hearing Homophony* (Oxford: Oxford University Press, 2020), 149.

music is largely at odds with the way some contemporary music theorists wrote about it, with writers such as Charles Butler condemning the 'effeminate' effect of accidentals, and William Prynne even describing 'Chromaticall harmonies' as 'whorish musicke crowned with flowers', as we saw above in Chapter 2: there is a gaping chasm between its usage in theory and in practice.[22] Moreover, chromaticism that appeared in one place in a piece of music as a means of enhancing textual expression can elsewhere serve simply as an enticing texture 'under the surface of the contrapuntal fabric',[23] as James Haar long since observed with regards to our humble false relation:

> This is a point that seems generally true of sixteenth-century composers: a turn of melody or harmony that could effectively underscore the meaning of a word of phrase could elsewhere be used for purely musical reasons. Music as the servant of the text, in other words, had its days off. Composers did not thus always use chromaticism for expressive purposes.[24]

Its expressive role was not simply a matter of capturing the gradient sweep of a rolling hill, the pain of heartbreak, or the pastoral frolic of shepherds and nymphs of Diana. Chromaticisms like false relations reacted with an entire other spectrum of textuality, also borne of the Reformation: the refrain, a kind of literacy more associated with secular song cultures, both contemporary and of the fifteenth and earlier sixteenth century.[25] Rhetorical figures like *hendiadys* (the substitution of a conjunction for a subordination, such as 'two for one'), *epizeuxis* (the repetition of word or phrase in quick succession), *antanaclasis* (the repetition of two homophonic words that sound the same but are different in meaning), *anaphora* (the repetition of words at the beginning of successive clauses), *epistrophe* (the repetition of words at the end of successive clauses), and *chiasmus* (the repetition of a phrase, grammatical elements or concepts in reversed order) were appropriated by William Tyndale and his successors in their efforts to forge a vernacular English devotional idiom as they translated the Bible from Latin to English.

---

[22] Charles Butler, *Principles of Musik, in singing and setting with the two-fold use thereof, ecclesiasticall and civil* (London: John Haviland, 1636), 96; William Prynne, *Histrio-Matrix* (London: Edward Allde and William Jones, 1633), 275; see also Larson, *Matter of Song*, 47. It should be noted that given that both of these texts appeared after the ascension of Archbishop William Laud to the see of Canterbury, it is likely that these descriptions in part have religio-political motivations.
[23] Haar, 'False Relations and Chromaticism', 415.
[24] Ibid, 404–405.
[25] Florence Hazrat, 'Fashioning Faith to Forms (Im)mutable: The Rondeau and Trust in the Poetry of Sir Thomas Wyatt', in *Shakespeare Quarterly*, 47: 2 (2018), 222–242.

Amongst these tropes, the refrain ruled supreme. We will have noticed, already, that Tomkins's slight textual adaptation of Psalm 149 allows a neat combination of *anaphora* and *epistrophe* that would have greatly appealed to listeners trained in this way of remembering, listening, thinking, and knowing. Tomkins's appeal to this mode of listening follows through into his tumbling cascade of jubilantly scrunchy alleluias, reiterated over and over and punctuated in almost every instance with a false relation. It is vital that we do not fall into the trap of unquestioningly accepting the rhetoric of the Reformists and the idea that clean, clear musical idioms such as homophony and the madrigal always make words more comprehensible.[26] These were not the only tactics available. Melisma is expressive and can often enhance meaning. A word peeping out from a dense texture of sound and interweaving voices, punctuated with false relations, can be just as semantically powerful as a clear-cut, sentence-length phrase with frequent cadences. In the next section of this chapter, we will briefly diverge from the false relation to the broader connection between musical and textual literacy during the English Renaissance, through the lens of the refrain.

Repeat Repeat

The boom in literacy as a result of the twin influences of the printing press and the reformation has been well established.[27] As we shall see in the next section of this chapter, these developments can offer us vital insight into the use of false relations in the English Renaissance, by virtue of the places that they appear in a text-setting. Brian Cummings has observed that the Reformation 'embodied a massive burgeoning of writing in general. Early modern religion is a religion of books: pre-eminently the Bible, but also a plethora of other books, devotional, doctrinal, controversial. Not only the spread of

---

[26] Indeed, such rhetoric is likely a part of the intricate operation of cultivated amnesia that drove so much of the Reformation in England. See Alexandra Walsham, Bronwyn Wallace, Ceri Law, and Brian Cummings (eds.), *Memory and the English Reformation* (Cambridge: Cambridge University Press, 2020).

[27] For more extended explorations of this, see, e.g., Brian Cummings, *The Literary Culture of the Reformation: Grammar and Grace* (Oxford: Oxford University Press, 2002); Alec Ryrie, *Being Protestant in Reformation Britain* (Oxford: Oxford University Press, 2013), 259–297; Kevin Sharpe, *Reading Revolutions: The Politics of Early Modern Reading* (New Haven, CT: Yale University Press, 2000); Ellen Spolsky, 'Literacy after Iconoclasm in the English Reformation', in *Journal of Medieval and Early Modern Studies*, 39: 2 (2009), 305–330; and Patrick Collinson, *The Birthpangs of Protestant England* (Oxford: Oxford University Press, 1972).

Protestantism, but its identity, is constituted by the exigencies of textual revolution.'[28] Within Protestant culture, certain relatively cheap and widely available books reigned supreme: the *Book of Common Prayer* (1549) and *The Whole Booke of Psalmes collected into English meeter* (1562).[29] One hundred and forty-three editions of the *Whole Booke of Psalmes* survive from the reign of Elizabeth;[30] it is beaten to the most-published spot only by the *Book of Common Prayer*, which reached around 525 editions in English alone by 1729.[31] By the end of the sixteenth century and due to a flooded market that testifies to its popularity, the *Book of Common Prayer* cost 10d—less than a pound of sugar and just more than a chicken.[32] These two books crucially permitted congregations to follow along with the liturgy, allowing them to piece together the words spoken with the visual marks inked on the page and inviting them, slowly but surely, into a new idiom of literacy. Writing about the evolution of the English ballett form, Lionel Pike has argued that the key inheritance from this tradition was the notion of the 'tune' established by the *Whole Booke of Psalmes* and the idea of the psalm tune:

> There were those—Byrd and Orlando Gibbons being the most notable—who preferred the older secular native English style, that of the consort song. In this type of composition the feeling of the text tended to be expressed in an overall way, while the classic Italian madrigal illustrated each element of the text individually, as it occurred. Thus the English secular style transferred more easily to instrumental performance, and had a

---

[28] Cummings, *Grammar and Grace*, 6.
[29] For more on the *Whole Book of Psalmes*, see Beth Quitslund and Nicholas Temperley, *The Whole Book of Psalms, Collected into English Metre by Thomas Sternhold, John Hopkins, and Others: A Critical Edition of the Texts and Tunes* (Tempe: Arizona Center for Medieval and Renaissance Studies, 2018); Katherine Larson, *Matter of Song*, 48–63; Richard M. Waugaman, 'The Sternhold and Hopkins Whole Book of the Psalms Is a Major Source for the Works of Shakespeare', in *Notes & Queries*, 56: 4 (2009), 595–604; Nicholas Temperley, '"Al skillful praises sing": How Congregations Sang the Psalms in Early Modern England', in *Renaissance Studies*, 29: 4 (2015), 531–553; Hannibal Hamlin, '"Very mete to be used of all sortes of people': The Remarkable Popularity of the 'Sternhold and Hopkins' Psalter', in *Yale University Library Gazette*, 75: 1&2 (2010), 37–51; Andrew Poxon, 'The Institutionalization of the Congregational Singing of Metrical Psalms in the Elizabethan Reformation', in *Studies in Church History*, 57 (2021), 120–141; Jonathan Willis, *Church Music and Protestantism in Post-Reformation England: Discourses, Sites and Identities* (Farnham: Ashgate, 2010), 121–128.
[30] Samantha Arten, 'The Origin of Fixed-Scale Solmization in the *Whole Booke of Psalmes*', in *Early Music*, 46: 1 (2018), 149–165, at 151.
[31] For a discussion of the life and development of some of the earlier editions, see Peter W. M. Blaney, *The Printing and the Printers of the Book of Common Prayer, 1549–1561* (Cambridge: Cambridge University Press, 2021).
[32] Daniel Swift, *Shakespeare's Common Prayers: The Book of Common Prayer and the Elizabethan Age* (Oxford: Oxford University Press, 2013), 30–31, at 31.

through-composed logic: Italian madrigals, being so closely tied to the text, were meaningless once that text was removed.

The consort song was more likely than the more 'literary' Italian madrigal to be contrapuntal and to pursue musical logic: but under the influence of the sturdy and attractive psalm-tune style of the protestant English church, there was a tendency in England towards the writing of one prominent part—a voice with the 'main tune'. This part at first had a character similar to that of the psalm tune. Thus Byrd's consort songs have a voice labelled 'the first singing part'—the part that must be sung even if all the others are performed instrumentally.

Such a concentration on a 'tune' is a factor leading away from the contrapuntal nature of much Renaissance music towards the idea of the 'tune with accompaniment' (or indeed, tune with basso continuo) of the baroque period. A fascinating feature of all music of the 'Golden Age of English Music' is the by-play that is traceable between the old native secular style and that of the Italian madrigal.[33]

However, it is clear that the gestural, performative aspect of both books was also immensely influential and deserves further, deeper exploration. Both establish a logic of call-and-response that was immensely influential to the musical culture of the English Renaissance. In turn, they infused into the rhythms of speech, phrase, and vernacular language in a manner that still leaves its traces today. Daniel Swift's analysis is particularly evocative and worth quoting in full:

> Its cadences echo through the popular devotions and supplementary prayers issued by the church; the prayer book's particular balance of exposition, confession, and petition came to structure a whole generation of devotion. [...] Each movement of the service builds upon the one previous. [...] The General Confession, which was added by Cranmer to the 1552 version, opens with two pairs of hendiadys, which is itself a figure of speech involving two elements. 'Almighty and most merciful', it begins, and 'erred and strayed from thy ways' with its internal rhyme, and from this doubling foundation builds to a simple simile: 'like lost sheep'. The passage is dense with allusion to Scripture. It is not quoting, yet it is meant to sound

---

[33] Lionel Pike, *Pills to Purge Melancholy: The Evolution of the English Ballett* (Farnham: Ashgate, 2004), 38.

like it might be, as the prayer book appropriates biblical commonplaces. 'Strayed from thy ways' recalls the biblical command to 'walk in the ways', a phrase scattered through the Bible, most frequently in the Psalms. It echoes through the prayer book, from the opening of Morning Prayer—'we might walk in thy laws'—to surface again in both the Communion rite and the Catechism at confirmation. The trail of echoes continues. [. . .] *For each new image, an older pattern; in every phrase, an allusion. The echoes build into a structure of recollection, where words and images gain rhetorical force through repetition.* All is familiar, for all is familial, and the relation between the prayer book and Bible is genetic, an issue of genealogy. These are not simple quotations. The General Confession is neither new nor old. *It is instead a tight palimpsest of phrases, remembered and reworked.* (my italics)[34]

This is the textual culture within which the false relation rose to prominence. As I stated above in the Introduction, the false relation appeared first in sacred repertoire. Its original context continued to flavour subsequent manifestations, be they within the context of devotion or straightforward recreation (although it should be observed, as demonstrated by Swift's exploration of the *Book of Common Prayer* and many other studies into early English Protestant culture, that devotion and recreation were by no means strictly divisible).[35] The *Book of Common Prayer* establishes a pattern of liturgy that requires the involvement of the worshipper, thus, as Swift notes, diffusing its single authority and laying the groundwork for its extension

---

[34] Daniel Swift, *Shakespeare's Common Prayers*, 31–38. See also Brian Cummings's comments on grammar and its importance to the textual cultures of the reformation: 'Grammar creates a less easily detectable undertow of meaning. If the first aim of this book is to provide a new visibility to the complex cultural processes of writing, the second is to illumine this neglected hinterland of grammar. The inclinations and deviations by which a sentence moves, the countervailing pressures of qualification of concession, the attenuating processes of conjunction or amplification, the rise towards peroration, the threat of sudden cadence, or a quizzical final resistance in defiantly dubious question, each denotes a different significance in the vexed economy of religious writing. Such processes can be as unknown and as baffling to their makers as to their readers. Grammar has the duplicity, and sometimes the advantage, of keeping some of its best secrets to itself. Not by the perilous byways of syntax only: the inflections of single verbs can, and should, give pause for thought.' Cummings, *Grammar and Grace*, 11.

[35] There is plentiful evidence of this phenomenon, and many studies into the textual, material, and visual remnants of this culture. A huge number of manuals of evangelical household management appeared during this period, from *A Glasse for Householders* (1542), *A Godly form of Householde Government* (which ran into nine editions between 1598 and 1624), and *Of Domesticall Duties* (which ran into three editions between 1622 and 1634). For two recent examples of studies into this phenomenon, see Tara Hamling and Catherine Richardson, *A Day at Home in Early Modern England* (London: Paul Mellon Centre for Studies in British Art, 2017); Alec Ryrie, *Being Protestant in Reformation Britain* (Oxford: Oxford University Press, 2013), especially 363–405.

beyond the physical bounds of the Church and into the home. It is a mode of rhetorical engagement that ensures that 'readers are not locked inside that which they read. Rather, they are freed by it, endowed with a vocabulary and a set of meanings, each twisted to a new purpose.'[36]

In such a context, the positioning of the false relations within Tomkins's 'O Sing unto the Lord' makes sense and allows us to approach the question of music, expressivity, and textual literacy in a new way. False relations shade out, variegate, and add complexity to the call-and-response structures of textuality borne out of the early Church of England liturgy, embellishing the rhetorical force gained through repetition, enhancing the presence of the older pattern and allusion within each new iteration of a refrain. Exploring the poetry of Thomas Wyatt, Florence Hazrat writes about 'the social eloquence of form in early modern poetry which particularly realises itself in the permutations of the refrain: Its circular, identical lines enable a certain way of thinking and knowing. The device assumes epistemological agency, affording the reader and poet the possibility of perceiving and understanding the world through form.'[37] Some of Wyatt's poetry admittedly predates the Reformation and the rise of the rhetoric of repetition, but Hazrat's point is nevertheless of use to the present investigation. The repeated inflections of Tomkins's alleluias with false relations does, indeed, invite performer and listener to perceive and understand through form: that of the hexachord, that of the act of devotion, and that of the word itself. David Collins has observed that the presence of the dissonant major second, the hallmark of the false relation, within works such as 'O Sing', is testament to Tomkins's great compositional skill and mastery of the strict imitative canon technique, another mode constructed around the repetition of form.[38] I briefly observed above that whilst Tomkins's enthusiasm for densely applied false relations is idiomatic (with the exception perhaps of his close contemporary Thomas Weelkes), his placement is certainly typical of the style of the English Renaissance. Farrant, for example, inflects his phrasal repetitions in 'Hide Not Thou Thy Face' (before 1580) with a non-simultaneous false relation between contratenor and tenor, delineating the phrasing with two separate sonic textures; Gibbons and Tallis use the same device to indicate a gathering together, a movement towards a new passage and an impending cadence,

---

[36] Swift, *Shakespeare's Common Prayers*, 40.
[37] Florence Hazrat, 'Fashioning Faith to Forms (Im)mutable: The Rondeau and Trust in the Poetry of Sir Thomas Wyatt', in *The Cambridge Quarterly*, 47: 3 (2018), 223.
[38] Collins, 'Thomas Tomkins' Canonic Additions', 352–354.

in 'O Clap Your Hands Together' (1622) and 'Hear the Voice and Prayer' (before 1551) and the substantial votive antiphon 'Ave rosa sine spinis' (before 1541), respectively. This usage is another manifestation of the rhetorical trope of *varietas* that we explored above: the pleasingly balanced variation that aided the beautiful *ductus* of eye (or ear) through a thing (a passage of music, piece of biblical text, a liturgical moment, a picture). Crucially, this is different from what Carl Dahlhaus has described as the shift from the paratactic phrase structure (whereby a phrase merely succeeds another) to the hypotactic (a phrase that is the consequence of the preceding one).[39] Rather, in each instance, the performer and listener are encouraged to experiment with and reflect upon potential meanings that can apply to each and every iteration, an active agent in the semantic product of the music as a whole, rather than a passive receiver.

The distinction between composition and performance and the concept of authorship were infamously blurred in the English Renaissance, as we have already explored above.[40] The enigma of the false relation is in no small part due to the way it plays into this musical culture, with the way it destabilizes the binary that has become a crucial tool in the way we conduct music analysis today. Throughout this most brief explanations of a single piece of music, we can begin to see that the textual function of false relations is far more subtle than previous interpretations would have us believe. When thinking about the phrases and places where false relations appear in works such as Tomkins's 'O Sing', it is clear that they indulge precisely in the requirement for involvement on the part of the performer and listener, a collaborative making of a given piece of music. In this way they are traces of the textual cultures of literacy cultivated by early Church of England Protestantism by documents such as the *Book of Common Prayer* and the *Whole Booke of Psalmes*. Their role, from the outset, was not of expression but rather of comprehension: they were aids to exegesis and the language of scripture.

The didactic purpose of both the *Book of Common Prayer* and the *Whole Booke of Psalmes* has been well established. Samantha Arten has convincingly demonstrated that fixed-scale solmization began not with William Bathe's *A Briefe Introduction to the Skill of Song* (c. 1597) and Thomas

---

[39] Carl Dahlhaus, *Studies on the Origin of Harmonic Tonality*, transl. Robert O. Gjerdingen (Princeton, NJ: Princeton University Press, 1990), 297–310.

[40] Kirsten Gibson, 'Author, Musician, Composer: Creator? Figuring Musical Creativity in Print at the Turn of the Seventeenth Century', in Rebecca Herissone and Alan Howard (eds.), *Concepts of Creativity in Seventeenth-century England* (Woodbridge: Boydell & Brewer, 2013).

Morley's *A Plaine and Easie Introduction to Practicall Musicke* (1597), as previously thought, but rather with the *Whole Booke of Psalmes* compiled by Thomas Sternhold and John Hopkins almost four decades earlier. The preface ('A shorte Introduction into the Science of Musicke') explains the purpose and working of the solmization syllables,

> for that the rude & ignorant in Song, may with more delight desire, and good wyl: be moved and drawen to the godly exercise of singing of Psalmes, as well in common place of prayer, where altogether one voice render thankes & prayses to God, as privately by themselves, or at home in their houses: I have set here in the beginning of this boke of psalms, an easie and moste playne way and rule, of the order of the Notes and Kayes of singing, which commonly is called the scale of Musicke, or the *Gamma ut*. Wherby & that also without ayde or helpe of any other teacher, attayne to a sufficient, knowledg, to singe any Psalme contained in thys Booke, or any suche other playne and easy Songes as these are.[41]

It does so both visually (see Fig. 3.1) and textually; surviving evidence of manuscript intervention into the *Whole Booke of Psalmes* suggests that the visual elements were particularly important to their initial readers (as evidenced in Fig. 3.2 and 3.2).[42] Later the technical wording was streamlined from a multi-page solmization preface into a 'To The Reader' preface. A representative example can be found in the 1569 imprint:

> TO THE READER
> Thou shalt understand (gentle Reader) that I have (for the helpe of those that are desirous to learne to sing) caused a new Print of Note to be made with letters to be joined to every Note: whereby thou mayst know how to call every Note by his right name, so that with a very little diligence (as thou art taught in the Introduction Printed heretofore in the Psalmes) thou mayst the more easily by the vieweing of these letters, come to the knowledge of perfect Solfyng: whereby thou mayst sing the Psalmes the more easier. The letters be these. U for Ut, R for Re, M for My, F for Fa, S. for Sol,

---

[41] Thomas Sternhold and John Hopkins, *The Whole Booke of Psalmes collected into Englysh metre* (London: John Day, dwelling over Aldersgate, 1562).

[42] For more discussion of this manuscript version, see Samantha Arten, 'The Whole Booke of Psalmes, Protestant Ideology, and Musical Literacy in Elizabethan England' (unpublished PhD diss., Duke University, 2018), 174.

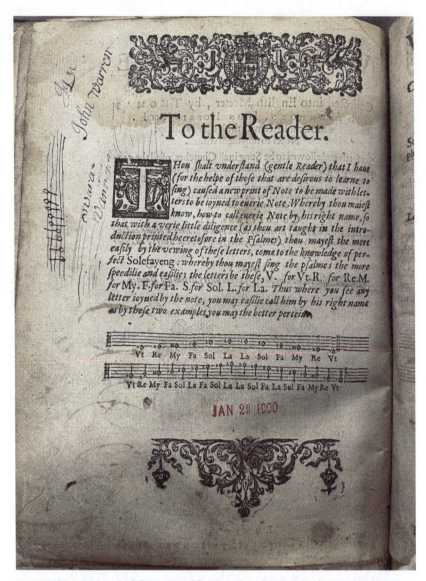

Fig. 3.1 'To the Reader' diagram of fixed-scale solmization, from Thomas Sternhold and John Hopkins, *The Whole Booke of Psalmes collected into English Meeter* (London: Company of Stationers, 1626). Cambridge, Cambridge University Library. Catalogue No. Syn.5.57.3. Photograph author's own.

Fig. 3.2 Manuscript addition of the fixed-scale solmization table in Thomas Sternhold and John Hopkins, *The Whole Booke of Psalmes collected into English Meeter* (London: John Day for Richard Day, 1591). London, British Library. Catalogue No. 3435.bb.29. Photograph author's own.

L. for La. Thus where you see any letter joined by the note. You may easily call him by his right name, as by these two examples you may the better perceive. Thus committing thee unto him that liveth for ever, who graunt that we may sing with our hartes and minds unto the glory of hys holy name. Amen.[43]

Sternhold and Hopkins make no mention of mutation or of hexachords; there is no need because, as Arten observes, 'every pitch is reliably given the same syllable, regardless of the final or the direction of motion': in other words, an absolute pitch.[44] This move appears to have been due to the desire to increase musical literacy such that its readership would be able to use the psalms 'privately for their solace & comfort' to 'with one voyce render thankes & prayses to God'. The *Whole Booke of Psalmes* is focused on monophonic unison singing, and so there are no false relations. Indeed, Arten notes that there are very few accidentals, and that there is little indication in the preface of what to do with them and how to solmize them, as she observes 'B-flats found in no-flat key signatures are all solmized as *fa* (obeying the rule of "Una nota supra la /Semper est canendum fa" or "A single note above la / Should always be sung as fa)", as is the psalter's single E-flat found in Psalm 130 (its identity as E-flat is due entirely to its syllable assignment, as the E has no accidental). No other accidentals appear in the solmization psalters.'[45] However, the *Whole Booke of Psalmes* does touch upon the question of solmization signatures and b-*mi* and b-*fa*:

> Here note that when *b, fa,* ♯, *mi,* is formed and signed in this maner, with this letter *b*, whiche is called *b*, flat, it must be expressed with this voice or note, *fa*, but if it be formed and signed with this forme ♯, whiche is called *b*, sharpe: or if it haue no signe at all, then must ye expres it in singing with thys voyce or Note. *mi.*[46]

The possibility of false relation is therefore established for the readership of the *Whole Booke of Psalmes*; a reader who had a particular collection of sonic, mathematical, and proportional proclivities could infer the rules that

---

[43] Sternhold and Hopkins, *The Whole Booke of Psalmes collected into Englysh metre*. See also Arten, 'Fixed Scale Solmization'.
[44] Arten, 'Fixed Scale Solmization', 153. Arten notes that this is entirely consistent across all editions of the *Whole Booke of Psalmes*, with the single exception of a setting of the Lord's Prayer.
[45] Ibid., 164–65, n. 12.
[46] Sternhold and Hopkins, *Whole Booke of Psalmes*, unpaginated.

permitted them with the information the book provides. The presence of this information indicates the vital importance of musical literacy for common people in Protestant ideology and, crucially, the idea of the accidental as a tool of explication.[47]

A Point

Reframing analysis of false relations and their textualities as a matter of *form*, rather than expression, offers some exciting possibilities. If false relations aid comprehension of a text (be it in Latin or in the vernacular), they are arguably structural in a sense that is concealed by their invisible, un-notated, inferable nature. Margaret Bent has argued that the analogy is in fact the most useful for understanding how false relations functioned within their original musical culture, and why and how their ambiguity came about and was tolerated:

> Notated 'accidentals' might be compared to written punctuation, equally variable over the centuries in amount and purpose. Just as a verbal sentence may be generously or sparsely punctuated, so may music. A literate reader who knows the language and the conventions can nearly always get the intended sense of under-punctuated written words, and communicate that sense by speech inflections. But there may be cases where punctuation fails to resolve an ambiguity; written sentences can change their meaning radically when given different spoken emphasis and inflection.[48]

Bent's interpretation, unsurprisingly given the above observations regarding chromaticism, focuses on punctuation as a means of expression; an accidental is an ordering element, assisting the general clarity of musical expression by emphasizing the basic structural principles and syntax of that particular system of musical language: in other words, its grammar. However, this approach sits uneasily with the textual culture of the English Renaissance. Recent research on voice and its vital role in the development of literacy during the sixteenth and seventeenth centuries has demonstrated that our understanding of reading has been heavily inflected by the

---

[47] Arten, 'Fixed Scale Solmization', 159.
[48] Margaret Bent, *Counterpoint, Composition and Musica Ficta* (London: Routledge, 2002), 5.

misleading way we associate reading with *silence*. Scholars such as Jennifer Richards, John Gallagher, and Richard Wistreich have all argued for the reintegration of voice into our understanding of early modern literacies, observing crucially that reading was by and large conducted *aloud*.[49] In the mesh of such logic, Richards observes that

> Punctuation—or pointing—was usually rhetorical, and not grammatical: the comma, the colon and the full stop, signal pauses of different lengths [... they are] potential cues for performance.[50]

In other words, the operation was precisely the inverse of that suggested by Bent. In Richards's model, punctuation does not dictate the ordering system, resolving ambiguity and predictable to all who are initiate in that mode of literacy: punctuation is the gateway towards the ambiguity that fuels the rhetorical art of *pronuntiatio* (delivery), performance, and its radical variety of potential inflections and emphases. The difference between these two interpretations is largely due to the different disciplinary angles from which Bent and Richards are writing (musicology and literary history with a background in rhetoric, respectively). However, they also differ in the way they interpret the matter of *text* (musical or verbal). Text entered Middle English from the Latin *textus*, *texere* (tissue, literary style, web, to weave) via the Old French *texte*.[51] Strictly speaking, therefore, the text is the construction or weaving together of semantic units—words, musical notes, punctuation, accidentals—as well as the tissue they ultimately become. Bent's interpretation of the musical text is just of the finished product, the notes on the page. Richards's, on the other hand, examines the process of *texere*, the texture of

---

[49] Jennifer Richards, *Voices and Books in the English Renaissance* (Oxford: Oxford University Press, 2019); Jennifer Richards, 'The Voice of Anne Askew', in *Journal of the Northern Renaissance*, Issue 9 (Autumn 2017), Special Issue: Early Modern Voices; Jennifer Richards and Richard Wistreich, 'The Anatomy of the Renaissance Voice', in Anne Whitehead, Angela Woods, Sarah Atkinson, Jane Macnaughton, and Jennifer Richards (eds.), *The Edinburgh Companion to the Critical Medical Humanities* (Edinburgh: Edinburgh University Press, 2016); Jennifer Richards and Richard Wistreich (eds.) *Voices and Books*, Special Issue of *Huntington Library Quarterly*, 81: 2 (2019); John Gallagher, *Learning Languages in Early Modern England* (Oxford: Oxford University Press, 2019). Gallagher calls for us to recognize 'language-learning not as a silent, scholarly activity, but as an endeavour that was oral, aural, and sociable: a kind of everyday work that made communication and conversation possible', 5–6. See also Laurie Maguire, *The Rhetoric of the Page* (Oxford: Oxford University Press, 2020).
[50] Richards, *Voices and Books*, 13.
[51] For more on this interpretation of text, see Hester Lees-Jeffries, 'A Subtle Point: Sleeves, Tents and "Ariachne's Broken Woof" (again)', in *Shakespeare Survey* (2009), 92–103; Susan Frye, *Pens and Needles: Women's Textualities in Early Modern England* (Philadelphia: University of Pennsylvania Press, 2013).

text and its textile, tactile semantic cousin: text as production, as construction, as fundamentally its performance or utterance. She describes books as 'choral' objects, created through use cumulatively and through collaboration, where voices join, respond, riposte, and complement each other.[52] The reader in this way can become the maker of the music, a 'choral' voice alongside the composers, scribes, and annotators. This subtle difference, although seemingly nearly imperceptible, greatly alters the way that literacy, and an individual's relationship to the text, functions. The latter approach acknowledges the dual identity of the text. Simultaneously, a text (musical or otherwise) is always the durable, printed or inscribed material, and the ephemeral concoction produced by the body of the performer(s).

What, then, of false relations and their punctuating capacity? 'Punctuation' in the sense we now use it, as the graphic marks used to divide sentences to clarify meaning, did not enter vernacular English usage until 1593.[53] Prior to that date, the appropriate term was 'distinction' or 'pointing'. The cognates of 'pointing' have variously continued or fallen out of use but are worth observing: to fill the lines of bricks or masonry with mortar, which the *Oxford English Dictionary* lists as in use from around 1375 and explicitly used from 1425; to mark out or clarify a piece of music, as in psalms (this sense used from around 1604). Another term sometimes used was to 'prick', as in 'pricksong'; again, this was used with similar connotations in musical and verbal notation.[54] Musical performance was thus key to the way that understanding of punctuation as a reading practice developed across the English Renaissance. In 1569, John Hart published his evocatively named *Orthographie conteyning the due order and reason, howe to write or paint thimage of mannes voice, most like to the life or nature*.[55] Amongst his many

---

[52] Richards, 'Voice of Anne Askew', 10. See also Gallagher's emphasis on linguistic competence as a social phenomenon; Gallagher, *Learning Languages*, 6. Another approach towards this chorality of texts can be found in, e.g., Katherine Acheson (ed.), *Early Modern English Marginalia* (London: Routledge, 2019).

[53] Neil Rhodes, 'Punctuation as Rhetorical Notation? From Colon to Semicolon', in *Huntington Library Quarterly* (Special Issue: Voicing Text 1500–1700), ed. Jennifer Richards and Richard Wistreich, 82: 1 (Spring 2019), 87–109, at 87. See John Eliot, *Ortho-epia Gallica* (London: 1593), sig. A4r.

[54] Rhodes, 'Punctuation', 89.

[55] John Hart, *An Orthographie conteyning the due order and reason, howe to write or paint thimage of mannes voice, most like to the life or nature* (London: Henry Denham for William Seres, dwelling at the west ende of Paules, at the signe of the Hedge-hogge, 1569). By the second decade of the seventeenth century things were radically different; see Jos Prat, *The Order of Orthographie: or, Sixty six rules shortly directing to the true writing, speaking and pronouncing of the English tongue* (London: Augustine Matthews for William Lee, and are to be sold at his shop in Fleete street, at the signe of the Golden Buck, neare Seriants Inne, 1622). 'The third is marked thus (.) with one point, and sheweth a full and perfect stop or stay, as if the sentence were ended, and it is named a *Period*' (unpaginated).

instructions as to how to 'write or paint the image of mannes voice', one key subject is salient for our present investigation into false relations and textuality: the comma (or *incisum* in Latin) is 'in reading the shortest rest, neare the time of a Crachet in musicke'.[56] This musical analogy is not isolated to Hart's account of 'pointing' or 'distinction'; Richard Mulcaster, in his *First Part of the Elementarie* (1582), similarly uses musical language: 'distinction' assists with the 'right and tunable uttering of our words and sentences' and can 'help a childes voice [. . .] be made swete, tunable and cunning'.[57] This is a visual as well as an oral/aural cue: reading and writing are merely the first two parts of Mulcaster's curriculum, followed by 'drawing, singing and playing'.[58] Literacy, orality, and visuality are closely linked: Mulcaster advocates the need to 'frame the childes hand right, to form and joyn letters well' and to develop a child's drawing skills 'while the finger is te[n]der, & the writing yet in hand, that both the pen & pe[n]cill, both the rule & co[m]pas, maie go forward together'.[59] Hart's choice of visual terminology in his title, describing his topic as how to '*paint* the *image* of mannes voice' (my italics), likewise supports this reading. We will return to Mulcaster's sentiments below in Chapter 5, but for the present it is worth observing that both writers saw musical metaphors as an important and useful way to contextualize their account of the 'pointing' or 'distinction' system, and that developments in the tonal musical system we know today occurred alongside the evolution in understanding around punctuation. By the second decade of the seventeenth century, orthographical descriptions are far more recognizable. Jos Prat, in his *Order of Orthographie* (1622), anatomizes the full or end stop in the following manner: 'the third is marked thus (.) with one point, and sheweth a full and perfect stop or stay, as if the sentence were ended, and it is named a *Period*'.[60] At the time that Hart and Mulcaster were writing, however, an accepted language and graphic convention had yet to be obtained; their descriptions are testament to the struggle to establish these conventions.

---

[56] Hart, *Orthographie*, fol. 40r–v. Compare to William Scott's 1599 definition, also evidently performance-inspired, of the comma as a 'breathing place'. William Scott, *The Model of Poesy* (1599), ed. Gavin Alexander (Cambridge: Cambridge University Press, 2013).
[57] Richard Mulcaster, *The First Part of the Elementarie* (London: Thomas Vautrollier, 1582), 148 and 28.
[58] Ibid., 53.
[59] Ibid., 56 and 58.
[60] Prat, *The Order of Orthographie*.

There are no explicit contemporary references to false relations or accidentals as a means of punctuation or distinction, in the manner that Bent describes them. However, it is clear from a brief examination of their usage in text settings like 'O Sing unto the Lord' (and its close cousin, 'Almighty God, the Fountain') that it is an appropriate way to interpret the textuality of false relations, and their rhetorical purpose within a texted piece of music. Notated accidentals should not be compared to written punctuation, but rather the other way round; punctuation should be compared to accidentals, because they were a key conceptual influence in their development of the visuo-graphical system. This is a subtly different way of thinking about their capacity for expressiveness: not just about expounding the meaning of a word, but shading out its many potential meanings, its flavours and inflections and semantic possibilities as today a modern comma, colon, semicolon, brace, slash, and interrobang can radically alter the meaning of a phrase or even a single word. The way that false relations mark the texture of a text (pun very much intended) speaks to an older concept of expression, thoroughly 'choral' and intricately tied to the literacies of early English Protestantism, bound as they were to the rhetoric of form: repetitions, reiterations, inversions, canonic transpositions. Megan Long has noted that popular musical forms (often built around repetition and refrain, such as the balletto, canzone, and canzonetta) enabled the shift towards the tonalities of the major-minor system.[61] Musical form would not emerge as an abstract, theorizable entity until the eighteenth century, but through the lens of the false relation and its relationship to text-setting, we can witness one of its seeds struggling to germinate as it chafes against the established concept of poetic form.[62]

Textualities extend beyond the words used to construct a phrase, sentence, verse, or song lyric. Equally important are the elements in between and the elements that join: the scaffolding that holds phrase, sentence, and so on together. The interaction between the false relation and the rhetorical logic of the *Book of Common Prayer*, with the developing system of distinction or pointing that governed the thresholds of phrases, is key for understanding its use and role within the musical culture of the English Renaissance and beyond. To acknowledge this interaction is to embrace the far more visual,

---

[61] Megan Kaes Long, *Hearing Homophony* (Oxford: Oxford University Press, 2020), 148–149. See also her analysis of Carl Dahlhaus's concept of the relationship between tonality and musical form, 199–200. Dahlhaus, *Studies on the Origin of Harmonic Tonality*, 318–319.

[62] Long, *Hearing Homophony*, 200–202.

embodied, material approach towards reading that characterized England in the first century of print, and to recognize that false relations are the trace of this older, richer approach. Form is important: it provides setting, context, and frame that heavily influence the meaning of any given word, musical trope, or phrase. Words and notes on the page are always (and in this culture especially) amplified by considerations to do with the *mise-en-page*, the space between that frames, allows breath, pause, and what we might think of as a graphic as well as aural silence.[63] In the next chapter, we will explore in greater depth the visual connotations touched upon in this chapter, and flesh out the styles of seeing in the English Renaissance.

---

[63] For more on this approach, see Adam Smyth, 'Book Marks: Object Traces in Early Modern Books', in Katherine Acheson (ed.), *Early Modern English Marginalia* (London: Routledge, 2019), 51–69; Maguire, *Rhetoric of the Page*; Megan Heffernan, *Making the Miscellany: Poetry, Print, and the History of the Book in Early Modern England* (Philadelphia: University of Pennsylvania Press, 2020), esp. 1–18.

4
Visualizing Falseness
Or, How to Look at a Discord

Discord: A Study in Silverpoint

She sits slightly turned away from us. One hand is elegantly draped across the strings of the lute, in the act of plucking the A string, the other fingering the frets to alter its pitch. She is loosely captured in dynamic, impressionistic strokes of pen and ink, an interplay of lines that tantalizingly gather in coils of hair pinned up on her head, echoing those that suggest her billowing sleeve. The pen strokes are so loose that they resolve halfway between the abstract and figurative, pattern, and representation everywhere apart from lute, hands, and face. She glances over her shoulder. It is only in meeting her eyes and appreciating the *chiaroscuro*, the play of dark and light between the intricately rendered expression on her face, her mouth open and seemingly still in the act of singing, her eyes lingering on us, and the sudden, jarringly large gap in the ink wash on that shoulder, that it becomes clear that something is wrong. The glow of skin on her shoulder, echoing the glow on her forehead, right cheek, hands, and crucially the soundboard of the lute itself, are unsettlingly at odds with the position of the rest of her body. The drawing is an early modern form of stereogram, snagging the eyes with two separate images, two separate perspectives, two separate visualizations of music-making that hinge on that shock of bare shoulder as it sits against the densely worked pegbox of the lute. This is Isaac Oliver (c. 1565–1617) and/or possibly his son Peter (c. 1589/1594–1648),[1] playing with the act of depicting dissonance.

Fig. 4.1, a tiny pen-and-ink wash drawing now in the Witt Collection at the Courtauld Gallery and dated c. 1610,[2] offers us an evocative window into

---

[1] Jeremy Wood, 'Peter Oliver at the Court of Charles I: New Drawings and Documents', in *Master Drawings*, 36: 2 (Summer 1998), 123–153.

[2] Witt Collection, Courtauld Gallery, London, c. 1610, 18.5c m × 14.7 cm: Object No. D.1952.RW.2390.2. See also Jill Finstein, *Isaac Oliver: Art and Courts of Elizabeth I and James I* (New York: Garland, 1981), Cats 201–205, 155–156, and 241.

Fig. 4.1 Attributed to Isaac Oliver and/or Peter Oliver, *Female Figure Playing the Lute*, c. 1610, pen and sepia ink; sepia and grey ink washes, drawn with point of brush on white (now discoloured) paper (London: Witt Collection, Courtauld Institute of Art), Object No. D.1952.RW.2390.2. Photograph author's own.

how the musical culture of the English Renaissance manifested in the visual arts. The looseness of Oliver's line creates a sense of constant, shifting movement; the figure's hair appears to be tumbling down from where it has been pinned, escaping its styled form, and the edges of her back, legs, and feet are blurred by the hatching, where the composition recedes into shadow. We might read this physiognomic disjunct as a sign of Oliver's error, but such an interpretation would be at odds with the other surviving drawings of the set, seemingly of the same figure, from the same period, which show no such anatomical errors.[3] Indeed, as Jill Finstein notes, they seem to be explicit explorations of the stylistic of Hendrik Goltzius, Jacques de Gheyn, and Leonardo, which likewise would discount the possibility of accidental 'error':

> The graphic style of the Witt drawings [. . .], the nervous, highly worked parallel hatching and stippling is a close approximation to Oliver's late miniature style. [. . .] Based on the engraved-type line drawings of Goltzius and de Gheyn—although Oliver's look more like etchings—these drawings with their heavily-worked linear patters foreshadow Oliver's very late miniature style. [. . .] Oliver makes not only a very similar visual effect—with generally the same graphic technique of parallel hatching strokes and delicate, curly outlines—but also equally pointed reference to Leonardo. [. . .] It is at this point a moot question whether Oliver arrived at Leonardo specifically via de Gheyn or whether these kinds of backward references to the great masters of the early sixteenth century were parallel expressions of a general phenomenon.[4]

Other surviving images of female figures playing the lute from the period are similarly accurately rendered; Isaac Oliver's teacher, Nicholas Hilliard, had produced a miniature of Elizabeth I playing a lute in 1575,[5] an anonymous frieze in the Great Chamber at Gilling Castle, Yorkshire

---

[3] Witt Collection, Courtauld Gallery, London: Object Nos. D.1952.RW.2390.1, D.1952.RW.2390.4, and D.1952.RW.2390.3.

[4] Finstein, *Isaac Oliver*, 241. Compare, e.g., Goltzius's portrait of Josina Hamels, which features a cartouche embellished with a lute player and singer. London: British Museum, Museum No. 1855,0414.229.

[5] Katherine Butler, *Music in Elizabethan Court Politics* (Woodbridge: Boydell, 2015), 17-19; Catherine Macleod, *Elizabethan Treasures: Miniatures by Hilliard and Oliver* (London: National Portrait Gallery, 2019).

140 SYRENE SOUNDES

(c. 1575–1585), and an anonymous monochrome wall-painting taken from the wall of 34 High Street, Thame in Oxfordshire, likewise depicted a carefully captured lute-playing figure (see Fig. 4.2). We will discuss the latter in greater detail later in this chapter; however, for the present

Fig. 4.2 Detail of monochromatic wall painting depicting music-making, cartouches, cornucopia, and strapwork and arabesque decoration taken from the upper room at 34 Upper High Street, Thame, Oxfordshire, c. 1560. Thame Museum, Thame, Oxfordshire. Photograph author's own.

context it is evidently unlikely that it was beyond either Isaac or Peter's skill to accurately capture the body position of a seated lute player. Indeed, such features were often deliberate, as Franciscus Junius, librarian of the Earl of Arundel, noted in 1638: 'It is in the meane time not onely tolerable but commendable also, and it addeth a singular grace to the worke, that there should sometimes appeare a certaine kinde of neglect in most excellent Pictures: a little sourenesse is otherwhiles pleasing in exquisite meats; and it doth not misbecome great wealth, to see something in it here and there carelesly scattered and neglected.'[6]

It is worth briefly pausing at this point to explain the attribution context of the drawing, in particular why it is unclear whether it is the work of father or son. When Isaac Oliver died in 1617, he left his 'drawings allreadye finished and unfinished' and his 'lymning pictures [miniatures], be they historyes, storyes or any thing of limning whatsoever of my owne hande worke as yet unfinished' to his eldest son (and apprentice) Peter.[7] This was likely in order to ensure that Peter could continue to hone his artistic craft using his father's materials, and possibly also to enable him to finish commissions; he completed at least one of Isaac's unfinished miniatures (an *Entombment* now in the Musée de Beaux-Artes in Angers, which Peter gifted to Charles I in 1636). The elision between the styles of the two is, therefore, inevitable and arguably deliberate. English Renaissance attitudes to authorship would not have been precious about such modern concepts as purity and sole creation, and so it is unlikely that anyone would have been concerned about a drawing or miniature being begun and finished by different hands. Jeremy Wood has reattributed the drawings with which Fig. 4.1 is mounted to Peter, due to their greater investment in Italianate (Florentine) draughtsmanship; recently Sophie Rhodes has noted that if one drawing in the mount can be attributed to Peter, it is likely that they all are. However, due to the deliberate blurring between Peter and Isaac's stylistic draughtsmanship it would be foolish to assume that Fig. 4.1 is not to some extent by Isaac. A couple of clues support the interpretation that this was one of the 'drawings allreadye finished and unfinished' bequeathed from father to son: the handling of line is somewhat loose and diaphanous, which is more characteristic of Isaac's draughtsmanship than Peter's,[8] and the lute has six courses and a relatively

---

[6] Franciscus Junius, *The Painting of the Ancients in Three Bookes: Declaring by Historicall Observations and Example* (London: Richard Hodgkinsonne, 1638), 205.

[7] Will of Isaac Oliver (4 June 1617), Public Office Record, London, Prob. 10/346.

[8] See, e.g., Isaac Oliver's portrait miniatures of an unknown woman (believed to be Lucy Harington, Countess of Bedford) of c. 1615, held in the Fitzwilliam Museum in Cambridge

short neck (rather than the greater number of courses and longer necks that came into fashion across the first decade of the seventeenth century),[9] which supports an earlier composition date. Although the father certainly had less exposure to Italian exemplars than the son,[10] a visit to Venice in 1596 and England's ongoing close relationship with the Dutch Republic (and artists such as Hendrik Goltzius and Jaques de Gheyn II, as mentioned by Finstein) would account for the slight continental flavours of the drawing. The drawing, moreover, bears significant resemblance to the securely attributed drawing *Antiope*, now in the British Museum.[11] For the purposes of this chapter, I will assume that Fig. 4.1 is predominantly the work of Isaac Oliver.

This diminutive drawing thus began its life, at least, as the work of a man embroiled in early Stuart court culture, the official limner to Queen Anna from 1605 and employed at the not inconsiderable sum of £40 per annum, closely connected to the Essex circle.[12] The 'rise, like cake dough, to become the last, sweetest desserts of royal entertainment' of the Masque form,[13] the great musical-visual expression of the English Renaissance, also occurred

(Museum No. 902), and of an unknown woman (formerly believed to be Frances Howard, Countess of Somerset), c. 1596-1600, now held in the Victoria & Albert Museum in London (Museum No. P.12-1971). By comparison, Peter Oliver's handling, in the study of heads in the Witt Collection, is considerably tighter.

[9] Matthew Spring, 'The Lute', in Michael Fleming and Christopher Page (eds.), *Music and Instruments of the Elizabethan Age: the Eglantine Table* (Woodbridge: Boydell & Brewer, 2021), 161-170, at 161-162. For comparison, see John de Critz's portrait of Mary Sidney, Countess of Pembroke with a fourteen-course theorbo lute (c. 1620, at Penshurst Place) and the anonymous *Portrait of Nicholas Lanier with Lute* (1613, and now in a private collection), in which Lanier holds a nine-course lute, of the kind that had been adapted for use in France by 1600, and had crossed the channel by 1603 to the extent that they are referenced in Thomas Robinson's *The Schoole of Musicke* (London: 1603). Benjamin M. Hebbert, 'A New Portrait of Nicholas Lanier', in *Early Music*, 38: 4 (November 2010), 509-522 and, 'The Lute and the Lutenist', in Katherine Ara (ed.), *Nicholas Lanier (1588-1666): A Portrait Revealed* (London: Weiss Gallery, 2010), 78-83, at 80. Roy Strong, moreover, has convincingly argued that the portrait is in fact by Isaac Oliver. Roy Strong, 'A Unique and Compelling Image', in Katherine Ara (ed.), *Nicholas Lanier (1588-1666): A Portrait Revealed* (London: Weiss Gallery, 2010), 29-38.

[10] In this Peter Oliver was likely greatly assisted by the aforementioned Nicholas Lanier, also a French Huguenot and whose family like the Olivers had emigrated from the city of Rouen. Lanier owned one of the largest collections of continental drawings in Stuart England, and in the 1620s was frequently sent to the continent to acquire drawings for Charles I. See Jeremy Wood, 'Nicholas Lanier (1588-1666) and the Origins of Drawing Collecting in Stuart England', in C. Baker, C. Elam, and G. Warwick (eds.), *Collecting Prints & Drawings in Europe c. 1500-1750* (Aldershot: Ashgate, 2003), 85-121.

[11] London: British Museum, Museum Number 1869,0612.295. The resemblance is particularly marked in the rendering of the hair, nose, and mouth.

[12] Catherine Macleod, 'Isaac Oliver and the Essex Circle', in *British Art Studies*, 17 (2020); Rab MacGibbon, 'The Most Ingenious Master and his Well-Profiting Scholar: Brief Lives of Nicholas Hilliard and Isaac Oliver', in Catherine Macleod (ed.), *Elizabethan Treasures*, 38.

[13] Patricia Fumerton, *Cultural Aesthetics: Renaissance Literature and the Practice of Social Ornament* (Cambridge; Cambridge University Press, 1991), 136. For more on the masque form,

during this period. Oliver is a ghostly presence in many of the surviving masques. Several of his miniatures in the early years of James I and VI's reign depict masquers, and senior members of the royal family and court in masqueing costume. Anna of Denmark and Prince Henry were both subjects of Oliver's masque miniatures.[14] Whilst no traces of Oliver's explicit involvement in masque production survive (in contrast to the well-documented contributions of his contemporaries such as Inigo Jones, Ben Jonson, Alfonso Ferrabosco the Younger, and Robert Johnson), it is clear that he would have witnessed preparation for, and performances of, masques.[15] Moreover, some of the most audaciously chromatic works of art music were composed in this environment. Such a context raises an alternative and exciting reading of Fig. 4.1: as a visualization of the culture that enshrined the false relation, an experiment in the picturing of musical falseness. The figure is in motion, as it were; caught between two separate positions, rather than in a static, frozen moment.[16] She is between the *mi–fa* interval, simultaneously both manifestations of the semitone interval. The dynamic is epitomized by her parted lips; we do not know if she is still singing along with the lute, or whether she has paused. The music continues to reverberate through each flourishing stroke of the pen.

This chapter seeks to explore the suggestive traces of responses, contemplations, and analogies of discord in the visual culture of the English Renaissance. In many places, these can be seen to offer evocative insight directly into the culture of false relation, through their suggestive inferences, and through their metaphorical and allegorical import. This chapter argues that solmization should be considered a matter of visual culture alongside musical culture, both in the context within which it was learned, and in the visuo-spatial demands it places upon a student learning to read music. It will

see Barbara Ravelhofer, *The Early Stuart Masque: Dance, Costume and Music* (Oxford: Oxford University Press, 2006); David M. Bevington and Peter Holbrook, *The Politics of the Stuart Court Masque* (Cambridge: Cambridge University Press, 1998).

[14] Catherine Macleod, *Elizabethan Treasures: Miniatures by Hilliard and Oliver* (London: National Portrait Gallery, 2019), 194–201.
[15] See, e.g., Andrew Sabol (ed.), *Four Hundred Songs and Dances from Early Stuart Masque* (Providence, RI: Brown University Press, 1978); Peter Walls, *Music in the English Courtly Masque 1604–1640* (Oxford: Clarendon Press, 1996); Sarah Schmalenberger, 'Hearing the Other in *The Masque of Blackness*', in Naomi Andre, Karen M. Bryan, and Eric Sayler (eds.), *Blackness in Opera* (Urbana: University of Illinois Press, 2012), 32–45.
[16] It is likely that the trope of sprezzatura is also at play. Kate Van Orden, 'Domestic Music', in Iain Fenlon and Richard Wistreich (eds.), *The Cambridge History of Sixteenth Century Music* (Cambridge: Cambridge University Press, 2019), 341–342.

explore ideas about the 'substance' of music as defined by Thomas Wright and by Campion, and the visual culture parallels to be found in thinking about what music was made of. Finally, returning to the pitch-space diagrams of William Bathe, Thomas Morley, and Thomas Campion, we will explore the visual implications of the practice of solmization and the *mi–fa* interval through the lens of the developing graphic, diagrammatic forms of visual culture enabled by the advent of the printing press.[17]

The ways in which artists and artisans sought to capture musical practice during the English Renaissance are far more diverse and varied than can be explored in this book. For the present investigation, it is important to note that Oliver's is (at the time of writing) a unique surviving example of an experimental, possibly preparatory sketch of a musical subject.[18] The appearance of music in the art objects of this period typically uses the allegorical or emblematic presence of a musical instrument to signify social or political harmony, ordered control and power; this much is certainly the undercurrent of Hilliard's 1575 miniature depiction of Elizabeth I with a lute. Fig. 4.1 instead uses music as a contemplative prompt, an exploration towards the limits of what it is possible to visually capture. This was an issue, too, in the visual field of musical notation. The practice of solmization through and with mutable hexachords had bequeathed the musical practitioners of the English Renaissance a sticky conundrum, as briefly explored above in Chapter 1: semitone intervals, and with them false relations, were frequently simply implied by the pattern of the given hexachord.[19] Their visual significance was dependent upon accurate interpretation of the correct hexachord. The ghost of this practice, as fixed-scale solmization came to supersede hexachord mutation, continued to linger over the semitone, chromatic styles, and the false relation itself.[20] The false relation was an issue of visual culture, just as much as it was an issue of musical culture.

---

[17] Christensen notes that the study of music was 'ineluctably' influenced by the invention of the printing press; Thomas Christensen, 'Music Theory and Pedagogy', in Iain Fenlon and Richard Wistreich (eds.), *The Cambridge History of Sixteenth Century Music* (Cambridge: Cambridge University Press, 2019), 414–438, at 414.

[18] It is also not listed in Christopher Page's survey of the imagery of the guitar and like instruments. See Christopher Page, *The Guitar in Tudor England* (Cambridge: Cambridge University Press, 2016).

[19] Margaret Bent, *Counterpoint, Composition and Musica Ficta* (London: Routledge, 2002), 2; Gregory Barnett, 'Tonal Organization in Seventeenth Century Music Theory', in Thomas Christensen (ed.), *The Cambridge History of Western Music Theory* (Cambridge: Cambridge University Press, 2002), 410.

[20] Note, e.g., Cristle Collins Judd's contention that we should approach musical notation as 'trace' rather than the concrete, absolute record of a piece of music. See Cristle Collins Judd,

VISUALIZING FALSENESS 145

Its visual dynamic, likewise, mirrors many of the other and hitherto better-known examples of the visual culture of the English Renaissance. Patricia Fumerton's analysis of the cultural aesthetics of the period is now three decades old but nevertheless still encapsulates the prevailing dynamic at the heart of many of its art objects. Writing of the striking semantic valency between the portrait miniature and the sonnet, Fumerton notes:

> The great form of Elizabethan retreat was *ornament*. The Elizabethan private self withheld itself paradoxically by holding forth in ostentatious, public showcases of ornament—some as large as architecture and some as small as jewelled lockets. The literary showcase most expressive of such self-representation was the ornamental little poem of love: the 'toyish' sonnet. [. . .] Nicholas Hilliard and Sir Philip Sidney—the leading contemporary artists of miniatures and sonnets, respectively—created precious, gemlike decorations that hid the self's 'secrets' behind a series of gorgeously ornate public rooms, cabinets, lockets, frames, paints, metaphors. [. . .] [Everything associated with miniature painting] suggests that its habit of public ornamentation kept, rather than told, private 'secrets'. Bedrooms displayed closed decorative cabinets; cabinets exhibited closed ivory boxes; boxes showed off covered or encased miniatures; and, when we finally set eyes on the limning itself, layers of ornamental colours and patterns only show the hiddenness of the heart. As seen in the frequent limning of 'miniatures-within-miniatures', indeed, the regress of concealing layers of ornament extended indefinitely. In Hilliard's *Man against a Background of Flames* for instance, a lover appears to literally bare his burning passion. His fine linen shirt, *en déshabillé*, opens wide to reveal his white breast and an enamelled gold locket hanging from a chain around his neck. Pressed against his heart, the locket undoubtedly contains a miniature of his mistress.[21]

The reader will already have noted the striking similarity between these social practices, and that of the false relation (not least in Fumerton's concept of the 'public showcases of ornament', and perhaps even the 'gemlike decorations that hid the self's 'secrets' behind a series of gorgeously ornate

'Introduction: Analysing Early Music', in Cristle Collins Judd (ed.), *Tonal Structures in Early Music* (New York: Garland, 2000), 5.

[21] Fumerton, *Cultural Aesthetics*, 69–70 and 84–85.

public rooms, cabinets, lockets, frames, paints, metaphors').[22] Like these objects of visual culture, the false relation's secretive nature was a guise: the openly displayed, openly known nature of both, withheld only as things seen or visualized, is the key to this aesthetic. There is, however, of course a crucial difference: the false relation's final line of defence was its ephemerality. Whereas the secrets of Nicholas Hilliard's *Man against a Background of Flames* (c. 1600) ultimately collapse into nothing more than the Ace of Hearts, the playing card on which Hilliard painted the miniature, the false relation is knowable.[23] Beyond the inaccessibility of a given performance after its moment of utterance, the intimate secret of the false relation and the slippage of the *mi–fa* interval was available to anyone versed in the practise of solmization.

Nevertheless, we should still take the intriguing valency between the visual dynamic of false relation, portrait miniature, and sonnet seriously.[24] Katelijne Schiltz has recently noted the importance of riddle culture to early modern music, and the way it interacted with the literary trope of *obscuritas* and the physical material of written, inscribed music:

> The key to a musical riddle always resides in the notation. It is the written form that the composer conceives as a conundrum that needs to be solved. The early modern period was the heyday of musical riddle culture. Composers revelled in wrapping their music in an enigmatic guise and leaving it up to the performer to figure out how to engage the performer in an insider's intellectual game, a process of obfuscation, discovery and delight.[25]

Schiltz argues that these practises arose precisely from the ambiguity of the musical notational culture of the sixteenth century, not least the compactness of the mensural system and the fact that 'a single note can have more than one meaning: it is a variable property. It is this flexibility between the note's visual appearance and its realization in sound that must have been

---

[22] Katelijne Schiltz, *Music and Riddle Culture in the Renaissance* (Cambridge: Cambridge University Press, 2015).

[23] Macleod, *Elizabethan Treasures*, 94–95. Note also the rendition of the same subject by Oliver, 'A Man Consumed by Flames', 70 × 56mm, National Trust (Ham House, Surrey), c. 1610.

[24] It is important to note that this is a distinctly English approach. See Jessie Ann Owens, 'Concepts of Pitch in English Music Theory c. 1540–1640', in Cristle Collins Judd (ed.), *Tonal Structures in Early Music*.

[25] Schiltz, *Music and Riddle Culture*, 2.

a major factor for composers and that inspired many riddles.'[26] Not least amongst these tantalizingly flexible variables is the *mi–fa* semitone: in effect, (an anachronous) Schrodinger's interval that plays with 'the radical promiscuity of musical meaning in early modern England'.[27] There is contemporary evidence, too, that musical culture was known for its obfuscation. Francis Bacon's disparaging comments in *Sylva Sylvarum* (1626) certainly suggest as much. For Bacon,

> MUSICKE in the *Practice*, hath bin well pursued; And in good Variety; But in the *Theory* and especially in the *Yeelding* of the *Causes* of the *Practique*, very weakly; Being reduced into certaine Mysticall Subtleties, of no use, and not much Truth.[28]

He does not explicitly name those 'certaine Mysticall Subtleties', but the spectre of solmization looms irresistibly large over his comments over the interaction between 'theory' and 'causes of the practique'. We might infer that he enjoyed certain aspects of his education at Cambridge more than others when he went up to Trinity College in 1573, and that the interaction between concealment and revelation at the heart of sixteenth-century musical notational culture is at the heart of Bacon's objections.

Oliver's study suggests a rather different attitude towards the 'certain Mysticall Subtleties' of music. The tug of war between concealment and revelation is the ineffable context of Fig. 4.1, and its choppy, shifting loose rendering. Its subject could well have been inspired by a technical element of musical culture, given Oliver's musical connections. Oliver married his third wife Elizabeth (1589–c. 1640) in 1606; she was the daughter of French Huguenot immigrant and court musician James Harding or Jacques Harden, and so (like Lanyer, as explored above) was likely versed in the practice of solmization and the intricacies of the *mi–fa* interval, amongst other musical

---

[26] Ibid., 74–75. Schiltz is inspired by James Haar's arguments around approaching notation as the centre of a composer's attention; see James Haar, 'Music as Visual Object: The Importance of Notational Appearance', in Renato Bordghi and Pietro Zappalà (eds.), *L'edizione critica tra testo musicale e testo letterario. Atti del convegno internazionale (Cremona 4–8 ottobre 1992)* (Lucca: Libreria Musicale Italiana, 1995), 97–128.

[27] Joseph M. Ortiz, *Broken Harmony: Shakespeare and the Politics of Music* (Ithaca, NY: Cornell University Press, 2011), 11.

[28] Francis Bacon, *Sylva Sylvarum* (London: 1626), fol. 1r. See Simon Smith's gloss on this; Simon Smith, *Musical Response in the Early Modern Playhouse, 1603–1625* (Cambridge: Cambridge University Press, 2017), 7–8.

knowledge.[29] Harding composed the popular five-part Galliard that Byrd would later arrange for keyboard, and which would survive in the Fitzwilliam Virginal Book;[30] unsurprisingly, given the period, it features stylistic use of false relation (in particular an English cadence to F, with an E♭ set against an E♮ in the Tenor). Fig. 4.1, dating from after Oliver's marriage to Elizabeth, reverberates suggestive traces of this musical connection. Indeed, it is possible that Elizabeth was the sitter for the drawing. There is a fleeting similarity between the figure's facial features and the surviving miniature thought to depict Elizabeth Oliver (dated 1610–1615 and now in the Portland Collection),[31] particularly in the shape of the sitter's eyes and brows. At some point before 1621 Peter Oliver also married Elizabeth's younger sister, Anne, meaning that the resemblance to Elizabeth might have been the result of Peter's later intervention (the facial features bear comparatively little resemblance to surviving images of Anne herself, and Peter's depiction of her).[32] The figure is evidently intended to be allegorical or mythological, but she is discreetly dressed in all sketches in the Witt Collection set, rather like a middle-class artisan's wife and unlike the comparable figure sketches in the British Museum, stylistically similar but which features the models' breasts bared.[33] However, in the absence of concrete evidence at present it is not possible to move beyond the evocative hint of resemblance. We are left, simply, with the hands of a practised lutenist, in the act of tuning a fret and plucking a string; not an empty mimicry, but the gesture she would adopt to produce a musical note. She is initiate in the musical culture, practices, and acts of reading and performing. In a very real sense, we are watching the unknowable shimmer between *mi* and *fa* in action.

All of this—Oliver's drawing, the 'public showcases of ornament[al privacy]'—might seem a far cry from the musicological matter of the false relation. But such a judgement is anachronistic; in the English Renaissance,

---

[29] MacGibbon, 'Brief Lives', 38; this musical connection also supports the theory that Isaac Oliver was the original draughtsman, and the earlier composition date, as it seems highly unlikely that Oliver would choose to depict a lute that was not at the height of fashion.

[30] Fitzwilliam Virginal Book, Cambridge: Fitzwilliam Museum, early seventeenth century, MU. MS.168. Another notable piece survives in an orphan partbook in the Bodleian Library, Mus.24.E (early seventeenth century). Andrew Ashbee, 'Harding, James', in *Grove Music Online* (2001) (accessed 09/05/2021).

[31] Macleod, *Elizabethan Treasures*, 138–139.

[32] Peter Oliver, *Portrait of Anne Oliver*, c. 1625–1630 (London: National Portrait Gallery), Museum No. NPG 4853a.

[33] 'Figure of Woman', London: British Museum, Museum No. 1946,0713.1170; 'Diana', London: British Museum, Museum No. Gg,3.360; and 'A Seated Woman', London: British Museum, Museum No. 1952,0121.9

music and the visual arts were seen as intricately entwined, in symbiosis, reciprocal, and part of the same endeavour to improve the self. Henry Peacham published his *Graphice: The Art of Drawing with the Pen, and Limning in Water Colours* in 1606. In it, Peacham establishes 'skil with the pencil' as comparable to 'insight into the Chords of musick', both being 'things of accomplement required in a Scholler or a Gentleman'.[34] Drawing and music are both genteel arts; they both contribute to the refinement and edification that makes a 'Scholler or Gentleman' and serve as building blocks for the conceptual architecture of the student in training. Returning to the explicitly musicological matter of the scale/gamut/pitch space diagrams used by Bathe, Morley, and Campion, it is clear that solmization should be considered a matter of visual acuity. As James Haar notes, the question of false relations is one of diagonal tonal relationship, and thus of inferring the correct oblique angle in order to achieve the sonic near-miss effect, rather than harmonic collapse.[35] A potential singer/musician's ability to read music is dependent upon their ability to visualize musical space and negotiate that visualization of musical space. Once the singer/musician had internalized the pattern, they were able to recreate more complicated musical forms. Peacham describes something very similar in *Graphice*:

> Having [your tools] in readiness, you shall practise for the space of a week or thereabouts, to draw Circles, Squares of all sorts, a Cylinder, the oval forme, with other such like solid and plaine Geometricall figures, till you can doe them indifferent wel, using the help of your rule and Compasse: the reason of exercising you first in these is, when as Symmetry or proportion is the very soule of picture, it is impossible that you should be ready in these bodies, before you can draw their abstract and generall formes, and have wanted and made your hand ready in proportions of all sortes, which are compounded of the same, as for example, your Circle will teach you, to draw even and truly all sphaericall bodies which are [. . .] of like parts and formes, as the Sun Moone, &c. The most flowers as the Rose, Marigold, Heliotropium, Daisie &c.: the most vessels as cups, Basons, Bowles, Bottles, &c. The Square will make you ready for

---

[34] Henry Peacham, *Graphice: The Art of Drawing with the Pen, and Limning in Water Colours* (London: Richard Braddock, 1606), in 'To the Reader'.

[35] James Haar, 'False Relations and Chromaticism in Sixteenth Century Music', in *Journal of the American Musicological Society*, 30: 3 (Autumn 1977), 391–418, at 413. Haar is writing explicitly about Zarlino. See also Dmitri Tymoczko, *A Geometry of Music: Harmony and Counterpoint in the Extended Common Practice* (Oxford: Oxford University Press, 2011).

all manner of compartments, bases, perystiles, plots, buildings &c.: your Cylinder for valuted turrets and round buildings; your Orthogonium and Pyramis, for sharpe steeples, turrets and all things [...] your Ovall forme will help you in drawing the face, a shield, or such like: so that you may reduce many thousand bodies to these few generall figures, as unto their principall heads and fountaine.[36]

The geometrical 'sphaericall', 'square', 'cylinder', 'orthogonium' and 'oval' forms that Peacham recommends to improve one's draughtsmanship are the analogues of the hexachord patterns and the practice of solmization. A student learning both at the same time, in their quest to become 'Scholler or Gentleman', would likely have experienced some radio interference between musical and visual practice, as it were. In approaching the musical culture of the English Renaissance, and the way it understood the act of reading music, it is vital that we take these connections seriously.

Picturing the 'Substance of Musicke'

We encountered two seemingly contrasting statements about the 'substance of music' above, in Chapter 2. A closer glance, more firmly located in the musical practice of the period, demonstrates that this contrast is, in fact, not quite so distinct as it first appears. The first is Thomas Wright's reflection, taken from his 1601 *Passions of the Minde in Generall*:

> What hath the shaking or artificiall crispling of the aire (which is in effect the substance of musicke) to doe with rousing up choler, afflicting with melanlancholie, jubilating of heart with pleasure, eleuating of soule with deuotion, alluring to lust, inducing to peace, exciting to compassion, inuiting to magnanimitie? It is not so great a meruaile, that meat, drinke, exercise, and aire set of aloft, for these are diuers waies qualified, and consequently apt to stirre up humors; but what qualitie carie simple single sounds and voices, to enable them to worke such wonders? [...] There is] a certaine sympathie, correspondence, or proportion betwixt our soules and musick: and no other cause can be yeelded. Who can give any other reason, why the loadstone draweth yron, but a sympathie of nature? Why

[36] Peacham, *Graphice*, 11–12, fol. C2v–C2r.

the Needle, toucht but with such a stone, should neuer leaue looking towards the North Pole; who can render other reason, than sympathie of nature?[37]

Passions of the Minde explores proto-scientific and philosophical interpretations of human nature, and the interaction between passions, soul, mind, and heart. For Wright the 'miraculous'[38] aspect of music is its relationship to the human soul: the 'certaine sympathie, correspondence or proportion betwixt our soule and musick', like the magnetic pull of a Needle on a compass. This is what enables the transformative power of 'simple single sounds and voices'. Without the sympathy between music and soul, the 'substance of music' is simply the 'shaking or artificiall crispling of the air' (crispling meaning, in this sense, to curl, coil or oscillate, as in 'shaking'). The reader will remember the 'artificial[ity]' of sugar sweetness as explored above in Chapter 2. The connection between the sugary falseness of the *mi–fa* relation and Wright's 'artificiall crispling' will be explored later in this chapter, but for the present it is important to note that he foregrounds the fact that it is man-made, a direct human intervention into the air.[39] Charles Butler uses identical language in his 1636 *Principles of Musik*, referring to the '*Artificial* works of [th]e best 'Au[th]ors' (my italics).[40]

On the other hand, we have Thomas Campion's claims for the 'substance of music', as listed in *A New Way of Making Fowre Partes in Counter-point* (1610):

The substance of all Musicke, and the true knowledge of the scale, consists in the observation of the halfe note, which is expressed either by Mi Fa or La Fa, and they being knowne in their right places, the other notes are easily applied unto them.[41]

---

[37] Thomas Wright, *The Passions of the Minde in Generall* (London: Valentine Simmes and Adam Islip for Walter Venge, 1604), 167–168.
[38] Ibid., 162.
[39] Scott Trudell, *Unwritten Poetry: Song, Performance and Media in Early Modern England* (Oxford: Oxford University Press, 2019), 34; see also Katherine R. Larson, *The Matter of Song in Early Modern England: Texts in and of the Air* (Oxford: Oxford University Press, 2019), 67–77.
[40] Butler, *Principles of Musik* (1636), 92. On the question of *imitatio* as a didactic tool in a slightly later context, see also Rebecca Herissone, *Musical Creativity in Restoration England* (Cambridge: Cambridge University Press, 2013), 3–15.
[41] Thomas Campion, *A New Way of Making Fowre Parts in Counter-Point by a most familiar, and infallible rule* (London: T. Snodham for John Browne, 1610), fol. B4r.

For Campion, the *mi–fa* interval is the substance, the crucial matter that allows for the practice of music. For our present purposes, however, it is important to note that Campion makes similar claims elsewhere in *A New Way*, as we saw above in Chapter 2:

> Of all things that belong to the making up of a Musition, the most necessary and useful for him is the true knowledge of the Key or Moode, or Tone, for all signifie the same thing, with the closes belonging unto it, for there is no tune that can have any grace or sweetnesse, unlesse it be bounded within a proper key, without running into strange keyes which have no affinity with the aire of the song.[42]

In other words, knowledge of the semitone and the potential for discord allows for the accurate 'observation' of their 'right places', the accurate interpretation of the hexachord pattern. This much is unsurprising. More surprising, perhaps, is the fact that both Campion and Wright appear to be writing about the same phenomenon (albeit Wright is in a more explicitly poetic, figurative register). The crucial facet is their relationship to the 'aire of the song'; that which is 'artificial[y] crispl[ed]', in Wright's account. The 'right place', with 'affinity' to the song, presupposes in strikingly visual terms a conceptual architecture of pitch space. We are accustomed to the imagined visualizations of solid pitch-space models (the Guidonian hand, the scala or ladder of the hexachord and scale, but also forms such as Robert Fludd's allegorized 'Temple of Music'; see Fig. 4.3), as Charles Simpson stated in his *Compendium of Practical Musick* (1667): 'a Pattern to imitate'.[43] Less familiar is the visual sense of the little ductile wiggle or segment of semantic bagginess, at the centre of the hexachord; the *mi–fa* interval that 'crispl[es]' the musical texture.

Once framed in this manner, it is possible to discern traces of the concept of the curling, coiling, undulating, twisting capacity of the *mi–fa* interval throughout the musical literature of the English Renaissance. This 'artificiall crispling' interacts fascinatingly with contemporary descriptions of how sound was produced. For Pierre de la Primaudaye, 'that which is framed in voice, & brought into use, is as a river sent from the thought with the voice, as

---

[42] Campion, *A New Way of Making Fowre Parts in Counter-Point*, fol. D4r.
[43] Charles Simpson, *Compendium of Practical Musick* (London, 1667), 117.

VISUALIZING FALSENESS 153

Fig. 4.3 Robert Fludd, the 'Temple of Music', from Robert Fludd, *Utriusque Cosmi Maioris Scilicet et Minoris Metaphysica* (Oppenheim: J. T. de Bry, 1617–1618), London: Wellcome Collection, EPB/D/2324/1.v1. Public Domain.

from his fountain'.[44] Likewise, John Davies's description (written in 1599) of how sound enters the ears:

> Should the voice directly strike the braine
> It would astonish and confuse it much;
> Therefore these plaites and folds the sound restrain,
> That the Organ it may more gently touch.
> As streames, which with their winding banks are
> stopt by their creeks run softly through the plaine,
> So in the Eares Labyrinth, the voice doth stray
> And doth with easie motion touch the braine.[45]

Elsewhere, Helkiah Crooke forms his analysis in rather more familiarly anatomical terms, in his *Mikrokosmographia* (1615).[46] Nevertheless the shadow of Davies's 'plaites and folds', 'winding banks', and Primaudaye's 'river' is still present; Crooke's ear is 'alwaies open and winding' and like a 'snaile-shel', and 'from the sinuing obliquitie of his passage [. . .] elegantly resembleth the winding of a Snayle or Perwinkle shell'.[47] This is echoed by Crooke's description of how the air is manipulated by the structure of the throat to produce sound as voice:

If these bodyes be polished and concauous or hollow, and of a solid and ayry matter, such as brasse and glasse is, then the sound will be greater, more plaine and delightsome, which may bee shewed in bels and musical instruments for such bodyes contain a great deale of ayre in them, which airy when it is moued and seeketh a vent, doth euery way strike about the sides and euery way causeth a resonance or resounding.[48]

The curls and 'plaites' are less explicit in Crooke's formulation, but the act of 'mov[ing] and seek[ing]' through the larynx, arytaenoides, 'gristles', and vuula, 'the quill of a Citterne in the forming of the voyce',[49] captures much the

---

[44] Pierre de la Primaudaye, *The Second Part of the French Academie* (London: G. B[ishop], R. N[ewbery] & R. B[arker], 1594), fol. 57r.
[45] John Davies, *Nosce Teipsum: this Oracle expounded in two elegies, 1) of Humane Knowledge, 2) Of the Soule of Man, and the Immortalitie thereof* (London: Richard Hawkins, 1599), 43.
[46] See also Larson, *Matter of Song*, 68.
[47] Helkiah Crooke, *Mikrokosmographia. A Description of the Body of Man* (London: William Iaggard dwelling in Barbican, 1615), 697 and 604.
[48] Ibid., 645.
[49] Ibid., 646.

Fig. 4.4 Ruff, linen with the initials 'CY' embroidered in red ink, c. 1615–1635, 3 cm × 38 cm/1950 cm × 13 cm (length) Amsterdam: Rijksmuseum, BK-NM-13112. Public Domain.

same concept of 'crispling' fluidity. Crooke's concept of the 'quill of the voyce' is also telling. The early modern English quill was not just a writing implement. The first instance listed above uses 'quill' as a form of plectrum (most commonly used to refer to the plectrums of keyboard instruments),[50] but at the time it also meant, in a verbal sense, the action of forming a fabric into the narrow, rounded folds and pleats of an elaborate ruff before starching (see Fig. 4.4),[51] similar to the craft of quilling or paper filigree still practised today.[52] It could serve as a synonym for 'coil', or describe multiple people acting in harmony, in both senses as an apparent borrowing from the Middle

---

[50] 'Quyll, with whiche a musician useth to play to save his fingers, or any lyke thinge, *plectrum*'. Richard Huolet, *Abecedarium Anglo Latinum* (London: G. Riddell, 1552).

[51] Ruff, linen with the initials 'CY' embroidered in red ink, c. 1615–1635, 3 cm × 38 cm/1950 cm × 13 cm (length) Amsterdam: Rijksmuseum, BK-NM-13112.

[52] E.g., 'He shall have garthes of all sortes, those for hunting or running of a wollen webbe, strongly quilled and joined to the lightest and sinest buckles.' Gervase Markham, *Cavelarice, or the English Horseman* (London: Edward White, 1607), 56.

French *cueillir*, to gather.⁵³ Hester Lees-Jeffries's account of the materiality of text and reading is of particular interest to the unravelling conundrum of the 'substance of music'. She notes the importance of considering the etymology of the Word in the Greek λόγος or *logos*. *Logos* is derived from *legein*, 'to gather, as wheat is gathered into sheaves, or as bits of string are gathered into hanks'.⁵⁴ Things become meaningful, as Word or *logos* or indeed as music, when the threads are gathered together into hanks, coils, or skeins. Such an interpretation is reflected in George Puttenham's 1589 account of the rhetorical figure of synecdoche or, as he terms it, 'the figure of quick conceit':

> If we use such a word [...] by which we drive the hearer to conceive more, or less, or beyond, or other than the letter expresseth [...] the Greeks then call it synecdoche, the Latins subintellectio or understanding, for by part we are enforced to understand the whole, by the whole part, by many things one thing, by one many, by a thing precedent a thing consequent.⁵⁵

A part stands for the whole, the hexachord in the 'quill of the voice'.

These 'crispling', quilling, 'plait[ing]' accounts of sound production come to vivid life when the matter of the *mi–fa* interval is brought into consideration. The clue lies again, in Crooke's anatomical discussion of the production of the voice and sound. Crooke talks about the need for moisture to ensure the 'polishing' of the vocal passages:

> Humidity is more aboundant within, yet so that in those which are sound it is neither more copious nor more scarse then the instrument of the voice doth require; by it also it is polished and so the voice is made pleasant and equal, for being moistened with a kinde of humidity it doth familiarly beate the aire, whence the sweetenesse of the voice proceedeth.⁵⁶

The 'sweetnesse of the voice' will immediately conjure the paradoxes of the literary trope of false, dissimulating, artificial sweetness of the concord

---

⁵³ See, e.g., 'Let's stand close, and then we may deliver our supplications in the Quill.' William Shakespeare, *Henry VI Part II*, 3.3, 1.

⁵⁴ Hester Lees-Jeffries, 'Ariachne', 94; J. Hillis Miller, 'Ariachne's Broken Woof', in *The Georgia Review*, 31 (1977).

⁵⁵ George Puttenham, *The Art of English Poesy*, first published 1589, this edition in Gavin Alexander (ed.), *Sidney's 'The Defence of Poesy' and Selected Renaissance Literary Criticism* (London: Penguin, 2004), 158. See also Raphael Lyne's account of synecdoche; Raphael Lyne, *Shakespeare, Rhetoric and Cognition* (Cambridge: Cambridge University Press, 2011), 75.

⁵⁶ Crooke, *Mikrokosmographia*, 644.

found in discord, as explored above in Chapter 2.[57] In the context of the rest of the passage and Crooke's recommendations for preventing the voice from producing 'unpleasant and harsh' sounds (also pitched through the analogy of musicians with their 'Pipes or Trumpets'), the question of the 'sweetnesse' or 'delectab[ility]'[58] of the voice is evidently a matter of appropriately shaping air; Crooke does not explicitly mention singing, but we can reasonably infer from the musical context of the passage that it is appropriate. It is the other key factor of this passage, however, that is of interest to the question of the shaping of the air and the shaping of the hexachord. 'Sweetnesse' is borne of the 'familiar [...] beat[ing of] the aire'. In this sense Crooke's concept of the 'sweetnesse of the voice' is related to Campion's requirement of 'affinity with the aire of the song': in other words, in its appropriate ductility.[59] An inappropriately, excessively coiling song fitted neither the 'plaites and folds' of the ear, nor the 'quill of the voyce'. However, a song should have some coils and 'crispl[es]', to aid its sweetness.

The theories of hearing and sound production are closely related to the concept of *ductus*, as explored by Mary Carruthers, Margaret Bent, Susan Rankin, and Elizabeth Eva Leach in a medieval context, and touched on briefly above in Chapter 1.[60] *Ductus*, as it appears in the devotional texts of the early medieval period, refers to the concept of the art object (musical, literary, and visual) as a journey. As Carruthers states, 'the experience of artistic form as an ongoing, dynamic process rather than as the examination of a static or completed object. *Ductus* is the way by which a work leads someone through itself: that quality in a work's formal patterns which engages an audience and then sets a viewer or auditor or performer in motion within its structures, an experience more like travelling through stages along a route than like perceiving a whole object.'[61] Rhetorically, *ductus* was an aspect of formal arrangement or disposition (*dispositio*); in contrast

---

[57] Lionel Pike, *Hexachords in Late-Renaissance Music* (London: Routledge, 1998), 32–33.

[58] Crooke, *Mikrokosmographia*, 644.

[59] Mary Carruthers, 'The Concept of Ductus, or Journeying through a Work of Art', in Carruthers (ed.), *Rhetoric beyond Words: Delight and Persuasion in the Arts of the Middle Ages* (Cambridge: Cambridge University Press, 2010), 1–19.

[60] Mary Carruthers (ed.), *Rhetoric beyond Words: Delight and Persuasion in the Arts of the Middle Ages* (Cambridge: Cambridge University Press, 2010). Margaret Bent, 'Grammar and Rhetoric in Late Medieval Polyphony: Modern Metaphor or Old Simile?', 52–71; Elizabeth Eva Leach, 'Nature's Forge and Mechanical Production: Writing, Reading and Performing Song', 72–95; Susan Rankin, '*Terribilis est locus iste*: The Pantheon in 609', 281–310, all in Carruthers (ed.), *Rhetoric beyond Words. Delight and Persuasion in the Arts of the Middle Ages* (Cambridge: Cambridge University Press, 2010).

[61] Carruthers, *Rhetoric beyond Words*, 190.

to our modern concept of formalism, this was a matter of active interaction between parts. Already in this brief account it is possible to see a clear interaction between the *ductus* and the practices of voice leading, tonal expectation, and cadential syntax as explored above.[62] The experience of listening or performing was one of following and navigating through the 'artificial crispling' of the air and the 'quill of the voyce'; in the act of listening, the semantic bagginess of the *mi–fa* interval serves, as Megan Kaes Long puts it, 'you are here' markers within the fabric of the musical composition.[63] They guide by their 'affinity' or 'familiarity' to the anatomical form of ear or throat, and the 'certaine sympathie, correspondence or proportion betwixt our soule and musick', like the magnetic pull of a Needle on a compass.[64]

The scantest visual traces of this way of thinking about the substance of music survive. We might interpret the G-clef as the most elucidated example; placing the original *mi–fa* interval at the very centre of the stave, it appears to have provided scribes with a lot of visual joy, as demonstrated by the wide variety of looping forms in which it survives. The varying forms of G-clef often strongly resemble the coiling spiral pattern that was popular in the decorative arts around the late sixteenth and early seventeenth centuries. The most explicitly musical example are the Westwood virginals (Fig. 4.5), which features this undulating, unfurling spiral pattern, picked out in segments of inlaid ivory; the instrument itself was created by Stefan Mutinensis in 1537, but it seems likely that the case was completed later in the century and by an English joiner, given the strong visual echoes with surviving objects such as Fig. 4.6, a sumptuously embroidered jacket dated c. 1615–1625, the exquisite mother-of-pearl and silver-gilt casket (Fig. 4.7, c. 1600) used to display sweetmeats at table (both now in the Victoria and Albert Museum), and indeed with the jacket worn by Elizabeth Oliver in her portrait miniature.[65] Close inspection of Fig. 4.5 reveals that the inlay has in fact been conceived in the manner of stitches, as discernibly discrete segments, suggesting that it was directly inspired by an embroidered precedent. Another possible musical

---

[62] Megan Kaes Long, 'Cadential Syntax and Tonal Expectation in Late Sixteenth-Century Homophony', in *Musical Theory Spectrum*, 40: 1 (2018), 52–83; Megan Kaes Long, *Hearing Homophony: Tonal Expectation at the Turn of the Seventeenth Century* (Oxford: Oxford University Press, 2020); David Huron, *Voice Leading: The Science behind a Musical Art* (Cambridge, MA: MIT Press, 2018); Elizabeth Eva Leach, 'Nature's Forge and Mechanical Production', 72–95.
[63] Long, *Hearing Homophony*.
[64] Wright, *Passions*, 168.
[65] Casket, c. 1600, Object No. M.245-1924.

Fig. 4.5 Anonymous, The Westwood Virginals, ivory inlay on wood (instrument by Stefan Mutinensis), 1537, National Trust Collection: Westwood Manor, Wiltshire. By kind permission of the National Trust.

example can be found in a set of the madrigal collection *The Triumphs of Oriana* (1601), now in Cambridge University Library (Fig. 4.8). This set is covered in repurposed proclamations from the early sixteenth century, with the blank sides as the covers and the written elements inside, turned upside down and serving as decorative endpapers through performance of their emptying of semantic content. Words have become simply marks on the page, unravelling lines of meaningless sound that contain meaningful sound: the madrigals in praise of Elizabeth I. These are disparate and largely undocumented instances of what might have been a musical-visual trend in the English Renaissance. Nevertheless, the suggestion of this conception of sound lives on in these scant surviving examples, and in the contemporary anatomical and musical accounts of sound production, the 'quill of the voice', the 'artificial crispling of the aire', and the 'plaites and folds' that 'elegantly resembleth the winding of a Snayle or Perwinkle shell'.

When thinking of the false relation and its potential visual culture, visual analogues, and visual echoes, the writing about how to musically and/or anatomically produce a sound can give a significant insight into the associations that may have been activated in the imaginations of listeners and performers in the English Renaissance. We saw above in Chapter 2 that the practice of the 'false' discord was frequently enjoyed

160 SYRENE SOUNDES

Fig. 4.6 Anonymous, waistcoat part, silver-gilt braid stitch to represent scrolling stems and a repeated pattern of strawberries in shades of pink and red silk floss to represent stages of ripening, in detached button-hole stitch on a linen ground, c. 1615, London: Victoria & Albert Museum, Accession Number T.259-1926. By kind permission of the Victoria & Albert Museum.

Fig. 4.7 Anonymous, casket, c. 1600, mother-of-pearl shell plaques set in a silver-gilt foot, with arabesque work silver-gilt cover, 8.5 cm × 12.9 cm × 7.5 cm, London: Victoria & Albert Museum, Accession Number M.245-1924. Reproduced by kind permission of the Victoria & Albert Museum.

as a guilty, sweet pleasure, combining both positive and negative aspects of artifice and luxurious indulgence. It was bound up in developing ideas about commodity, and as we have seen in the preceding sections of this chapter, privacy and secrecy. In this way, it was emblematic of many of the characteristics of English Renaissance culture and its shifting economic and social dynamics. By its very visual connotations, the false relation is a distant conceptual cousin of the sonnet and the miniature. However, this connection goes deeper. For those who had inherited with the concept of sound discussed above the act of performing or listening to a false relation felt like a material intervention into a physical matter, the 'substance' of music. Born of artifice and cultures of ornament, the voluminousness of the *mi–fa* interval is visually related to the pleat or 'quill' in a bolt of fabric. The false relation, the diagonal or oblique joining/disjoining of *mi* and

162 SYRENE SOUNDES

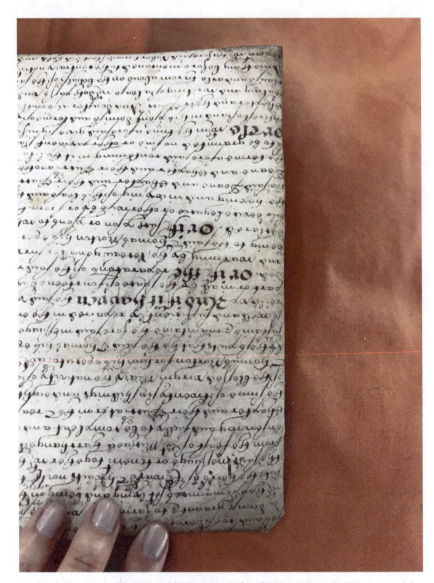

Fig. 4.8 Anonymous, covers of *The Triumphs of Oriana* (1601), Cambridge: Cambridge University Library. Catalogue No. Syn.7.60.203. Photograph author's own.

fa (as Crooke states, the 'sinuing obliquity' that seems to imply Wright's 'certaine sympathie, correspondence, or proportion betwixt our soules and musick')[66] is like the shaping of diaphanous fabric to produce the fashionably billowy full sleeves, skirts, and breeches, the 'head-on-a-plate' broad ruffs and other popular sartorial bodily distortions of Elizabethan and early Stuart dress.[67] Such pleats and quills simultaneously reveal and conceal the fullness of cloth and the richness of the musical texture and the dense array of pitches it contains, hidden beneath the rigid structure of the scala, ladder, hexachord. All these connotations are contained in the metaphors used by Wright, Campion, Davies, and Crooke to describe the way that human beings produce sound and shape it into music or 'sweetnesse'.

Reframing our understanding of the false relation in terms of its visual implications (the way it fitted into existing imagined-visual models of pitch space, the ways that it complemented, distorted, and manipulated these models) can provide key insight into how and why they came to be such prized stylistic elements of musical culture. Taking into account how sound was thought to be produced and shaped provides a visual account, but one that is never intended to be made material. In this sense, the frequent lack of explicit notation for accidentals to signal the *mi* or *fa* degree chimes directly with such a conceptualization of sound and, as Katherine Larson notes (specifically of ornamental devices such as the trill, but also including the improvised elements such as accidental inflection), 'the vital tension between notational trace and embodied performance that characterized musical circulation in sixteenth- and seventeenth-century England. [. . .] The notation of vocal ornament stretches musical signification to the breaking point. While providing a vital visual cue for the singer, in performance ornaments are more elastic than the rigidity of musical notation suggests, drawing attention to the inability of a score to capture or fully represent a voice'.[68] The act of mutating a hexachord to place the *mi–fa* interval away from B-*mi*/B-*fa*,

---

[66] Crooke, *Mikrokosmographia*, 604; Wright, *Passions*, 167–168; Haar, 'False Relations and Chromaticism', 413.

[67] Susan Vincent, *Dressing the Elite: Clothes in Early Modern England* (Oxford: Berg, 2003). For more on English Renaissance fashion, see Hester Lees-Jeffries, *Textile Shakespeare* (Oxford: Oxford University Press, forthcoming); Ann Rosland Jones and Peter Stallybrass, *Renaissance Clothing and the Materials of Memory* (Cambridge: Cambridge University Press, 2000).

[68] Larson, *Matter of Song*, 79–81. See also Richard Wistreich, 'Vocal Performance in the Seventeenth Century', in Colin Lawson and Robin Stowell (eds.), *The Cambridge History of Musical Performance* (Cambridge: Cambridge University Press, 2012), 398–420.

and the act of performing or hearing a false relation, would have provoked a broad range of dimly registering associations, available in the metaphorical language that describes the visual placement and shaping of sound into music. Such associations are of vital use to us in the twenty-first century, as we examine musical-visual objects like the pitch space diagrams of Campion, Morley, and Bathe, and seek to re-access the musical culture of the English Renaissance.

Picturing Discord

There is one element indisputably shared between the musical and visual cultures of the English Renaissance, by dint of its all-encompassing influence: that of the printing press. This technological innovation altered the visual expectations of readers, viewers, and listeners beyond the form of the book or pamphlet. The impact of the advent of print upon verbal literacy is well established.[69] Less well explored is the parallel impact that it had upon visual literacy across the sixteenth and into the early seventeenth centuries. Print vastly altered how people received information, the way they thought about things like taste, decoration, and recreation, and vitally, how they thought about space and the distribution of things (motifs, people, buildings, musical notes) within that space.

In some areas of musical culture, it was a long time before the innovation of print was adopted wholeheartedly. Indeed, manuscript continued to be an important medium of musical dissemination well into the seventeenth century, as testified to by the high number of musical manuscript examples in this book. There were a number of likely contributing factors, not least the difficulty of typesetting music and the increased number of impressions (and with it, the increased potential for error) brought about by the process. Nevertheless it is evident that print had a pervasive (albeit slow) impact upon the musical culture of the English Renaissance, such that a number of the manuscripts contained in this book (such as the Hamond set, as we will see in Chapter 5), are written onto the printed music papers produced by Thomas East following his association with Tallis and Byrd and the royal

---

[69] Elizabeth Eisenstein, *The Printing Revolution in Early Modern Europe* (Cambridge: Cambridge University Press, 1983); John Man, *The Gutenberg Revolution: The Story of a Genius and an Invention That Changed the World* (London: Review, 2002); Neil Rhodes and Jonathan Sawday (eds.), *The Renaissance Computer: Knowledge Technology in the First Age of Print* (London: Routledge, 2000).

granting of their music printing monopoly in 1575.[70] Another vital clue lies in the extremely careful integration of textual and visual elements in musical printed texts such as Morley's *Plaine and Easie Introduction to Practicall Musicke*, Campion's *New Way of making fowre parts in counter-point*, and Bathe's *Skill of Song*, at the end of the sixteenth and the turn of the seventeenth centuries.[71] By this point, there was evidently an expectation of how music education and instruction should be conducted, and one that had been heavily influenced by the technology of print with the expectation that visual diagrammatics were a necessary didactic inclusion.[72] Towards the end of the sixteenth century, music books had become the site of many of the most innovative graphic formats and *mise-en-page* set-ups, as demonstrated by the rise of the table book format (see MS 31390 in Chapters 5 and 6, Morley's *Plaine and Easie Introduction*, later editions of Charles Butler's musical-beekeeping treatise *The Feminine Monarchie* of 1609, and Dowland's 1609 translation of *Micrologus*).[73]

Music books were not the only places in which novel graphic formats became increasingly popular across the English Renaissance. Katherine Acheson has argued that the 'visual rhetoric' by which the diagrammatic images that developed across the late sixteenth and seventeenth centuries sought to form a new language of representation.[74] Examining visual objects such as tables, plans, and schemes, Acheson looks directly at the 'patterns, categories and methods of inference; training in a range of representational conventions; and experience, drawn from the environment, in what are plausible ways of visualizing what we have incomplete information about'[75] used in a diverse range of practical manuals at the turn of the seventeenth

---

[70] Katherine Butler, 'Printed Borders for Sixteenth-Century Music or Music Paper and the Early Career of Music Printer Thomas East', in *The Library*, 19: 2 (June 2018); Iain Fenlon and John Milsom, '"Ruled Paper Imprinted": Music Paper and Patents in Sixteenth-Century England', in *Journal of the American Musicological Society*, 37 (1984), 139–163. See also Tessa Murray, *Thomas Morley: Elizabethan Music Publisher* (Suffolk: Boydell and Brewer, 2014), particularly 71–73.

[71] A new exploration of the integration of graphic elements is forthcoming by Jessie Ann Owens and John Milsom.

[72] It is worth noting that despite the immense amount of care that went into Morley's *Introduction*, the first impression was still full of mistakes, as testified to by the errata appended to the earlier impressions and the manuscript corrections still to be found in a number of surviving copies (see Douce M 750 in the Bodleian Library in Oxford, and Hirsch I 416, k.3/m/6 and 59.c.16 in the British Library). Tessa Murray, *Thomas Morley*, 78–79 and 160–161.

[73] John Dowland, *Andreas Ornithoparcus his Micrologus* (London: Thomas Snodham for Thomas Adams, 1609).

[74] Katherine Acheson, *Visual Rhetoric and Early Modern English Literature* (Farnham: Ashgate, 2013).

[75] Michael Baxandall, *Painting and Experience in Fifteenth-Century Italy* (Oxford: Oxford University Press, 1972), 32.

century to convey dense amounts or new forms of information using the graphic forms made available to them by the printing press.[76] Focussing on the importance of diagrams for military strategy, garden design and technical works, all 'devices that enabled users [...] to flatten three-dimensional forms into two-dimensional representations',[77] she explores the way that print innovations significantly altered the methods of inference available to infer order to visual experience. Her analysis of the visual form of the table is of particular use to the present investigation:

> [Tables] provide the *method* for the acquisition of information and the establishment of relationships that constitute bodies of knowledge. They are, in short, epistemological forms: because they entail particular relationships between cause and effect, parts and wholes, and plots and narrative, *they powerfully shape the nature of the fields in which they are used and the minds of those who produce and consume knowledge through them.* (my italics)[78]

Acheson's argument, pitched to provide tools that 'allow us to interpret visual phenomena as visual phenomena, rather than as versions of things that could be as well or even better said in words',[79] provides a tantalizing way to approach the pitch space diagrams of the *Whole Booke of Psalmes* from the mid-sixteenth century onwards and of Bathe, Morley, and Campion, as discussed above. We will explore the table in greater detail below, in Chapter 5, with regards to its educational efficacy. For the present, however, it is worth observing that its rise in dominance is possibly due to the limiting factors of print technology. Given the difficulty in producing musical type, and the way that printed music lagged behind other forms of print, it is likely that the use of the scale derived directly from the limitations of print: technically speaking, it was harder to produce a woodblock of the Guidonian hand than the scale.[80] Scalar diagrams had long existed in tandem with the

---

[76] This has been explored in greater depth as a literary phenomenon by Claire M. L. Bourne, *Typographies of Performance in Early Modern England* (Oxford: Oxford University Press, 2020); and Rachel Stenner, *The Typographic Imaginary in Early Modern English Literature* (London and New York: Routledge, 2018).

[77] Acheson, *Visual Rhetoric*, 44.

[78] Ibid., 6.

[79] Ibid., 4.

[80] There were plenty of printed Guidonian hands, but in continental and earlier sources. Jane D. Hatter, 'Constructing the Composer: Symbolic Use of the Hexachord in Compositions c. 1500', in *Composing Community in Late Medieval Music: Self-Reference, Pedagogy, and Practice* (Cambridge: Cambridge University Press, 2019).

Guidonian hand, but before the second half of the sixteenth century they were broadly complementary graphic forms rather than representations of gradually diverging conceptualization of pitch space. The Guidonian hand had gradually slipped out of favour as a pitch-mapping form across the English Renaissance, as the preference began to be for scalar models. Whilst we certainly should not assume that it ceased to be adopted in musical education and in conjunction with the ladder/scale formats used by Bathe, Morley, and Campion, this shift is important. The pitch space diagrams of the turn of the seventeenth century are crucial steps towards the pitch space diagrams based on the keyboard and string instruments that would rise to popularity later in the seventeenth century, and which would afford a far broader range of tonal movement.[81]

We should not underestimate the impact of the English Renaissance table, and with it the printed musical scale upon the musical imagination. To state as much might appear boringly obvious, but this is to underestimate the influence it had upon the directional, navigational facets of musical pitch space. In other words, creating a musical imaginary that is scalar vitally affects the way that a potential singer/performer (and indeed listener) will think about their movement between pitches, and the potential paths that a melodic line can take. On the Guidonian hand (see Fig. 1.1), these paths are by their inherent nature more malleable: the movement from Gamut in stepwise terms to A-*re*, B-*mi*, and so on, right up to gg-*solreut*, is a serpentine but inflexible twist across the joints of the hand, coiling back in on itself to express the full range of musical pitches. Each finger enables the reading across hexachords (*molle, naturale, durum*), whilst having a fixed finger joint and pitch at which it is possible to move from contains the potential for movement. In a scalar diagram of pitch space, the only possible movements are orthogonal: up, down, or (in the case of the *mi–fa* interval), across, oblique. This is not to mention the difference between learning a pattern of pitch space from the physical hand of a Director of Music, Master of the Choristers, or Music Tutor, and from a printed diagram (be it hand or scalar). The shift away from the body to the woodblock-printed paper page gradually built a collective understanding of the pattern of pitch space that 'powerfully shape the nature

---

[81] Long, *Hearing Homophony*, 44. Harold Powers, 'From Psalmody to Tonality', in Cristle Collins Judd (ed.), *Tonal Structures in Early Music* (London: Routledge, 1998), 276. See also Samantha Arten, 'The Origin of Fixed-Scale Solmization in *The Whole Booke of Psalmes*', in *Early Music*, 46: 1 (February 2018), 149–165. See also Richard Robinson, '"A perfect-full harmonie": Pitch, Tuning and Instruments in the Elizabethan and Jacobean Mixed Consort', in *Early Music*, 47: 2 (May 2019), 199–223.

of the fields in which they are used and the minds of those who produce and consume knowledge through them'. As Samantha Arten notes, the earliest instances of these sorts of diagrams are to be found in editions of the *Whole Booke of Psalmes*,[82] demonstrating the desire to reach a far broader audience than had been possible before the advent of print and induct them into a new way of musical seeing, knowing, and imagining. The page, increasingly more widely available to a broader body of musical readers and performers, offered a crucial abstracted space within which to experiment with tonal possibility.

The pattern of pitch space made possible by the scalar model allowed for far greater freedom of movement, and for the potential placement of other pitches within its structure. In this sense the scalar model was aided by the developing visual culture of its disciplinary relation, mathematics. Across the second half of the sixteenth century, mathematics began to be understood as a tool for practical usage, rather than theoretical purposes; aided by translations into the English vernacular by practitioners such as Robert Recorde and Leonard Digges, it was transformed from a kind of sixteenth-century sudoku into a method to aid the work of joiners, masons, tailors, broderers, printers, and other craftsmen, as well as the professions that would come to be known as 'scientific' later in the seventeenth century.[83] By and large this shift was achieved by careful usage of craft metaphors to describe the actions and properties of the geometrical elements, the point, the line, the 'surface' or 'platte' (now more generally known as the plain), and the body.[84] Such an alteration laid the groundwork for the development of analytic, abstract geometry. However, it also heavily influenced the patterns of pitch space that evolved across the sixteenth century, tied to the scalar model as first seen in the *Whole Booke of Psalmes* (as we saw in Chapter 3). Of particular interest is the interaction between the line and the surface, and the metaphors used to build an imaginary of their relationship. Sixteenth-century English vernacular mathematical texts follow the standard

---

[82] Arten, 'Fixed-Scale Solmization'.

[83] For more on this, see Henry S. Turner, *The English Renaissance Stage: Geometry, Poetics, and the Practical Spatial Arts* (Oxford: Oxford University Press, 2006); Yelda Nasifoglu, 'Reading by Drawing: The Changing Nature of Mathematical Diagrams in Seventeenth-Century England', in Philip Beeley, Yelda Nasifoglu, and Benjamin Wardhaugh (eds.), *Reading Mathematics in Early Modern Europe: Studies in the Production, Collection and Use of Mathematical Books* (London: Routledge, 2021); Jennifer M. Rampling, 'The Elizabethan Mathematics of everything: John Dee's "Mathematicall Praeface" to Euclid's *Elements*', in *Journal of the British Society for the History of Mathematics*, 26: 3 (2011).

[84] Eleanor Chan, *Mathematics and the Craft of Thought in the Anglo-Dutch Renaissance* (London: Routledge, 2021), 3–10.

Aristotelian formula of defining the line as an accumulation of points: 'Nowe of a great number of these prickes, is made a Lyne, as you may perceive by this form ensuing . . . .'.[85] Their concept of how lines accumulate to become surfaces or lates, however, is a new invention: lines are meshed, woven, or twisted to become a surface, as threads are to create cloth. This is the way that Robert Recorde frames the importance of geometrical knowledge at the outset of his *Pathway to Knowledge* (1551):

> Carpenters, Carvers, Joiners and Masons,
> Painters and Limners with suche occupations,
> Broderers, Goldsmithes, if they be cunning,
> Must yelde to Geometrye thankes for their learning [...]
> So weavers by Geometrye hade their fondacion,
> Their Loome is a frame of strange imaginacion.[86]

Recorde's 'Loome' or 'frame of strange imaginacion' is, of course, of use to another group of people whom he does not mention: musicians, amateur and professional. John Dee makes no such omission in his 'Mathematicall Praeface' to Henry Billingsley's *Euclid* (1570): 'Musicke is a Mathematicall Science, which teacheth, by sense and reason, perfectly to judge, and order the diversities of soundes hye and low [...] from audible sound, we ought to ascende, to the examination: which numbers are *Harmonious*, and which are not.'[87]

The 'loome' or 'frame of strange imaginacion' is visually related to the scalar models of pitch space we encountered above. The resemblance is unsurprising: the Classical concept of the Quadrivium, still in use in universities in the English Renaissance, interpreted music as a sub-branch of mathematics along with geometry, and so the two subjects were closely related. However, Recorde's concept raises an intriguing slant on how one was expected to traverse the scale. His 'loome' presupposes a mesh or web of warp and weft threads

---

[85] Robert Recorde, *The Pathway to Knowledge, Containing the First Principles of Geometrie* (London: Reginald Wolfe, 1551), 1; Aristotle, *De Lineis Insecabilibus*, in Jonathan Barnes (ed.), *The Complete Works of Aristotle*, Vol. 2 (Princeton, NJ: Princeton University Press, 1984). Recorde also uses the traditional Euclidean formulation of the line as being 'Lengthe withoute breadth'. Intriguingly, in his geometrical work, *Problematum Geometricum*, Simon Stevin makes no attempt to define the point at all. This is presumably due to the fact that it was composed in Latin, and therefore for people who had ready access to the Latin translation of Euclid's *Elementes*, which had been widely available in scholastic circles for almost a hundred years; see Simon Stevin, *Problematum Geometricum* (Antwerp: Ioannem Bellerum, 1583).

[86] Recorde, *Pathway to Knowledge*, fol. g.ii.

[87] John Dee, 'Mathematicall Praeface', in Henry Billingsley, *Elements of Euclid* (London: John Daye, 1570), fol. Biii. See also fol. Diiij.

that are fundamentally malleable rather than rigidly immobile.[88] To assert as much in a mathematical context may seem peculiar, but returning to the ways that Recorde and his contemporaries define geometrical elements it is clear that mutability (that very hexachord-related word) was an inherent part of how they imagined the geometrical system, and with it the properties of all the mathematical arts. Recorde lists, amongst permissible geometrical lines, the 'croked' line (a spiral form) and a 'twiste or twine' line, wrapped around a Doric column.[89] Digges, likewise, writes that 'the shortest drawen between two Poyntes is a straight line, the contrary are crooked lines'.[90] As a related mathematical art, music in the English Renaissance was likewise inflected by this interpretation of the way that geometrical elements interacted, and could be used to produce a table, chair, a bridge, the constituent elements of a building, a painting or limning, an embroidered garment, and, crucially, a piece of music. If one could geometrically construct in between warp and weft, and by manipulating warp and weft, then one could lead a melodic line through a conduit that pulled the gaps between their analogues, full tone placement on the scale, tighter or looser, 'hye or low'. A culture that could conceive of the geometrical potential of a 'twiste', 'twine', and 'croked' line would not have interpreted solmization scales as strict records of pitch relations. This is supported by the anonymous *Praise of Musicke*'s very textile, and loosely pliable definition of concord as 'unlike voyces within themselves, *tackt together, sweetly sounding unto the eare*' (my italics).[91] Ironically, the move to fix pitch space on printers' woodblocks led to an increased sense of a singer/performer/composer's agency to intervene in the pattern of pitch space, and to fashion it to their will.[92]

Visual depictions of musical subjects testify to the impact that these graphic shifts had upon the English Renaissance imagination. Fig. 4.9 is a large and elegantly monochrome wall-painting now in Thame Museum, Oxfordshire, taken from a first floor chamber at 34 Upper High Street, Thame (c. 1560). The wall-painting spreads across three walls and the ceiling and depicts a variety of scenes

---

[88] Vincent, *Dressing the Elite*, 53.
[89] Recorde, *Pathway to Knowledge*, 8.
[90] Leonard Digges, *A Geometrical Practice, named Pantometria* (London: Henrie Bynneman, 1571), unpaginated.
[91] Attributed to John Case, *The Praise of Musicke* (Oxford: Joseph Barnes, 1586); for more on this see Linda Phyllis Austern, *Both from the Ears and Mind: Thinking about Music in Early Modern England* (Chicago: University of Chicago Press, 2020), 100.
[92] Herissone's arguments about the understanding of creativity and authorship in the late seventeenth century demonstrate that this continued to be an important facet of the development of patterns of pitch space for a long time after the period in question. Herissone, *Musical Creativity*, 1–3.

Fig. 4.9 Anonymous, monochromatic wall painting depicting music-making, cartouches, cornucopia, and strapwork and arabesque decoration taken from the upper room at 34 Upper High Street, Thame, Oxfordshire, c. 1560. Thame Museum, Thame, Oxfordshire. Photograph author's own.

from domestic life, collapsed into one eternal moment and gathered around a scrolled circular cartouche.[93] The cartouche reads, in blackletter script:

<blockquote>
The First E
Of Saint Paule for romans
O the depnes of the aboundant
Wisdom of God: howe uncerchable
Are his judgements & his ways paste
Finding out: for who hathe knwen ye
minde of ye Lord? Or who was his con
celoure? Other who hathe given unto
Him first that he might be recompencyd a
</blockquote>

---

[93] Tara Hamling and Catherine Richardson, *A Day at Home in Early Modern England* (London: Paul Mellon Centre for Studies in British Art, 2017), 202–206.

gayne? For of him, and through him
And for him are all things
To him be glory for
Ever and ever
Amen.[94]

To the right at the bottom of the wall is another, damaged cartouche, which collapses two sentences from Pythagoras and Aristotle, which had been published by William Baldwin in his *Treatise of Morall Philosophie* (1547). It reads:

Desire nothing of God,
Save what is profitable.
Science is had by diligence:
But discretion and wisdom cometh from God.[95]

Above this second cartouche are cornucopia swags, and the trace of faces gazing up at the text, and across back to the central cartouche and the figures that surround it. To the left of the central text sits a woman playing or tuning a lute, in a pose that echoes Oliver's Fig. 4.1, and two children reading from a partbook; echoing them, on the other side, is the fragment of the neck, nuts, pegbox and scroll of a bass viol, and another fragment of the edge of its body (the remainder was lost when the wall-painting was uncovered). Their gazes do not cross or interact, but rather direct the eyes of the viewer to yet more elements of the composition. Above them, fragments of moresque/strapwork patterning decorate the ceiling, containing the scene as a whole and providing the sense of an edge.[96] Tara Hamling and Catherine Richardson note that this chamber, beside the bedchamber on the first floor, was likely a multi-functional space where the family came together to pray, eat, and make music, amongst other things, and so that the theme of social harmony is particularly apposite.[97] The painted musical figures sit enmeshed in the interplay of gazes, deictically drawing the eye to other elements within the wall painting as a whole, across and indeed outwards to the room that

---

[94] Ibid., 205.
[95] Ibid.
[96] Katherine Butler, 'Printed Borders for Sixteenth Century Music or Music Paper and the Career of Music Printer Thomas East', in *The Library*, 19: 2 (June 2018), 174–175 and 205. See also Juliet Fleming, *Cultural Graphology: Writing after Derrida* (Chicago: University of Chicago Press, 2016), and 'How to Look at a Printed Flower', in *Word & Image*, 22: 2 (2006).
[97] Hamling and Richardson, *A Day at Home*, 206.

no longer exists beyond. Fig. 4.9 very palpably imitates the interpersonal dynamic of a consort group, keeping time and pitch together whilst simultaneously reaching out to their audience. In its lack of hierarchical planarity, it quite literally creates a venue for cross-relations.[98]

The surviving two-dimensional art objects of the English Renaissance were for many years derided for their queasy, skewed perspectives, their refusal to adhere to fixed-point perspective and proportion. It is now clear that what appears visually dissonant to our eyes, trained in a 'cognitive style'[99] influenced by the Italian Renaissance and its descendants, was in fact a combination of deliberate trends and techniques. One need look no further than the fashions of the period, and the above-mentioned head-on-a-plate aesthetic of the large, diaphanous yet stiff ruff, often paired with an elongated torso and puffed sleeves, skirts, and breeches: the English Renaissance eye was accustomed to distortion, and far more invested in what things looked like from multiple perspectives, as one moved, rather than from a frozen fixed point. Fig. 4.9 is certainly not the most audaciously skewed, when compared to *Four Children Making Music* by the Master of the Countess of Warwick (c. 1565, Fig. 1.2), but it captures something of that understanding of how to compose a picture.

I stated above that the visual art objects of the English Renaissance betray very little interest in fixed-point perspective and are instead interested in pattern, depth as the texture of sumptuous fabrics and furnishings, and a multiplicity of perspective points and temporal moments (as epitomized by Fig. 1.2, and the anonymous *Life of Sir Henry Unton*, c. 1596, Fig. 4.10). David Evett has defined this approach to visual composition as 'parataxis', images 'built up by the serial addition of elements of relatively equal importance, rather than by the formal as well as the logical subordination of some elements to others', which 'in effect trusts viewers to place their own emphasis'.[100] Michel Foucault suggests something similar in his concept of the 'grid of resemblance' that constitutes the 'renaissance episteme':

> Up to the end of the sixteenth century, resemblance played a constructive role in the knowledge of Western culture [...] it was resemblance that

---

[98] Tim Shephard, *Echoing Helicon: Music, Art and Identity in the Este Atudioli, 1440–1530* (Oxford: Oxford University Press, 2014), 141–142.
[99] Michael Baxandall, *Painting and Experience in Fifteenth-Century Italy* (Oxford: Oxford University Press, 1972), 32.
[100] David Evett, *Literature and the Visual Arts in Tudor England* (London: University of Georgia Press, 1990), 10 and 235.

Fig. 4.10 Anonymous, *The Life of Sir Henry Unton*, oil on panel, c. 1596, London: National Portrait Gallery, Object No. NPG710. Public domain.

organized the play of symbols, made possible knowledge of things visible and invisible, and controlled the art of representing them. The universe was folded in upon itself: the earth echoing the sky, faces seeing themselves reflected in the stars, and plants holding within their stems the secrets that were of use to man. Painting imitated space. And representation—whether in the service of pleasure or of knowledge—was posited as a form of repetition.[101]

Both models of the alternative approach to visual space are compelling, but of course are not without their problems, particularly in a musical context. Evett's 'paratactic' approach in particular sits uneasily with the developing hierarchical models of composition that underlay the move towards tonality and indeed Carl Dahlhaus's use of the term 'parataxis' (as encountered above in Chapter 3), and Foucault's 'representation as repetition' is based on now outmoded interpretations of the Scientific Revolution as the great paradigm shift of the early modern period; scholarship of the last forty years has revealed that the groundwork for the Scientific Revolution occurred across the sixteenth century.[102] Nevertheless, both accounts provide useful ways into understanding the approach to picturing adopted by visual artists in the English Renaissance, and the logic behind art objects like Figs. 4.9, 1.1, and 4.10.

We have strayed far from the visual acuity required by the shift from musical hand to musical scale. To return, explicitly, to the impact of the scalar model of pitch space, and the visual effect of its pattern as the fundamental shape of the musical system: models such as Evett's 'parataxis' and Foucault's grid of resemblance can help us understand the impact that the graphic shift in conventions of representing pitch space had upon the musical imaginary, and in turn how the false relation interaction might have been visualized. In the context of visual art objects with musical subjects such as Figs. 4.9 and 1.1, we should take the representation of pitch space as a key contextual element. Fig. 4.9 appears to be heavily influenced by the visual appearance and appeal of print, due not only to its choice of elegantly restrained monochrome but also to the fragmentary evidence that it was once framed or

---

[101] Michel Foucault, *The Order of Things: An Archaeology of the Human Sciences* (London: Routledge, 2002), 19.
[102] Deborah Harkness, *The Jewel House: Elizabethan London and the Scientific Revolution* (New Haven, CT: Yale University Press, 2007); Turner, *English Renaissance Stage*; Sachiko Kusukawa, *Picturing the Book of Nature: Image, Text, and Argument in Sixteenth Century Human Anatomy and Medical Botany* (Chicago: University of Chicago Press).

bordered by strapwork and moresque edges, mirroring the printer's flowers that were used to mark the edge of the musical text and prevent smudging during multiple print impressions. Monochrome moresque or strapwork 'damask papers' were a common interior design feature in the sixteenth century, decorative papers that could be used for wallpapers, lining papers, book bindings, and pattern sheets.[103] Blackwork embroidery also became increasingly popular across the English Renaissance (Fig. 4.11). Its aesthetic of black-dyed silk thread in strapwork[104] and moresque[105] motifs on linen was a cost-effective way of mimicking the visual appearance of lace (which was heavily taxed) as well as a nod to the burgeoning taste for the 'exotic', strange, or foreign, as demonstrated by the term 'moresque' and the apocryphal origins of the blackwork trend in the arrival of Catherine of Aragon in England in 1501, bringing with her the North African decorative art form. This trend likely increased the desire for printer's flowers as a mark of restrained opulence. By means of the quotation of the visual appearance of print, the wall painting as a whole becomes a form of echo of the printed page; its layers, an analogue of the stave. The relationship between the two children with the partbook and the lute-playing female figure is generated not simply by the fact that they are thematically allied, but also because they are positionally allied, too. The singing children are above the lute-playing female figure. The edges of their bodies, left 'white' or unpainted against the stark wash of black to their left, follow the rhythmic line of the curve of the strapwork cartouche that frames the melded quotation from Pythagoras and Aristotle. Following the logic of the 'paratactic' perspective, that imagines multiple viewing perspectives in one collapsed moment, they accompany each other, both physically and musically: they are beside each other, behind and in front of each other as well as above and below. They are of a piece. They do not look at each other, because they do not need to; they are united by the implied music that they are playing. They combine to create the same imagined musical texture, the same inferred polyphony. In this way we can read them as notes or even short motives on a staff, in the way that they interact, bolster, and complement each other within the structure of the

---

[103] Juliet Fleming, 'Damask Papers', in Emma Smith and Andy Kesson (eds.), *The Elizabethan Top Ten: Defining Print Popularity in Early Modern England* (London: Routledge, 2013), 179–192.

[104] Ethan Matt Kavaler, 'Ornament and Systems of Ordering in the Sixteenth-Century Netherlands', in *Renaissance Quarterly*, 72: 4 (2020), 1269–1325.

[105] 'Moreske worke; a rude, or anticke painting, or caving, wherein the feet and tayels of beasts &c., are intermingled with, or made to resemble, a kind of wild leaves, &c.'; Randle Cotgrave, *A dictionarie of the French and English tongues* (London: Adam Islip, 1611).

Fig. 4.11 Anonymous, smock part embroidered in blackwork embroidery with black silk floss on bleached linen, 1575–1585, London: Victoria & Albert Museum, Accession Number: T.113 to 118-1997. By kind permission of the Victoria & Albert Museum.

image. Across the cartouche is a literal 'cross' relation, what presumably were another group of musical figures now represented solely by the remnants of the bass viol; our eyes are directed towards the lost grouping by the gaze of a figure to the bottom right of its fragmentary outline. In this way, Fig. 4.9 allegorizes the music-making culture that enshrined false relations as a mark not only of skill[106] but also of the unity of the musical ensemble that was able to perform them without losing the key.

Juliet Fleming has written of the way that printed flowers, or type ornament, undercut the binary between word and image in early modern books. Her analysis is of use when attempting to understand the way of seeing invited by a picture like Fig. 4.9, and the elaborate interplay between printed text as appearance, printed text as idea, and printed text as semantic import:

> To understand type ornament in this way is to be able to see the printed page not as site for information but as a visual field whose intricate black lines and white spaces provoke sensations of movement and light and whose vibrating surface combines regularity and recurrence with a commitment to systemic local variance. Making the visual proposition 'this is what writing looks like' even as it continues to manifest its own isotropic beauty, type ornament encourages readers to think about writing under the aspect of appearance, and by turning the page into nonpurposive space it breaks the stranglehold that the semantic function otherwise exerts over phonetic writing. [. . .] Still, it is worth remarking that, to the untrained eye of most readers, type letters and type ornament do not stay combined but separate like poorly made mayonnaise. It is even true to say that the decorative and the semantic elements are never *seen* together (even where, in a well-formed letter, they are the same thing). For where text is read, its beauties will be overlooked; and where its beauties are studied, the text disappears.[107]

In less abstract theoretical terms, this is similar to her claims about the damask papers that the remaining ceiling fragments so strongly resemble:

> Patterns are collocations of visual, affective and cognitive resources, so even if we could separate the contents of 'lasting' poems or wallpaper designs from the sheets of paper that gave them material support we would still be unable to discriminate between them in terms of their influence or endurance.[108]

Fleming is writing specifically about the nature of writing through the lens of Derrida's assertion in his *Grammatology* that we fundamentally do not

---

[106] Larson, *Matter of Song*, 80.
[107] Fleming, *Cultural Graphology*, 84.
[108] Fleming, 'Damask Papers', 180.

know where writing begins and ends.[109] In a musical context this semantic/decorative leakiness is compounded by the fundamental question of the ramifications that this model has on the act of reading: of reading music, of reading an accidental (through the processes discussed above in Chapter 1), and of reading a musical performance as an audience member/spectator. We cannot directly translate Fleming's statement: where music is read, its beauties will be overlooked; and where its beauties are studied, the music disappears. It does not work in a musical context, because of the question of utterance, voice, and the ephemerality of the performance.[110] A musical text is never without sound. One does not unproblematically reproduce or represent the other, but they are semantically complementary.[111] In this sense, Fig. 4.9 captures the tensions at the heart of a printed page of music and the way that it generates meaning: a tension that in turn is the essence of the false relation, the slippery *mi–fa* interval, and the culture of discord.[112]

A group of singers or instrumental musicians join together to make music, under, around, beside a cartouche that proclaims the 'ways paste [/] Finding out: for who hathe knwen ye [/] minde of ye Lord?'. One of those 'ways' is mirrored in the partbook held by the small children. The notation is not quite legible and there are only three stave lines instead of five, but close inspection reveals that some effort has gone into making it appear authentic and the trace of some diamond-shaped note heads are visible (see Fig. 4.9). The appearance of notation within the fabric of the wall painting thus explicitly alludes to the need to read *through* the musical notation to the shape of the music to be performed. Like the bodies beneath the diaphanous folds of linen worn by the musicians themselves in shirt collars, cuffs, sleeves, the notation, and Fig. 4.9 in the way that it depicts and contemplates music-making, assumes a visuality that reads between the lines to the music that unites the surviving figures of the children and the lute-playing female figure, and their lost companions to the left of the wall painting.

Such traces of the structure of visual expectation and convention with an object of English Renaissance musical visual culture are important. They tell us that many of the conventions of musical culture associated specifically

[109] Ibid., 28.
[110] Jennifer Richards has recently, importantly, argued that we should not ignore the role of the voice in reading in general. See Jennifer Richards, *Voices and Books in the English Renaissance* (Oxford: Oxford University Press, 2019).
[111] For more on this, see Herissone, *Musical Creativity*, 61, 70, and 119.
[112] For more on the way the enjoyment of musical ambiguity permeated into the broader culture of the English Renaissance, see Ortiz, *Broken Harmony*, 2–5.

with the performance of false relations infused into the way that images of music-making were conceived as visual compositions. They also tell us that music was understood to be a visual phenomenon, one that required a certain way of seeing and knowing. This way of seeing and knowing extended beyond the practice of solmization and the ability to read music as notes on the page to the 'Mysticall Subtleties' that Bacon complained of. It fed the eyes as well as the ears and mind, and the *mi–fa* interval and all the sonic slippages it gave rise to were emblematic of this visual frisson, the hidden riddle, the secret, the inferred wrinkle, pleat, quill, in the pattern of the hexachord. This chapter has moved across a variety of visual sources, from Oliver's evocative sketch to the very visual metaphors of music and sound, to the intricate musical scene of the Thame wall painting. In each, the way that music is imagined is shaped by the parameters set by its inherent ephemerality; each riffs on the fleeting, evasive, dissimulating capacity of the musical system. The tantalizing interplay between what is visible and what is not, what is audible and what is not, evidently proved fertile food for thought for those producing objects of visual culture, just as it was for those producing objects of musical culture. This much is made palpable by the shifting perspective of Oliver's lute-playing female figure, the elegant Thame wall-painting, and the accounts of sound production, all of which search for ways to depict the intangible aspects of reading, performing, and listening to music in the English Renaissance. These visual art objects may seem a far cry from the practices that enshrined false relations as a key stylistic feature of musical culture. However, to ignore extant objects from the further reaches of this culture of false relation is to overlook vital traces into the ways of thinking, seeing, and knowing that fed into making that culture a source of delight to listeners and performers. Looking at visual art objects like Figs. 4.1, 4.9, and 1.2 with a critical eye allows us to adopt the rose-tinted spectacles that allowed people to look with fondness on the accidental by-products impelled by the logic of voice leading, and with nostalgia on the older models of reading and composing music as they slowly but surely became redundant. It is vital, as we turn to the more traditional musicological material in the second section of this book, that we keep these lessons from the broader visual culture in mind.

SECTION II
PERFORMING

5
How to Train Your Discord

Performing Falseness

Miscellaneity, Mélange, Melée

On the inside cover of the Cantus book from the Hamond partbooks, someone has drawn two little birds. Perhaps it is Philip Hamond, the name rehearsed again and again in pen trials across the same page—or perhaps his child, or another child from the household. What is certain is the genesis of the birds; that their little knock-knee joints began their lives as two lozenge-form minims, also carefully if shakily rehearsed elsewhere on the page and yet to receive their full avian form. This is just one instance of marginalia to be found in the upper two partbooks from the 'Hamond' set, and the trace of the role they once played. The *idea* of musical notation has suffused beyond its textual musical content, into the metaphorical. Was the doodler inspired by the visual resemblance between the lozenge notation shapes and the knock-knees of birds? Perhaps the idea of bird song? Or indeed, the pun between 'Byrd' (five pieces by the composer William Byrd appear in the partbook) and 'bird'? The bird itself appears to be fantastical, vacillating somewhere between an ostrich, a grebe, and a plover. However, I would hazard that the actual species of bird evoked is not the point of this doodle. It is an imaginative prompt, the record of a singer-reader being imaginatively prompted: an invitation to think beyond the music as notated.[1]

Such speculation may appear merely incidental to the musicological meat of the Hamond set. However, throughout this chapter I will argue that it is in fact a key clue to unravel in our efforts to understand false relations in the English Renaissance and their connection to the broader culture. Katherine Butler has established that the 'Hamond' set began life as a 'liturgical and educational collection for the training of choirboys'.[2] By the time the set had

---

[1] I discuss the connotations of approaching marginalia as a visual extra-notational form in my article, 'Scrollwork: Visual Culture of Musical Notation and Graphic Materiality in the English Renaissance', in *Journal of Medieval and Early Modern Studies*, 53: 2 (May 2023), 347–377.

[2] Katherine Butler, 'From Liturgy and the Education of Choirboys to Protestant Domestic Music-Making: The History of the "Hamond" Partbooks (GB-Lbl: Add. MSS 30480-4)', in *Royal Musical*

entered the collection of Thomas Hamond, its first recorded owner and perhaps the grandson of the Philip Hamond who rehearsed his name so diligently, the partbooks were already around forty-five years old. Throughout those forty-five years between c. 1570 and 1615 (when the partbooks entered the Hamond collection), they had by no means been static entities. No fewer than four layers of copying are evident, with the situation 'further complicated by the exceptionally numerous text and notation hands—many belonging to inexperienced copyists judging by their awkwardly formed note shapes—and a copying span of nearing 50 years'.[3] The experience of making music from the 'Hamond' set, neither elegant nor especially coherent, would have been one that consistently and forcibly reminded the singer of the collaborative nature of music, and that a piece of music was never fully finished or completed at the moment that it was committed to the page.

The Hamond set presents us with an array of tantalizing potential insights into the false relation, not least the question of how they were introduced to those learning music in the English Renaissance, and how it might have influenced and impelled certain educational practices and structures. The education of choristers forms the most well-documented type available to us today, and so it is this matter that we will explore in most depth; whilst Morley's premise is of an adult amateur learning music for the first time, it is clear from Morley's own background and the apparent pastiche he creates of a fusty if slightly arch music master that he is drawing upon the education of choristers. As Jane Flynn has established, the education of choristers can be divided into two main periods: the approach adopted before around 1565, and the approach adopted afterwards. The early to mid-sixteenth-century approach began at around the age of seven with 'song', a combination of Latin grammar and chant.[4] Choristers were taught to read and write, and to

---

Association Research Chronicle, 50: 1 (2019), 29–93. For older research on the partbooks, see May Hofman, 'The Survival of Latin Sacred Music by English Composers 1485–1610' (unpublished DPhil diss., University of Oxford 1977), 70–85 and 250–260; Warwick Edwards, 'The Sources of Elizabethan Consort Music' (unpublished PhD diss., University of Cambridge, 1977), 121–126.

[3] Butler, 'History of the Hamond Partbooks', 30.

[4] Jane Flynn, 'The Education of Choristers in England during the Sixteenth Century', in John Morehen (ed.), *English Choral Practice 1400–1650* (Cambridge: Cambridge University Press, 1996), 180–199, at 182. See also Susan Boynton and Eric Rice (eds.), *Young Choristers, 650–1700* (Woodbridge: Boydell & Brewer, 2012); Jane Flynn, 'Thomas Mulliner: An Apprentice of John Heywood?', in Susan Boynton and Eric Rice (eds.), *Young Choristers, 650–1700* (Woodbridge: Boydell & Brewer, 2012), 173–194; Anne Heminger, 'Music Theory at Work: The Eton Choirbook, Rhythmic Proportions and Musical Networks in Sixteenth-Century England', in *Early Music History*, 37 (2018), 141–182; Jonathan Willis, *Church Music and Protestantism in Post-Reformation England: Discourses, Sites and Identities* (Farnham: Ashgate, 2009) 169–172.

memorize the psalms with their psalm tones; at this stage they were taught the gamut and basic solmization in order to enable them to memorize intervals. From here, they would advance to the visual forms of mensural music or 'pricksong', by memorizing tables of prolation and mensuration from the practise of singing canons. Once an aspiring chorister had internalized these processes and was able to read and sing chant in rhythmicized ways, they moved onto improvisation in forms such as faburden, initially using solmization syllables, either unmeasured or with figuration, before moving on to descant.[5] It was in these last two forms of improvisation that the matter of false relations would begin to come into play, as Thomas Morley's Master Gnorimus notes, 'it should seem that it was by means of the Descanters who, striving to sing harder ways upon a plainsong than their fellows, brought in that which neither could please the ears of other men, nor could be themselves be defended by reason'.[6]

The bridging of theory to performance was vital for the artful execution of false relations and all associated elements of improvisation. In the preceding chapters we have looked at and played with the idea of the reception of musical falseness and the false relation; how it might have been imagined, visualized, talked about, textualized. In this chapter, we will return to the crucial question of how it was learned, and what a pair of case studies can tell us about the conceptual architecture that went into inferring when and where to place a false relation. We shall do so by examining a pair of musical manuscripts begun at opposite ends of the 1570s: the 'Hamond' set, and *A Booke of In nomines & other solfainge songes of v: vi: vii: & viii pts for voyces or Instrumentes*, alias British Library Add. MS. 31390 (c. 1578).[7] First, however, we will briefly explore the concept of musical education in the English Renaissance, and what it was for.

Learning the Notes

An important thing to note at the outset is that the disorder of the Hamond partbooks would not have been viewed as a negative thing by its original readers/performers at any point in its forty-five-year copying span. In fact,

---

[5] Flynn, 'The Education of Choristers', 182–190.
[6] Thomas Morley, *A Plaine and Easie Introduction to Practicall Musicke* (London: Peter Short, 1597), 90.
[7] British Library, GB-Lbl Add. MS 31390.

the case would likely have been the complete opposite. We encountered the aesthetic taste for eclecticism and lack of fixed, hierarchical direction with which to visually engage above, in Chapter 4; as Megan Heffernan has recent argued, this extended beyond the strictly visual and material into the poetic and the rise of the miscellany across the second half of the sixteenth century. Following the publication of Richard Tottel's *Songes and Sonnets* in 1557, the first poetry miscellany in the vernacular, taste for the miscellaneous slowly but steadily grew through collections such as Isabella Whitney's *A Sweet Nosgay, or Pleasant Posye*, George Gascoigne's *A Hundred sundrie Flowres bounde up in one small Poesie* (both published 1573), and Richard Edwards's (onetime master of the choristers at the Chapel Royal) *The Paradise of Dainty Devices* (1576).[8] The poetics of gathering epitomized in the slippage between 'poesie'/'posye' and posy (both a gathering of disparate flowers and poetry itself) drove a love of variety and, as Heffernan describes it, 'delight in disorder', figuring disorder as

> form in potential, a legible trace of other figurations [...] not pejorative, as it might now seem, but rather a simpler observation about the lack of any set sequence or organization, often because the final state of the compilation reflected the process of making it. Poets and compilers alike approached the open, modular design of the printed book as a tool that could serve both their own expressive purposes and the desires of readers. [. . .] For readers seeking poetic variety, disorder was actually promoted as a benefit because it allowed any single book to be approached from multiple different perspectives.[9]

Due to the palpably visible distinctions between each layer of copying evident in the Hamond set, these 'multiple different perspectives' are especially available to its readers, singers, and appreciators. Fascinatingly, the diversity of 'disorder' was also inherent to the set's use as a didactic tool, as we shall discover below.

The learning of certain forms of music and musical styles was of immense religiopolitical importance throughout the English Renaissance. Amanda

---

[8] Isabella Whitney, *A Sweet Nosgay, or Pleasant Posye* (London: Richard Jones, 1573); George Gascoigne, *A Hundredth sundrie Flowres bounde up in one small Poesie* (London: Richard Smith, 1573); Richard Edwards, *The Paradise of Dainty Devices* (London: Henry Disle, 1576).

[9] Megan Heffernan, *Making the Miscellany: Poetry, Print and the History of the Book in Early Modern England* (Philadelphia: University of Pennsylvania Press, 2020), 10–11.

Eubanks Winkler, Hannibal Hamlin, Christopher Marsh, and Jonathan Willis have all argued for the immense importance of group singing of psalms in constructing an English Protestant identity.[10] In the many grammar schools founded across the sixteenth century, the practice of psalm singing was deemed so important to the education of young Protestants that it can be found written into the statutes.[11] As Eubanks Winkler has observed, the books from which grammar school (both male and female) students learned was likely the Sternhold and Hopkins *Whole Booke of Psalmes* we explored above in Chapter 3, with its handy 'Short Introduction to the science of music' in the preface. Learning Protestant modes of music was seen as an immensely important facet of constructing a Protestant mindset that would ultimately enable the perpetuation of the Church of England. The schoolmaster John Brinsley's 1612 *Ludus literarius, or, the grammar schoole* advocated that elder children should assist the younger in their singing of the psalms in order to ensure that 'they will all learne to give the tunes sweetely'.[12] Music was so important, and so contested, that Catholic communities in the wake of the Reformation used similar tactics. As recently explored by Emilie Murphy, post-Reformation English Catholic musical miscellanies were vital tools of commemoration both individual and social: as well as recording personal experiences in music, these miscellanies were also used for 'the composition of music that represented and remembered religious change, which includes music that evoked nostalgia for a pre-Reformation past, and music which voiced communal protests about the contemporary situation'.[13] There are tantalizing traces of the vital impact that these musical practices had upon the broader musical culture of the English Renaissance, which will be discussed in greater detail below in Chapter 6. For the present, however, it is important to note the primacy that music (and learning music) had for the ideological formation of English identity following the break from Rome. In the case of children, the next generation of good English Protestants (or Catholics), music had a huge amount of potential power.

---

[10] Amanda Eubanks Winkler, *Music, Dance, and Drama in Early Modern English Schools* (Cambridge: Cambridge University Press, 2020); Hannibal Hamlin, *Psalm Culture and Early Modern English Literature* (Cambridge: Cambridge University Press, 2004); Christopher Marsh, *Music and Society in Early Modern England* (Cambridge: Cambridge University Press, 2010); Willis, *Church Music and Protestantism*.

[11] Eubanks Winkler, *Music, Dance and Drama*, 40–42.

[12] John Brinsley, *Ludus literarius: or, the grammar schoole* (London, 1612), 298. Quoted in Eubanks Winkler, *Music, Dance and Drama*, 40.

[13] Emilie K. Murphy, 'Making Memories in Post-Reformation English Catholic Musical Miscellanies', in Alexandra Walsham, Bronwyn Wallace, Ceri Law, and Brian Cummings (eds.), *Memory and the English Reformation* (Cambridge: Cambridge University Press, 2020), 403–421.

188　SYRENE SOUNDES

Evidence of this way of thinking can be found in Thomas Tallis and William Byrd's *Cantiones sacrae* (1575), one of the biggest music publication projects of the day, and widely accepted as a key effort in the attempt to establish the concept of musical Englishness. Amongst the prefatory matter is a dedicatory poem by Richard Mulcaster, headmaster of Merchant Taylors' School from 1561 and high master of St Paul's from 1596, whom we encountered above in Chapter 3.

> Quanti sit precis res Musica, quamque, regendis
> Insansis animi motibus apt a, docent,
> Qui numeros formæ sedem cuiuslibet esse,
> E quibus efficitur Musica forma, docent.
> Quid? Quod nemo docet, quonam Respublica pacto
> Formando, & quonam prima iuuent a modo,
> Quin idem doceat, primam quod Musica sedem
> Obtineat, promo sit que docenda loco.

> Of how great a price musical enterprise is, and how fit for ruling
> unsound movements of the spirit, they teach
> Who teach that numbers are the seat of every form,
> from which (numbers) Musical form is brought about.
> Note that no one teaches by whatever pact a state
> and by whatever manner first youth is to be formed,
> But also teaches that Music should obtain the first seat,
> and it should be taught in first place.[14]

Mulcaster was the author of the *Positions* (1581) and the *Elementarie* (1582), two of the most influential didactic publications of the sixteenth century. In the latter, Mulcaster is yet more explicit about the importance of music for a basic education and the excellent grounding that it would provide for later life. Music numbers amongst the four main educational elements, along with reading, writing, and drawing.[15] Not only does Mulcaster's concept of music include the finding of the correct musical instrument and 'due

---

[14] Thomas Tallis and William Byrd, *Cantiones sacrae* (London: Thomas Vautrollier, 1575), sig. Aiiir. Transcription from John Milsom, *Thomas Tallis & William Byrd: Cantiones Sacrae* (Early English Church Music 56) (London: Stainer & Bell for the British Academy, 2014).

[15] 'This therfore shall suffise now, that children are to be trained vp in the Elementarie schoole, for the helping forward of the abilities of the minde, in these fower things, as commaunded vs by choice and commended by custome. *Reading*, to receiue that which is bequeathed vs by other, and to serue our memorie with that which is best for vs. *VVriting* to do the like thereby for others, which

compass' (the correct part, with the correct range) for a child's voice, but also the 'matter' of music: the 'setting and discant', for, he argues, a child will become a better singer if they are aware of the principles of setting text to music. He follows Plato in the concept of music as doing for the mind what gymnastics would do for the body, the 'natural sweeter for our sour life in anie mans judgement'.[16]

> I will also set down so manie chosen lessons for either of them, as shall bring the young learner to plaie reasonable well on them both, tho not at the first sight, whether by the ear, or by the book, allwaie prouided that priksong go before plaing. All which lessons both for instument & voice, I will not onelie name, and set the learner ouer to get them, where he can, in the writen song books set furth by *musik* masters, but I will cause them all to be prikt and printed in the same principle of *musik*, that both the reader maie iudge of them, and the scholer learn by them.[17]

---

other haue done for vs, by writing those thinges which we daily vse: but most of al to do most for our selues: *Drawing* to be a directour to sense, a delite to sight, and an ornament to his obiectes. *Musick* by the instrument, besides the skill which must still encrease, in forme of exercise to get the vse of our small ioyntes, before they be knitte, to haue them the nimbler, and to put Musicianes in minde, that they be no brawlers, least by some swash of a sword, they chaunce to lease a iointe, an irrecouerable iewell vnaduisedly cast away.' Mulcaster, *Positions* (London: Thomas Vautrollier for Thomas Chard, 1581), 40-41.

[16] Richard Mulcaster, *The First Part of the Elementarie* (London: Thomas Vautrollier, 1582), 9 and 26.
[17] Ibid., 59-60. Mulcaster precedes this passage with lengthy recommendations as to how to begin the practical, performance aspects of musical education, both for instrument and voice. 'As for *Musik*, which I have deuided into voice and instrument, I will kepe this currant. The training vp in *musik* as in all other faculties, hath a speciall eie to these thre points: The childe himself, that is to learn: the matter it self, which he is to learn: and the instrument it self, whereon he is to learn. Wherein I will deall so for the first and last, that is for the childe and the instrument, as neither of them shall lak, whatsoeuer is nedefull; either for framing of the childes voice, or for the righting of his finger, or for the prikking of his lessons, or for the tuning of his instrument. For in the voice there is a right pitch, that it be neither ouer nor vnder strained, but delicatelie brought to his best ground, both to kepe out long & to rise or fall within dew compas, and so to becom tunable, with regard to helth, and pleasant to hear. And in the fingring also, there is a regard to be had, both that the childe strike so, as he do not shufle, neither spoill anie sound, and that his finger run so both sure and sightiie, as it cumber not it self with entangled deliuerie. Where of the first commonlie falleth out by to much hast, in the young learner, who is euer longing vntill be a leauing: the second falt coms of the master himself, who doth not consider the naturall dexteritie, and sequele in the ioynts, which being vsed right, & in a naturall consequence, procureth the finger a nimblenesse with ease, and helpeth the deliuerie to readinesse without pain, as the vntoward fingring must nedes bring in corruption, tho corrupt vse do not vse to complain. For the matter of *musik*, which the childe is to learn, I will set it down how, and by what degres & in what lessons, a boy that is to be brought vp to sing, maie & ought to procede by ordinarie ascent from the first term of Art, & the first note in sound, vntill he shalbe able without anie often or anie great missing, to sing his part in priksong, either himself alone, which is his first in rudenesse, or with some companie, which is his best in practis. For I take so much to be enough for an Elementarie

Mulcaster does not mention the *Whole Booke of Psalmes*, but it is likely that it played a part in ensuring a child avoided 'entangled delivery'. The last few sentences of this passage are crucial; Mulcaster believes it is enough to establish the basics because in time 'the hole bodie of music will come, and crave place'. Likewise, introducing music to a young mind would not be corrupting, as, according to Mulcaster in his earlier work *Positions*, it was its misuse rather than its inherent quality that produced dire consequences.

> For which cause *Musick* moueth great misliking to some men that waye, as to great a prouoker to vaine delites, still laying baite, to draw on pleasure: still opening the minde, to the entrie of lightnesse. And in matters of religion also, to some it seemes offensiue, bycause it carieth awaye the eare, with the sweetnesse of the melodie, and bewitcheth the minde with a *Syrenes* sounde, pulling it from that delite, wherin of duetie it ought to dwell, vnto harmonicall fantasies, and withdrawing it, from the best meditations, and most vertuous thoughtes to forreine conceites, and wandring deuises. [...] Nay which of all our principles shall stand, if the persons blame, shal blemish the thing? We read foolish bookes, wherat to laugh, nay wherein we learne that, which we might & ought forbeare: we write strange thinges, to serue our owne fansie, if we sway but a litle to any lewde folly: we paint and draw pictures, not to be set in Churches, but such as priuate houses hide with curtaines, not to saue the colours, but to couer their owners, whose lightnesse is discouered, by such lasciuious obiectes. Shall reading therfore be reft from religion? shall priuate, and publike affaires, lease the benefit of writing? shall sense forgoe his forsight, and the beautifier of his obiect? Change thou thy direction, the thinges will follow thee more swifte to the good, then the other to the bad, being capable of both, as thinges of vse be, and yet bending to the better. Mans faulte makes the thing seeme filthie. Applie thou it to the best, the choice is before thee. It is the ill in thee, which seemeth to corrupte the good in the thing, which good, though it be defaced by thy ill, yet shineth it so cleare, as it bewraieth the naturall beautie, euen thorough the cloude of thy greatest disgracing. *Musick* will

---

institution, which saluteth but the facultie, tho it perfit the princple, & I refer the residew for setting & discant to enciease of cunning, which dailie will grow on, & to further years, when the hole bodie of *musik* wil com, & craue place. And yet bycause the childe must still mount somwhat that waie, I will set him down some rules of setting & discant, which will make him better able to iudge of singing being a setter himself, as in the tung, he that vseth to write, shal best iudge of a writer,' 58–59.

not harme thee, if thy behauiour be good, and thy conceit honest, it will not miscary thee, if thy eares can carie it, and sorte it as it should be.[18]

In other words, a musical seed established in the mind of a child and nurtured in the right manner would be enough to establish a musical (and Protestant devotional) habit for the rest of the child's lifetime. The 'syrenes sounde' that 'carieth awaye the eare', like the 'lascivious objectes' and 'foolish' books that enable a listener, viewer, reader to learn 'that which we might and ought [to] forbear': they train a student to recognize music, visual art, and words for what they are, rather than squeamishly avoid them.

All of this—the primacy of pricksong, the question of miscellaneity, and the devotional importance of musical education—is crucial for how we interpret the teaching of false relations to aspiring musicians, adult and child alike. We have already explored how Sternhold and Hopkins's *Whole Booke of Psalmes* served as a tool of musical education, to such a successful extent that its model of fixed-scale solmization had become an accepted norm by the turn of the seventeenth century. In the midst of its instructions, as we saw in Chapter 3, was the trace of the visual logic of the hexachord and solmization in the form of b-*mi* and b-*fa*:

> Here note that when *b*, *fa*, ♯, *mi*, is formed and signed in this maner, with this letter *b*, whiche is called *b*, flat, it must be expressed with this voice or note, *fa*, but if it be formed and signed with this forme ♯, whiche is called *b*, sharpe: or if it haue no signe at all, then must ye expres it in singing with thys voyce or Note. *mi*.[19]

This passage, as well as allowing for the possibility of false relation, crucially introduces the aspiring musical student to all of the musical knowledge they would need in order to solmize one or insert one into the shape of any music they encountered beyond the bounds of the *Whole Booke of Psalmes*. Though its explicit purpose was to supersede solmization, it had the potential to function as an invitation into the surprising, destabilizing delights of the sonic aesthetic of false relation. This chapter will linger over the implications of the continued presence of solmization signatures within the developing new performance conventions of the hexachordal model of

---

[18] Ibid., 38–39. The concept of training in surprise is a topic that is currently receiving a lot of attention in cognitive literary studies. See Vera Tobin, *Elements of Surprise: Our Mental Limits and the Satisfactions of Plot* (Cambridge, MA: Harvard University Press, 2018).
[19] Sternhold and Hopkins, *Whole Booke of Psalmes*, unpaginated.

reading music, and the impact on how students (child and adult alike) were introduced to the concept of false relations. Building upon the arguments regarding the visual appeal of the pattern of the hexachord and the ocular engagement it invited explored above in Chapter 4, it will focus on how students of music were introduced to the false relation, how they were invited to internalize the visual/aural patterns of hexachordal solmization, and how they built an 'audiation'[20]—that is, 'a faculty of hearing in the mind that either recollects acoustic experience or, in some cases, can produce an experience of inward hearing that has little or no relation to sensory sound perception [...] the sonic, aural equivalent to imagination' of false relation.[21] Audiation includes, equally, the shape of the musical style of the English Renaissance and features such as the minim-footed bird in the Hamond partbook. This chapter suggests that this playfulness and intellectual liveliness is crucial to establishing the mindset of the false relation. It will do so through exploring one of the most avant-garde compositions of the English Renaissance, and one that was explicitly used in the education of choristers in the *Booke of In nomines & other solfainge songes of v: vi: vii: & viii pts for voyces or Instruments*: William Byrd's 'O salutaris hostia a 6'.

(P)laying the Table: 'O salutaris hostia'

The origins of Byrd's six-part setting of the 'O salutaris hostia' text (Appendix II) are unknown, although certain provocative and speculative accounts have been suggested. The lyrics are as follows:

O salutaris hostia	O redeeming sacrifice
quae empi pandis ostium,	who opens the gate of heaven,
bella premunt hostilia:	hostile wars press on us:
da robur, fer auxilium	give strength, bring aid.
Uni trinoque Domino	To the Lord, three in one,
sit empiternal gloria,	Be everlasting glory,
qui vitam sine termino	for life without end
nobis donet in patria.	He gives to us in his Kingdom.

---

[20] My thanks to Emilie Murphy for bringing my attention to this concept.
[21] Lucia Martinez Valdivia, 'Audiation: Listening to Writing', in *Modern Philology*, 119: 4 (May 2022), 555–579, at 557.

It survives in three sources dating from after Byrd's conversion to Catholicism in the 1570s: *A Book of Solfaing Songes* (c. 1578), the Baldwin Partbooks (1575–1581), and an orphan partbook now in a private collection (c. 1595–1613).[22] It may have been a student work produced by Byrd whilst under the tutelage of Tallis, Sheppard, or Mundy at the Chapel Royal, a possibility cautiously floated by Kerry McCarthy:

> [Byrd's] six-voice setting of 'O salutaris hostia' is one of the strangest things he ever wrote. Unlike almost all his other surviving six-part motets, it was passed over in discreet silence when he published his six-part anthology in the 1591 *Cantiones sacrae*. The omission is not too surprising. 'O salutaris hostia' is a three-voice canon at various pitch levels, interwoven with three freely-composed parts, all undertaken with the breeziest possible attitude toward dissonance treatment. The result is layer upon layer of grating discord and tonal instability. It may well be the most appallingly dissonant piece of sacred music written in the sixteenth century. The music still has an unmistakable confidence—even authority although it is hardly the kind of thing Byrd would have composed (much less circulated) later in life. Could this have been another student work of his, perhaps written at the age of seventeen or eighteen, while the Latin motet was still universal currency among English musicians? The taste for acrid false relations and irregular suspensions was doubtless something Byrd picked up from his London colleagues in the 1550s, though it must be said that even Sheppard never wrote anything quite like this.[23]

Distinctive as 'O salutaris hostia' is, it is not entirely out of place amongst Byrd's compositional approach from this period (and arguably later). His contribution to *Similes illis fiant* (c. 1557–1558, preserved in the Gyffard

---

[22] British Library, GB-Lbl Add. MS 31390, fol.17v–18r; Christ Church Oxford, Och 979–983 (Baldwin), fol. 266–267 and Wimbourne (Private Collection), GB-Lmcghie s. s., fol. 153–154. For more on the *Booke of In nomines & other solfainge songes* alias Add. MS. 31390, see Richard Rastall, 'Spatial Effects in English Instrumental Consort Music, c. 1560-1605', in *Early Music*, 25: 2 (1997), 268–290.

[23] Kerry McCarthy, *Byrd* (Oxford: Oxford University Press, 2013), 19–20. See also Peter le Huray, 'Some Thoughts about Cantus Firmus Composition, and a Plea for Byrd's *Christus Resurgens*', in Alan Brown and Richard Turbet (eds.), *Byrd Studies 48* (Cambridge: Cambridge University Press, 1992), 1–23. For more on Byrd's later use of canonic imitation in his secular works, see Jeremy L. Smith, *Verse & Voice in Byrd's Song Collections of 1588 and 1589* (Woodbridge: Boydell & Brewer, 2016), 83 and 207–208.

Part Books, now Add. MS. 17802–17805 in the British Library),[24] composed with William Munday and John Sheppard, features a fast-and-loose treatment of pitch; McCarthy notes the manner in which the alto F at the beginning of the first 'alleluia' 'smashes unceremoniously' into the cantus-firmus E, and his general prioritization of voice-leading in canonic imitation, a trait that continued into his mature works.[25] Twenty-first-century fans of Byrd are left with a conundrum in 'O salutaris hostia'. It bears little resemblance to Byrd's four-part setting of the same text, built instead around a canonic structure that, in overlaying and repeating one monodic sequence, evokes the sinuous, intertwining, and rounded effect of polyphony.[26] Rigid adherence to the canon brings about the false relations. As a result, one could argue that in the context of the extremely early and experimental 'O salutaris hostia' they are not intentional at all. However, given the skilled composer Byrd would later become and how that skill frequently involved the elegant (albeit admittedly restrained) deployment of false relations (as in, for example, 'Tribue, Domine' and 'Ave Verum Corpus'), it seems highly unlikely that the piece was not a honing of technique and style: an exploration into just how far the combination of canonic structure and acrid false relation could be pushed. In whatever context Byrd composed this, the effect is of dramatizing the unravelling of musical form and tonal structures, the interchanging gaping space and tightly, intarsia-flush textures brought about by the *mi–fa* relation. As a result, it is incredibly hard to recreate 'O salutaris hostia' as a modern editor of early music (and was presumably tricky to solmize as a student, for whom *A Booke of In nomines & other solfainge songes* [c. 1578] appears to have been compiled), because of the competing factors at play. For example, does one prioritize the *ficta* or does one prioritize the canon? Should the canon pursued be exact, or diatonic? Does choosing exact canon over diatonic truly compromise the effect of the piece as a whole, or is it the entire point of how Byrd composed it? The C in bar 24 in the sexta pars is C♮/*fa* by the rules of solmizing *ficta*, but a C♯/*mi* by the canonic relation between the sexta pars and discantus parts (see b. 23),

---

[24] For more on the Gyffard partbooks see David Mateer, 'The Compilation of the Gyffard Partbooks', in the *Royal Musical Association Research Chronicle*, 26: 1 (1993), 19–43.

[25] Ibid., 15.

[26] Edward Wilson-Lee, 'Tables of the Mind', in Michael Fleming and Christopher Page (eds.), *Music and Instruments of the Elizabethan Age: The Eglantine Table* (Suffolk: Boydell & Brewer, 2021), 219–230, at 227. See also John Milsom, 'The Music in Staff Notation', in Michael Fleming and Christopher Page (eds.), *Music and Instruments of the Elizabethan Age: The Eglantine Table* (Woodbridge: Boydell & Brewer, 2021), 69–100, at 75.

and so it grates against the Tenor C♯ (see Appendix II). At bar 30, one has to choose whether to solmize the F in the discantus or follow the canonic precedent of the superius; to solmize it as F♯ is to scrape it against the superius F♮. These are merely two examples of the many shot through the fabric of 'O salutaris hostia' like a contrast weft of silk, lending the piece its glinting flares of scrunchy iridescence. All offer an insight into the composer at work, experimenting at the limits of dissonance treatment that would later result in such carefully executed works as the Agnus Dei of his four-part mass setting. This is not to mention the places where such features interact with cadential tropes, which further complicate the matter. Which inflection should be chosen? Should it be left to the discretion of the performer, and how should one signify this sonic ambiguity?

This ambiguity, I would argue, is the entire point of a piece like 'O salutaris hostia'. It is not just an experiment in composition, and not just for the benefit of the young Byrd himself. It can also be productively approached as an experiment in how to teach English Renaissance musical style, because in posing the paradox of canon and false relation it offers its performer/readers the chance to immerse themselves in the sheer variety of things that can be done with imitative counterpoint, whether they are aspiring professionals or amateurs making casual music after dinner. In so doing, it introduces its performer/reader to possibility; to the experience of navigating between the twin poles of canon and *ficta* or false relation. Peter Urquhart's recent and thorough exploration of canon and accidental deployment, albeit in Franco-Flemish repertoire from the first half of the sixteenth century, is worth noting here.[27] Urquhart notes that despite the fact that canonic imitation was predicated on obscurity, deception, games, or voice parts that were to be derived rather than written out, canon is a useful device for understanding how accidentals functioned in the music of the fifteenth and sixteenth centuries, and the tension that they brought about between melodic (linear) and harmonic (vertical) considerations.

> The modern view of '*musica ficta*' in the performative sense, in which all harmonic flaws could be repaired by a performer, predisposes one to the view that diatonic canon was the norm, and that exact canon may have been a special case, the result of unusual linear constraints, or a special

---

[27] Peter Urquhart, *Sound and Sense in Franco-Flemish Music of the Renaissance: Sharps, Flats and the Problem of 'Musica Ficta'* (Leuven: Peeters, 2021), 401–490.

conceit created by the composer. But this is not the case. [...] The nature of the canon, 'hiding behind a certain obscurity', when combined with modern insensitivity to the practice of solmization by musicians of the period, results in a loss of the precise pitch content of the work. Modern '*musica ficta*' practice then covers the loss with a muffling blanket of what is assumed to be proper harmonic content.[28]

The harmonic piquancy of 'O salutaris hostia' should not be considered a juvenile failing by a composer who had yet to hit their masterful stride, but rather a dramatization of the collision between the melodic and harmonic aspects inherent in canonic imitation as an inherited and developing form. Diminished fifths (alias the infamous tritone) and augmented octaves can be integral parts of this musical culture and should not automatically be considered problematic and to be avoided.[29] 'O salutaris hostia' is designed to allow the performer to learn the feel of that paradox, and when and where a false relation will be expressive, meaningful (indeed useful), or surplus to requirements. In other words, it is a training exercise in the compositional and performance skills and English Renaissance musical style that well-coached choristers (and future flagbearers of the English choral tradition) in the late 1550s and early 1560s required.

The educational potential of 'O salutaris hostia' becomes clear when turning to one of its material sources: Add. MS 31390, or *A Booke of In nomines & other solfainge songes*. It is telling that we find this motet in the *Booke*. The *Booke* is a manuscript miscellany of music designed for the education of aspiring choristers.[30] This was a topic close to Byrd's heart, as we know from his 'Reasons briefely set downe by th'aucthor, to perswade every one to learne to sing' in the preface of his *Psalms, Sonnets and Songs of Sadness and Pietie* (1588).

> First, it is a knowledge easely taught, and quickly learned, wher ther is a good Master, & an apt Scoler.
> 2 The exercise of singing is delightful to Nature, and good to preserve the health of man.

---

[28] Ibid., 403 and 413.
[29] Ibid., 436–439.
[30] Butler, 'From Liturgy', 53; Flynn, 'The Education of Choristers', 196; Warwick Edwards, 'The Performance of Ensemble Music in Elizabethan England', in *Proceedings of the Royal Musical Association*, 97 (1970–1971), 113–119.

3 It doth strengthen all parts of the brest, & doth open the pipes.
4 It is a singular good remedie for a stutting & stamaring in the speech.
5 It is the best meanes to procure a perfect pronunciation, and to make a good Orator.
6 It is the onely way to know where Nature hath bestowed the benefit of a good voyce: which gift is so rare, as ther is not one among a thousand that hath it: & in many that excellent gift is lost, because they want art to expresse Nature.
7 Ther is not any Musicke of Instruments whatsoever, comparable to that which is made of the voyces of men, wher the voices are good, & the same wel sorted and ordered.
8 The better the voyce is, the meeter it is to honour & serve God therewith: and the voice of man is chiefly to be imployed to that end.

> Since singing is so good a thing,
> I wish all men would learne to sing.[31]

Towards the end of the *Booke of In nomines* there is a chart explaining note values and mensuration signatures (see Fig. 5.1), which surely would not have been necessary if the book were compiled with experienced performers in mind.[32] Moreover, the fact that it is described explicitly as a collection of 'solfaing songs', to be solmized (or sight-read), likewise suggests that it was intended for training purposes. However, recalling the recommendations of Mulcaster and Brinsley, this approach is not out of keeping with the musical education of England in the sixteenth century. The more surprising thing is, rather, the presence of overtly Marian music in collections that appear to have had no explicit Catholic connection or purpose.[33] As Daisy Gibbs notes, the copying of music with Marian or Catholic connections as instrumental pieces or solfaing songs was a way of removing the problematic issue of the words.[34] This might have briefly deflected from the issue, but as we explored above in Chapter 3, the question of the meaningfulness of text extended far beyond the individual words, and well into the fabric of

---

[31] William Byrd, *Psalms, Sonets and Songs and Sadnes and Piete, Made into Musicke of Five Parts* (London: Thomas East, 1588).
[32] British Library, GB-Lbl Add. MS 31390, Fol. 127.
[33] For more on the continued use of music written for the Catholic liturgy, see Daisy M. Gibbs, '"Your Muse Remains Forever": Memory and Monumentality in Elizabethan Manuscript Partbooks', in *Early Music* (1 February 2022). See also Kerry McCarthy, 'Evidence of Things Past', in *Journal of the Royal Musical Association*, 135 (2010), 405–411.
[34] Gibbs, 'Memory and Monumentality', 3.

198 SYRENE SOUNDES

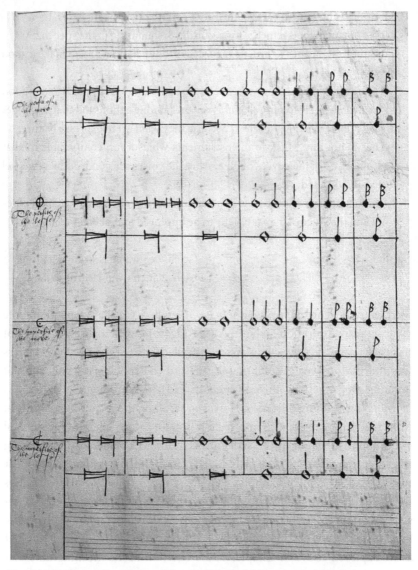

Fig. 5.1 Anonymous, Chart of Note Values and Mensuration Signatures, from *A Booke of In nomines* (1578), London: British Library, Add. MS 31390. Photograph author's own.

the music and its structure. Music laden with 'acrid false relations and irregular suspensions' likely continued to be redolent of Popery regardless of whether or not they were attached to the words. We will explore the connotations of this idea further below in Chapter 6 with an exploration of Thomas Tallis's 'O sacrum convivium', which in the *Booke of In nomines & other solfainge songes* appears with a fifth voice part only extant in one other contrafact.[35] The other pieces included in the manuscript are similarly radical; Osbert Parsley's 'Spes nostra', Brewster's 'In nomine a 5', Clement Woodcock's 'Browning My Dear' and Picforth's 'In nomine a 5' all pull at the seams of rhythmic (and, to an extent, pitch) decorum, although none to quite the extent of Byrd. Clement Woodcock was in all likelihood closely associated with the compiler of the manuscript, given that it spent the early decades of its existence in the region of Chichester, and the relatively high number of his compositions that it contains; however, copies of his autograph in the archives at Canterbury Cathedral suggest that Woodcock was not the copyist himself. Woodcock had served as lay clerk at King's College, Cambridge and Canterbury Cathedral before being appointed Organist (and later Master of the Choristers) at Chichester Cathedral in 1570, where he possibly commissioned the *Booke of In nomines & other solfainge songes* to train his choristers (amongst whom may have been Thomas Weelkes, born near Chichester and baptized in the neighbouring parish of Elsted in October 1576).[36] Its very purpose might, then, perhaps have been to expose choristers to music that 'carieth awaye the eare, with the sweetnesse of the melodie, and bewitcheth the minde with a *Syrenes* sounde, pulling it from that delite, wherin of duetie it ought to dwell, vnto harmonicall fantasies, and withdrawing it, from the best meditations, and most vertuous thoughtes to forreine conceites, and wandring deuises'. Doing so would not only have (in theory) bolstered choristers against the seductions of pre-reformed religion; it would also, as Gibbs suggests, have offered a sense of their place and heritage within the English musical tradition.[37]

Such a dynamic may have been engrained in the material, visual structure of the *Booke of In nomines & other solfainge songes*, and the performance practices that it compelled. The *Booke of In nomines* is a table book, designed

---

[35] See also Eleanor Chan, 'The Etymology of the English Cadence', in *Music & Letters*, 104: 3 (August 2023); Magnus Williamson, 'Queen Mary I, Tallis' *O Sacrum convivium* and a Latin Litany', in *Early Music*, 44: 2 (2016), 251–270, at 251; John Milsom, 'A Tallis fantasia', in *Musical Times*, 126 (1985), 658–662; Milsom, *Thomas Tallis and William Byrd*, 128–167.

[36] Rastall, 'Spatial Effects', 271.

[37] Gibbs, 'Memory and Monumentality', 12–14.

to be laid on a table and performed in the round.[38] It is one of few surviving manifestations of this format, the others including Morley's *Introduction*, Dowland's *First Booke of Aires* (1597), and *Lachrimae, or Seaven Teares* (printed in 1605); it is the only surviving English manuscript conceived around this format. The relative lack of other surviving table book sources is intriguing to say the least, given that recreational performance was often done around a table, as depicted in the anonymous *Life of Sir Henry Unton* of 1596 (Fig. 5.2), and implied by the inclusion of a legible contrafact of Tallis's 'O Lord in Thee Is All My Trust' on the Eglantine Table (c. 1567) at Hardwick Hall (Fig. 5.3).[39] Richard Rastall notes the importance of the 'pattern of physical disposition of the players' in the table book format, clearest in the six-part music; it ensures clear physical separation between pairs of voices that are close together in pitch, with, for example, parts III and IV separated by the length of the table, and parts I and II placed diagonally across the table, as far apart as the remaining positions permit.'[40] This pattern of placement would have greatly aided performance, with the added effect that it would also have increased the legibility of the music as the students solmized it. To this day, choral singers observe the importance and usefulness of knowing the precise physical position of each of the voice parts and how this aids their ability to read music. By plotting his musical manuscript in table book format, Woodcock offered his choristers the chance to experience the texture of this musical style from deep within its very midst: an immersive, three-dimensional, and heavily somatic mode of reading music (see Fig. 5.4).

The table book would have brought with it a variety of other connotations to the performers who encountered it in the late sixteenth and early seventeenth centuries, which are vital to any attempts to unpack the way that this particular contrafact of 'O salutaris hostia' would have made meaning. As we saw above in Chapter 4, tables were a semantically loaded concept in the English Renaissance, both as an analytical space and as an imaginary space in which knowledge could be ordered, demarcated, and brought into line.[41] They had been important to Western culture from Plato's *Republic* and later Aristotle's *On Interpretation*, as the standard object with which to think about form and

---

[38] For more on the table book format, see Milsom, 'The Music in Staff Notation', 69–100, at 71.
[39] Milsom, 'The Music in Staff Notation', 69–100.
[40] Rastall, 'Spatial Effects', 271.
[41] Edward Wilson-Lee, 'Tables of the Mind', in Fleming and Page (eds.), *Music and Instruments of the Elizabethan Age*, 219–230, at 220. For more on the concept of the table, see also Peter Stallybrass, Roger Chartier, J. Franklin Mowery, and Heather Wolfe, 'Hamlet's Tables and the Technologies of Writing in Renaissance England', in *Shakespeare Quarterly*, 55: 4 (2004), 379–419.

Fig. 5.2 Detail of music-making section of *The Life of Sir Henry Unton*, c. 1596, London: National Portrait Gallery, Object No. NPG710. Public domain.

Fig. 5.3 Anonymous, copy of Thomas Tallis's 'O Lord in Thee Is All My Trust' rendered in inlay and etching on the Eglantine Table, c. 1567, National Trust: Hardwick Hall. By kind permission of the National Trust.

Fig. 5.4 William Byrd's 'O salutaris hostia a 6' in table book format, from *A Booke of In nomines*, c. 1578, London: British Library, Add. MS 31390. Photograph author's own.

essence.[42] Well into the middle ages, wax tablets were used as pedagogical tools, account books, and notebooks for drafts of poems or letters.[43] The case was such that Richard and Mary Rouse argue that 'as a support for the written word, wax tablets had a longer uninterrupted association with literate Western civilization than either parchment or paper, and a more intimate relationship with literary creation'.[44] In c. 1599 Shakespeare has Hamlet imagine his memory as a 'table' (generally accepted by scholars of Renaissance literature as a stage-prop as well as a metaphorical table) which he can wipe clean.

> Remember thee?
> Yea, from the table of my memory
> I'll wipe away all trivial fond records.
> All saws of books, all forms, all pressures past
> That youth and observation copied there,
> And thy commandment all alone shall live
> Within the book and volume of my brain
> Unmix'd with baser matter. (1.5, 97–104).

Writing about this moment, Peter Stallybrass, Roger Chartier, J. Franklin Mowery, and Heather Wolfe observe that erasable notebooks or tables (with pages that bore remnants of a hard coating) do appear to have survived within the archives. In some examples, these treated pages bore visual evidence of having been repeatedly wiped, although faint traces of writing remained, as in a palimpsest.[45] This aspect, in particular, was crucial for the way that the table (both physical and conceptual) was experienced in the English Renaissance. As Juliet Fleming notes, 'to cross or expunge ("prick out") writing is to mark it, more or less memorably, for erasure: it is, in effect, to *write it again*'.[46] Tables were things, both material and metaphorical, durable and ephemeral, that preserved the memory of what had been written before.

---

[42] Wilson-Lee, 'Tables of the Mind', 220–221; Plato, *Republic*, V, 596b; Aristotle, *On Interpretation*, 19b; Jocelyn Penny Small, *Wax Tablets of the Mind: Cognitive Studies of Memory and Literacy in Classical Antiquity* (London: Routledge, 1997).

[43] Stallybrass et al., 'Hamlet's Tables', 383. See also Juliet Fleming, 'Graffiti Futures', in *Journal of Early Modern Studies*, 9 (2020), 29–36, and *Graffiti and the Writing Arts of Early Modern England* (New York: Reaktion, 2001), especially Chapter 2, 'Whitewash'; Hester Lees-Jeffries, *Shakespeare and Memory* (Oxford: Oxford University Press, 2013), 22–26.

[44] Richard H. Rouse and Mary A. Rouse, 'The Vocabulary of Wax Tablets', in Olga Weijers (ed.), *Vocabulaire du Livre et de l'Ecriture au Moyen Age* (Turnhout: Brepols, 1989), 220–230, at 220.

[45] Stallybrass et al., 381–382.

[46] Fleming, *Graffiti and the Writing Arts*, 76.

What does this mean for this contrafact of 'O salutaris hostia', and, more generally, for *A Booke of In nomines & other solfainge songes*? How would it have felt to solmize and perform from its pages? With its emphatic insistence on the form, concept, and connotations of the table, it would likely have activated a strong musical-visual response in the choristers and consorts who originally used it as part of their musical training, and which could have fed into how they thought about the act of performance for the rest of their musical lives. Recreational music was often practised around a table, after a meal; this is the situation in which the imagined conversation between the initially very un-musical Philomathes and the music master Gnorimus takes place outside a pseudo Gresham College, in Thomas Morley's *Plaine and Easie Introduction to Practicall Musicke set downe in forme of a dialogue*:

> PHILOMATHES Among the rest of the guestes, by chaunce, master *Aphron* came thether also, who falling to discourse of Musicke, was in an argument so quickely taken up & hotly pursued by *Eudoxus* and *Calergus*, two kinsmen of *Sophobulus*, as in his owne art he was ouerthrowne. But he still sticking in his opinion, the two gentlemen requested mee to examine his reasons, and confute them. But I refusing & pretending ignorance, the whole companie condemned mee of discurtesie, being fully perswaded, that I had beene as skilfull in that art, as they tooke mee to be learned in others. *But supper being ended, and Musicke bookes, according to the custome being brought to the table*: the mistresse of the house presented mee with a part, earnestly requesting mee to sing. But when after manie excuses, I protested vnfainedly that I could not: everie one began to wonder. Yea, some whispered to others, demaunding how I was brought up: so that upon shame of mine ignorance I go nowe to seeke out mine olde frinde master *Gnorimus*, to make my selfe his scholler (my italics).[47]

'Dialogue' is the crucial aspect of this interaction: it is both a theoretical dialogue and dialogue in performance. Katie Bank and Cristle Collins Judd

---

[47] Morley, *Plaine and Easie Introduction*, sig. B2.

have observed the fundamental importance of the dialogue format to English Renaissance musical culture, from Morley's to Martin Peerson's 1620 collection *Private Music, or the First Booke of Ayres and Dialogues*.[48] Bank argues that 'dialogue is found not only in the printed documents of the past, but like musical experience, in those ephemeral things less easily preserved in tangible and lasting forms. It is through an examination of *experience* that literature like dialogue can be more fully understood.'[49] The audiation—the sonic, aural equivalent of imagination that does not necessarily have any connection to things physically heard through sensory sound perception— evoked by the *Booke of In nomines & other solfainge songes* enmeshes the dialogic aspects of music. This is present in two aspects. The first of these are the 'spatial effects' of the *Booke*, or in other words the manner in which its very physical form places performers in close, choreographed proximity, emphasizes the effect of dialogue and of music as conversation by foregrounding the interaction of parts. The second is the *miscellaneous* nature of the *Booke*, activating the 'delight in disorder' described by Heffernan above. I refer to the miscellaneity not just as the book itself, a miscellany by merit of the fact that it contains an array of works by different authors, but also to the connotations of the visual 'table' form of the book. The table, site of music-making and music-thinking, erasable and re-inscribable, also carried a palimpsested miscellany: a miscellany of previous performances, ephemeral and lost but resurrected within each new performance, each new solmization, each new audiation.

These are complex concepts for the twenty-first-century mind, but it is worth observing that these associations would have come naturally to the people of the English Renaissance. Hamlet's passing reference to erasable tables demonstrates that this was assumed knowledge. As a training document, *A Booke of In nomines & other solfainge songes* is firmly situated within the educational culture of the period and interacts with its tropes and approaches as laid out by Mulcaster and Brinsley, but also as depicted in the literature of the period. False relations, borne of the slippage between *mi* and *fa* in solmization, were a necessary part of the musical education of choristers and aspiring amateurs. To learn how to execute them in performance a number of

---

[48] See Katie Bank, *Knowledge Building in Early Modern English Music* (London: Routledge, 2020), 188–236; and Cristle Collins Judd, 'Music in Dialogue: Conversational, Literary, and Didactic Discourse about Music in the Renaissance', in *Journal of Music Theory*, 52: 1 (2008), 41–74. Martin Peerson, *Private Music, or the First Booke of Ayres and Dialogues, contayning songs of 4, 5 or 6 parts, of several sorts and being verse and chorus, is fit for voyces and viols* (London: Thomas Snodham, 1620).

[49] Bank, *Knowledge Building*, 192.

skills were necessary, amongst them crucially the intricate awareness of how the dissonant part interacted within the dialogue of shifting parts. Byrd's 'O salutaris hostia' offers the ideal opportunity for exploring this kind of awareness. The tension between canonic structure and *ficta* (the eternal *mi* or *fa* question) is staged within the very *mise-en-page* of the *Booke of In nomines & other solfainge songes*. In its manifestation within the *Booke*, 'O salutaris hostia' performs its identity as 'choral' text-as-*texere*, created through use cumulatively and through collaboration, where voices join, respond, riposte, and complement each other, which we encountered in Chapter 3.[50] It seeks to train its readership to bridge the gap between the theory of solmization, and the performance practice of them. It can offer us an unparalleled, if tantalizingly fragmentary insight into the way that false relations were learned in the English Renaissance.

Reading Miscellaneity

The *Booke of In nomines & other solfainge songes* and the contrafact it contains of Byrd's 'O salutaris hostia' is one distinctive example among many surviving (albeit fragmentary) experiments in musical education that bridges theory and performance. Returning to the Hamond partbooks and their awkwardly formed note shapes, it is possible to discern traces of the same approaches that are perceptible in 'O salutaris hostia'. However, the difference is that part of the musical lesson is scribal: these documents preserve the act of choristers learning to transcribe music, as they learn to read and perform it. There are plenty of instances within the Hamond partbooks (particularly in the upper two parts of Discantus and Altus) of scribal error. This includes both places where words have been omitted and where pitches have been incorrectly transcribed into a space between ledger lines and amended with a hastily applied ledger line with no reference to which one it refers. These tiny, incidental, seemingly insignificant details potentially betray something rather exciting: it may be a trace of a child solmizing (e.g., in Osbert Parsley's 'Flat Service: Te Deum', unsuccessfully as *mi*, and

---

[50] Jennifer Richards, 'The Voice of Anne Askew', in *Journal of the Northern Renaissance* (Special Issue: Early Modern Voices), Issue 9 (Autumn 2017), 10. See also Gallagher's emphasis on linguistic competence as a social phenomenon; Gallagher, *Learning Languages*, 6. Another approach towards this chorality of texts can be found in, e.g., Katherine Acheson (ed.), *Early Modern English Marginalia* (London: Routledge, 2019).

then successfully as *re*) in order to transcribe.[51] In other words, it offers us a chance to witness the audiation of a trainee musician in action, across the centuries.

In order to assess this possibility in greater detail, it is necessary to step back and take a broader view of the partbook set. Butler observes that the Hamond partbooks are the only major manuscript source of Protestant service music from the first decades of Elizabeth's reign,[52] and indeed, service music forms the first section of the Discantus, Altus (Add. MS. 30481), Tenor (Add. MS 30482), Bassus (Add. MS. 30483) partbooks, and in the later addition Quintus partbook (Add. MS 30484). The books then progress to a miscellaneous mid-section featuring sacred songs, consort songs, and textless pieces, before concluding in a back section with textless music of various genres; this section, due to the large number of page turns required, was likely not for viol consort but rather a training repertoire, to be solmized or sung *sol-fa*.[53] Previous accounts of the Hamond set have been in disagreement as to how the copying process functioned; May Hofman interpreted the process as front-to-back with some later infill, whereas Warwick Edwards argued that the back section and service music were begun by the same scribal hand.[54] Both Hofman and Edwards focused upon the textless back section of the set, and thus on the notation hands; Butler's approach examined both the text hands and the notation hands to identify a vast number of scribal hands better grouped into 'families' of related hands using the same model script rather than individual hands, and is thus should be considered the most accurate.[55] Crucially, Butler's approach has revealed that suppositions by Hofman, Peter Le Huray, and most recently John Milsom that the set bore traces of having been a domestic collection were correct.[56] Her analysis, moreover, reveals the possible route by which the partbooks entered into the

---

[51] Add. MS 30480 (Discantus of the Hamond Partbooks), 1560–1590, fol. 4r.
[52] Butler, 'From Liturgy', 30.
[53] Ibid., 54; Morley, *Plaine and Easie Introduction*, 179.
[54] Butler, 'From Liturgy', 33; May Hofman, 'The Survival of Latin Sacred Music by English Composers 1485–1610' (DPhil diss., University of Oxford, 1977), ii, 250–260; Warwick Edwards, 'The Sources of Elizabethan Consort Music' (DPhil diss., University of Cambridge, 1974), I, 121–125.
[55] Butler, 'From Liturgy', 36.
[56] Milsom had argued that the set had begun life under a church roof before entering into domestic usage, whereas Hofman and Le Huray interpreted the partbooks as solely a domestic, non-liturgical collection. John Milsom, 'Sacred Songs in the Chamber', in John Morehen (ed.), *English Choral Practice 1400–1650* (Cambridge: Cambridge University Press, 1995), 161–179, at 169; May Hofman, 'The Survival of Latin Sacred Music', ii, 70; Peter Le Huray, *Music and the Reformation in England 1549–1660* (Cambridge: Cambridge University Press, 1978), 98.

collection of Thomas Hamond in 1615, via what she identifies as Phase IV of the copying (a Master of Music and his Choristers).

A large number of novice scribal hands are in evidence in pieces such as Thomas Causton's 'Service for Children', Adam's 'Venite', Christopher Tye's 'From the Depths', and Johnson's 'Deus misereatur'.[57] Wobbly, irregularly slanting hands and inconsistent diamond shapes slipping into the more easily formed round hand before reverting to diamond shapes can be found in all of these pieces, as the choristers slowly but surely mastered the art of writing notation. The Discantus and Altus partbooks are also littered with childish features such as extravagantly elongated custodes, dotted ditto marks and trial directs, extended 'finininininis' at the end of the 'Service for Children', and the declaration that John Sheppard's 'Kyrie Paschali' is 'the best songe in Englande'. Similar declarations can be found in the rather more sophisticated Dow partbooks (c. 1581), where Robert Dow marks the end of Byrd's 'In resurrection tua' with an epigram in his honour:

Birde suos iactet si Musa Britanna clientes;
Signiferum turmis te creet illa suis.

You who are a glory to our (British) race, and a nightingale to our people,
Byrd, I pray that you may make music with voice and hand for a long time.[58]

In the Hamond set we witness a childish imitation of this, and a rehearsal and internalizing of what it means to be part of the English choral tradition. Taken together, these are traces of the new turn in choral education from around 1565 explored above: the move away from the learning of complex methods of improvising performance during the liturgy, towards the learning of how to write music for the liturgy.[59]

Towards the turn of the seventeenth century, musical writing became a vital aspect of musical education and the cultivation of musical literacy. However, as we have seen throughout the course of this book, scholars of writing have recently, and frequently, demonstrated that in the sixteenth century the written word (and by extension, note) was rarely just visuo-graphic

---

[57] Add. MS 30482 (Altus), fol. 7r; Add. MS 30483 (Tenor), fol. 47r; Add. MS 30481 (Discantus), fol 76r.
[58] The Dow Partbooks, Contratenor, Christ Church MSS 986, 66; translation in Daisy Gibbs, 'Memory and Monumentality', 13.
[59] Flynn, 'Education of Choristers', 194.

entities. It was constituted of visual forms that destabilized the boundary between meaningful and meaningless; these forms were a provocation to vocalize and perform, rather than the silent process we know it as today.[60] Forming note-shapes enabled choristers to learn crucial skills such as the deployment of *musica ficta* not just as singers and improvisers, but also as scribes, and as composers who could take a score's-eye view of a piece, intricately conscious of its intervallic content. Learning to write in the English Renaissance was a sonic matter, a performance matter, just as much as the ability to hold and guide the pen into uniform lozenge-shaped noteheads. The scribal layer of the Hamond partbooks associated with the choristers and their master dates from the very beginning of the period at which musical copying would have been important to a choral education, identified by Jane Flynn as in approximately 1565. Thus, the evocative and fragmentary scribal hands identified by Butler offer an exciting possibility: the choristers may not have been copying from visual exemplars, but rather from ear (either performance, or aural memory). In this way, the Hamond partbooks might in fact offer a record of the audiation—'the sonic, aural equivalent to imagination'[61] of a community of choristers in this crucial, transitionary phase in choral education.

In such a context, the miscellaneity of the collection and of the hands provides a valuable musical lesson. It preserves the spectral vestiges of past solmization errors, and in so doing it offers an additional framework by which a young chorister could 'read' a piece of music. Modern choral singers will recognize the experience of being handed a copy of sheet music that is well-worn, taped at the seams where it is beginning to come apart, and scrawled across with past performance instructions from past years or even decades; often these extend from simple dynamics to the matter of error, where those past performer/s have frequently misread a note or phrase and written or drawn increasingly frantic directives to themselves, 'No!', 'E-*flat*', 'FOCUS', and so on. The Hamond partbooks, in all their effusive and chaotic glory, offer a particularly early and particularly poignant manifestation

---

[60] Juliet Fleming, *Cultural Graphology: Writing after Derrida* (Chicago: University of Chicago Press, 2016); 'Damask Papers', in Andy Kesson and Emma Smith (eds.), *The Elizabethan Top Ten: Defining Print Popularity in Early Modern England* (Farnham: Ashgate, 2013); Jennifer Richards, *Voices and Books in the English Renaissance* (Oxford: Oxford University Press, 2019); John Gallagher, '"To Heare It By Mouth": Speech and Accent in Early Modern Language Learning', in *Huntington Library Quarterly*, 82: 1 (Spring 2019), 63–86; Neil Rhodes, 'Punctuation as Rhetorical Notation? From Colon to Semicolon', in *Huntington Library Quarterly*, 82: 1 (Spring 2019), 87–100.

[61] Valdivia, 'Audiation: Listening to Writing', 557.

of this phenomenon. Within their pages, Heffernan's delight in disorder translates into a cognition of disorder: a recognition of all that seeps into the edges of musical performance, and a bringing-in of an array of useful, redolent inferences to aid the reader's comprehension of its contents by providing an additional framework of extra-notational visuo-graphic features that lead beyond the page.[62] This chapter has aimed to flesh out the possible conditions and structures by which aspiring musicians, professional and amateur, adult and child, learned how to perform false relations. It has done so by taking a pair of material remnants and seeking to reinvigorate them and the connotations suggested by these material, visual conditions. It has demonstrated that learning how to successfully perform false relations required a musical knowledge that was somatic, spatial, and embedded within the imagined (audiated) soundscape of a given music book; it also, vitally, thrived off the spectral remnants of past failures as part and parcel of the guiding structure of the music. In turning to the final chapter of this book, an exploration of the *una nota supra la/semper est canendum fa* (the note above *la* must be sung as *fa*) rule and its afterlives, it is important that these somatic, spatial, imagined substructures be kept in mind. It is only through appreciating their role in the musical education of the people of the English Renaissance that we can begin to approach *fa* above *la* and its associated tropes as they once might have been heard, in sixteenth- and early seventeenth-century spaces.

---

[62] Mind-wandering has recently garnered much attention in cognitive literary studies; see Raphael Lyne, *Memory and Intertextuality in Renaissance Literature* (Cambridge: Cambridge University Press, 2016). For a cognitive definition of mind-wandering see Paul Seli, Evan F. Risko, Daniel Smilek, and Daniel L. Schacter, 'Mind-Wandering with and without Intention', in *Trends in Cognitive Sciences*, 20 (2016), 605–617; Michael C. Corballis, *The Wandering Mind: What the Brain Does When You're Not Looking* (Chicago: University of Chicago Press, 2015).

6
Una nota supra La/Semper est canendum Fa
A Tale of Two Semitones

Exit La, pursued by Pha

Let us move forwards several decades from the genesis of the Hamond partbooks and *A Booke of In nomines & other solfainge songes* to an episode in the mid-seventeenth century. At the tail end of the English Renaissance, as William Laud came to prominence as Archbishop of Canterbury[1] and a new set of religio-political concerns began to govern the sacred music of the realm, another musical theoretical treatise was published. This is Charles Butler's *Principles of Musik, in singing and setting with the two-fold use thereof, ecclesiasticall and civil* (1636):

> The number of Notes Musical is therefore divided by Septenriz; because there are in nature but 7 distinct sounds, exprest in Musik, by 7 distinct notes, in the 7 several Cliefs of the scale. [...] These seven Notes (as the Cliefs wherein they stand) are discerned by their Places. A Place is either Rule or Space. In eleven Rules with their Spaces is comprehended the whole Scale.[2]

> [...]
> The names of the Notes were invented for more easy and speedy instruction of Skollars in Tuning them: that being taught the Names and Tunes together; when they are perfect in [agreement], they might, by the help of them, known these more readily.
> For the 7 Notes there are but six several Names: [*Ut, re, MI, fa, sol, la*.] The seventh Note, because it is but a half-tone above *la*, as the four[th] is

---

[1] Charles Carlton, *Archbishop William Laud* (London: Routledge and Kegan Paul, 1987).
[2] Charles Butler, *The Principles of Musik, in singing and setting with the two-fold use thereof, ecclesiasticall and civil* (London: John Haviland, 1636), 10.

above *MI*; (whereas the rest are all whole tones) is fitly called by the same Name: the which being added, the next Note will be an Eight or Diapason to the first; and consequently placed in the same Letter of Clief, and called by the same Name.

Of the seven Notes thus Named, *MI* is the principal, or Master-note: which being found, the six several Notes doo follow, (both ascending and descending) in their order.[3]

So goes Butler's elucidation of the *una nota supra la/semper est canendum fa* rule, inherited from late-medieval practices of solmization and the age-old Guidonian Gamut.[4] His elucidation is uncontroversial, and, as we shall see in this chapter, it follows that of his forebears. However, one details stands out: his squeamish avoidance of the very naming of the note *fa* which, although notated in his diagrams of solmization, are studiously substituted instead for 'the seventh note [. . .] a half-tone above *la*' and 'the four[th]', almost as though, like Voldemort, they could be summoned by the very act of naming. Butler's gold standard 'Master-note'[5] is instead *mi*,[6] the unproblematic, unambiguous whole tone counterpart to the lascivious, promiscuous, slippery *fa*; this is in a marked contrast to, for example, Thomas Campion, for whom 'the substance of musicke' is 'the observation of the halfe note, which is expressed either by *Mi Fa* or *La Fa*'.[7] Yet even by his insistence that *mi* is the 'principal, or Master-note' of the 'seven distinct sounds, exprest in Musik' and his refusal to acknowledge its shady half-tone counterpart, Butler conjures the spectre of *fa/pha* and its pervasive, seductive power over the music of the English Renaissance. In the preceding chapters we have seen how the *mi–fa* interval inflected musical thought, shaped the imagination of

---

[3] Ibid., 11.

[4] Karol Berger, *Musica Ficta: Theories of Accidental Inflections in Vocal Polyphony from Marchetto Da Padova to Gioseffo Zarlino* (Cambridge: Cambridge University Press, 1987), 77–79; Stefan Mengozzi, '"Clefless" Notation, Counterpoint and the fa-Degree', in *Early Music*, 36: 1 (2008), 51–66; Nicholas Routley, 'A Practical Guide to *Musica Ficta*', in *Early Music*, 13: 1 (1985), 59–72; Robert Wienpahl, 'Modality, Monality and Tonality in the Sixteenth and Seventeenth Centuries II', in *Music and Letters*, 53: 1 (1972), 59–73.

[5] We should note that this is not a direct equivalent of the 'key note', although it bears some conceptual resemblance. See Megan Kaes Long, 'What Do Signatures Signify? The Curious Case of 17th-Century English Key', in *Journal of Music Theory*, 64: 2 (2020), 147–201.

[6] It is worth noting that Jessie Ann Owens interprets Butler's insistence on *Mi* as the 'master-note' is as a substitute for *Ut* as a means of defining the scale. See Jessie Ann Owens, 'Concepts of Pitch in English Music Theory c. 1540–1640', in Cristle Collins Judd (ed.), *Tonal Structures in Early Music* (New York: Garland, 2000), 211.

[7] Thomas Campion, *A New way of Making Fowre Parts in Counter-Point by a most familiar, and infallible rule* (London: T. Snodham for John Browne, 1610), fol. B4r.

musical space, and transformed an impelled transgression into a key stylistic feature. In this final chapter we will investigate the rise of *la–fa*, the seventh pitch extension of the hexachord, unpacking the associations it inherited from *fa*, marrying its expressive function for the early music revival as simultaneously the modern jazz blue seventh[8] and the relic of an early medieval musical theoretical rule. For the sake of avoiding confusion, I will follow Butler in referring to the seventh as *pha*, 'which is the first syllable of Pharos, the name of a high tower, and of an upper garment'.[9]

It is worth rehearsing the rule of '*Una nota supra La/Semper est canendum Fa*' or *fa*-above-*la* to appreciate just how central the *fa*-degree is to its very conception, and how distinctive is Butler's omission. Rather than mutate to a different *recta* (authorized) or *ficta* hexachord, the performer could assume the seventh solmization degree that extended the hexachord as a second *fa*-degree, that is, a flattened form. The rule in effect provides a seventh, *ficta* degree to the six-syllable solmization scale, thus equipping the performer with something that vaguely resembles the closed circle of the octave now in use in the Western tradition of music. It is of vital importance that this is kept in mind as the main context of *pha*: *pha* is not a solmization syllable in its own right, or even strictly a proto-seventh, but an extension of the hexachord, allowing a mutation to a different recta hexachord. Butler's diagram of the 'Tonorum Cyclus' or Tonal Cycle (see Fig. 6.1) epitomizes this logic. Likewise, as Karol Berger emphasizes, it is vital that we do not interpret the *fa*-above-*la* rule as a separate, stand-alone entity in and of itself, a pothole that awaited reconstructing editors of early music in the mid twentieth century due to the dogmatic assertions of music theorists such as Butler and Morley.[10] Though there were many in the sixteenth century, notes Berger, who adopted the rule indiscriminately, it was strictly a spin-off of the prohibition of the tritone.[11] The eclectic use of the *fa*-above-*la* appears to be an entirely sixteenth century innovation, and not isolated to any particular geographical area or decades within the century.[12] Nevertheless, we can surmise that the musicians of the English Renaissance were particularly fond of it given their penchant for what would anachronously become known as the 'English' cadence, more of which later in this chapter. As for the tritone itself,

---

[8] Ben Curry, 'Two Approaches to Tonal Space in the Music of Muddy Waters', in *Music Analysis*, 36: 1 (2017), 37–58.
[9] Butler, *Principles of Musik*, 15.
[10] Berger, *Musica Ficta*, 77.
[11] Ibid., 78.
[12] Ibid., 78.

Cap. I I.   Of Singing.   13

of de Moonts in de yeer˄) is most˄ fitly exemplifyed in dat Figur˄, wie hat˄ no˄ end˄.

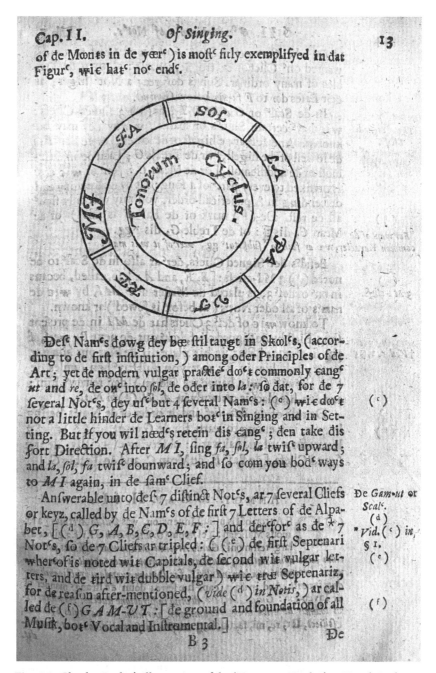

Des˄ Nam˄s dowg dey bee stil taugt in Skool˄s, (according to de first institution,) among oder Principles of de Art; yet de modern vulgar practie˄ doo˄t commonly cang˄ *ut* and *re*, de on˄ into *sol*, de oder into *la*: so dat, for de 7 several Not˄s, dey us˄ but 4 several Nam˄s: (ᶜ) wie doo˄t not a little hinder de Learners bot˄ in Singing and in Setting. But if you wil need˄s retein dis cang˄; den take dis sort Direction. After *M I*, sing *fa, sol, la* twis˄ upward; and *la, sol, fa* twis˄ dounward; and so coom you bod˄s ways to *M I* again, in de sam˄ Clief.

(ᶜ)

Answerable unto des˄ 7 distinct Not˄s, ar 7 several Cliefs or keyz, called by de Nam˄s of de first 7 Letters of de Alpabet, [(ᵈ) *G, A, B, C, D, E, F :*] and der˄for˄ as de * 7 Not˄s, so de 7 Cliefs ar tripled: ((ᵉ) de first Septenari wher˄of is noted wit Capitals, de second wit vulgar letters, and de tird wit dubble vulgar) wie tree Septenariz, for de reason after-mentioned, (vide (ᵈ) in *Notis*,) ar called de (ᶠ) *G A M-U T*: [de ground and foundation of all Musik, bot˄ Vocal and Instrumental.]

De *Gam-ut* or *Scal˄*.
(ᵈ)
* *Vid.* (ᶜ) in § 1.
(ᵉ)

(ᶠ)

B 3   De

Fig. 6.1 Charles Butler's illustration of the 'Tonorum Cyclus' or Tonal Cycle. From Charles Butler, *Principles of Musik* (London: John Haviland, 1636), fol. B3r. London, British Library. Catalogue No. 1608/4719. Photograph author's own.

theoretically permitted only when properly resolved, the *fa*-degree is the vacillating unspoken aspect at its core as a matter of horizontal relation, via the mnemonic taught to students of music in the English Renaissance: '*Mi contra fa diabolus est in musica*', *mi* against *fa* is the devil in music, not just the tritone but also the major third (from the durum hexachord) against the minor third (from the molle hexachord).[13] The *fa*-degree is the cynosure of the instability of musical meaning, the lesser evil that provides the basis for the musical theoretical rules that permit false relation in particular, chromaticism in general, and Campion's 'strange keyes'.

Elsewhere in *The Principles of Musik*, Butler's avoidance of *fa* is not quite so punctilious. In describing solmization signs, Butler cannot avoid mention of the problematic interval:

> There belong to Notes [thus described by their Number, Names, Tune and Time] these 7 things: a Flat, a Sharp, a Ligature, a Repeat, a Pauze, a Direct, and a Cloze.
> A Flat changes *Mi* into *fa*, making him half a Tone lower: and is thus marked
> A Sharp raises *fa* or *ut*, half a Tone higher, not changing their names: and is thus marked[14]

The reader will notice that *fa* is also nameable when it comes to the question of the sharp (formerly the *mi*-solmization sign, as we explored in Chapters 1 and 5) as it is in the question of the flat (formerly the *fa*-solmization sign). The distinction and the context in which Butler deems it appropriate to name *fa* are of vital importance in understanding how the people of the English Renaissance thought about the semitone and *fa*-above-*la* in practice.

At this point it is worthwhile to step back and examine Butler the man, and in so doing gain greater understanding of his motivations for describing an old, inherited rule in this idiosyncratic manner. From humble origins Butler became a chorister at Magdalen College, Oxford, in 1579; he matriculated two years later and received his BA at the remarkably young age of fifteen in 1584 and MA in 1587, before joining the priesthood.[15] During his time as

---

[13] Lionel Pike, *Hexachords in Late-Renaissance Music* (London: Routledge, 2020), 97–98. See also Carl Dahlhaus, *Studies on the Origin of Harmonic Tonality* (Princeton, NJ: Princeton University Press, 1990), 153–248, at 181–182, and 249–324, at 249–250.
[14] Charles Butler, *Principles of Musik*, 35, fol. E2r.
[15] A. H. Bullen and Karl Showler, 'Charles Butler (1560–1647)', in *Oxford Dictionary of National Biography* (accessed 6 August 2021).

Rector at Nately Scures and Wootton St Lawrence, Butler published a diverse arrange of works: *Two Books of Ramean Rhetoric* (1597), a school textbook which utilized the diagrammatic philosophy of Petrus Ramus; *The Feminine Monarchie* (1609, and much revised 1623 and 1634), the first work on bee-keeping in the English language and which posited his theory about the generation of beeswax and included musical notation of a healthy hive, which we briefly encountered above; and *The English Grammar* (1633), in which he sought to establish a standardized phonetic alphabet to assist spelling (this last work was published together with the final revised *Feminine Monarchie* in 1634).[16] Despite the fact that the *Principles of Musik* was published several decades after the majority of the music explored in this book, it is of great use to us in understanding a lot of this material. Not only was Butler singing in one of the centres of music-making, at a key time in the English Renaissance; this formative experience appears to have translated into a life-long fascination with the standardization of sound as meaningful and unambiguous, as demonstrated by his *English Grammar*: 'for solution of which doubt, it is meet that, where we have generally, or in the more civil parts (as the Universities and Cities) forsaken the old pronunciation; there we conform our writing to the new sound, and write as we speak'.[17] In other words, Butler sought specifically to evade the frustrating multiplicity of meaning, and close what Joseph M. Ortiz has referred to as 'the gap between the *logos* of meaningful language and the *materia* of musical sound'.[18] Still in the mid-1630s, the bewitching semantic slipperiness of *fa* was emblematic of this gap.

Butler's treatment of *fa* (and, implicitly, *pha*) provides a fascinating insight into one of the fundamental issues and appeals of the false relation in the English Renaissance: the inability to control sound and so manage the thoroughly blurred threshold between unruly noise and mannered musical sound. Take, for example, his interpretation of the 'music' of a healthy beehive and the way he notates it. The 'princesse' bee begins 'the od minim in A-*lamire*' and 'tuneth the rest of her notes in C-*solfa*', whilst the Queen 'in a deeper voice thus' (thus indicating F-*faut*) 'continuing the same, some foure or five semibriefes, and sounding the end of every note in C-*solfaut*'. In other words, every sound emitted by the bees adheres closely to the musical gamut

---

[16] Charles Butler, *Rameae rhetoricae libri duo* (Oxford: Joseph Barnes, 1597); *The Feminine Monarchie* (Oxford: Joseph Barnes, 1609); *The English Grammar, or Institution of Letters, Syllables and Words in the English Tongue* (Oxford: William Turner, 1633).
[17] Butler, *English Grammar*, 3, fol. A2r.
[18] Joseph M. Ortiz, *Broken Harmony: Shakespeare and the Politics of Music* (Ithaca, NY: Cornell University Press, 2011), 3.

as understood in the early seventeenth century. There are strong moral theological motivations for Butler's choice, as well as philosophical. As in his *English Grammar,* in the *Feminine Monarchie* Butler seeks to establish a hard and fast boundary between meaningful (musical) sound and meaningless (unmusical) noise. The natural, pleasant sound of the beehive is, for Butler, of course contained within one of the authorized hexachords and within the proper, authorized musical gamut. *Fa* and *pha,* on the other hand, disturb the hard and fast boundary between the musical and the unmusical, the meaningful and the meaningless. By its very ambiguity, only patchily signified by the conventions of the way the music is written, they do not 'conform [its] writing to the new sound, and write as we speak'. *Mi* was far more reliable. In many ways this is another (albeit later) expression of the neuroses surrounding B-*fa* discussed above in the Introduction and Chapter 2. However, it is important to note that it is in striking contrast to the approach of Butler's closest contemporary, Campion, and that the question of appropriately styled *expression* and meaning appear to be the fundamental motivation behind Butler's approach.

Butler's concern with musical decorum, appropriate stylization, and meaning encapsulate the themes that have recurred throughout this book: those of the rapidly shifting sands of musical literacy, and the tension between inherited conventions and new innovations in musical signification as developments such as the printing press, musical genres from the continent, and ideas about key exerted their influence over the musical culture of the English Renaissance. These concerns come to a head in the form of *pha* and the indiscriminate application of the *fa-above-la* rule throughout the latter half of the sixteenth century and into the seventeenth century.[19] As a result, we find Campion listing the rule as follows (see also Fig. 6.1):

> First observe the places of the halfe Notes, which are marked with a halfe circle, and remember that if the lowest be Mi Fa, the upper halfe Note is La fa, and contrariwise if the lowest halfe Note be La Fa, the upper must be Mi Fa.
>
> It will give great light to the understanding of the scale, if you trye it on a Lute, or Voyall, for there you shall plainely perceive that there goe two frets to the raising of a whole Note, and but one to a halfe Note, as on the Lute in this manner the former eight may be expressed.[20]

---

[19] Berger, *Musica Ficta,* 78.
[20] Campion, *A New Way,* unpaginated.

For Campion, *la fa* or *pha* is simply a fact of the scale, and the fixed-scale solmization that the tradition has developed from the *Whole Booke of Psalmes* onwards. The approach is similar to Thomas Morley's of fourteen years earlier, in the *Plaine and Easie Introduction to Practicall Musicke*, as the Master introduces Philomathes to the basics of solmization. This is the episode in the *Introduction* that Morley glosses as '*what to sing above la*':

MASTER   Take this for a generall rule, *that in one deduction of the sixe notes, you can have one name but once used*, although in deed (if you could keepe right tune) it were no matter now you named any note. But this wee use commonly in singing, that *expect it be in the lowest note of the part wee never use ut.*
[...]
PHILOMATHES   But now I am out of my byas [bias, inclination or 'comfort zone'], for I know not what is above *la. Ut re me fa sol la.*
MASTER   Wherein standeth the note whereof you doubt?
PHILOMATHES   In F fa ut.
MASTER   And I praie you, *F fa ut,* how many cliefes and how manie notes?
PHILOMATHES   One cliefe and two notes.
MASTER   Which be the two notes?
PHILOMATHES   *Fa* and *ut.*
MASTER   Now if you remember what I told you before concerning the singing of *ut*, you may not sing it in this place: so that of force you must sing *fa*.[21]

Likewise, William Bathe's *Skill of Song* (1597) provides an account that chimes with both Campion and Morley:

When you haue in this sort found out the *vt*, you must vnderstand that euery note that standeth in the next place aboue it is named *re*, euery note that standeth in the next place to that is named *mi*, in the next to that *fa*, then *sol*, then *la*, then *fa*, ascending vp alwaies orderly, counting the rules, and spaces: then next aboue that againe is *vt*: for you shall finde that place, which is the eight place from that wherein your other *vt* stood, to begin with

---

[21] Thomas Morley, *A Plaine and Easie Introduction to Practicall Musicke* (London: Peter Short, 1597), 3 and 5.

the same letter: So that if the rules & spaces were infinite, you might in this manner giue euery note his right name: and as you did count vpward *vt, re, mi, fa, sol, la, fa,* and so come againe to *vt*: so must you come downeward from *vt*, the same way backward, by *fa, la, sol, fa, mi, re, vt*. And so come to *fa*, againe.[22]

We will explore these passages in greater depth later in the chapter. For now it is worth observing that none makes mention of the origin of the *la*-above-*fa* rule, in the prohibition of the tritone. This absence is peculiar, as we shall see, as it goes some way to explaining why this particular semitone appears to have escaped the pejorative connotations of its companion concept, the *mi–fa* interval and the lascivious b-*fa*. *Fa*-above-*la* was easily avoidable by either mutating to an appropriate hexachord rather than stretching the limits of the existing one with *pha*, or by the rubric of the leading note which ordained that a pitch be raised a semitone where it featured in an ascending passage in order to 'lead' to the next.[23] Overt indulgence in *Fa*-above-*la* gave rise to a number of tropes, not least the kitschy froth of what became known four centuries later as the 'English' cadence. To adopt an undeniably provocative term from Robert Wienpahl, *pha* was a key stylistic to the 'monality' of English Renaissance music, and its bricolage of older, inherited, and newer, innovated, styles.[24] In the following section of this chapter we will use the 'English' cadence as a route towards understanding the phenomenon of *pha* and false relations in general. In many ways it is the most basic and familiar of the false relation tropes, but as we shall see this renders it a particularly enlightening (if not rather prismatic) lens into attitudes towards false relation in the English Renaissance, and how we have been encouraged by its historiographical reception to imagine the musical culture that allowed it to namelessly flourish.

---

[22] William Bathe, *A Briefe Introduction to the Skill of Song* (London: Thomas Este, 1596), unpaginated.

[23] Simon Jackson, 'Double Motion: Herbert and Seventeenth Century Polyphonic Practice', in *George Herbert Journal*, 37: 1–2 (Fall 2013–Spring 2014), 146–161, at 150. The leading note, of course, was not without its provocations; see Elizabeth Eva Leach, 'Gendering the Semitone, Sexing the Leading Tone: Fourteenth Century Music Theory and Directed Progression', in *Music Theory Spectrum* 28 (2006), 1–21.

[24] Robert S. Wienpahl, 'Modality, Monality and Tonality in the Sixteenth and Seventeenth Centuries', in *Music & Letters*, 52: 4 (1971), 407–417, and 'Modality, Monality and Tonality in the Sixteenth and Seventeenth Centuries II', in *Music & Letters*, 53: 1 (1972), 59–73.

A Cadence by Any Other Name Would Smell as Sweet

'Robbed out of a capcase of an old organist' and a 'deformitie [. . .] hidden by flurish', the so-called English cadence (see Ex. 6.1) was thus banished to the odds and ends bin of the English Renaissance by Thomas Morley's officious fictional music master, Gnorimus.[25] In modern terms it is innocuous enough: a perfect authentic cadence constructed around the V–I chord progression, inflected by a dominant chord in which the third of the chord is heard in both major and minor forms, thereby creating a false relation, sometimes in adjacent sonorities and sometimes simultaneous. The minor third typically sounds at the peak of a five- or seven-note melodic curve, which stretches over the 4-3 suspension over the dominant and heightens or leans towards its dissonance.[26] In sixteenth-century terms, it is an execution of the *fa*-above-*la* rule that enshrines *pha* (minor third) at the peak of a melodic curve and thwarts expectations of the leading note (major third); the melodic curve is itself an illustration of the elastic ductility of the hexachord,

Ex. 6.1 Example of an English Cadence (from 'a Kyrie by Taverner'), from Thomas Morley, *A Plaine and Easie Introduction to Practicall Musicke* (London: Peter Short, 1597).

[25] Morley, *Plaine and Easie Introduction*, 154.
[26] Eleanor Chan, 'The English Cadence: Reading an Early Modern Musical Trope', in *Early Music*, 49: 2 (2021), 19.

running *sol la pha la sol fa mi* in its full form, pitching the forms of the *molle* and *durum* hexachords against each other and refusing to resolve into the leading note and pull more satisfactorily towards the 'key' note of *ut*. The melodic curve serves as a catchy refrain, increasing the memorability of the phrase and the text that its sets. The classically fifteenth- and sixteenth-century 4-3 suspension obfuscates the origin of the dissonance and the false relation between major and minor third, seemingly amplifying, echoing, and at the same time displacing the discordance; listening to an English cadence, we are briefly unaware of the precise interaction of notes that has produced the dissonance, which renders the *pha* degree both more and less at odds with the harmonic texture of the piece. Megan Long has noted that the tonal expectation generated by the I–V–I tonal plan—period-like phrasing, highly segmented musical surface, efficient text-setting, frequent cadences, and audible phrase boundaries—of homophonic partsong at the turn of the seventeenth century was a vital step towards the tonal strategies which are still in use today; these repertoires invited listeners and performers to hear and interpret regularities, and to enjoy the neatly formed fulfilment of expectation mapped out tonally by the above listed features.[27] The 'English' cadence is part and parcel of this musical style, merely one of many strategies to create a sense of carefully curated tonal scheme, design, draft, plot.[28] The additional spiciness of the false relation between major and minor third, the push-pull between leading note and *pha*, simply adds the frisson of a twist to the V–I progression; a secret revelation, like the puffs of silk through a fashionably slashed sleeve, the glimpse of extra space between *mi–fa* or *la–fa*.

Thus described the 'English' cadence appears merely innocuous. What was it about the 'English' cadence that Morley's Master Gnorimus found so objectionable? Little did Gnorimus know how much he let slip by framing the trope as archaic ('robbed [. . .] from an old organist', 'deformitie [. . .] hidden by flurish'); nor, indeed, how much enchantment it would hold for those of the early music revival rediscovering the music of Morley and his contemporaries for themselves, and for choristers across the land to this very day. We might be forgiven for wondering if in choosing these criticisms, the Master (or whoever he was intended to performatively pastiche) in fact deliberately intended to provoke these very cultural associations.[29] Only twenty years earlier, Bess of Hardwick had commissioned an appliqué series of

---

[27] Megan Kaes Long, *Hearing Homophony: Tonal Expectation at the Turn of the Seventeenth Century* (Oxford: Oxford University Press, 2020), 18–19.

[28] Michael Baxandall, 'English Disegno', in Edward Chaney and Peter Mack (eds.), *England and the Continental Renaissance* (Woodbridge: Boydell Press, 1990).

[29] Katie Bank, *Knowledge Building in Early Modern English Music* (London: Routledge, 2020).

hangings depicting the 'Virtues and Heroines' (as the mythical and historical figures of Penelope, Artemisia, Cleopatra, Lucretia, Zenobia) and furnishing panels of the Liberal Arts, composed of damasked scraps covered all over in flourishing strapwork patterns and taken from ecclesiastical vestments both as plunder from the Dissolution of the Monasteries in the early sixteenth century and from earlier, medieval vestments of *opus anglicanicum*.[30] In other words, precisely the kind of thing that might have been found in the capcase (used to carry items of apparel like collars, caps, gloves, 'lace, pinnes and needles')[31] of an old organist. The 'Virtues and Heroines' hangings were particularly prized by Bess, such that in 1601 (a mere four years after the publication of Morley's *Plaine and Easie Introduction*) they were the only tapestries or hangings to be itemized in detail, rather than under a collective heading.[32] 'Garment[s] of strange fashion', 'deformitie[s] hidden by flurish', and so on were continually recycled, reused, and repurposed in the late sixteenth and early seventeenth centuries. Bess was by no means an outlier; indeed, the visual art of the English Renaissance is characterized by a passion for eclectic borrowings from various archaic idioms into a bricolage of forms to a far greater extent than that of its continental contemporaries, a curiosity which resulted in the art historians of the twentieth century interpreting English visual tastes as a kind of 'anorexia', the product of ignorance rather than preference.[33] The continual reuse, recycling, and reapplication of older decorative forms was a key aspect of the visual cultures of the English Renaissance; the architecture of the period, for example, continued to use gothic forms alongside neoclassical well into the seventeenth century.[34] Indeed Morley's Gnorimus is a peculiarity in this respect. He is dismissive of 'old stale fashion' and compositional approaches that have 'many times [been] compelled'.[35] His vehement objection to the two-flat key signature, well established in

---

[30] Margaret Ellis, 'The Hardwick Hall Hanging: An Unusual Collaboration in English Sixteenth-Century Embroidery', in *Renaissance Studies*, 10: 2 (1996), 284. For more on the role of textiles, their reuse, and their self-fashioning role in sixteenth century society, see Ann Jones and Peter Stallybrass, *Renaissance Clothing and the Materials of Memory* (Cambridge: Cambridge University Press, 2001); and Hester Lees-Jeffries, *Textile Shakespeare* (Oxford: Oxford University Press, forthcoming 2024).

[31] Thomas Dekker, *The Belman of London* (London: 1608), sig.D4v.

[32] Eleanor Chan, *Mathematics and the Craft of Thought in the Anglo-Dutch Renaissance* (London: Routledge, 2021), 167.

[33] For this art historical approach, see Patrick Collinson, *The Birthpangs of Protestant England: Religious and Cultural Change in the Sixteenth and Seventeenth Centuries* (Basingstoke: Macmillan, 1988); Mack and Chaney (eds.), *England and the Continental Renaissance*. For early arguments that countered this approach, see Lucy Gent (ed.), *Albion's Classicism: The Visual Arts in Britain 1550–1660* (London: Yale University Press for the Paul Mellon Centre for Studies in British Art, 1995).

[34] Ethan Matt Kavaler, *Renaissance Gothic* (New Haven, CT: Yale University Press, 2012).

[35] Morley, *Plaine and Easie Introduction*, 156.

English choral music from at least the 1540s, is strikingly in contrast to the general acceptance of the practice and not to mention Campion and Butler's relative silence on the subject.

> Such shiftes the Organistes are many times compelled to make for ease of the singers, but some haue brought it from the Organe, and haue gone about to bring it in common use of singing with bad successe if they respect their credit, for take me any of their songes, so set downe and you shall not find a musicion (how perfect soeuer hee be) able to *sol fa* it right, because he shall either sing a note in such a key as it is not naturally as *la in C sol faut, sol in b fa b my, fa in alamire.* or then hee shall be compelled to sing one note in two seueral keyes in continual deduction as *fa in b fa b mi*, and *fa in A la mi re* immediatlie one after another, which is against our very first rule of the singing our sixe notes or tuninges, and as for them who haue not practised that kind of songes, the verie sight of those flat cliffes (which stande at the beginning of the verse or line like a paire of staires, with great offence to the eie, but more to the amasing of the yong singer) make them mistearme their notes and so go out of tune.[36]

We cannot hope to reach towards even a fragment of the contemporary understanding of this criticism until we recognize the full array of associations that Morley invites his readership into, and the collective palimpsestic cultural landscape which he and his readership occupied.

There are technical, music-theoretical reasons behind the objection to the English cadence. However, before we examine the structure of the cadence in any detail, it is worth lingering over how we know it was received in late sixteenth-century England and focusing on the cultural reasons for Morley/Master Gnorimus' objections. Morley's is the only contemporary description of the cadence. The names which he gave it have had little impact on the name chosen by the historical musicologists of the latter half of the twentieth century, and by which we know it today.[37] It has been a platitude of the early twenty-first century that the 'English' cadence is, of course, not even really 'English'; its naming is arguably the by-product of the historiographical desire to find an English Renaissance musical style to feed into the English musical tradition that composers were attempting to forge in the late nineteenth and early

---

[36] Morley, *Plaine and Easie Introduction*, 156.
[37] Jeremy Summerly, 'The English Cadence', in *Leading Notes*, 6: 1 (1996), 7–9, at 8.

twentieth centuries.[38] Nevertheless, by focusing in on this single aspect of the 'English' cadence we arguably miss the fascinating tensions at play behind the façade of the simple question of English or not-English. As we explored in the preceding chapters, the attempt to establish a discrete 'English' identity by both Elizabeth I and James I in the face of colonial activity was a crucial backdrop to the music of this period. This is an undercurrent that is alive and well in Morley's choice of adjective: the 'garment of *strange* fashion' (my italics). 'Strange' entered English in the thirteenth century from the French *estrange*, meaning external, strange, foreign, alien, belonging to another country, 'unknown to the locality', 'belonging to others'.[39] Randle Cotgrave's 1611 *Dictionarie of the French and English Tongues* defines *estrange* and its cognates as variously 'strange, uncouth, unusuall; forraine, alien, outlandish; unaccustomed, unacquainted; also, harsh, rude, od', 'strangely, unusually, wonderfully; out of ordinarie course in an uncouth manner', 'strangeness, unwontedness', 'a rare, or wonderfull matter', 'harshnesse, forwardness, perverseness', and 'a stranger, alien, forreiner, an outlander, or outlandish man'.[40] Already in this early seventeenth-century lexicographical definition of the strange we can witness many of the tropes still peddled today surrounding the foreign (their supposed 'harshnesse', 'pervers[ity]', 'rude[ness]' crossed with the 'wonder' and rarity that they provide). It is probable that 'unusual' was the chief connotation that Morley intended with Master Gnorimus' description of the 'garment of strange fashion', but it is clear that the other meanings are seeping into the edges of the critique, fed by the complex entanglement of associations surrounding the early modern English 'strange'.[41] Incredibly, this means that the question of English or not-English has been a dynamic of the English cadence since at least 1597: it is inherent to its appeal.

---

[38] Sarah Collins, 'The National and the Universal', in P. Watt, S. Collins, and M. Allis (eds.), *The Oxford Handbook of Music and Intellectual Culture in the Nineteenth Century* (Oxford: Oxford University Press, 2020).

[39] Oxford English Dictionary Online, https://www.oed.com/view/Entry/191244?rskey = LCVJIf&result = 1&isAdvanced = false#eid, accessed 16 August 2021.

[40] Randle Cotgrave, *A Dictionarie of the French and English Tongues* (London: Adam Islip, 1611), unpaginated. See also Onyeka Nubia on the meanings of strangeness in Tudor society; Onyeka Nubia, *England's Other Countrymen: Black Tudor Society* (London: Zed Books, 2019), 141–144.

[41] For a nuanced discussion of this dynamic, see Callan Davies's discussion of the use of the term 'strange' and 'stranger' in theatrical performance: 'Certainly, at heart, as with the etymological roots of the term that fix it in questions of belonging and identity, strangeness was closely associated with foreignness. The practical and political charge of "strange", "stranger" and strangeness sounds loudly throughout the entirety of Elizabethan and early Jacobean England. Used to describe residents who are not local to the parish as well as those hailing from outside the realm, the idea of the "stranger" elicited a great deal of anxiety throughout the period, and the term itself is sometimes censored on stage, as evidenced by the manuscript of *The Book of Sir Thomas More* that bears the Master of the Revels Edmund Tilney's emendations. [. . .] The crossover of social, political and

What are we to make of this undercurrent of strangeness, foreignness, alienness at the heart of the English cadence? As Onyeka Nubia states, the term was not quite as pejorative as it might first appear to the twenty-first-century eye.[42] It was used to describe anyone not of the parish, or not English, and so was often applied to the immigrant Dutch and French Huguenot craftsmen who had come to England fleeing from religious persecution throughout the sixteenth century.[43] Many of the court musicians employed by Henry VIII and inherited by Edward VI, Mary, and ultimately Elizabeth were from across Europe, including Aemilia Lanier's ancestors the Bassano family.[44] At the time of writing, the earliest instances of the cadence are in the work of Josquin des Prez (c. 1450–1521); thus we can interpret the cadence as a Franco-Flemish export alongside the artisanal skills that entered England from the Low Countries and Spain in the sixteenth century.[45] Another early set of instances can be found in the collection of madrigals by the Franco-Flemish composer Phillipe Verdelot (c. 1480–c. 1540), gifted to Henry VIII by the City of Florence in c. 1527/early 1528 whilst Verdelot was Maestro di Cappella at the Baptistry of S. Maria del Fiore and the Duomo itself; this collection appears to have remained in the music library of the Chapel Royal for the duration of the sixteenth century, and is now known to us as the Newberry-Oscott partbooks.[46] The collection was painstakingly identified by H. Colin Slim in 1972; the missing Altus part was subsequently discovered in the library of St Mary's College, Oscott. The partbooks feature a number of swaggering English cadences, such as the one

dramatic anxiety centred on the notion of "strangeness" provides an important backdrop to Jacobean notions about strange language and spectacle. Indeed, immigration—both from provincial England and from foreign countries—was a particular concern in London, especially during this period of steady urbanisation and population growth. While the swell of apparent popular opinion altered periodically throughout the Elizabethan and Jacobean periods, it remained consistently a time of conflicted attitudes towards immigration. Throughout the entirety of Elizabethan reign, the City of London Corporation discussed measures to curb, control and navigate immigrant labour, as well as attempting to manage anti-immigration sentiments.' Callan Davies, *Strangeness in Jacobean Drama* (London: Routledge, 2021), 9–10. See also Ayanna Thompson, *Passing Strange: Shakespeare, Race and Contemporary America* (Oxford: Oxford University Press, 2011).

[42] Nubia, *England's Other Countrymen*, 141. See also Lien Luu, *Immigrants and the Industries of London 1500–1700* (Aldershot: Ashgate, 2005).
[43] Nubia, *England's Other Countrymen*, 143.
[44] Katherine Butler, *Music in Elizabethan Court Politics* (Woodbridge: Boydell, 2015), 80.
[45] An earlier instance in the work of Guillaume de Machaut is wrongly attributed to Apel and Binkley; they do not, in fact, mention an English cadence in Machaut. Apel and Binkley, *Italian Violin Music of the Seventeenth Century*, 56.
[46] I am grateful to David Skinner for bringing this connection to my attention. Newberry Library, Chicago, MS minus VM 1578 .M91. David Skinner, album notes for *Philippe Verdelot: Madrigals for a Tudor King*, Alamire directed by David Skinner, Obsidian Records CD703, 2007; H. Colin Slim, *A Gift of Madrigals and Motets* (Chicago: University of Chicago Press, 1972).

in *Italia mia benche 'lparlar sia indarno*.[47] One English occurrence predates the arrival of the Newberry-Oscott partbooks in England at around the turn of 1528: William Cornysh's (1465–1523) 'Ah Robin Gentle Robin', which survives in the so-called Henry VIII Manuscript, compiled between 1515 and 1520 and now in the British Library.[48] It is unclear whether Cornysh and Verdelot met, but it seems likely they knew of each other; Cornysh was in charge of the musical entertainments at the Field of the Cloth of Gold in 1520 (at which point Verdelot may have still been in France) and travelled throughout the Holy Roman Empire, so it is feasible that his travels took him to Florence and the Cattedrale di Santa Maria del Fiore.[49] Likewise it is also possible that Cornysh came across the cadence as a musical figure in Josquin's work; as Kerry McCarthy has recently demonstrated and contrary to prior opinion, Josquin's music did appear to circulate to an extent in English circles.[50] In any case, attempting to ascertain whether their adoption of the cadence was influenced by one or the other, or a delight in the *fa*-above-*la* rule as it became more and more detached from its original purpose of maintaining harmonic decorum, proves ultimately futile. English cadences begin to appear in works by English composers at this point; it features, for example, in Thomas Tallis's Mass 'Puer natus est nobis' (c. 1554); John Sheppard's 'Deus misereatur' (before 1558); William Byrd's 'O God Give Ear' (1588), 'Civitas sancti tui' (1589), and 'Sacerdotes Domini' (1605); John Wilbye's 'I Live and Yet Methinks I Do Not Breathe' (1598); Martin Peerson's 'Laboravi in gemitu' (c. 1620s); the Nunc dimittis of Richard Ayleward's *Short Service*; Thomas Tomkins's Voluntary in D; and Robert White's 'Tota pulchra est'. As a musical trope, the English cadence is thus arguably in equal parts stranger and native.

The mythical origins of the 'English' cadence do little to explain quite why Morley, or rather the persona he adopted in writing the character of Master Gnorimus, objected to it quite so vehemently. As we have seen throughout this book, 'strangers' brought many of the things that were highly prized by people of both the high and middling sort in the English Renaissance: musical forms like the madrigal; strapwork and arabesque patterns that soon covered

---

[47] Susan McClary, *Modal Subjectivities: Self-fashioning in the Italian Madrigal* (Berkeley: University of California Press, 2004), 38–56.
[48] Add. MS 31922, London: British Library, Fols. 53r–54v.
[49] It also seems likely that Cornysh's earlier work would have been known in the Holy Roman Empire. See Daisy M Gibbs, 'England's Most Christian King: Henry VIII's 1513 Campaigns and a Lost Votive Antiphon by William Cornysh', in *Early Music*, 46: 1 (2018), 131–148.
[50] Kerry McCarthy, 'Josquin in England: An Unexpected Sighting', in *Early Music*, 43: 3 (August 2015), 449–454. This is contrary to the previous belief that England was isolated from continental musical exemplars for much of the sixteenth century; see Sarah Schmalenberger, 'Hearing the Other in the *Masque of Blackness*', in Naomi Andre, Karen M. Bryan, and Eric Sayler (eds.), *Blackness in Opera* (Urbana: University of Illinois Press, 2012), 35.

the masonry, wooden, textile, paper, gold, silver, and steel surfaces across the country; artisanal techniques like blackwork; foodstuffs like sugar; and the musical font of the Huguenot Thomas Vautrollier, one of only two full sets in England in the late 1570s and the one carefully selected by Tallis and Byrd for their *Cantiones sacrae* in 1575. Morley's faulty example is taken from a Kyrie by John Taverner (1490–1545). Taverner was entirely native and so much admired that one of his 'Missa Gloria Tibi Trinitas' spawned the 'In nomine' genre, much loved of composers throughout the sixteenth century; certainly not the 'old organist' of odds and ends conjured up by Morley's/Gnorimus' description. There is perhaps an inference of reformist zeal and anti-papistry, but as historians of religion such as Alexandra Walsham and Brian Cummings have demonstrated over the past decade, this is not in keeping with the character of the English reformation.[51] Besides this, between 1526 and 1530 Taverner was the inaugural Organist and Master of the Choristers at Christ Church, Oxford (then Cardinal College, named after its founder Cardinal Wolsey); it appears likely that Taverner was sympathetic to the reformist cause.[52] Master Gnorimus' confused criticism rages against an entirely fictional organist enamoured of the old religion, its vestments, and its musical practices, rather than the historical figure who composed the faulty example itself (Ex. 6.1). It brings us no closer to understanding Morley's objections (or rather, performed objections) to the English cadence. A better clue can be found in the adjective 'old'. To call something 'old' or archaic is another form of othering, another way of making 'strange', 'forraine', 'alien', 'outlandish', 'unaccustomed'.

Alongside the movement to establish the category of 'stranger' or 'other' as non-English rather than 'not from the parish',[53] another project was afoot in the English Renaissance: the project to establish a coherent narrative around the English past. These two forms of alterity served as useful points of comparison that ultimately built into an overall understanding of the 'forraine' as exotic, primitive, uncivilized, 'rude', and/or 'perverse'. We need look no further than colonial governor and artist John White's (c. 1539–c. 1593) watercolours of (real) native Americans (see Fig. 6.2) and the (imagined) images of ancient Britons they inspired (see Fig. 6.3),

---

[51] Alexandra Walsham, Bronwyn Wallace, Ceri Law, and Brian Cummings (eds.), *Memory and the English Reformation* (Cambridge: Cambridge University Press, 2020); Harriet Lyon, *Memory and the Dissolution of the Monasteries in Early Modern England* (Cambridge: Cambridge University Press, 2021); Margaret Aston, *Broken Idols of the English Reformation* (Cambridge: Cambridge University Press, 2015); Alexandra Walsham, *The Reformation of the Landscape: Religion, Identity and Memory in Early Modern Britain and Ireland* (Oxford: Oxford University Press, 2011).
[52] Hugh Benham, *John Taverner: His Life and Music* (London: Routledge, 2003).
[53] Nubia, *England's Other Countrymen*, 93–94, 31–34, and 141–144.

Fig. 6.2 John White, 'A Wyfe of an Timucuan chief of Florida', watercolour over graphite, 1585–1593, 25 cm × 14 cm. London: British Museum. Object No. 1906,0509.1.23. By kind permission of the British Museum.

Fig. 6.3 Jacques Le Moyne de Morgues (formerly attributed to John White), 'A Young Daughter of the Picts', watercolour and gouache, touched with gold on parchment, c. 1585, 26 cm × 18 cm. Yale Center for British Art: Paul Mellon Collection. Object No. B1981.25.2646. Public Domain.

which present one blended concept of otherness. The English Renaissance witnessed the rise of a taste for the archaic as a fetishized and often heavily embellished past or collective history, epitomized by Raphael Holinshed's *Chronicles* (1577),[54] William Camden's *Britannia* (1586), and Richard Verstegan's *Restitution of Decayed Intelligence* (1605) alongside the continuing influence of the romance genre in works such as Edmund Spenser's *Faerie Queene* (1590–1596),[55] which sees the mythical female knight and founder of the English race, Britomart, on a quest to find her predestined husband after seeing his face in an enchanted mirror. English passion for the archaic was only intensified when James I came to the throne in 1603 and began his campaign to establish the concept of 'Great Britain', a term that was not legally recognized until 1707 but which gained much of its political capital as a result of James's energies in forging a 'British' subjectivity as an English, Scottish, and Irish entity discrete from other potential national subjectivities.[56] To a considerable extent this was motivated by a desire to assuage the anxieties surrounding James's right to succession and the fact that he simply did not fit the mould and mythology of English sovereignty that Elizabeth had established: he, after all, was a stranger, 'forraine', 'alien'. As Kim F. Hall notes, 'rhetorically and politically, the Jacobean fascination with otherness was the logical successor to Elizabethan insularity. [...] The maintenance of England's borders through figurations of Elizabeth as the pure and fair national body only helped produce a void of English whiteness that her successor, himself a foreign other, could not fill. English identity comes to rely on both the appropriation and the denial of differences troped through blackness in order to fill this void and preserve a sense of self.'[57] Elizabeth had constructed a model of sovereignty based on her appropriation of the cult of the Virgin Mary and her role as the 'pearl [/] whom God and man doth love'; only James's complexion allied him to this imagery of English monarchy.[58]

---

[54] Raphael Holinshed, *The First Volume of the Chronicles of England, Scotlande, and Irelande* (London: Lucas Harrison, 1577).

[55] Edmund Spenser, *The Faerie Queene* (London: Richard Field for William Ponsonbie, 1596).

[56] A project to explore the musical, material, and visual ramifications of this passion for the archaic is in early stages of planning by the author. It is likely that the passion for the archaic originated in the dissolution of the monasteries; see Harriet Lyon, *Memory and the Dissolution*.

[57] Kim F. Hall, *Things of Darkness: Economies of Race and Gender in Early Modern England* (Ithaca, NY: Cornell University Press, 1995), 129. See also Helen Cooper, *The English Romance in Time: Transforming Motifs from Geoffrey of Monmouth the Death of Shakespeare* (Cambridge: Cambridge University Press, 2004).

[58] Anonymous, *Lo, Here the Pearl, who Man and God Doth Love* (London, 1563), unpaginated.

Both forms of 'strange[ness]' are at play in the 'English' cadence. By the time that Morley published *A Plaine and Easie Introduction to Practicall Musicke* in 1597, the cadence was archaic. It is a moot point whether or not this would have been interpreted as a good or bad thing; the music of Taverner was still being copied into manuscript collections such as the Sadler, Baldwin, and the Peterhouse (latter Caroline set) Partbooks, so was evidently still performed and learned. It is also a figure that is bound to the continental polyphonic style established by Josquin and his (continental) contemporaries, if not necessarily 'invented' on the continent; concepts of musical authorship throughout this period were, as we explored above, extremely contentious and very different from our modern concept.[59] However, this double strangeness did not prevent James I from apparently selecting Thomas Weelkes's virtuosic and English cadence-laden *Ninth Service* (c. 1603) for use in his coronation service (see Appendix III); the *Ninth Service* shares two substantial passages with Weelkes's 'O Lord Grant the King a Long Life', one ten-bar passage shared with the Magnificat and the Amen of the Nunc dimittis, and both are written for seven voices.[60] From this we might reasonably surmise that the 'garment of strange fashion', 'robbed from the capcase of an old organist', the 'deformitie [...] hidden by flurish' was received by contemporary readers as a reference to its origins in England's pre-Reformation past, more a matter of archaic strangeness rather than the 'forraine'. Already in 1603, James I was seemingly relying upon the inherent Englishness of the 'English' cadence.

What are we to make of this trope, at the same time so significant to the English Renaissance imagination and yet so apparently devoid of significance as to be virtually undocumented? How can it inform our understanding of false relations as they were used and thought about at the time? At this most crucial point in English history, we find it adopted in one of the most important state ceremonies and integrated into the rich tapestry of performance (alongside allegorical masques by Thomas Dekker and Ben Jonson)[61] used to

---

[59] Rebecca Herissone, *Musical Creativity in Restoration England* (Cambridge: Cambridge University Press, 2013); Jessie Ann Owens (ed.), *Composers at Work: The Craft of Musical Composition 1450–1600* (Oxford: Oxford University Press, 1997); Rob Wegman, 'From Maker to Composer: Improvisation and Musical Authorship in the Low Countries, 1450–1500', in *Journal of the American Musicological Society*, 49, 3 (1996), 409–479; M. Everist, *Discovering Medieval Song: Latin Poetry and Music in the Conductus* (Cambridge: Cambridge University Press, 2018), 151–180.

[60] David Brown, *Thomas Weelkes: A Critical Study and Biography* (London: Faber & Faber, 1969), 186–187, 191.

[61] Alan Stewart, *The Cradle King: A Life of James VI and I* (London: Chatto & Windus, 2003), 172–173; Anne Lancashire, 'Dekker's Accession Pageant for James I', in *Early Theatre*, 12: 1 (2009), 39–50; Heather C. Easterling, 'Reading the Royal Entry (1604) in/as Print', in *Early Theatre*, 20: 1 (2017), 45–75.

establish James I's divine right to rule. On 25 July 1603 in Westminster Abbey, the 'English' cadence was one of the many cultural factors and signs at play to contribute to a carefully choreographed atmosphere. It was part of the rhetorical work of the spectacle of coronation and kingship, used to entwine James within a display of Englishness to insist upon his belonging. In this way it functioned like the visual art form of the tapestry and the way that it was used to signal the presence of the monarch, constantly unhung and rehung to cover the walls of whichever space the monarch was passing through.[62] To state as such is no mere fanciful claim: in the English Renaissance, tapestry was experienced in three dimensions and a highly involved, tactile manner. It took a large number of people to hang a tapestry given their typically immense size; they would be moved from residence to residence and room to room within residences, used to conceal doors (and indeed courtiers, as they waited upon the monarch).[63] Weelkes's thoroughly contrapuntal *Ninth Service*,[64] weaving the threads of six voice parts together in a manner that lends itself to the thematic repetition more typical of the polyphony of the early sixteenth century, creates a dense and intricate texture of sound that vacillates between the semantic and asemantic musical sound. It recalls Fleming's observations on the relationship between writing and type ornament that became a key stylistic of the book in English Renaissance print: 'The decorative and the semantic elements are never *seen* together (even where, in a well-formed letter, they are the same thing). For where text is read, its beauties will be overlooked; and where its beauties are studied, the text disappears.'[65] In this way Weelkes's use of the cadence plays with the very idea of its status as superficial 'garment', a trifle (derived from the Old French *trufler*, to mock or deceive, another falsehood) that belonged in the 'capcase of an old organist'. Elsewhere in the shared passage between the *Service* and its companion anthem 'O Lord Grant the King a Long Life', Weelkes leans heavily on the *pha* degree at salient moments of text underlay, 'that his years may endure', 'throughout all generations', 'alway sing and praise', and the 'amen', which constantly threatens to break into the melodic curve of the English cadence (see Ex. 6.2). Thus Weelkes creates a bewitching valency between concepts of continuation: continuation

---

[62] Rebecca Olson, *Arras Hanging: The Textile That Determined Early Modern Literature and Drama* (Newark: University of Delaware Press, 2013); Eleanor Chan, *Mathematics*, 43.

[63] Olson, *Arras Hanging*, 24.

[64] David Brown notes that the *Ninth Service* is one of the most contrapuntal of Weelkes's prolific output. See David Brown, *Thomas Weelkes*, 191–192.

[65] Juliet Fleming, *Cultural Graphology: Writing after Derrida* (Chicago: University of Chicago Press, 2016), 84.

Ex. 6.2 Thomas Weelkes, 'O Lord Grant the King a Long Life', c. 1603, bb. 10–15, which plays on the expectation of the flat seventh and the melodic curve of the English cadence, after Thomas Weelkes, *Collected Anthems*, transcr. and ed. David Brown, Walter Collins, and Peter le Huray, *Musica Britannica*, 23 (London, 1966).

of monarchy; elastic continuation of hexachord into *pha* above *la*, and indeed the continuation of a musical theoretical rule borne of Guido's early medieval hand. Largely undocumented the 'English' cadence may be, but it is clear that audiences of the English Renaissance received it as an appropriately elaborate flourish with which to bring in the reign of a celebrated new monarch.[66] In addition to connoting the visual form of an 'ornamental curve', a 'flourish' is also of course the fanfare of trumpets to introduce someone of importance.[67]

'Deformitie hidden by Flurish'

We have unpacked some of the broader cultural associations of Morley/ Master Gnorimus' description of the 'English' cadence, and explored some of the pejorative connotations that it aimed to invoke. As we have seen, these objections would not have been uncontroversial or universally accepted in 1597; they directly undermine the contemporary taste for the archaic, contemporary understanding of what a 'garment of strange fashion' would have been in the English Renaissance imagination. However, the context of Morley's broader musical work makes the rhetorical work of his description of the 'English' cadence somewhat less surprising. In the following section, we will investigate the technical musicological reasons behind Morley/ Master Gnorimus' objections and how these musical theoretical objections interact with the cultural objections explored above. Largely, as we shall see, this is driven by Morley via Gnorimus' desire to do away with the older, obsolete aspects of solmization and retain only elements of the early modern musical style that corresponded to how the music theory was observed in practice. This much is unsurprising given Morley's efforts to bring Italianate musical forms such as the madrigal into England.[68] What is surprising is the endurance of the older, solmization-inspired models of music well into the

---

[66] Thomas Dekker's account should perhaps be taken with a pinch of salt, as it is evidently in part a bid for patronage, but it is clear that James was well received by the English public if only for the fact that no conflict preceded his accession. See Thomas Dekker, *The Magnificent Entertainment* (London: Thomas Creede, 1604).

[67] Michael Tilmouth, 'Flourish', in *The Grove Music Dictionary Online*, https://www.oxfordmusiconline.com/grovemusic/view/10.1093/gmo/9781561592630.001.0001/omo-9781561592630-e-0000009879?rskey = 2NBz87&result = 1 (accessed 21 August 2021).

[68] See, e.g., Morley's enthusiastic response to the first madrigal collection, *Musica Transalpina* (1588). For more on Morley's enthusiasm for Italianate forms, see Lionel Pike, *Pills to Purge Melancholy: The Evolution of the English Ballett* (Farnham: Ashgate, 2004), 39–128; and Tessa Murray, *Thomas Morley*, 124–128. For more on this collection, see Alfred Einstein, 'The Elizabethan Madrigal and "Musica Transalpina"', in *Music & Letters*, 35: 2 (1944), 66–77.

seventeenth century, in the works of Henry Purcell, John Blow, and their contemporaries. The bricolage approach towards musical style continued even as such corresponding trends in the visual and literary cultures fell away, merely adopting the new forms introduced by Morley and combining them to create a distinctly English mélange of tropes and figures. First, however, we shall turn again to the musical theoretical accounts.

The 'English' cadence is absent from the other musical theoretical treatises of the period, but the language with which Morley through Master Gnorimus describes it is certainly not. The 'garment of strange fashion' has its echoes in Thomas Campion's criticism of the 'strange keys' which can occur without proper knowledge of the *mi–fa* and *la–fa* intervals and their placement in the scale:

> [. . .] bounded within a proper key, without running into *strange keyes* which have no affinity with the aire of the song.[69]
>
> Relation or reference, or respect not harmonicall is *Mi* against *Fa* in a crosse forme, and it is foure Notes, when one being considered crosse with the other doth produce in the Musicke a *strange discord*.[70] (my italics)

Butler, likewise, adopts language that chimes with this particular phrase. In his explanation of why he chose the term *pha* to describe *fa*-above-*la* he states that it is taken from the Greek *Pharos*, 'the name of a high tower, and of an *upper garment*' (my italics).[71] In these two accounts we catch the faintest, shimmering glimpse of a common language of music criticism: the 'strange discords' of *mi–fa* and *la–fa* are strange for their superficiality, their elaborate, ornamental nature that does not fit within the bounds of the structure of music.[72] As we explored above in Chapter 1, this entirely belies the origin of the false relation; nevertheless it is tantalizing to find this rhetorical disavowal in the musical theoretical writing of the English Renaissance. William Bathe's *Briefe Introduction to the Skill of Song* (1597) gives us a somewhat more sympathetic approach to 'strangeness' in music, referring to 'some strange markes and knitting of notes which time I doubt not will cut off' (in reference to prolation, perfection, and imperfection) and the 'strange flat'

---

[69] Campion *A New Way*, fol. D4r.
[70] Ibid., fol. E1v.
[71] Butler, *Principles of Musik*, 15.
[72] For more on this idea with relation to visual culture, see Chan, 'The English Cadence', 21–29.

impelled by the shape of the polyphony, which is best made 'sharp, unlesse it bee in such places as a strange flat will doe well to come in'.[73] Together with Campion's dedicatory poem included in the prefatory material to Thomas Ravenscroft's *Briefe Discourse* 1614, Bathe's account gives us a clear context for the precise connotations of the musical 'strange':

> The *Markes* that limit *Musicke* heere are taught,
> So fixt of ould, which none by right can change,
> Though *Use* much alteration hath wrought,
> To *Mosickes Fathers* that would now seeme strange.
> The best embrace, which herein you may finde,
> An *Author* praise for his good *Worke*, and *Minde*.[74]

The 'markes' of notation, 'so fixt of ould' but which through 'use much alteration hath wrought', have become 'strange' to 'Mosickes Fathers'; these 'markes and knittings' are 'strange', but 'time' will 'cut' them off. Thus, that which is musically 'strange' is strange because it is out of its time, archaic. This is the context in which we should read the trope that became the 'English' cadence. The archaically strange and exotically strange are two sides of the same coin for the reasons explored above, but it is important that this is the inflection adopted by the language of the contemporary musical theoretical treatises.

In this context, we can begin to see the sketchy outline of a rationale for the musical theoretical objections to the cadence. Note that Karol Berger, in discussing the use of the *fa*-above-*la* rule, observed that its use had become completely indiscriminate and separate from the question of avoiding tritones by the sixteenth century.[75] False relations and figures and tropes constructed around them, like the 'English' cadence, originated in the prioritization of counterpoint over harmony. As Morley himself observed, they came about 'for lack of other shift'. We do not know what Bathe, Campion, Ravenscroft, or Butler thought about the 'English' cadence.[76] Arguably we do not know what Morley thought of them, or his purpose behind denouncing

---

[73] William Bathe, *A Briefe Introduction to the Skill of Song* (London: Thomas Este, 1596), unpaginated.
[74] Thomas Campion, 'O This Ensuing Discourse', paratext to Thomas Ravenscroft, *A Briefe Discourse of the True (but neglected) use of charact'ring the degrees* (London: Edward Allde for Thomas Adams, 1614), unpaginated.
[75] Berger, *Musica Ficta*, 78.
[76] Perhaps we can reasonably infer from Tomkins's annotations in Morley; see Dennis Collins, 'Thomas Tomkins' Canonic Additions to Thomas Morley's "A Plaine and Easie Introduction to Practicall Musicke"', *Music & Letters*, 76: 3 (1995).

them through Master Gnorimus; Morley uses one in precisely the manner he objects to in his madrigal 'Round around about a Wood', suggesting that the above passage is to be taken with a pinch of salt.[77] However, what we can with relative certainty deduce is that part of the furore surrounding false relations in the English Renaissance was to do with the fact that they were, fundamentally, old-fashioned, and detached from their original purpose: they are relics of a scalar model prior to the advent of fixed-scale solmization.[78] To assert as much is perhaps to state the obvious. However, it is interesting that this sentiment is markedly at odds with the general attitude towards objects from the past, as explored above with regards to the Hardwick Hall hangings. Largely this was due to music's privileged place within the English Renaissance imagination. Music provided a direct route to the Divine. In the context of the Reformation and the ongoing deconstruction of modes of worship that took place across the sixteenth century, older styles of music could be politically dangerous. For the composers who came of age through the turbulent upheaval of Edwardian reform, Marian restoration, and eventual Elizabethan moderation, their works and sonic inheritance bore the marks of this constant revision and circumvention of undesirable musical styles.

A compelling example of this dynamic can be found in the evolution of one of Tallis's 'evergreen' motets, from its origins in the 1550s to the form he ultimately published and circulated in the *Cantiones sacrae* of 1575: 'O sacrum convivium' or 'I Call and Cry to Thee, O Lord'.[79] The motet appeared in various collections as three vernacular anthems, and began its life as a fantasia laden with the melodic curves of the 'English' cadence, before its ultimate reworking as the piece familiar from choral repertoires to this day.[80] It is, in other words, an analogue of Bess of Hardwick's gorgeous appliqué recyclings of ecclesiastical vestments and altar cloths, a patchwork of older forms made new by their combination. Why, though, did Tallis ultimately remove the 'English' cadences? It seems a peculiar move given that they were a key stylistic feature in his forty-voice motet 'Spem in alium', probably first performed in the late 1560s and which would later be given pride of sonic

---

[77] Thomas Morley, *Madrigals to Foure Voices* (London: Thomas Este, 1600), No. 21.
[78] Samantha Arten, "The Origin of Fixed-Scale Solmization in *The Whole Booke of Psalmes*," *Early Music* 46: 1 (2018), 149–165.
[79] Kerry McCarthy, *Tallis* (Oxford: Oxford University Press, 2020), 110–111 and 165–166.
[80] Magnus Williamson, 'Queen Mary I, Tallis' *O Sacrum convivium* and a Latin Litany', *Early Music*, 44: 2 (2016), 251–270, at 251; John Milsom, 'A Tallis Fantasia', *Musical Times*, 126 (1985), 658–662; John Milsom, *Thomas Tallis and William Byrd: Cantiones Sacrae 1575*, Early English Church Music 56, (London: Stainer & Bell, 2014), 128–167.

place and much admired at the investiture of Henry, Prince of Wales, in 1610.[81] Magnus Williamson notes that the instrumental fantasia contrafact of 'O sacrum convivium' found in Add. MS 31390 and in fragmentary form at the end of MS Harley 7578 is likely a relic of the Marian restoration of the 1550s; it is suited to the Eucharistic theology of this period, but not necessarily associated with a specific event.[82] Despite the fact that in its motet form it appears quintessentially Elizabethan for its heavy use of imitation and of five voice parts, Williamson argues that 'O sacrum convivium' is evidently a much older piece by merit of its inclusion in MS Harley 7578, which was compiled by the 1550s at the latest;[83] given the fact that it had been contrafacted into this instrumental fantasia by c. 1555 (in MS Harley 7578), Tallis's prototype work could easily be Edwardian or even Henrician.[84] The piece's stylistic similarity to Tallis's Mass 'Puer natus est nobis' (c. 1554) would certainly appear to support an earlier composition date, both constructed of 'large slabs of sound adorned with repetitive decoration'.[85] Thus, the versions preserved in Add. MS 31390 and MS Harley 7578 offer a tantalizing glimpse into shifting attitudes towards false relations and what they came to represent for listeners and performers in the English Renaissance. It is possible that the ornamentation of the cadences to make ostentatious use of the *pha* degree was a result of scribal interference;[86] however, the fact that they appear in both sources suggests that they were likely a feature intended by Tallis himself, and indeed there is no reason to presume that they were not. Likewise, we should not assume that the 1575 version was anything other than a politically whitewashed version given that the *Cantiones* were being dedicated to Elizabeth I; it would certainly be a mistake to conclude that it

---

[81] Thomas Wateridge, a student at the Inns of Court, reported the anecdote in 1611 (possibly second or third hand): 'In Queen Elizabeth's time there was a song sent into England of 30 parts (whence the Italians obtained the name to be called the Apices of the world) which being sung made a heavenly harmony. The Duke of ____, bearing a great love to music, asked whether none of our Englishmen could set a good song, and Tallis, being very skillful, was felt to try whether he would undertake the matter, which he did, and made one of 40 parts which was sung in the long gallery at Arundel House, which so far surpassed the other that the Duke, hearing of the song, took his chain of gold from off his neck, and gave it him: which song was again sung at the Prince's coronation.' Cambridge University Library MS Dd.5.14, fol. 73v. Quoted in McCarthy, *Tallis*, 191-194.

[82] Williamson, 'O Sacrum Convivium', 263.

[83] British Library, MS Harley 7578, fols. 92r-93r; John Milson, 'A Tallis Fantasia', 658.

[84] Williamson, 'O Sacrum Convivium', 270, n. 70.

[85] McCarthy, *Tallis*, 185. See also David Humphreys, 'Why Did Tallis Compose the *Missa Puer Nobis Natus Est*?', in *The Musical Times*, 157 (2016); and Joseph Kerman, 'The *Missa Puer Nobis Natus Est* by Thomas Tallis', in *Write All These Down: Essays on Music*, (Berkeley: University of California Press, 1994), 125-138.

[86] Milson, 'A Tallis Fantasia', 662.

Ex. 6.3 Thomas Tallis's revisions of 'O sacrum convivium' between (a) the 1550s instrumental fantasia, preserved in Add. MS 3130, c. 1578, and (b) the version printed in the *Cantiones sacrae* (1575), after Thomas Tallis and William Byrd, *Cantiones sacrae 1575*, transcr. and ed. John Milsom, *Early English Church Music* 56 (London, 2014), 158–159.

was the final, fixed form intended by Tallis, or indeed even his 'preferred' form simply because it was printed.[87] The English cadence and its indulgent use of the *pha* degree was not universally problematic even in the context of the *Cantiones*, given that Tallis uses one in the final measures of 'Salvator mundi I', also included in the volume. Instead, the move towards the version ultimately printed in the *Cantiones sacrae* appears to have been motivated by a desire to achieve what was believed to be greater clarity in text-setting (see Ex. 6.3a and b) and a politically astute decision to eschew excessive use of the

---

[87] Again, see Owens, *Composers at Work*; and McCarthy, *Tallis*, 164–165. Andrew Johnstone, *William Byrd: Eight Fragmentary Songs Edited and Reconstructed by Andrew Johnstone* (London: Fretwork, 2020), ii–iii.

stylistic features of earlier Henrician and Marian musical culture, steeped as it was in the Latin liturgy. The indulgent use of false relations, particularly of unnecessary instances such as the *pha* degree where there was no danger of the tritone, appears to have fallen squarely in this category.

It would be disingenuous to present the English Reformation and the gradual move towards Protestantism as a neat, clear-cut, or even objective matter: evidently for many in the late sixteenth century, false relations did not retain the savour of recusancy and were charmingly, if perhaps quaintly, nostalgic musical tools for expression. But it is evident that for some excessive use of the *mi–fa* and *la–fa* relation bore connotations of the older style of worship. This much is made evident by Erasmus' (1466–1536) infamous interruption of his annotations of Corinthians I to deliver an impromptu critique of English choral culture in 1515, which it is worth returning to in full:

> We have brought into sacred edifices a certain elaborate and theatrical music, a confused interplay of diverse sounds, such as I do not believe was ever heard in Greek or Roman theatres. [. . .] These activities are so pleasing to monks, especially the English, that they perform nothing else. Their song should be mourned; they think God is pleased with ornamental neighings and agile throats. In this custom also in Benedictine Colleges in Britain young boys, adolescents, and professional singers are supported, who sing the morning service to the Virgin mother with a very melodious interweaving of voices and organs.
>
> [...]
>
> Those who are more doltish than really learned in music are not content on feast days unless they use a certain distorted kind of music called *Fauburdum* [sic]. This neither gives forth the pre-existing melody nor observes the harmonies of the art. In addition, when temperate music is used in church in this way, so that the meaning of the words may come more easily to the listener, it also seems a fine thing to some if one or other part, intermingled with the rest, produces a tremendous tonal clamour, so that not a single word is understood. Thus the whims of the foolish are indulged and their baser appetites are satisfied.[88]

---

[88] Desiderius Erasmus, *Opera Omnia*, ed. J. Clericus (Leiden, 1703–1706), VI, 731C–732C. Quoted in Clement A. Miller, 'Erasmus on Music', in *The Musical Quarterly*, 52: 3 (1966), 338–339; see also McCarthy, *Tallis*, 6; and Rob Wegman, *The Crisis of Music in Early Modern Europe, 1470–1530* (London: Routledge, 2005), 164.

Erasmus makes no direct reference to false relations, but they dance through his accounts of 'tremendous tonal clamour', 'a certain distorted kind of music called *Fauburdum*', 'ornamental neighings', and the 'confused interplay of diverse sounds'. His critique is not that of an inexperienced amateur; Henricus Glareanus claimed that Erasmus had spent a couple of years of his childhood as a choirboy under Jacob Obrecht at the Domkerk in Utrecht.[89] Likewise, whilst he cannot be unproblematically associated with Protestantism due to his theological stance, Erasmus' sentiments certainly laid the groundwork for later Reformed thought on a number of subjects, not least music; as Long notes, the strategies of homophony (predictable V–I progressions, frequent cadences, and so on) came about as a way to increase the comprehensibility of text settings 'so that the meaning of the words may come more easily to the listener'. Tallis evidently wished to avoid invoking the ire of the more vehemently reformist factions of the Elizabethan court; by and large, the pieces he selected for inclusion in the *Cantiones* were arranged with a clearly audible text setting and little in the way of 'a confused interplay of diverse sounds'. McCarthy states that they are 'built on the same principle as the visual art of Tudor court miniaturists such as Levina Teerlinc [...] and Nicholas Hilliard: fine workmanship on a tiny canvas'.[90] However it is important to remember that each of these pieces, 'O sacrum convivium', 'Absterge Dominum', 'Salvator mundi', contains the spectral remains of the 'elaborate and theatrical' predecessors from which they were adapted.[91] For those well-versed in the performance practices of the day, it is easy to reinsert the melodic curves of the 'English' cadence into 'O sacrum convivium' by merit of the structure of the piece and the spaces left by their absence by the popular tropes of the 4-3 suspension and/or tonal expectation of the V–I progression.[92] For those who had lived through the Dissolution, and for their children, grandchildren, wards, and students, the ghosts of early sixteenth-century musical culture would have been omnipresent, inherent in any encounter with a musical text or performance.[93]

---

[89] Gustav Reese, *Music in the Renaissance* (New York: W. W. Norton, 1959), 107.
[90] McCarthy, *Tallis*, 183.
[91] Ibid., 165; Milsom, *Thomas Tallis and William Byrd*, 1–81, 128–167, 308–320.
[92] Chan, 'English Cadence', 19.
[93] Hester Lees-Jeffries addresses this with her evocative description of the Guild Chapel in Stratford-upon-Avon, which John Shakespeare oversaw the whitewashing of in 1563. 'William Shakespeare was born a few months after the Doom was whitewashed. Visitors to the chapel today look at the wall that he would have looked at on an almost daily basis as a schoolboy, but see something that he never saw. Yet he would have known that there was *something* behind its whitewashed surface, and perhaps heard it described by Stratford's older inhabitants, or by his father. The Doom

Through the lens of the vexed 'English' cadence, the false relation resolves itself into a hallmark of the intimate interplay between remembering and forgetting, oblivion and recollection, that is so typical of the English Renaissance as it progressed inchmeal through the Reformation.[94] Examples of the cadence in Elizabethan and Stuart music cluster overwhelmingly in the sacred, rather than secular, repertoires; in Byrd's responses, in the anthems of Gibbons, Byrd, and Weelkes. Bittersweet, the presence of *mi–fa* and *la–fa* teetered on a tightrope between acceptable and indulgent decadence, a wallowing at the very edges of meaningful, musical sound: the instrument both of commemoration and of obliteration. William Barley's ill-fated musical treatise, *The Pathway to Musicke*, offers a particularly charged insight into this tension. Despite his lack of musical expertise, Barley was quick to take advantage of the end of Byrd's monopoly on general music printing in 1596, and brought out the *Pathway*, along with *A New Booke of Tabliture*, which instructed the reader in the rudiments of how to play the lute and other string instruments. His lack of music font, indiscriminate borrowing from sources such as *The Praise of Musicke* (1586), and the numerous errors in both render them difficult documents to deal with, both presumably for aspiring musicians at the time and for those attempting to understand English Renaissance musical culture now.[95] However, it does give us something of a hint of the doublethink required in the case of false relations. Barley follows the *Praise of Musicke* in defining concord as 'a concord of unlike voyces within themselves, tackt together; [sweetly?] sounding unto the eare'. Dissonance is 'a combination of divers sounds, *naturallie* offending the eare' (my italics).[96] In other words, meaningful music is enshrined by nature, as Butler believed that the buzzing of bees could be mapped onto the gamut and the *durum* hexachord. Meaningful music can be distinguished by what the human ear is naturally inclined towards, by the shape of the human ear. As we explored above in Chapter 4, the ear is 'alwaies open and winding' and like a 'snaile-shel', and 'from the sinuing obliquitie of his passage [. . .]

---

represented the end of time, its visual depiction of a cosmic future, of life after death, now available only as a memory, and second-hand'. Hester Lees-Jeffries, *Shakespeare and Memory* (Oxford: Oxford University Press, 2013), 92–93.

[94] Ibid., 92.
[95] Gerald D. Johnson, 'William Barley, Publisher and Seller of Books', in *The Library*, 11: 1 (1989), 10–46, at 23.
[96] William Barley, *The Pathway to Musicke containing sundrie familiar and easie rules for the readie and true understanding of the scale, or gamma-ut* (London: J. Danter for William Barley, 1596), unpaginated. See also Johnson, 'William Barley', 10–46.

elegantly resembleth the winding of a Snayle or Perwinkle shell'[97] and the 'substance' of music, the 'crispling of the aire'[98] or 'the observation of the halfe note'.[99] In describing how to produce a 'descant', Barley states that it is 'grounded' in 'consonances and disonences'; the interplay between sounds that offend and delight the ear is the key to a successful and pleasant musical experience, governed by human reason and its fundamental connection to, and resemblance to, the Divine. A tantalizing relic of this way of thinking survives in the Waltham Abbey manuscript (now known as Lansdowne MS 763) of twenty diverse musical theoretical treatises from the fourteenth and fifteenth centuries, which Tallis salvaged from the Dissolution in 1540, and which later ended up in the possession of Morley as he composed his *Introduction*.

> The seven spheres of the seven planets revolve with the sweetest harmony. [...] Just as the universe is adorned by seven tones, and our music by seven notes, the framework of our body is united by seven modes when the body with its four elements is joined to the soul with its three powers, reconciled naturally by musical art. Thus man is called a microcosm, that is, a little universe.[100]

Cosmological accounts of music were incredibly important to a nation still scarred from the wounds of a long century of ongoing Reformation; as Linda Phyllis Austern notes, 'Pythagorean cosmology [. . .] to many early modern thinkers still maintained order over chaos through the perfect precision of arithmetic number, geometric proportion, and everlasting harmony'.[101] For the people of the English Renaissance, labouring under the collective loss of older practices of remembering, marking time, and observing their relationship to God, the false relation is thus a crucial emblem of humanity's place in the designed cosmos, of the ability to stray from the natural and *musica recta*, and return.

These are the spectral associations that teem beneath the surface of the 'English' cadence trope, the melodic curve that stretches over the V–I perfect

---

[97] Helkiah Crooke, *Mikrokosmographia. A Description of the Body of Man* (London: William Iaggard dwelling in Barbican, 1615), 697 and 604.
[98] Thomas Wright, *The Passions of the Minde in Generall* (London: Valentine Simmes and Adam Islip for Walter Venge, 1604), 167–168.
[99] Campion, *A New Way*, fol. B4r.
[100] British Library, Lansdowne MS 763, fol. 52r–52v. Kerry McCarthy, *Tallis*, 24–29 and 183.
[101] Linda Phyllis Austern, *Both from the Ears and Mind: Thinking about Music in Early Modern England* (Chicago: University of Chicago Press, 2020), 90.

authentic progression, the brief frustration of tonal expectation and the shimmer of cognitive dissonance as the brain hears the discord of the 4-3 suspension and affixes it to the *pha* degree at the peak of the melodic curve. It would be foolish to claim that any or all of these associations would have been activated with every hearing and every performance of the cadence, not least given the fact that it is so little documented. But these are all feasible connections that may very easily have been felt, as distant echoes or as memories of a musical culture lost and past. In this way the musical theoretical rules of the time took on shades of the contemporary events; what was 'forbidden' or permissible where there was 'lack of other shift' took on added weight of meaning, moral, cultural, and political. In the final section of this chapter, we will explore an example of this dynamic at play, and how thwarting or playing with these rules could influence ideas about character. Enter again the shady figure of Thomas Weelkes, aloft.

A Leading Note: Enter Weelkes, Aloft

We know vanishingly little of the life of Weelkes, and what we do know paints him as fundamentally disreputable. Here is a quote regarding his antics from 1619:

> Most of the choir and other officers of the same (as many as come to Divine Service) demean themselves religiously all the time of prayers, save only Thomas Weelkes, who divers times and very often come[s] so disguised eyther from the Taverne or Ale house into the quire as is muche to be lamented, for in these humours he will both curse and swear most dreadfully, & so profane the service of God) especially on the Sabbath Days) as is most fearful to hear, and to the great amazement of the people present. And though he hath been often times admonished by the late Lord Bishop, the Dean and Chapter to refrain these humours and reform himself, yet he daily continues the same, and is rather worse than better therein. [. . .] I know not of any of the choir or other the officer of the Church to be a common drunkard but Mr Weelkes.[102]

---

[102] Brown, *Thomas Weelkes*, 43; Katie Bank, *Knowledge Building in Early Modern English Music* (London: Routledge, 2020), 47.

Weelkes's drunken frolics culminated in an incident for which he is still notorious: being dismissed as organist, Sherbourne Clerk, and Master of the Choristers at Chichester Cathedral for urinating on the Dean from the organ loft. He was ultimately reinstated. Visitors to Chichester Cathedral seeking to soak up the atmosphere of the scene of this infamous crime will be puzzled; although the loft itself has been moved, the constituent architectural elements remain unchanged and the angle required for a man to successfully urinate upon the Dean's seat is one that has not, any time before or after, been known to be humanly possible. David Brown also notes that the senior clergy of Chichester were prone to making accusations of drunkenness and debauchery, likely in order to purge their choir stalls; lay officials at the cathedral were frequently and repeatedly in trouble, and a complaint against six of the choristers for negligence of their duties in 1608 does not include Weelkes's name, though he had been at Chichester since around 1602–1603.[103] Moreover, reports of bad behaviour amongst the choir date well back into the 1590s. One could speculate that Weelkes perhaps found more sympathy with Anthony Watson and Lancelot Andrewes, Bishops of Chichester between 1596–1605 and 1605–1609 respectively, than he did with Samuel Harsnett, who translated to the see in 1609.

Of Weelkes's work we know rather more: his predilection for chromaticism, his joyous playfulness with the parameters of form, pitch, and rhythm, and his love of the English cadence as demonstrated by his *Ninth Service*, discussed above.[104] The two aspects (reputed drunkard, and skilful inverter, subverter and converter of the musical forms of his day) sit uneasily together. The dangers of equating a composer's way of life with their music have been well established; however, the architectural fact of the placement of the organ loft and choir stalls in Chichester Cathedral suggest that there may have been something rather more political at play in accounts of Weelkes's disreputableness. A clue lies in one of the aforementioned Bishops of Chichester, under whom Weelkes served: Lancelot Andrewes. Andrewes is renowned as an avant-garde conservative reformist who paved the way for the Laudian ecclesiology that would go on to be a significant aggravating factor in the English Civil War. He was, moreover, educated by Richard Mulcaster (whom

---

[103] Brown, *Thomas Weelkes*, 31–33. For more on Weelkes see Philip Brett, 'The Two Musical Personalities of Thomas Weelkes', in *Music & Letters*, 53: 4 (1972), 369–376; Eric Lewin Altschuler and William Jansen, 'Thomas Weelkes's Text Authors: Men of Letters', *The Musical Times*, 143: 1879 (2002), 13–24; Lionel Pike, *Pills to Purge Melancholy* (Aldershot: Ashgate, 2004).

[104] Long, *Hearing Homophony*, 166.

we encountered above in Chapter 5) at the Merchant Taylors' School and evidently greatly influenced by his positive attitude towards music; Andrewes vehemently advocated for music in liturgy with a fervour that Natalya Din-Kariuki and Peter McCullough note was particularly intense between 1605 and 1610, coinciding with his time at Chichester.[105] This is an excerpt from his *Sermon upon the nativity*, preached to the court of James I and VI at Whitsun 1608, speaking on the 'love knott of the two natures united in Christ' and Acts 2, 1–4:

> To both *senses* is the *Holy Ghost* presented. To the *eare* which is the sense of *faith*: To the *eye*, which is the sense of *love*. The *eare*, that is the ground of the *word*, which is audible: the *eye*, which is the ground of the *Sacraments*, which are *visible*: To the *eare*, in a *noise*; To the *eye*, in a *shew*: A noise, of a *mighty Wind*. A shew, of *fiery Tongues*. The *noise*, serving as a *Trumpett*, to awake the World, and give them warning, He was come.
>
> [...]
>
> And so, by speaking all tongues, they have gathered a Church, that speaketh all tongues; a thing much tending to the glorie of GOD. For, being now converted to CHRIST, they ascend up daily to heaven, so many *tongues*, there to praise His name; as He, this day, sent downe to earth, to convert them withall to His truth. And indeed, it was not meet, one *tongue* onely should be imployed that way, as (before) but one was: It was too poore, and slender; like the musick of a *monochord*. Farre more meet was, that many *tongues*; yea, that *all tongues* should doe it; which (as a consort of many instruments) might yield a full harmonie.[106]

The 'full harmonie' as opposed to the 'poore', 'slender' 'musick of a monochord'; the word which was 'audible [. . .] noise [. . .] a mighty Wind

---

[105] Natalya Din-Kariuki, '"This Musique Hath Life in It": Harmony in Lancelot Andrewes's Preaching', in *Huntington Library Quarterly*, 85: 2 (Summer 2022), 241–258; and Peter McCullogh, 'Music Reconciled to Preaching: A Jacobean Moment?', in Natalie Mears and Alec Ryrie (eds.), *Worship and the Parish Church in Early Modern Britain* (Farnham: Ashgate, 2013), 109–129. For more on Andrewes's devotional stance, see Joseph Ashmore, 'Faith in Lancelot Andrewes's Preaching', in *The Seventeenth Century Journal*, 32: 2 (2017), 121–138, and 'Attending to the Passion in Early Modern England: Lancelot Andrewes' Good Friday Sermons', in *Journal of Medieval and Early Modern Studies*, 53: 2 (May 2023), 379–404; Sophie Read, 'Lancelot Andrewes' Sacramental Wordplay', in *The Cambridge Quarterly*, 36: 1 (2007), 11–31. See also Harry Spillane, 'Eucharistic Devotion and Textual Appropriation in Post-Reformation England', in *The Seventeenth Century Journal* (Dec 2020), 1–24.

[106] Lancelot Andrewes, *XCVI sermons by the Right Honorable and Reverend Father in God, Lancelot Andrewes* (London: George Miller for Richard Badger, 1623), 600–601 and 613.

[...] serving as a Trumpett' all combine to create a subtle but markedly positive interpretation of intricate polyphonic music as a route towards understanding the Divine. In 1603, in a nation relieved to find itself under another Protestant monarch in James I, Weelkes's elaborate, nostalgic polyphony and pastiches of early sixteenth-century styles, forms, and tropes (like the *Ninth Service* but also like his *Service for Trebles*, a format not attempted by any of his contemporaries) were a charming throwback and a reassurance of continuity. By 1609, such indulgence in proto-Laudian approaches had seemingly gained far more potential to upset or be divisive. In much the same way that differences in musical worship formats still hold the capacity to cause conflict in the Church of England in the twenty-first century, in the second and third decades of the seventeenth century, music had the power to be immensely contentious. Weelkes's older contemporary Byrd was, by this point, treading the perilous tightrope between writing and producing music for use in recusant circles and somehow avoiding inciting the wrath of those of a more reformist bent. Some of Byrd's offerings for the *Cantiones sacrae* in 1575 have been read as provocative, but by the publication of the *Gradualia* in 1605 and 1607 (with a reprint to meet demand in 1610), his devotional preferences were overt: pieces such as 'Christus resurgens' are dense with complex, elaborate polyphony constructed around the cantus firmus technique of pre-Reformation musical liturgy, and the chosen text settings tend to revolve around the oppression and struggles of the chosen people.[107] Weelkes was certainly not as provocative as Byrd, but in other ways his flaunting of age-old musical theoretical rules (from his playful manipulation of *mi* and *fa* in 'As Vesta Was from Latmos Hill Descending' [1601], to his swaggering English cadences in 'O God Grant the King' and the *Ninth Service* [c. 1603], to his exuberant mixing of secular with sacred language, forms and tropes in works such as his frolicking madrigal 'Hark All Ye Lovely Saints Above' [1598]), it is likely that he was just as aggravating to his ecclesiastical colleagues. Thus, it is perfectly possible that the attempts by senior clergy at Chichester to discredit Weelkes were borne of an objection to his simultaneously irreverent and nostalgic musical style, rather than his personal behaviour. As Brian Hyer recently noted, 'tonality is an ideological as

---

[107] Jackson, 'Double Motion', 152–154. See also Craig Monson, 'Reading between the Lines: Catholic and Protestant Polemic in Elizabethan and Jacobean Sacred Music', in Jessie Ann Owens (ed.), *Noyses, Sounds and Sweet Aires: Music in Early Modern England* (Washington, DC: Folger Shakespeare Library, 2006), 78–89, at 79–82.

well as theoretical construct'.[108] It is no very great stretch of the imagination to entertain the possibilities of what tussles over its direction at the turn of the seventeenth century might have influenced, the trace of which is lost to posterity because its history was written by the 'winners'.

False relations have the potential to be so much more than stylistic features, or by-products of a musical theoretical system. They are windows into moments that have shaped our musical history, and the political, religious, visual, and literary influences that have guided these developments and ways of thinking. By seeking to adapt our eyes, ears, and minds to their intricate, evocative choreography we can begin to appreciate just how important musical falseness was to the culture of the English Renaissance. They sat squarely in the centre of the debate over music and its role in devotional practice, ideas about the scientific connotations of *musica speculativa*, as a guiding structural principle that governed the cosmos. Allowing *pha* and its transgressions space to breathe provides us with a fascinating insight into corners of musical culture that can otherwise appear innocuous or mundane: the editorial, revisionary practices that composers exercised upon their own works throughout their careers; the evolution of musical reputations; the understanding of national boundaries and identities. Their notated or implied presence within musical repertoire is like a barometer; their brief, embellishing destabilization of what would come to be known as the tonal centre, far more than a sonic 'near-miss', are emblems of the status of music in the English Renaissance.

---

[108] Brian Hyer, 'Tonality', in Thomas Christensen (ed.), *The Cambridge History of Western Music Theory* (Cambridge: Cambridge University Press, 2002), 747.

Afterword

'The Bitter-Sweetest Achromaticke'

Around twenty years after the Interregnum, twenty years after the choir stalls had fallen silent and the musical landscape of England seemed, briefly, to have changed forever, a five-part setting of Psalm 122 appeared. It has variously been attributed to John Blow (1649–1708) and to Henry Purcell (1659–1695), but its authorship is still uncertain; this authorial confusion dates back to contemporary accounts, with the sole surviving manuscript naming Blow as the composer, but eyewitness accounts naming Purcell.[1] It uses the wording from the 1662 *Book of Common Prayer*, which is as follows:

> I was glad when they said unto me: We will go into the house of the Lord.
> [...]
> For thither the tribes go up, even the tribes of the Lord: to testify unto Israel, to give thanks unto the Name of the Lord.
> For there is the seat of judgement: even the seat of the house of David.
> O pray for the peace of Jerusalem: they shall prosper that love thee.
> Peace be within thy walls: and plenteousness within thy palaces.
> [...]
> Glory be to the father, and to the son, and to the Holy Ghost;
> As it was in the beginning, is now, and ever shall be, world without end. Amen.

What we do know for certain is that it was used as an anthem at the coronation of the ill-fated James II on 23 April 1685,[2] the last Catholic monarch of

---

[1] Attributed to 'Dr Blow', 'I Was Glad', in Cambridge University Library, Ms. EDC 10/7/6 (c. 1705–1713), 210. See also Francis Sandford's account of the coronation, *The History of the Coronation of the Most High, Most Mighty, and Most Excellent Monarch, James II* (London: 1687).

[2] Matthias Range, 'The 1685 Coronation Anthem "I Was Glad"', *Early Music*, 36: 3 (2008), 397–408. Range notes that the anthem clearly predates the coronation, as Lionel Pike has identified an earlier copy at the Barber Institute of Fine Arts in Birmingham (MS.5001), dating from around 1682–1683. Lionel Pike, 'The Ferial Version of Purcell's *I was glad*', in *Royal Musical Association*

England, Scotland, and Ireland, and son of the equally ill-fated Charles I. We also know that it features several English cadences and highly mannered, ornately framed false relations. It was sung as the introit as James and his queen, Mary of Modena, entered Westminster Abbey, establishing a precedent that would later be recreated at Queen Anne's coronation in 1702 and George I's in 1714 with a setting by Francis Pigott, at George III's coronation in 1761 with a setting by William Boyce and finally a setting of the text that would be composed some two centuries later by one Charles Hubert Parry, and used for the coronations of Edward VII (1902), Elizabeth II (1952), and Charles III (2023). It was suitably if indulgently extravagant, and it raised many of the phantoms that had lingered around the false relation, redolent as incense, since the break from Rome. James had ascended to the throne on the death of his elder brother, Charles II; Charles had converted to Catholicism on his deathbed. Within merely three years, James would be deposed in favour of his Protestant daughter Mary and her husband William of Orange. With his deposition came an end to the relentless back-and-forth between Protestant and Catholic devotional approaches, and the gradual dwindling of the Reformation that his great-great-uncle Henry VIII had set in motion almost 160 years earlier.

As Matthias Range notes, Charles II had been notoriously averse to counterpoint and so 'the extrovert use of polyphony in a coronation anthem for his successor might be a sign that the composer was enjoying the new freedom, and perhaps expecting a change in style; overall, the lavish musical programme at this coronation may have been the composers' way of showing James II the values of his Chapel Royal, as they must have realised that the new, Catholic, king would have little interest in this Protestant institution'.[3] It is far beyond the scope of this conclusion or even this book to consider the many afterlives of the English Renaissance love of false relation, but it is worth lingering briefly on this one, intriguing, star-crossed incarnation. Regardless of whether it was the work of Blow or Purcell, it follows the exemplars of its Chapel Royal predecessors by placing the melodic curve in the middle parts, the Alto and the Treble 2. It is frustrated in the Alto at 'plenteousness within thy palaces' (bb. 84–85) as only a partial curve but with a

---

Research Chronicle, 35 (2002), 41–59; Rebecca Herissone, '"Fowle Originalls" and "Fayre Writing": Reconsidering Purcell's Compositional Process', in *Journal of Musicology*, 13: 4 (2006), 569–619, at 575; Ian Spink, *Restoration Cathedral Music 1660–1714* (Oxford: Oxford University Press, 1995), 84.

[3] Range, 'The 1685 Coronation Anthem', 406.

direct clash between Alto and Treble 2 (see *Musica Britannica 50*); it passes evocatively between the Alto and Treble 2 parts throughout the concluding 'Amen' section, where, in the final Treble 2 entry at bars 110–111 it decorates the resolution of a I–IV6/4–I progression rather than the more typical V–I:[4] Blow or Purcell pulling at the stitching of the English cadence trope and repurposing it for a new setting, a new context, a new monarch.

There, at the heart of another important ceremonial occasion, are the false relations. In this instance they were almost certainly the sole choice of the musicians of the Chapel Royal (whereas, in the case of Weelkes's contribution for the coronation of James I and VI in 1603,[5] or Tallis's for the investitures of Prince Henry in 1610, Prince Charles in 1616, and the future Charles II in 1638 as Prince of Wales, it is possible that the monarchs or perhaps their favoured courtiers were invited to advise on the musical choices). Range's speculation is that the Chapel Royal was likely using the occasion as an opportunity to demonstrate their musical (rather than ecclesiastical) value. Nevertheless, it is fascinating that false relations (and the by now long-favoured false relation trope, the 'English' cadence) as a device are at play within this vital project. We have no record of the music performed at Elizabeth I's coronation, but we do know that it took the form of a full Catholic mass because of the practical issues involved in trying to reintroduce Protestant ceremony following Mary I's brief but intensely iconoclastic reign.[6] As a result, James's coronation was the first fully Protestant coronation service and the first to be conducted in English, rather than Latin.[7] We might speculate that by 1685 false relations played a similar role to that of the vernacular, and the 'Englysh metre' that Tallis and Byrd sought to promote in the *Cantiones sacrae*.

England was still scarred by the Civil War, and those scars were evidently a motivating factor in James's deposition. Nevertheless, he was openly welcomed and celebrated as an overtly Catholic monarch in 1685. Amidst the pomp and circumstance of his ceremonial welcome and installation, the use of false relations suggests that a subtle shift in meaning

---

[4] I am grateful to Alan Howard for pointing this out to me. Eleanor Chan, 'The "English" Cadence: Reading an Early Modern Musical Trope', in *Early Music*, 49: 1 (2021), 19.

[5] Janet Leeper, 'Coronation Music', in *Contemporary Review*, 151 (1937), 554–562, at 556. Roy Strong, *Coronation: A History of Kingship and the British Monarchy* (London: HarperCollins, 2005), 260.

[6] Matthias Range, *Music and Ceremonial at British Coronations: From James I to Elizabeth II* (Cambridge: Cambridge University Press, 2012), 10.

[7] Alice Hunt, *The Drama of Coronation: Medieval Ceremony in Early Modern England* (Cambridge: Cambridge University Press, 2008), 174.

had taken place across the seventeenth century. False relations had ceased to be predominantly redolent of Catholicism (either as a nostalgic throwback, or as Mulcaster's 'syrenes sounde' that 'carieth awaye the eare' and can train the brain in resilience against its seductions).[8] They had, instead, become markers of an English choral tradition, and an inheritance that transcended the Reformation. They had become features of a native style (with Byrd as 'ensign of the troops to the British Muse', according to Robert Dow)[9] which, building out from the musical fashions and tastes of the Chapel Royal, had become available to a rapidly broadening collection of listeners and performers due to the boom in the musical printing trade.

By the last quarter of the seventeenth century, the hexachordal system and the solmization technique of reading had by and large fallen out of use. Nevertheless, the ghost of its forms and its demands upon visual acuity lingered. Purcell's anthems are littered with carefully curated proximate instances; we find them in 'Remember Not Lord Our Offences' and 'Hear My Prayer, O Lord', typically divided by a crotchet longer than might have been adopted by his earlier seventeenth-century forebears, sonic near-misses rather than direct scrunches.[10] A setting of Ariel's 'Full Fathom Five' song from *The Tempest* (c. 1670–1712), sometimes attributed to Purcell, likewise features the melodic curve of an 'English' cadence as a set piece, a bridge between verse and chorus that stages the layering of fairyland over England described by William N. West, a *copresence* with England rather than a differing presence that overlays and 'gaps' into its landscape.[11] These late instances, and the context elucidated by West, offer a crucial insight and possibility for the way that false relations created meaning in the English Renaissance. West notes that fairyland is a way of claiming indigeneity and of celebrating Tudor and Stuart aristocracy; this much is clear from Spenser's narrative surrounding Artegall and Britomart, as the founders of the British race,[12] and indeed much later in Thomas Hobbes's use of fairyland as a metaphor for exploring the Catholic church:

---

[8] Richard Mulcaster, *Positions* (London: Thomas Vautrollier for Thomas Chard, 1581), 38–39.
[9] The Dow Partbooks, Contratenor, Christ Church MSS 986, 66.
[10] MS 88, Cambridge: Fitzwilliam Museum.
[11] William N. West, 'England/Faerie lond/Ireland: Physics/Metaphysics/Colony', Renaissance Society of America Annual Meeting (Dublin, 2022), 31 March 2022.
[12] Kent R. Lehnhof, "Britomart and the Birth of the British Empire in Edmund Spenser's The Faerie Queene," in Lisa Bernstein (ed.), *(M)Othering the Nation: Constructing and Resisting National Allegories through the Maternal Body* (Cambridge: Cambridge Scholars, 2008), 12–22.

For so must all things excellent begin,
And eke enrooted deepe must be that Tree,
Whose big emboldened braunches shall not lin,
Till they to heavens hight forth stretched bee.
For from thy wombe a famous Progenie
Shall spring, out of the aunctient Troian blood,
Which shall revive the sleeping memorie
Of those same antique Peres, the heavens brood,
Which Greeke and Asian rivers stained with their blood.
[...]
It was not, Britomart, thy wandering eye,
Glauncing unawares in charmed looking glas,
But the straight course of heavenly destiny,
Led with eternall providence, that has
Guided thy glaunce, to bring his will to pas:
Ne is thy fate, ne is thy fortune ill,
To love the prowest knight, that ever was.
Therefore submit thy ways unto his will,
And do by all dew meanes thy destiny fulfil.
(*The Faerie Queene*, Cantos 22 and 24).

The ecclesiastics have their cathedral churches, which, in what town soever they be erected, by virtue of holy water, and certain charms called exorcisms, have the power to make those towns, cities, that is to say, seats of empire. The fairies also have their enchanted castles, and certain gigantic ghosts, that domineer over the regions round about them.
[...]
To this and such like resemblances between the papacy and the kingdom of fairies may be added this, that as the fairies have no existence but in the fancies of ignorant people, rising from the traditions of old wives or old poets: so the spiritual power of the Pope (without the bounds of his own civil dominion) consisteth only in the fear that seduced people stand in of their excommunications, upon hearing of false miracles, false traditions, and false interpretations of the Scripture.

It was not therefore a very difficult matter for Henry the Eighth by his exorcism; nor for Queen Elizabeth by hers, to cast them out. But who knows that this spirit of Rome, now gone out, and walking by missions through the dry places of China, Japan, and the Indies, that yield him little fruit, may not return; or rather, an assembly of spirits worse than he enter and inhabit this clean-swept house, and make the end thereof worse than the beginning?[13]

Placed side by side, these passages reveal the conceptual slippage between England's Catholic past, the alterity of fairyland, and the projection of a magnificent future for England under a continuing Tudor/Stuart dynasty. Britomart's 'charmed looking glas' is a manifestation of fairyland, and of the relics of the Catholic church. Such a context is shot through the usage of false relations throughout the sixteenth and well into the seventeenth century: the spectral remnants of the hexachordal system and its impelled visual acuity were another trace of fairyland and another palimpsest of England's past.

In Chapter 6 we briefly encountered James I and VI's project to establish Great Britain, and his interest in colonial expansion. In considering the possibilities listed above, it is worth exploring these matters in further detail. The term 'Great Britain' was not legally recognized until 1707 but gained considerable political capital as a result of James's energies in forging a 'British' subjectivity as an English, Scottish, and Irish entity discrete from other potential national subjectivities;[14] in turn, James built upon the taste for mythologizing the past that had burgeoned across the late sixteenth century, with the British 'race' as the last great descendant of the Trojans as the lodestar for this passion. These concepts, however, had impelled a similarly voracious taste for self-fashioning that went deeper than associating inhabitation with citizenship. Race as a category had been gaining traction since the early medieval period. The beginning of the seventeenth century, however, marked a serious departure in the way it was conceptualized: it was the last period in which ethnicity could be fluidly understood, and the first in which race could be read as analogous to difference.[15] The cultural products

---

[13] Thomas Hobbes, 'Comparison of Papacy with the Kingdome of the Faeries', from Chapter 47, *Leviathan or the Matter, Forme, & Power of a Common-Wealth Ecclesiastical and Civill* (London: Andrew Crooke at the Green Dragon in St Paul's Churchyard, 1651).

[14] A project on the musical, material, and visual ramifications and manifestations of this project is in the early stages of planning by the author. It is likely that the passion for the archaic originated in the dissolution of the monasteries; see Harriet Lyon, *Memory and the Dissolution of the Monasteries in Early Modern England* (Cambridge: Cambridge University Press, 2021).

[15] Ania Loomba, *Shakespeare, Race and Colonialism* (Oxford: Oxford University Press, 2005), 22–44; Mathieu Chapman, *Anti-Black Racism in Early Modern English Drama: The Other 'Other'* (London: Routledge, 2017), 2–3. Margo Hendricks, '"Obscured by dreams': Race, Empire, and Shakespeare's *A Midsummer Night's Dream*', in *Shakespeare Quarterly*, 47: 1 (1996), 37–60; Kim F. Hall, *Things of Darkness: Economies of Race and Gender in Early Modern England* (Ithaca, NY: Cornell University Press, 1995), 127–176.

of this period—literary, visual, material, and musical—all bear witness to the gradual marking out of the limits of what constituted Englishness and Britishness, and what did not.[16] In negotiating this sense of racial edge, limit, and parameter, the musical texts and objects of the English Renaissance fed into this dialogue, reiterating and consolidating ideas about what an English/British tradition of music constituted, and what an 'English metre' might look like. False relations are a part and parcel of this dialogue as, governed first by the tastes of the Chapel Royal and then percolating beyond, they became hallmarks of an English musical style that transcended the Reformation and devotional divides, stretching back across an imaginary time immemorial and into a fantasized, fairyland past.

Musical figurations of race were gathering apace in the English Renaissance. On the continent, Orlande de Lassus had been experimenting with *moresche* songs across the sixteenth century. *Moresche*, a form of *villanelle*, originated in Naples and staged imagined courtship scenes between the stock Afro-Neapolitan characters Giorgio and Catalina, complete with 'thick, mock-African accents'.[17] *Moresche* made their way to the English consciousness; Noémie Ndiaye has recently demonstrated that the 'Willow' song, sung by Desdemona in *Othello* (1603) and learned from her mother's maid Barbary, can be productively approached as *moresche*-inspired, a 'musical conjuration' that 'thicken[s] the play's ambivalent racial discourse with a poignant degree of irony that does not sound foreign to Shakespeare'.[18] In the projective dreaming space of Venice, the parameters of Englishness and non-Englishness were delineated in a musical idiom that audiences would increasingly recognize as signifying a ventriloquized African musical 'culture', as contrasted to the musical culture of England.

The self-fashioning of English, white, Christian, male identity against an imagined Other and what Ayanna Thompson refers to as the 'white/right gaze' is merely one amongst the many that were being cultivated during this period, and which are important in the formation of the modern

---

[16] For a recent and excellent exploration of the vocabularies of race in this period, see Nandini Das, João Vicente Melo, Haig Smith, and Lauren Working, *Keywords of Identity, Race and Human Mobility in Early Modern England* (Amsterdam: Amsterdam University Press, 2021).

[17] Noémie Ndiaye, 'Off the Record: Contrapuntal Theatre History', in Tracy C. Davis and Peter Marx (eds.), *The Companion to Theatre and Performance Historiography* (London: Routledge, 2020), 229–248, at 229.

[18] Ibid., 234. See also Ayanna Thompson, *Performing Race and Torture on the Early Modern Stage* (London: Routledge, 2008), 4; Ralph P. Locke, *Music and the Exotic from the Renaissance to Mozart* (Cambridge: Cambridge University Press, 2015).

concept of race; as Matthieu Chapman argues, Moors, Jews, Turks, and indeed England's continental neighbours used discourses of otherness in their nation-building and often the English were the explicit other.[19] Crucially, however, this was the period in which the English established their identity as associated with rationality, objectivity, and what would become known as scientific endeavour through the collapsing of the etymological root, *scientia*, certain knowledge (of which the ultimate was that attainable through theology), into the modern science (an approach that aspires towards an unattainable absolute objectivity and prioritizes the epistemological).[20] It aided the construction of conceptual whiteness as a socially constructed identity, and one that explicitly fashioned itself as the default, prevailing, and paradoxically exceptional position.[21] As Sara K. Ahmed defines it:

Whiteness is invisible and unmarked, as the absent centre against which others appear only as deviants, or points of deviation. Whiteness is only invisible for those who inhabit it, or those who get so used to its inhabitance that they learn not to see it, even when they are not it.[22]

In time, the whiteness of the musical theoretical system constructed upon the accounts of Morley, Campion, and Butler would come to form the rules of the Western musical tradition. Terminology that focused on the strangeness, the 'lasciviousness', and the femininity of false relations or the musical features that aid and feed into false relation were already at play in the medieval period. As we have seen throughout this book, these ideas were slowly but surely becoming consolidated into a fully elucidated discourse. False relations, however, briefly prevailed as an acceptable strangeness, archaism, and repudiation of the tonal system.

We have come full circle and returned to the questions surrounding the musical golden age of Tudor and Stuart England, and the fascination of composers such as Ralph Vaughan Williams, Gustav Holst, Frederick Delius, Edward Elgar, and later Benjamin Britten and Herbert Howells with the musical style of this period. We will remember Cooke's analysis

---

[19] Chapman, *The Other 'Other'*, 2–24, at 4.
[20] See, e.g., Deborah Harkness's concept of the 'scientific renaissance' in Harkness, *The Jewel House*.
[21] For more on the foundational concept of whiteness, see Frantz Fanon, *Black Skin, White Masks* (first published 1958, this edition London: Pluto, 2008).
[22] Sara Ahmed, 'A Phenomenology of Whiteness', in *Feminist Theory*, 8: 2 (2007), 149–168, at 157.

of Howells's *Gloucester Service*, which we encountered in Chapter 1, and his description of the way it represents simultaneously 'otherness' and a 'continuum of tradition'. I stated there that the traditional/other dichotomy has inflected understanding of the false relation from the very moment that they became hallmarks of the English Renaissance choral style. False relations offer us a vital (if admittedly splintered) lens into the formation of the concept of Englishness in this period. They are cultural barometers over a fractious century of what was permissible and what was not, and of the steady formation of the sense of a limit to the categorization of Englishness. They demonstrate how the English negotiated the ongoing aftereffects of the Reformation, and how carefully cultivated amnesia melded with imagination enabled these operations in a musical context. False relations, ultimately, demonstrate that the question of how the English musical (and specifically choral) tradition developed is far from simply answered.

The example of the Blow/Purcell setting of 'I Was Glad', with which this afterword opened, makes clear how successfully false relations had insinuated their way into the English choral tradition as a feature of 'native', appropriated, even colonized style. As borrowings from fifteenth-century Franco-Flemish polyphony, exploitations of the by-products of the earlier medieval musical system of reading music through solmization and the mutable patterns of hexachords, false relations were entwined in ideas of heritage and continuation with the past. At the same time, as we have seen throughout this book, the musicians of the English Renaissance used them as tools to innovate, experiment, and subvert. The concept of dissonance and discordance, throughout an immensely politically dissonant/discordant period of time, became of fundamental importance to the way the people of the English Renaissance conceptualized their history. As one distinctive variety of musical dissonance, false relations played a quiet but crucial role in this process.

We can witness this interaction in the final case study of this book. In 1614, chorographer, surveyor, and antiquary John Norden (c. 1547–1625) published his *Labyrinth of Mens Life*. Norden's true passion was in cartography and his planned but never fully completed *Speculum Britanniae* (parts published in 1593 and 1598) and maps contributed to the fifth edition of William Camden's *Britannia* (1607); however, his income by and large came from devotional works like the *Labyrinth*. Indeed, his *Pensive Mans Practise* (1584) reached forty editions before his death in 1625. As distinct as these projects might seem to have been, they were separate strands of the same endeavour: to cultivate a separable, discrete, and recognizable Englishness, both as Protestant and as autochthonous, deeply connected to the English landscape and territory. His association with Camden, for example, is illuminating. In his address 'To the Reader' in the 1610 edition of *Britannia*, Camden announced that he has sought 'after the Etymologie of Britaine' and 'attained some skill of the most ancient British and English-Saxon tongues'.[23] He aims to 'restore antiquity to Britaine, and Britain to his antiquity'. Norden follows Camden's lead by elucidating the Saxon alphabet, and by elucidating Britain's heritage in a manner that foregrounds the Saxon shaping of county boundaries, but which ultimately originates with Brutus, son of the Trojan Aeneas.

> Thus is our *Britannia* forced to sustaine sundry titles vnder one truth as *Brytannia, Pritania, Prid-caine* or *Pridayne, Brithtania, Brutania, Bridania*, and such like: according to as manie sundrie mens conceits. But were not *Brute* so generally reiected in these our daies, I could verie easely be drawne to assure me that it might be most truly *Brutania* of *Brute* the supposed conquerour, and that Greeke worde *tania* a kingdome, though *Brute* were no Greeke, yet might he fitly conioyne this worde *tania* vnto his name *Brute*, and so conclude it *Brutania, Bruti regnum,* the kingdome of *Brute*.[24]

It is worth noting here that the two terms 'England' and 'Britain' were conceptualized as the same geographical territory during this period, and were thus physically indistinguishable; Britain referred to the historic region of 'antiquity', whereas 'it is at this day called ENGLAND, *Anglorum terra*'.[25] Norden also observes that there is a possibility that the story of Brutus is 'Poeticall (fabulous) rather than a true hystorie', but that its importance

---

[23] William Camden, 'To the Reader', in *Britain, or a Chorographicall Description of the most flourishing Kingdomes, England, Scotland, and Ireland, and the lands adjoining, out of the depth of Antiquitie* (London, 1610). For an explanation of the misleading nature of the term 'English Saxon' and 'Anglo-Saxon', see Allen J. Frantzen, *Desire for Origins: New Language, Old English, and Teaching the Tradition* (New Brunswick, NJ: Rutgers University Press, 1990); Donna Beth Ellard, *Anglo-Saxon(ist) Pasts, postSaxon Futures* (Earth, Milky Way: Punctum Books, 2019); Mary Rambaran-Olm, M. Breann Leake, and Micah James Goodrich, 'Medieval Studies: The Stakes of the Field', in *postmedieval*, 11 (2020), 356–370; and Mary Rambaran-Olm and Erik Wade, 'The Many Myths of the Term 'Anglo-Saxon', *Smithsonian Magazine* (14 July 2021).

[24] John Norden, *Speculum Britanniae. The first parte an historicall, chorographicall description of Middlesex* (London: Eliot's Court Press, 1593), 2.

[25] Ibid., 3.

lies in the fact that it is 'what antiquitie hath left, and wee by tradition have received'.

Steeped in this context of mythologized, chorographical antiquity, we find a tantalizing possible trace of false relation, in Norden's *Labyrinth*. 'Discord' is the metaphor by which Norden establishes his sense of limit. It is never just musical—the visual context is overlayed and melded in a realization of the trope of *varietas* Norden advocates—but music glints throughout his couplets.

> Without a discord can no concord be,
> *Concord* is when contrary things agree:
> But these two contraries that guide the mind,
> Are so disiunct can neuer be combin'd:
> [...]
> And contraries by art be made agree:
> Of coulours mixed, meerely contraries,
> She moldes and makes most pleasing decencies,
> The eye beholdes the mixtures with delight,
> If they haue beauty, and be exquisite,
> But if the growndes, as white, or black, or blew,
> Exceed too much, it marres the mixed hew.
> Drugges farre vnlike, in hot, cold, moyst and dry,
> Are brought by art to true Congruity:
> *Musicke*, the medicine of heauy hearts,
> Makes concord, only of discording partes,
> As high and low, as longs and shortes agree,
> So harsh, or sweet, is musicke found to be.
> No contraries appeare in perfect kind,
> But seene together, or by art combind,
> Vnlike to these are inward qualities,
> The hart indureth not her contraries:[26]

The idea of false relation percolates through Norden's description, as the two contraries are brought to agree to create 'concord', but only 'of discording partes' that 'can never be combin'd' present the distorted reflections of *mi*

---

[26] John Norden, *The Labyrinth of Mans Life, Or Vertues Delight and Envies Opposite* (London: George Eld for John Budge, to be solde at the great south doore of Paules, and at Brittaines Bursse, 1614), unpaginated.

and *fa* and their evocative slippage. There are of course other connotations at play, for example temporal dissonance in the form of suspensions and syncopations, in the 'long and shortes' that 'agree'. However, it is important that we entertain the possibility that false relations are one of the threads shot through and shimmering, briefly, in Norden's account of discord.

Indeed, there is an instance (almost precisely contemporaneous) that supports such a reading: Henry Peacham's emblem book *Minerva Britanna, or a garden of heroicall deuises* (1612). The *Minerva* was dedicated to Prince Henry and is believed to have been based upon a manuscript presented to Henry in 1610, around the time of his investiture as Prince of Wales. It is, states Peacham,

> a Subiect very rare. For except the collections of Master *Whitney*, and the translations of some one or two else beside, I know not an *Englishman* in our age, that hath published any worke of this kind.[27]

Minerva Britanna was indeed the first original vernacular emblem book since Geoffrey Whitney's *A Choice of Emblemes* (1586), but what is most striking in Peacham's claim (along with the rather telling title) is its Englishness.[28] The prefatory matter emphasizes this theme, with E.S.'s 'To Master Henry Peacham, A Vision Upon This His Minerva' describing Peacham as 'infuse[d]' with the 'Enthean soule' of Trojan genius as the 'English muse'.[29] Peacham's own emblem 'ad Jacobum Regem,' envisioning James as a modern Orpheus, is also telling:

> While I lay bathed in my natiue blood,
> And yielded nought saue harsh, & hellish soundes:
> And saue from Heauen, I had no hope of good,
> Thou pittiedst (Dread Soveraigne) my woundes,
> Repair'dst my ruine, and with Ivorie key,
> Didst tune my stringes, that slackt or broken lay.

---

[27] Henry Peacham, *Minerva Britanna, or a garden of heroicall deuises, and adorned with emblems and impresa's of sundry natures, newly devised, moralised and published* (London: Printed in Shoe-lane at the signe of the Faulcon by Wa. Dight, 1612).

[28] For more on this idea, see Julie Corre, 'Le concept de "Britishness" dans les emblèmes de Henry Peacham (1612): vers une reconquête identitaire?', in *Revue LISA (Littératures, histoire des idées, Images et Sociétés du monde Anglophone)*, 13: 3 (2015).

[29] Peacham, *Minerva Britanna*, unpaginated.

> Now since I breathed thy Roiall hand,
> And found my concord, by so smooth a tuch,
> I giue the world abroade to understand,
> Ne're was the musick of old Orpheus such,
> As that I make, by meane (Deare Lord) of thee,
> From discord drawne, to sweetest vnitie.[30]

James is imagined, within the fabric of the *Minerva*, as the Thracian bard Orpheus, the Argonaut who, according to Apollonius' *Argonautica* (Ἀργοναυτικά) enabled his captain Jason and fellow crew to pass by the Sirens by drowning out their bewitching songs with sweeter, more beautiful music. He repairs the harmony of the speaker, 'tun[ing] my stringes' and shifting away from 'harsh & hellish soundes', drawing out of 'discord' the 'sweetest unitie' and allows the ship to move onwards, closer to its goal of capturing the golden fleece.

The emblem 'ad Jacobum Regem' does not offer any detailed sense of what discord specifically means, beyond a metaphor for cosmic and national, political, and religious harmony. However, Peacham's emblem 'Tanto Dulcius', or 'Such Sweetness' (see Fig. 7.1), provides a literalization of what 'discord' connotes in the *Minerva Britanna*.

> The mortall strifes that often doe befall,
> Twixt loving Bretheren, or the private frend,
> Doe prove (we say) the deadliest of all:
> Yet if compos'd by concord, in the end
> They relish sweeter, by how much the more
> The jarres were harsh, and discordant before.[31]

Emblems as a form were importantly enigmatic, designed to provoke their readers into drawing connections between word and image to puzzle out the emblem's meaning.[32] The pictorial element of the emblem is musical notation, within which, as Peacham notes in the margin, 'the first Discord here taken is from the eleventh to the tenth, that is from b-*fa* b-*mi*, unto a-*lamire*, a tenth to f-*fa ut* in the Base, the second from the ninth, or second to the 8, or

---

[30] Ibid., 31.
[31] Ibid., 204.
[32] For more on emblems, see Ludwig Volkmann, *Hieroglyph, Emblem, and Renaissance Pictography* (Leiden: Brill, 2018).

Fig. 7.1 Henry Peacham's emblem illustration for 'Tanto Ducius', from Henry Peacham, *Minerva Britanna, or a garden of heroicall deuises, and adorned with emblems and impresa's of sundry natures, newly devised, moralised and published* (London: Printed in Shoe-lane at the signe of the Faulcon by Wa. Dight, 1612). Washington, DC, Folger Shakespeare Library. Photograph author's own.

unison'. The placement of the C-clef appears, unusually, to be placed over a space of the stave rather than on the more conventional ledger line, meaning that there is an F♮ in the top part against the F♯ in the bottom. In other words, Peacham's first discord is implicitly a non-simultaneous false relation. Reading across these two emblems produces a complex, indeed mercurial interpretation of discord and false relation. It repeats the medieval trope of sweetness produced by a pleasant resolution of 'harsh jarres' into concord but weaves it into an allegory of James out-playing the Sirens, with his seductive mending of strings and harsh sounds 'with Ivorie key'. It encapsulates the paradox at the heart of the false relation.

We have seen throughout this book that false relations offer a tantalizing, kaleidoscopic if fragmented lens into the conceptual architecture of sixteenth- and early seventeenth-century England. These 'syren[e] sounde[s]' both subvert and enrich the metaphor of musical harmony that governed so much of the political and religious discord of the period; they glint throughout its visual, material, and textual remnants, often in objects with an evident musical theme but sometimes, surprisingly, in places that seem not to have any musical relevance at all. They shed light on the developing discourses surrounding the acts of reading and writing, and the question of literacy; they show us something of how people might once have interacted with notes on the page, and the visual acuity that enabled the leap from music as abstract to music as performance. They provide a glimpse into the carefully cultivated amnesia of the English Reformation and the deep nostalgia for the musical tropes and devotional approaches of the Catholic past; in turn, they aided the development of the mythologized English-as-British past, and burgeoning theories of English exceptionalism that fuelled colonization. These innocuous tropes thus linger at the conceptual fringes of much of England's most problematic episodes during this period, lending a striking truth to Mulcaster's observation: '*Musick* will not harme thee, if thy behauiour be good, and thy conceit honest, it will not miscary thee, if thy eares can carie it, and sorte it as it should be.'[33] False relations were infused into the English Renaissance imagination. They were the scraps, the effluvium of the solmization system, and yet they accumulated into treasured

---

[33] Mulcaster, *Positions* (London: Thomas Vautrollier for Thomas Chard, 1581), 38–39. The concept of training in surprise is a topic that is currently receiving a lot of attention in cognitive literary studies. See Vera Tobin, *Elements of Surprise: Our Mental Limits and the Satisfactions of Plot* (Cambridge, MA: Harvard University Press, 2018).

feature of English Renaissance musical style, and the English choral tradition. Approaching them as entities that possess a pertinence that extends beyond the musical to the visual, material, and conceptual allows us to appreciate the enigmatic, palimpsestic beauty of false relations as they blossomed across the pages, spaces, and minds of the English Renaissance.

APPENDIX I

O sing unto the Lord

272 APPENDIX I

APPENDIX I 273

APPENDIX I 275

APPENDIX I 277

278 APPENDIX I

APPENDIX I 279

APPENDIX I 281

APPENDIX I 283

APPENDIX I 285

APPENDIX II

O salutaris hostia [6vv]

288 APPENDIX II

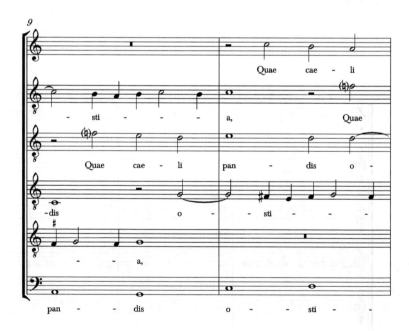

APPENDIX II 289

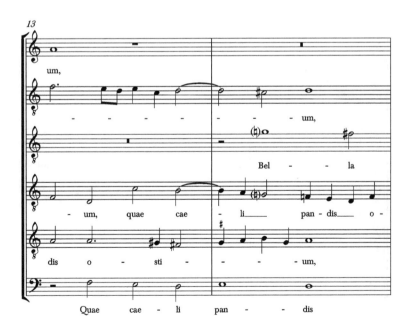

APPENDIX II 291

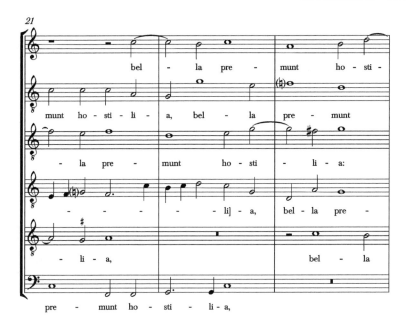

APPENDIX II

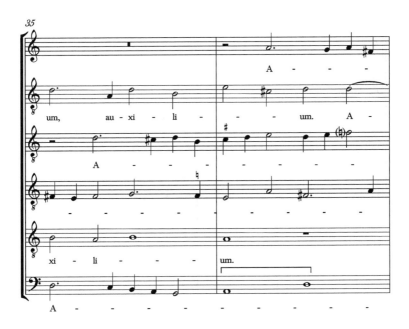

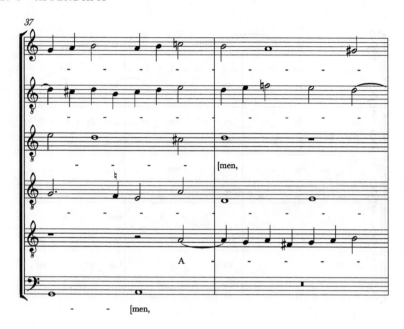

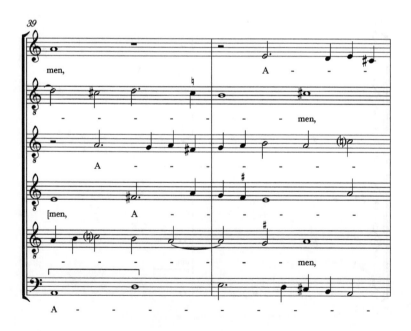

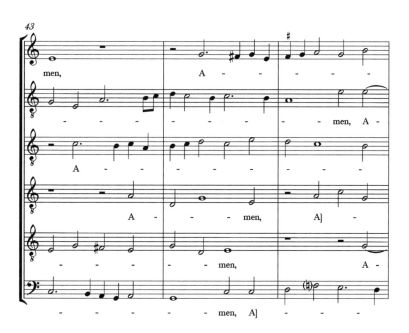

296 APPENDIX II

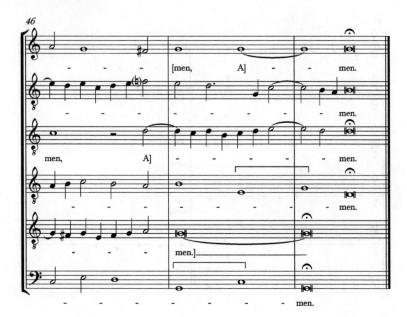

APPENDIX III

Ninth Service

Magnificat

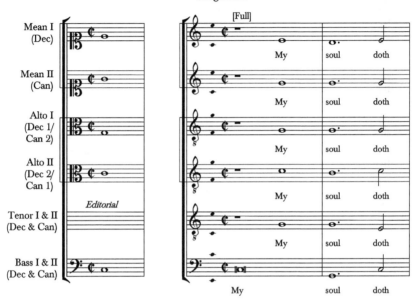

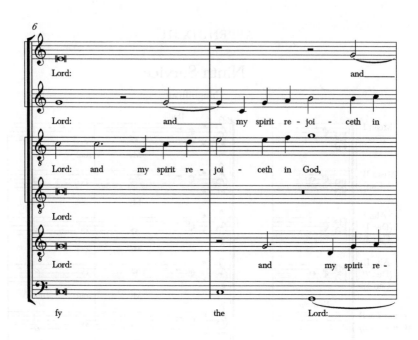

APPENDIX III 299

300 APPENDIX III

APPENDIX III 301

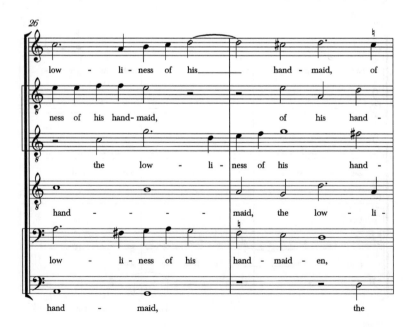

APPENDIX III 303

304 APPENDIX III

306 APPENDIX III

APPENDIX III 309

APPENDIX III 311

APPENDIX III 313

APPENDIX III 315

316 APPENDIX III

APPENDIX III 317

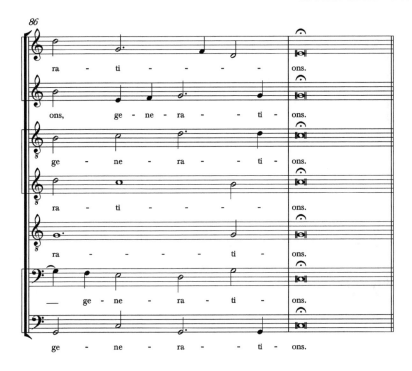

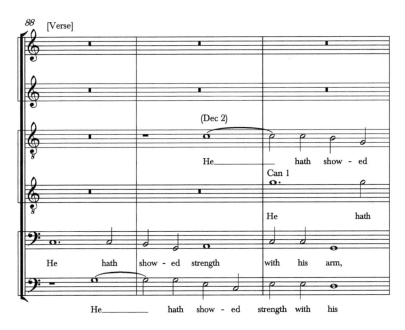

APPENDIX III 319

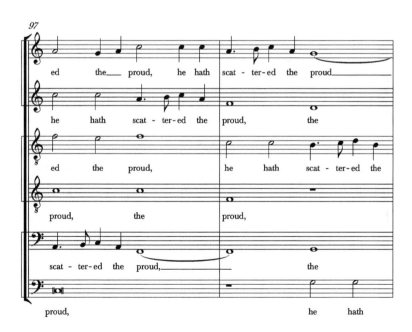

320 APPENDIX III

APPENDIX III 323

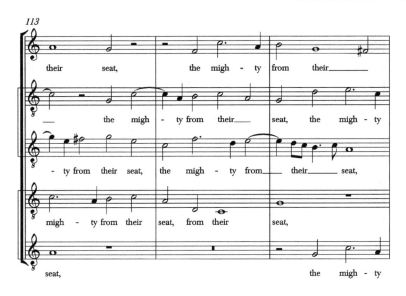

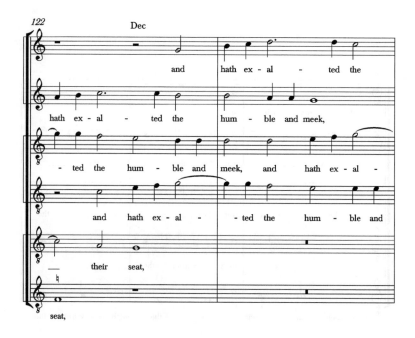

APPENDIX III 325

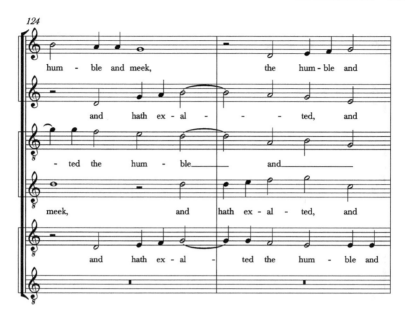

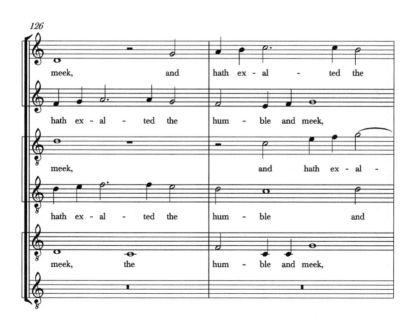

326 APPENDIX III

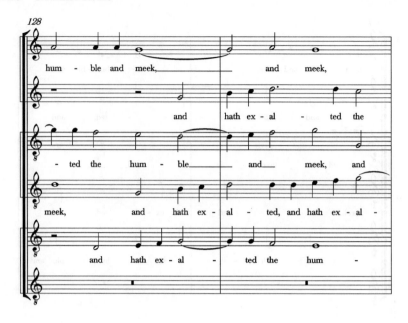

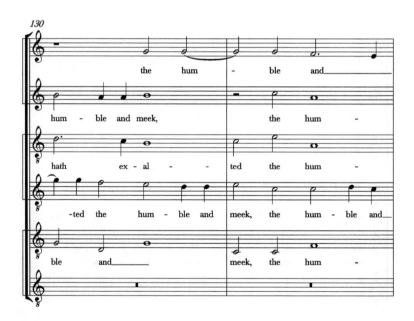

APPENDIX III 327

330 APPENDIX III

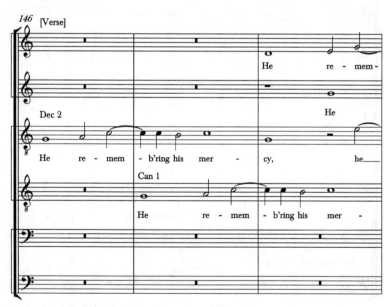

APPENDIX III 331

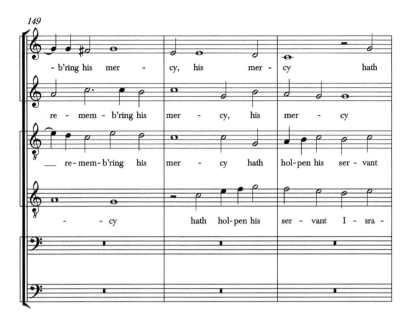

APPENDIX III 333

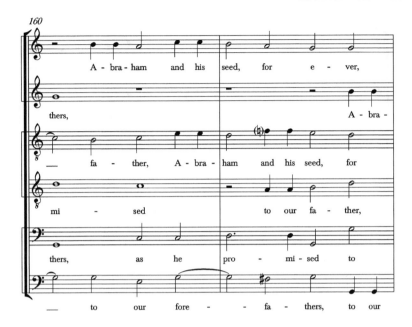
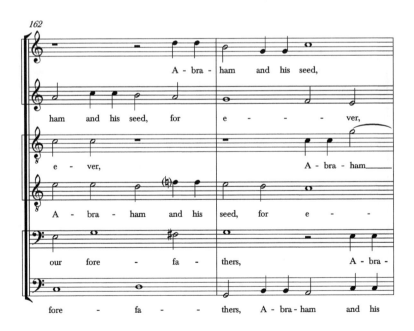

APPENDIX III 337

APPENDIX III 339

APPENDIX III 343

346 APPENDIX III

APPENDIX III

Nunc dimittis

APPENDIX III 349

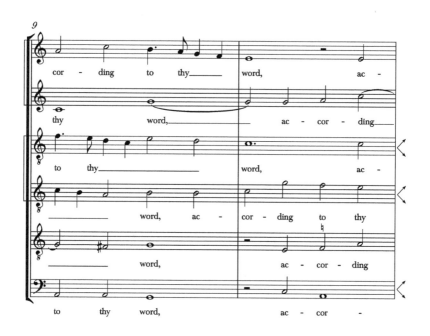

APPENDIX III 351

APPENDIX III 353

354 APPENDIX III

356 APPENDIX III

APPENDIX III 357

358 APPENDIX III

360   APPENDIX III

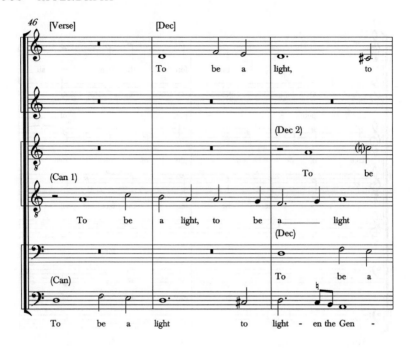
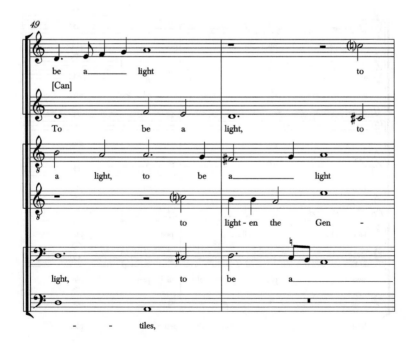

APPENDIX III 361

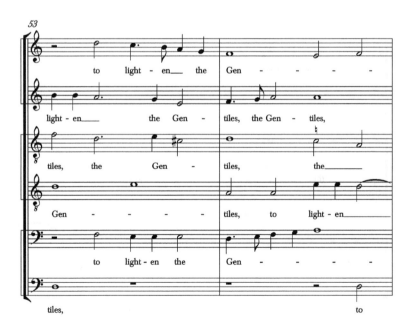

APPENDIX III

APPENDIX III 363

364 APPENDIX III

APPENDIX III 365

APPENDIX III 367

368 APPENDIX III

APPENDIX III 369

APPENDIX III 371

APPENDIX III 373

376 APPENDIX III

378 APPENDIX III

APPENDIX III

APPENDIX III 383

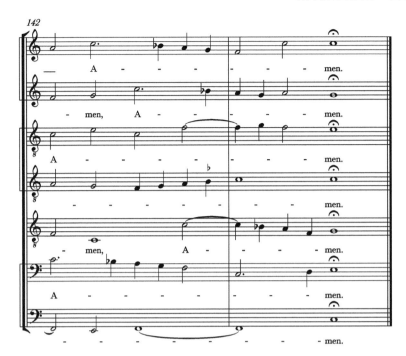

Bibliography

Primary Sources

Manuscripts

Add. MS 22597, c. 1565–1585, London: British Library.
Add. 2765, c. 1530, Cambridge: Cambridge University Library.
Add. MS 32377, c. 1585–1590, London: British Library.
Add. MS 34191, early sixteenth century, London: British Library.
Add. MS 47844, 1581, London: British Library.
The Anne Boleyn Songbook, MS 1070, 1533–1536, London: Royal College of Music.
The Baldwin Partbooks, Och 979–983, Oxford: Christ Church.
The Batten Organ Book, MS Tenbury 791, c. 1630–1640, Oxford: Bodleian Library.
A Booke of In nomines & other Solfainge Songes of v: vi: vii: & viii pts for voyces and Instrumentes, Add. MS 31390, 1578, London: British Library.
The 'Braikenridge Manuscript', Tenbury 1486, mid-to-late sixteenth century, Oxford: Bodleian Library.
Caius Choirbook, MS 667/760, late 1520s, Cambridge: Gonville & Caius College.
Dd. 13. 27, contratenor partbook, c. 1525–1530, Cambridge: Cambridge University Library.
The Dow Partbooks, MSS. 984–988, Oxford: Christ Church.
The Gyffard Partbooks, Add. MS 17802–17805, c. 1570–1585, London: British Library.
The Forrest-Heather Partbooks, Mus. Sch. e. 376–381, c. 1525–1530, 1553–1558, 1590s, 1615–1625, Oxford: Bodleian Library.
The Hamond Partbooks, Add. MS 30480–30484, 1560–1590, London: British Library.
Harley 1709, c. 1525–1530, London: British Library.
The Henry VIII Manuscript, Add. MS 313922, London: British Library.
MS 234, c. 1525–1530, Cambridge: St John's College.
MS. Tenbury 341–344, early seventeenth century, Oxford: Bodleian Library.
The Mulliner Book, Add. MS 305153, London: British Library.
Newberry-Oscott Partbooks, MS minus VM 1578 M.91, c. 1527, Chicago: Newberry Library and Case B No. 4, Sutton Coldfield: Oscott College Old Library.
Old Library G.14.17, c. 1636, Cambridge: Queens' College Library.
Peterhouse Partbooks (Former Caroline Set), copied c. 1625–1640, assembled c. 1635–1643, MS 33, 34, 38, 39, 47, 49 (Cantoris Bass, Medius and Contratenor and Decani Medius, Contratenor and Bass), Cambridge: Peterhouse, Perne Library.
The Sadler Partbooks, Mus. e. 1–5, 1580–1585, Oxford: Bodleian Library.
The Southwell Tenor Book, MS. Tenbury 1382, c. 1617 with seventeenth- and eighteenth-century additions, Oxford: Bodleian Library.
Tristitiae Remedium of Thomas Myriell, Discantus partbook from a set of six, Add. MS 29372, 1616–1618, London: British Library.
Wanley Partbooks, MS Mus. Sch. e. 420–422, c. 1549–1552, Oxford: Bodleian Library.
Willmott Manuscript, Mus. c. 784, 1591, Oxford: Bodleian Library.
Winchester Partbooks, MS 153, 1564–1566, Winchester: Winchester College, Warden and Fellows Library.

Printed Sources

Richard Allison, *The Psalmes of David in Meter* (London: William Barley for Thomas Morley, 1599).
Anonymous, *Bel-vedere, or The Garden of the Muses* (London: F.K. for Hugh Astley, 1600).
Anonymous, *A Very Proper Treatise wherein is briefly set for the the arte of Limming* (London: Richard Tottil, 1573).
Francis Bacon, *Sylva Sylvarum* (London: J. H. for William Lee, 1626).
William Baldwin, *The Canticles or Balades of Solomon, phraselyke declared in Englysh metres* (London: William Baldwin servant with Edwarde Whitchurche, 1549)
William Barley, *The Pathway to Musicke, Contayning Sundrie Familiar and Easie Rules for the Reading and Understanding of the Scale* (London: William Barley, 1596).
William Bathe, *A Briefe Introduction to the Skill of Song by William Bathe* (1586); ed. Kevin C. Carnes (Music Theory in Britain, 1500–1700: Critical Editions; Aldershot: Ashgate, 2005).
Lewis Bayly, *The Practise of Piety* (London: Thomas Snodham, 1613).
Francis Beaumont, *The Knight of the Burning Pestle* (London: Nicholas Okes for Walter Burre, 1613).
John Bennet (c. 1575–1615), *Madrigals to Foure Voyces* (London: Printed in little Sainte Hellens by H. Ballard for William Barley, the assigne of Thomas Morley, 1599).
Joachim Burmeister, *Musica Poetica* (Rostock, 1606); ed. Rainer Bayreuther, repr. (Laaber: Laaber, 2004); ed. and trans. Benito V. Rivera as *Music Poetics* (New Haven, CT: Yale University Press, 1993).
Charles Butler, *Rameae rhetoricae libri duo* (Oxford: Joseph Barnes, 1597).
Charles Butler, *The Feminine Monarchie* (Oxford: Joseph Barnes, 1609).
Charles Butler, *The English Grammar, or Institution of Letters, Syllables and Words in the English Tongue* (Oxford: William Turner, 1633).
Charles Butler, *The Principles of Musick* (London: John Haviland, 1636).
William Byrd, *Psalms, Sonets and Songs and Sadnes and Piete, Made into Musicke of Five Parts* (London: Thomas East, 1588).
William Byrd, Psalmes, *Songs and Sonnets: Some Solemne, Others Ioyfull, Framed to the Life of the Words* (London: Thomas Snodham, 1611).
William Camden, *Britain, or a Chorographicall Description of the most flourishing Kingdomes, England, Scotland, and Ireland, and the lands adjoining, out of the depth of Antiquitie* (first published 1586; this edition London: George Bishop, 1607).
Thomas Campion, *Observations in the art of English poesie* (London: R. Field for A. Wise, 1602).
Thomas Campion, *A New Way of Making Fowre Parts in Counter-Point* (London: T. Snodham for John Browne, 1610).
Thomas Campion, 'O This Ensuing Discourse', paratext to Thomas Ravenscroft, *A Briefe Discourse of the True (but neglected) use of charact'ring the degrees* (London: Edward Allde for Thomas Adams, 1614).
John Case, *The Pathway to Musicke* (Oxford: Joseph Barnes for the Universitie, 1586).
Robert Cawdrey, *A Table Alphabeticall of Hard Usual English Words* (this edition London: T. S. for Edmund Weaver, 1617).
Henry Cockeram, *The English Dictionarie, or, An Interpreter of Hard Wordes* (London: Nathaniel Butter, 1623).
Randle Cotgrave, *A Dictionarie of the French and English Tongues* (London: Adam Islip, 1611).
Helkiah Crooke, *Mikrokosmographia. A Description of the Body of Man* (London: William Iaggard dwelling in Barbican, 1615).
William Daman, *The psalms of David in English meter* (London: John Daye, 1579).
William Daman, *The Former Booke of the Musicke of M. William Damond* (London: Thomas East, 1591).
Samuel Daniel, *A defence of ryme against a pamphlet entitled: Observations in the art of English poesie* (London: Valentine Simmes, 1603).

Samuel Daniel, *The Tragedie of Cleopatra*, in *Certaine small works heretofore divulged by Samuel Daniell* (London: J[ohn] L[egat] for Simon Waterston, 1611).
John Davies, *Orchestra or a Poeme of Dauncing. Judicially proving the true observation of Time and Measure, in the authenticall and laudable use of Dauncing* (first published London: I. Robarts for N. Ling, 1596).
John Davies, *Nosce Teipsum: this Oracle expounded in two elegies, 1) of Humane Knowledge, 2) Of the Soule of Man, and the Immortalitie thereof* (London: Richard Hawkins, 1599).
John Dee, 'The Mathematicall Praeface', in Henry Billingsley, *Elementes of Euclid of Megara* (London: John Day, 1570).
Thomas Dekker, *The Magnificent Entertainment* (London: Thomas Creede, 1604).
Thomas Dekker, *The Belman of London* (London: Nathaniel Butter, 1608).
Thomas Dekker and Thomas Middleton, *The Roaring Girl* (London: Nicholas Okes for Thomas Archer, 1611).
Leonard Digges, *A Geometrical Practice, named Pantometria* (London: Henrie Bynneman, 1571).
John Dowland, *Andreas Ornithoparcus his Micrologus* (London: Thomas Snodham for Thomas Adams, 1609).
Thomas East, *The Whole Booke of Psalmes: with their wonted tunes* (London: Thomas East, 1592).
Thomas Elyot, *The Boke of the Governor* (London, 1530).
John Gerard, *The Herball or Generall Historie of Plantes* (London: John Norton, 1597).
John Hart, *An Orthographie* (London: [Henry Denham] for William Seres, 1569).
Richard Haydocke, *A Tracte Concerning the Artes of Curious Paintinge Carvinge & Buildinge, written first in Italian by Jo. Paul Lomatius painter of Milan* (Oxford: Joseph Barnes, 1598).
Raphael Holinshed, *The First Volume of the Chronicles of England, Scotlande, and Irelande* (London: Lucas Harrison, 1577).
Richard Huolet, *Abecedarium Anglo Latinum* (London: G. Riddell, 1552).
Franciscus Junius, *The Painting of the Ancients in Three Bookes: Declaring by Historicall Observations and Example* (London: Richard Hodgkinsonne, 1638).
Aemilia Lanier, *Salve Deus Rex Judaeorum* (London: Valentine Simmes, 1611).
Gervase Markham, *Cavelarice, or the English Horseman* (London: Edward White, 1607).
Gervase Markham, *Countrey Contentments, or the English Huswife* (London: John Beale, 1623).
John Marston, *The Malcontent* (London: Valentine Simmes for William Aspley, 1604).
Thomas Middleton, *Your Five Gallants* (London: George Eld for Richard Bonlan, 1608).
Thomas Morley, *The Firste Booke of Balletts to Five Voyces* (London: Thomas East, 1595).
Thomas Morley, *Canzonets or Litle short aers to five and sixe voices* (London: Peter Short, 1597).
Thomas Morley, *A Plaine and Easie Introduction to Practicall Musicke* (London: Peter Short, 1597).
Thomas Morley, *Madrigals to Foure Voices* (London: Thomas Este, 1600).
Thomas Morley, *Canzonets or little short songs to three voyces* (London: Thomas East, 1606).
John Norden, *Speculum Britaaniae. The first parte an historicall, chorographicall description of Middlesex* (London: Eliot's Court Press, 1593).
John Norden, *The Labyrinth of Mans Life, Or Vertues Delight and Envies Opposite* (London: George Eld for John Budge, to be solde at the great south doore of Paules, and at Brittaines Bursse, 1614).
John Palsgrave, *Lesclarcissement de la langue francoyse* (London: J. Hakuyns, 1530).
Henry Peacham, *Graphice: The Art of Drawing with the Pen, and Limning in Water Colours* (London: Richard Braddock, 1606).
Henry Peacham, *Minerva Britanna, or a garden of heroicall deuises, and adorned with emblems and impresa's of sundry natures, newly devised, moralised and published* (London: Printed in Shoe-lane at the signe of the Faulcon by Wa. Dight, 1612).
Henry Peacham, *The Compleat Gentleman* (London: Francis Constable, 1622).
Hugh Plat, *Delightes for Ladies to Adorne their Persons, Tables, Closets and Distillatories with Beauties, Perfumes and Waters* (London: Peter Short, 1602).
John Playford, *A Breefe Introduction to the Skill of Musick* (London: John Playford, 1654).

Owen Price, *The Vocal Organ, or A new art of teaching the English orthographie by observing the instruments of pronunciation* (Oxford: William Hall for Amos Curteyne, 1665).

Pierre de la Primaudaye, *The French Academie Wherein is Discoursed the Institution of Maners*, transl. Thomas Bowes (London: Edmund Bollifont for George Bishop, 1586).

Pierre de la Primaudaye, *The Second Part of the French Academie* (London: G. B[ishop], R. N[ewbery] & R. B[arker], 1594).

William Prynne, *Histrio-Matrix* (London: Edward Allde and William Jones, 1633).

George Puttenham, *The Art of English Poesy*, first published 1589, this edition in Gavin Alexander (ed.), *Sidney's 'The Defence of Poesy' and Selected Renaissance Literary Criticism* (London: Penguin, 2004).

Thomas Ravenscroft, *A Briefe Discourse of the True (but neglected) use of charact'ring the degrees* (London: Edward Allde for Thomas Adams, 1614).

Robert Recorde, *The Pathway to Knowledge, Containing the First Principles of Geometrie* (London: Reynold Wolfe, 1551).

Thomas Robinson, *The Schoole of Musicke wherein is taught, the perfect method, of true fingering of the lute, pandora, orpharion and viol de gamba; with most infallible generall rules, both easie and delightful* (London: Thomas East, 1603).

Thomas Salter, *A mirrhor mete for all mothers, matrones, and maidens, intituled the Mirrhor of Modestie no lesse profitable and pleasant, then necessarie to bee read and practiced* (London: J. Kingston for Edward White, at the little Northdore of Paules at the signe of the Gun, 1579).

William Samuel, *The abridgemente of goddess statutes in myter* (London: Robert Crowley, 1551).

William Shakespeare, *An excellent conceited tragedie of Romeo and Juliet as it hath been often (with great applause) plaid publiquely* (London: John Danter, 1597).

William Shakespeare, *Mr William Shakespeares comedies, histories and tragedies Published according to the true originall copies* (London: Isaac Iaggard, and Ed. Blount, 1623).

Philip Sidney, *The Defense of Poesy*, first published 1590, this edition ed. Gavin Alexander, *Sidney's 'Defence of Poesy' and Selected Renaissance Literary Criticism* (London: Penguin, 2004).

Charles Simpson, *Compendium of Practical Musick* (London: William Godbid, 1667).

Edmund Spenser, *The Faerie Queene* (London: Richard Field for William Ponsonbie, 1596).

John Taverner, *On the Origin and Progress of the Art of Music*, 1611, ed. Joseph M. Ortiz (London, Routledge, 2018).

Johannes Tinctoris, *The Art of Counterpoint* (Liber de Arte Contrapuncti), translated and edited by Albert Seay (Musicological Studies and Documents 5; American Institute of Musicology, 1961).

Nathaniel Tomkins and Thomas Tomkins, *Musica Deo Sacra & ecclesiae Anglicanae, or, Musick dedicated to the honour and service of God, and to the use of the cathedral and other churches of England, especially of the Chappel-Royal of King Charles the First* (London: William Godbid, 1668).

Thomas Tomkins, *Songs of 3, 4, 5 and 6 parts* (London: Thomas Snodham, 1622).

Thomas Tomkis, *Lingua, or Combat of the Tongue* (London: G. Eld., 1607).

Thomas Tusser, *Five Hundred pointes of good Husbandrie* (London: Henrie Denham, 1580).

Christopher Tye, *The Actes of the Apostles, translated into Englyshe Metre* (London: Wyllyam Seres, 1553)

John Webster, *The Duchess of Malfi*, 1614 (first published London: Nicholas Ores, 1623).

Thomas Weelkes, *Balletts and Madrigals to Five Voyces* (London: Thomas East, 1598).

Thomas Weelkes, *Madrigals of 5 and 6 parts* (London: Thomas East, 1600).

Thomas Weelkes, *Ayeres or phantasticke spirites for three voices* (London: William Barley, 1608).

Geoffrey Whitney, *A Choice of Emblemes* (Leiden: Christopher Plantin, 1586).

Isabella Whitney, *A Sweet Nosgay* (London: R. Jones, 1573).

Thomas Wright, *The Passions of the Minde in Generall* (London: Valentine Simmes and Adam Islip for Walter Venge, 1604).

Secondary Sources

Katherine Acheson, *Visual Rhetoric and Early Modern English Literature* (Farnham: Ashgate, 2013).
Sylvia Adamson, Gavin Alexander, and Katrin Ettenhuber (eds.), *Renaissance Figures of Speech* (Cambridge: Cambridge University Press, 2007).
Sara Ahmed, 'A Phenomenology of Whiteness', in *Feminist Theory*, 8: 2 (2007), 149–168.
Patricia Akhimie, *Shakespeare and the Cultivation of Race: Race and Conduct in the Early Modern World* (New York: Routledge, 2018).
Gavin Alexander, 'The Elizabethan Lyric as Contrafactum: Robert Sidney's "French Tune" Identified', in *Music & Letters*, 84: 3 (2003), 378–402.
Eric Lewin Altschuler and William Jansen, 'Thomas Weelkes's Text Authors: Men of Letters', in *The Musical Times*, 143: 1879 (2002), 13–24.
Sydney Anglo, 'The *British History* in Early Tudor Propaganda', in *Bulletin of the John Rylands Library*, 44 (1961), 17–48.
Willi Apel, *The Notation of Polyphonic Music, 900–1600* (Cambridge, MA: Mediaeval Academy of America, 1961).
John Aplin, '"The Fourth Kind of Faburden": The Identity of an English Four-Part Style', in *Music & Letters*, 61 (1980), 260–261.
John Aplin, 'The Origins of John Day's "Certaine Notes"', in *Music & Letters*, 62 (1981), 295–299.
Katherine Ara (ed.), *Nicholas Lanier (1588–1666): A Portrait Revealed* (London: Weiss Gallery, 2010).
Dennis M. Arnold, 'Thomas Weelkes and the Madrigal', in *Music and Letters*, 30: 1 (January 1950), 1–12.
Samantha Arten, 'The Origin of Fixed-Scale Solmization in *The Whole Booke of Psalmes*', in *Early Music* 46: 1 (2018), 149–165.
Samantha Arten, 'Singing as English Protestants: *The Whole Booke of Psalmes*' Theology of Music', in *Yale Journal of Music and Religion* 5: 1 (2019), 1–34.
Samantha Arten, '"To be songe to the tune of [the] 25th psalme": Adapting *The Whole Booke of Psalmes* for Personal Devotion and Communal Singing', in *Reformation*, 27: 1 (May 2022), 65–84.
Andrew Ashbee, 'Groomed for Service: Musicians in the Privy Chamber at the English Court c. 1495–1558', in *Early Music*, 25 (1997), 193–194.
Joseph Ashmore, 'Faith in Lancelot Andrewes's Preaching', in *The Seventeenth Century Journal*, 32: 2 (2017), 121–138.
Joseph Ashmore, 'Attending to the Passion in Early Modern England: Lancelot Andrewes' Good Friday Sermons', in *Journal of Medieval and Early Modern Studies*, 53: 2 (May 2023), 379–404.
Margaret Aston, *Broken Idols of the English Reformation* (Cambridge: Cambridge University Press, 2015).
Linda Phyllis Austern, '"Alluring the Auditorie to Effeminacie": Music and the Idea of the Feminine in Early Modern England', in *Music & Letters*, 74: 3 (August 1993), 343–354.
Linda Phyllis Austern, '"Sweet Music with Sour Sauce": The Genesis of Musical Irony in English Drama after 1600', *Journal of Musicology*, 4:4 (1986), 472–490.
Linda Phyllis Austern, *Both from the Ears and the Mind: Thinking about Music in Early Modern England* (Chicago: University of Chicago Press, 2020).
Linda Phyllis Austern, Candace Bailey, and Amanda Eubanks Winkler (eds.), *Beyond Boundaries: Rethinking Music Circulation in Early Modern England* (Bloomington: Indiana University Press, 2017).
Patrick Ball, 'The Playing Cards and Gaming Boards', in Michael Fleming and Christopher Page (eds.), *Music and Instruments of the Elizabethan Age: The Eglantine Table* (Suffolk: Boydell & Brewer, 2021), 47–56.
Katie Bank, *Knowledge Building in Early Modern English Music* (London: Routledge, 2020).
Katie Bank, '(Re)creating the Eglantine Table', in *Early Music*, 48: 3 (2020), 359–376.

Katie Bank, 'Truth & Travel: The *Principal Navigations* and "Thule, the Period of Cosmographie"', in *Journal of the Hakluyt Society* (July 2020), 1–22.
Nicholas Baragwanath, *The Solfeggio Tradition: The Forgotten Art of Melody in the Long Eighteenth Century* (Oxford: Oxford University Press, 2020).
Gregory Barnett, 'Tonal Organization in Seventeenth Century Music Theory', in Thomas Christensen (ed.), *The Cambridge History of Western Music Theory* (Cambridge: Cambridge University Press, 2002), 407–455.
Dietrich Bartel, *Musica Poetica: Musical Rhetorical Figures in German Baroque Music* (Lincoln: University of Nebraska Press, 1997).
Ben Barton and Elizabeth Scott-Baumann (eds.), *The Work of Form: Poetics and Materiality in Early Modern Culture* (Oxford: Oxford University Press, 2014).
Marisa Bass (eds.), *Conchophilia: Shells, Art and Curiosity in Early Modern Europe* (Princeton, NJ: Princeton University Press, 2021).
Michael Baxandall, *Painting and Experience in Fifteenth-Century Italy* (Oxford: Oxford University Press, 1972).
Michael Baxandall, 'English *Disegno*', in Edward Chaney and Peter Mack (eds.), *England and the Continental Renaissance* (Woodbridge: Boydell Press, 1990), 203–214.
Hugh Benham, *John Taverner: His Life and Music* (London: Routledge, 2003).
Margaret Bent, 'Diatonic *Ficta*', in *Early Music History*, 4 (1984), 1–48.
Margaret Bent, *Counterpoint, Composition and Musica Ficta* (London: Routledge, 2002).
Margaret Bent, 'Grammar and Rhetoric in Late Medieval Polyphony: Modern Metaphor or Old Simile?', in Mary Carruthers (ed.), *Rhetoric beyond Words: Delight and Persuasion in the Arts of the Middle Ages* (Cambridge: Cambridge University Press, 2010), 52–71.
David M. Bevington and Peter Holbrook, *The Politics of the Stuart Court Masque* (Cambridge: Cambridge University Press, 1998).
Gurminder Bhogal, *Details of Consequence: Ornament, Music and Art in Paris* (Oxford: Oxford University Press, 2013).
Bonnie J. Blackburn, 'The Lascivious Career of B-Flat', in Bonnie J. Blackburn and Laurie Stras (eds.), *Eroticism in Early Modern Music* (Farnham: Ashgate, 2015), 19–42.
Anthony Boden (ed.), *Thomas Tomkins: The Last Elizabethan* (London: Routledge, 2005).
Claire M. L. Bourne, *Typographies of Performance in Early Modern England* (Oxford: Oxford University Press, 2020).
Philip Brett, Joseph Kerman, and Davitt Moroney, 'The Two Musical Personalities of Thomas Weelkes', in *Music & Letters*, 53 (1972), 369–376.
Dennis Britton, *Becoming Christian: Race, Reformation and Early Modern English Romance* (New York: Fordham University Press, 2014).
Thomas Brothers, *Chromatic Beauty in the Late Medieval Chanson: An Interpretation of Manuscript Accidentals* (Cambridge: Cambridge University Press, 2006).
David Brown, 'The Anthems of Thomas Weelkes', in *Proceedings of the Royal Musical Association*, 91: 1 (1964), 61–72.
David Brown, *Thomas Weelkes: A Biographical and Critical Study* (London: Faber & Faber, 1969).
Michael Buchler, 'Ornamentation as Gesture in Atonal Music', in *Music Theory Spectrum*, 42: 1 (2019), 24–37.
L. Poundie Burstein, 'The Half Cadence and Other Such Slippery Events', in *Music Theory Spectrum*, 36: 2 (2014), 203–227
Katherine Butler, 'In Praise of Music: Motets, Inscriptions and Musical Philosophy in Robert Dow's Partbooks', in *Early Music*, 45: 1 (2017), 89–101.
Katherine Butler, 'Printed Borders for Sixteenth-Century Music or Music Paper and the Early Career of Music Printer Thomas East', in *The Library*, 19: 2 (June 2018), 29–93.
Katherine Butler, 'From Liturgy and the Education of Choirboys to Protestant Domestic Music-Making: The History of the "Hamond" Partbooks', in *Royal Musical Association Research Chronicle*, 50: 1 (2019), 29–93.

Katherine Butler, 'Creating a Tudor Musical Miscellany: The McGhie/Tenbury 389 Partbooks', *Music & Letters* (29 March 2021).
Mary J. Carruthers, 'Varietas: A Word of Many Colours', in *Poetica*, 41: 1 and 2 (2009), 11–32.
Mary Carruthers, 'The Concept of Ductus, or Journeying through a Work of Art', in Mary Carruthers (ed.), *Rhetoric beyond Words: Delight and Persuasion in the Arts of the Middle Ages* (Cambridge: Cambridge University Press, 2010), 1–19.
Mary Carruthers (ed.), *Rhetoric beyond Words: Delight and Persuasion in the Arts of the Middle Ages* (Cambridge: Cambridge University Press, 2010).
Urvashi Chakravarty, *Fictions of Consent: Slavery, Servitude and Free Service in Early Modern England* (Philadelphia: University of Pennsylvania Press, 2022).
Eleanor Chan, *Mathematics and the Craft of Thought in the Anglo-Dutch Renaissance* (London: Routledge, 2021).
Eleanor Chan, 'The English Cadence: Reading an Early Modern Musical Trope', in *Early Music*, 49: 2 (February 2021), 17–34.
Eleanor Chan, '{Not}ation: the In/Visible Visual Cultures of Music Notation in the English Renaissance', in *Arts* (Special Issue: Im/Materiality in Renaissance Arts, ed. Lisa Pon and Kate van Orden) (April 2023).
Eleanor Chan, 'Scrollwork: Visual Culture of Musical Notation and Graphic Materiality in the English Renaissance', in *Journal of Medieval and Early Modern Studies*, 53: 2 (May 2023), 347–373.
Eleanor Chan, 'The Etymology of the "English" Cadence', in *Music & Letters*, 104: 3 (August 2023), 414–438.
Matthieu Chapman, *Anti-Black Racism in Early Modern English Drama: The Other 'Other'* (New York: Routledge, 2017).
Matthieu Chapman, 'Whitewashing White Permanence: The (Dis)/(Re)membering of White Corporeality in Early Modern England', in *Literature Compass* (5 December 2022), 1–14.
Thomas Christensen, 'Music Theory and Pedagogy', in Iain Fenlon and Richard Wistreich (eds.), *The Cambridge History of Sixteenth Century Music* (Cambridge: Cambridge University Press, 2019), 345–355.
Emily Cockayne, *Hubbub: Filth, Noise and Stench in England 1600–1770* (New Haven, CT: Yale University Press, 2020).
Suzanne Cole, *Thomas Tallis and His Music in Victorian England* (Woodbridge: Boydell & Brewer, 2008).
Rosalie L. Colie, *Paradoxia Epidemica* (Princeton, NJ: Princeton University Press, 1966).
Dennis Collins, 'Thomas Tomkins' Canonic Additions to Thomas Morley's "A Plaine and Easie Introduction to Practicall Musicke"', in *Music & Letters*, 76: 3 (1995), 369–386.
Sarah Collins, 'The National and the Universal', in P. Watt, S. Collins, and M. Allis (eds.), *The Oxford Handbook of Music and Intellectual Culture in the Nineteenth Century* (Oxford: Oxford University Press, 2020).
Patrick Collinson, *The Birthpangs of Protestant England: Religious and Cultural Change in the Sixteenth and Seventeenth Centuries* (Basingstoke: Macmillan, 1988).
Philip A. Cooke, 'A "Wholly New Chapter" in Service Music: Collegium Regale and the Gloucester Service', in Philip A. Cooke and David Maw (eds.), *The Music of Herbert Howells* (Woodbridge: Boydell & Brewer, 2008), 86–99.
Helen Cooper, *The English Romance in Time: Transforming Motifs from Geoffrey of Monmouth to the Death of Shakespeare* (Cambridge: Cambridge University Press, 2004).
Michael C. Corballis, *The Wandering Mind: What the Brain Does When You're Not Looking* (Chicago: University of Chicago Press, 2015).
Julie Corre, 'Le concept de "Britishness" dans les emblèmes de Henry Peacham (1612): vers une reconquête identitaire?', in *Revue LISA (Littératures, histoire des idées, Images et Sociétés du monde Anglophone)*, 13: 3 (2015), 224–235.
Brian Cummings, *The Literary Culture of the Reformation: Grammar and Grace* (Oxford: Oxford University Press, 2002).

Ben Curry, 'Two Approaches to Tonal Space in the Music of Muddy Waters', in *Music Analysis*, 36: 1 (2017), 37–58.

Carl Dahlhaus, *Studies on the Origin of Harmonic Tonality* (Princeton, NJ: Princeton University Press, 1990).

Nandini Das, *Courting India: England, Mughal India and the Origins of Empire* (London: Bloomsbury, 2023).

Nandini Das, João Vicente Melo, Haig Smith, and Lauren Working (eds.), *Keywords of Identity, Race and Human Mobility in Early Modern England* (Amsterdam: Amsterdam University Press, 2021).

Callan Davies, *Strangeness in Jacobean Drama* (London: Routledge, 2021).

Ruth I. DeFord, *Tactus, Mensuration and Rhythm in Renaissance Music* (Cambridge: Cambridge University Press, 2015).

Flora Dennis, 'Scattered Knives and Dismembered Song: Cutlery, Music and the Rituals of Dining', in *Renaissance Studies* 24: 1 (2010), 156–184.

Edward J. Dent, 'On the Composition of English Songs', in *Music & Letters*, 6: 3 (1925), 280–300.

Matthew Dimmock, *Elizabethan Globalism: England, China and the Rainbow Portrait* (New Haven, CT, and London: Yale University Press for the Paul Mellon Centre for Studies in British Art, 2019).

Natalya Din-Kariuki, '"This Musique Hath Life in It": Harmony in Lancelot Andrewes's Preaching', in *Huntington Library Quarterly*, 85: 2 (Summer 2022), 241–258.

Holly Dugan, *The Ephemeral History of Perfume: Scent and Sense in Early Modern England* (Baltimore: Johns Hopkins University Press, 2011).

Theodor Dumitrescu, *The Early Tudor Court and International Musical Relations* (Aldershot: Ashgate, 2007).

Heather C. Easterling, 'Reading the Royal Entry (1604) in/as Print', in *Early Theatre*, 20: 1 (2017), 45–75.

Warwick Edwards, 'The Performance of Ensemble Music in Elizabethan England', in *Proceedings of the Royal Musical Association*, 97 (1970–1971), 113–119.

Warwick Edwards, 'The Sources of Elizabethan Consort Music' (DPhil diss., University of Cambridge, 1974).

Elizabeth Eisenstein, *The Printing Revolution in Early Modern Europe* (Cambridge: Cambridge University Press, 1983).

Donna Beth Ellard, *Anglo-Saxon(ist) Pasts, PostSaxon Futures* (Earth, Milky Way: Punctum Books, 2019).

Margaret Ellis, 'The Hardwick Hall Hanging: An Unusual Collaboration in English Sixteenth-Century Embroidery', in *Renaissance Studies*, 10: 2 (1996), 352–353.

David Evett, *Literature and the Visual Arts in Tudor England* (London: University of Georgia Press, 1990).

Christina J. Faraday, *Tudor Liveliness: Vivid Art in Post-Reformation England* (London and New Haven, CT: Yale University Press for the Paul Mellon Centre for Studies in British Art, 2023).

Iain Fenlon and John Milsom, '"Ruled Paper Imprinted": Music Paper and Patents in Sixteenth-Century England', in *Journal of the American Musicological Society*, 37 (1984), 139–163.

Iain Fenlon and Richard Wistreich (eds.), *The Cambridge History of Sixteenth Century Music* (Cambridge: Cambridge University Press, 2019).

Kenneth Fincham, 'Contemporary Opinions of Thomas Weelkes', in *Music and Letters*, 62: 3–4 (1981), 165–187.

Kenneth Fincham and Nicholas Tyacke, *Altars Restored: The Changing Face of English Religious Worship, 1547–1700* (Oxford: Oxford University Press, 2007).

Jill Finstein, *Isaac Oliver: Art and Courts of Elizabeth I and James I* (New York: Garland, 1981).

Juliet Fleming, 'How to Look at a Printed Flower', in *Word and Image*, 22: 2 (April–June 2006), 345–371.

Juliet Fleming, 'How Not to Look at a Printed Flower', in *Journal of Medieval and Early Modern Studies*, 38: 2 (Spring 2008), 48–64.
Juliet Fleming, 'Changed Opinions as to Flowers', in Helen Smith and Louise Wilson (eds.), *Renaissance Paratexts* (Cambridge: Cambridge University Press, 2011), 179–192.
Juliet Fleming, 'Damask Papers', in Andy Kesson and Emma Smith (eds.), *The Elizabethan Top Ten: Defining Print Popularity in Early Modern England* (Farnham: Ashgate, 2013), 377–394.
Juliet Fleming, 'The Renaissance Collage: Signcutting and Signsewing', in *Journal of Medieval and Early Modern Studies*, 45: 3 (September 2015), 443–456.
Juliet Fleming, *Cultural Graphology: Writing after Derrida* (Chicago: University of Chicago Press, 2016).
Juliet Fleming, 'Graffiti Futures', in *Journal of Early Modern Studies*, 9 (2020), 29–36.
Michael Fleming and Christopher Page (eds.), *Music and Instruments of the Elizabethan Age: The Eglantine Table* (Suffolk: Boydell & Brewer, 2021).
Jane Flynn, 'The Education of Choristers in England during the Sixteenth Century', in John Morehen (ed.), *English Choral Practice, 1400–1650* (Cambridge: Cambridge University Press, 1995), 80–99.
Jane Flynn, 'Thomas Mulliner: An Apprentice of John Heywood?', in Susan Boynton and Eric Rice (eds.), *Young Choristers, 650–1700* (Woodbridge: Boydell & Brewer, 2012), 173–194.
Valerie Forman, 'Marked Angels: Counterfeits, Commodities, and *The Roaring Girl*', in *Renaissance Quarterly*, 54 (2001), 1531–1560.
Michel Foucault, *The Order of Things: An Archaeology of the Human Sciences* (London: Routledge, 2002).
Allen J. Frantzen, *Desire for Origins: New Language, Old English, and Teaching the Tradition* (New Brunswick, NJ: Rutgers University Press, 1990).
Susan Frye, *Pens and Needles: Women's Textualities in Early Modern England* (Philadelphia: University of Pennsylvania Press, 2010).
Patricia Fumerton, *The Broadside Ballad in Early Modern England: Moving Media, Tactical Publics* (Philadelphia: University of Pennsylvania Press, 2020).
Patricia Fumerton, *Cultural Aesthetics: Renaissance Literature and the Practice of Social Ornament* (Chicago: University of Chicago Press, 1991).
Patricia Fumerton, *The Broadside Ballad in Early Modern England: Moving Media, Tactical Publics* (Philadelphia: University of Pennsylvania Press, 2020).
John Gallagher, *Learning Languages in Early Modern England* (Oxford: Oxford University Press, 2019).
John Gallagher, '"To Heare It by Mouth": Speech and Accent in Early Modern Language Learning', in *Huntington Library Quarterly*, 82: 1 (Spring 2019), 63–86.
Lucy Gent, *Picture and Poetry 1560–1620: Relations between Literature and the Visual Arts in the English Renaissance* (Leamington Spa: James Hall, 1981).
Lucy Gent, 'The Rash Gaze: Economies of Vision in Britain, 1550–1660', in Lucy Gent (ed.), *Albion's Classicism: The Visual Arts in Britain, 1550–1660* (Studies in British Art 1) (London: Paul Mellon Centre, 1995), 19–46.
Daisy M. Gibbs, 'England's Most Christian King: Henry VIII's 1513 Campaigns and a Lost Votive Antiphon by William Cornysh', in *Early Music*, 46: 1 (2018), 131–148.
Daisy M. Gibbs, '"Your Muse Remains Forever": Memory and Monumentality in Elizabethan Manuscript Partbooks', in *Early Music*, 50: 1 (February 2022), 33–50.
I. Godt, 'John Bennet and the Directional Convention: An Introduction to Madrigalism', in Paul Laird (ed.), *Words & Music* (Binghamton, NY: Binghamton University, 1990), 121–146.
E. H. Gombrich, *Art and Illusion* (New York: Phaidon, 1959, this edition 2002).
E. H. Gombrich, *The Sense of Order: A Study in the Psychology of Decorative Art* (London: Phaidon, first published 1979, this edition 2002).
Christine Göttler, 'Vapours and Veils: The Edge of the Unseen', in Christine Göttler and Wolfgang Neuber (eds.), *Spirits Unseen: The Representation of Subtle Bodies in Early Modern European Culture* (Leiden: Brill, 2008), 165–2016.

Penelope Gouk, *Music, Science and Natural Magic in Seventeenth-Century England* (New Haven, CT: Yale University Press, 1999).

Antony Grafton, *Inky Fingers: The Making of Books in Early Modern Europe* (Cambridge, MA: Harvard University Press, 2020).

Roger Mathew Grant, *Beating Time and Measuring Music in the Early Modern Era*, Oxford Studies in Music Theory (Oxford: Oxford University Press), 2015.

James Haar, 'False Relations and Chromaticism in Sixteenth Century Music', in *Journal of the American Musicological Society*, 30: 3 (Autumn 1977), 391–418.

James Haar, 'Music as Visual Object: The Importance of Notational Appearance', in Renato Bordghi and Pietro Zappalà (eds.), *L'edizione critica tra testo musicale e testo letterario. Atti del convegno internazionale (Cremona 4–8 ottobre 1992)* (Lucca: Libreria Musicale Italiana, 1995), 97–128.

Imtiaz Habib, *Black Lives in the English Archives 1500–1677: Imprints of the Invisible* (Farnham: Ashgate, 2008).

Helen Hackett, *The Elizabethan Mind: Searching for the Self in the Age of Uncertainty* (New Haven, CT: Yale University Press, 2022).

John Haines (ed.), *The Calligraphy of Medieval Music* (Turnhout: Brepols, 2011).

Kim F. Hall, *Things of Darkness: Economies of Race and Gender in Early Modern England* (Ithaca, NY: Cornell University Press, 2018).

Hannibal Hamlin, *Psalm Culture and Early Modern English Literature* (Cambridge: Cambridge University Press, 2004).

Tara Hamling, *Decorating the Godly Household: Religious Art in Post-Reformation Britain* (London and New Haven, CT: Paul Mellon Centre, 2010).

Tara Hamling, 'Living with the Bible in Post-Reformation England', in J. Doran, C. Methuen, and A. Walsham (eds.), *Religion and the Household* (Woodbridge: Boydell & Brewer, 2014), 210–239.

Tara Hamling, 'Memorable Motifs: The Role of "Synoptic" Imagery in Remembering the English Reformation', in Alexandra Walsham, Bronwyn Wallace, Ceri Law, and Brian Cummings (eds.), *Memory and the English Reformation* (Cambridge: Cambridge University Press, 2020), 185–206.

Tara Hamling and Catherine Richardson, *A Day at Home in Early Modern England* (London: Paul Mellon Centre for Studies in British Art, 2017).

Deborah Harkness, *The Jewel House: Elizabethan London and the Scientific Revolution* (New Haven, CT: Yale University Press, 2007).

E. Ruth Harvey, *The Inward Wits: Psychological Theory in the Middle Ages and the Renaissance* (London: Warburg Institute, 1975).

Jane D. Hatter, 'Constructing the Composer: Symbolic Use of the Hexachord in Compositions c. 1500', in *Composing Community in Late Medieval Music: Self-Reference, Pedagogy, and Practice* (Cambridge: Cambridge University Press, 2019), 217–236.

Florence Hazrat, '"Fashioning Faith to forms (im)mutable": The Rondeau and Trust in the Poetry of Sir Thomas Wyatt', in *The Cambridge Quarterly*, 47: 2 (2018), 222–242.

Florence Hazrat, '"The wisedome of your feete": Dance, Rhetoric, and Cognition', in Lynsey Culloch, and Brandon Shaw (eds.), *The Oxford Handbook of Shakespeare and Dance* (Oxford: Oxford University Press, 2019), 726–752.

Benjamin M. Hebbert, 'The Lute and the Lutenist', in Katherine Ara (ed.), *Nicholas Lanier (1588–1666): A Portrait Revealed* (London: Weiss Gallery, 2010), 78–83.

Benjamin M. Hebbert, 'A New Portrait of Nicholas Lanier', in *Early Music*, 38: 4 (November 2010), 509–522.

Megan Heffernan, *Making the Miscellany: Poetry, Print and the History of the Book in Early Modern England* (Philadelphia: University of Pennsylvania Press, 2021).

Anne Heminger, 'Music Theory at Work: The Eton Choirbook, Rhythmic Proportions and Musical Networks in Sixteenth-Century England', in *Early Music History*, 37 (2018), 141–182.

Anne Heminger, 'Musical Devotions for Mixed Audiences: Printed Metrical Song in the Edwardian Reformation', in *Reformation*, 27: 1 (May 2022), 45–64.
Margo Hendricks, '"Obscured by dreams": Race, Empire, and Shakespeare's *A Midsummer Night's Dream*', in *Shakespeare Quarterly*, 47: 1 (1996), 37–60.
Margo Hendricks, *Race and Romance: Coloring the Past* (Chicago: University of Chicago Press, 2022).
Rebecca Herissone, *Music Theory in Seventeenth-Century England* (Oxford: Oxford University Press, 2000).
Rebecca Herissone, '"Fowle Originalls" and "Fayre Writeing": Reconsidering Purcell's Compositional Process', in *Journal of Musicology*, 13: 4 (2006), 569–619.
Rebecca Herissone, *Musical Creativity in Restoration England* (Cambridge: Cambridge University Press, 2013).
May Hofman, 'The Survival of Latin Sacred Music by English Composers 1485–1610' (DPhil diss., University of Oxford, 1977).
John Hollander, *The Untuning of the Sky: Ideas of Music in English Poetry 1500–1700* (Princeton, NJ: Princeton University Press, 1961).
Paul Hopwood, 'Polite Patriotism: The Edwardian Gentleman in English Music, 1904 to 1914', in *Nineteenth-century Music Review*, 16: 3 (2019), 383–416.
Meirion Hughes and Richard Stradling, *The English Musical Renaissance 1840–1940: Constructing a National Music* (Manchester: Manchester University Press, 2001).
David Humphreys, 'Why Did Tallis Compose the *Missa Puer Nobis Natus Est*?', in *Musical Times*, 157 (2016), 9–15.
Alice Hunt, *The Drama of Coronation: Medieval Ceremony in Early Modern England* (Cambridge: Cambridge University Press, 2008).
Katherine Hunt, 'The Art of Changes: Bell-Ringing, Anagrams, and the Culture of Combination in Seventeenth-Century England', in *Journal of Medieval and Early Modern Studies*, 48: 2 (2018), 387–412.
Katherine Hunt, 'What Did Didactic Literature Teach? Change-ringing Manuals, Printed Miscellanies, and Forms of Active Reading', in *Renaissance Studies*, 36: 5 (November 2022), 686–704.
David Huron, *Voice Leading: The Science behind a Musical Art* (Cambridge, MA: MIT Press, 2018).
Jenni Hyde, 'Mere Claptrap Jumble? Music and Tudor Cheap Print', in *Renaissance Studies*, 35: 2 (April 2021), 212–236.
Brian Hyer, 'Tonality', in Thomas Christensen (ed.), *The Cambridge Companion to Western Music Theory* (Cambridge: Cambridge University Press, 2002), 3–13.
John Irving, 'Thomas Tomkins' Copy of Thomas Morley's *A Plaine and Easie Introduction to Practicall Musicke*', in *Music & Letters*, 71: 4 (1990), 483–493.
Simon Jackson, 'Double Motion: Herbert and Seventeenth Century Polyphonic Practice', in *George Herbert Journal*, 37: 1–2 (Fall 2013–Spring 2014), 146–161.
Simon Jackson, *George Herbert and Early Modern Musical Culture* (Cambridge: Cambridge University Press, 2022).
Gerald D. Johnson, 'William Barley, Publisher and Seller of Books', in *The Library*, 11: 1 (1989), 10–46.
Ann Jones and Peter Stallybrass, *Renaissance Clothing and the Materials of Memory* (Cambridge: Cambridge University Press, 2001).
Emily Griffiths Jones, *Right Romance: Heroic Subjectivity and Elect Community in Seventeenth-Century England* (Philadelphia: University of Pennsylvania Press, 2019).
Cristle Collins Judd, 'Introduction: Analysing Early Music', in Cristle Collins Judd (ed.), *Tonal Structures in Early Music* (New York: Garland, 2000), 395–426.
Cristle Collins Judd, 'Music in Dialogue: Conversational, Literary, and Didactic Discourse about Music in the Renaissance', in *Journal of Music Theory*, 52: 1 (2008), 41–74.
Cristle Collins Judd, *Reading Renaissance Music Theory* (Cambridge: Cambridge University Press, 2006).

Ethan Matt Kavaler, *Renaissance Gothic* (New Haven, CT: Yale University Press, 2012).

Ethan Matt Kavaler, 'Ornament and Systems of Ordering in the Sixteenth-Century Netherlands', in *Renaissance Quarterly*, 72: 4 (2020), 1269–1325.

Matthew Kendrick, '"So strange in Quality": Perception, Realism and Commodification in *The Roaring Girl*', in *Criticism*, 60: 1 (2018), 99–121.

Neil Kenny, *Curiosity in Early Modern Europe: Word Histories* (Wiesbaden: Harassowitz, 1998).

Andy Kesson and Emma Smith (eds.), *The Elizabethan Top Ten: Defining Print Popularity in Early Modern England* (Farnham: Ashgate, 2013).

Hyun-Ah Kim, *The Praise of Musicke, 1586: An Edition with Commentary* (London: Routledge, 2017).

Marius Kozak, *Enacting Musical Time* (Oxford: Oxford University Press, 2020).

Gloria Kury, '"Glancing Surfaces": Hilliard, Armour and the Italian Model', in Lucy Gent (ed.), *Albion's Classicism: The Visual Arts in Britain 1550–1660* (London: Paul Mellon Centre, 1995), 395–426.

Sachiko Kusukawa, *Picturing the Book of Nature: Image, Text, and Argument in Sixteenth Century Human Anatomy and Medical Botany* (Chicago: University of Chicago Press, 2012).

Anne Lancashire, 'Dekker's Accession Pageant for James I', in *Early Theatre*, 12: 1 (2009), 39–50.

Katherine R. Larson, *The Matter of Song in Early Modern England: Texts in and of the Air* (Oxford: Oxford University Press, 2019).

Elizabeth Eva Leach, 'Gendering the Semitone, Sexing the Leading Tone: Fourteenth Century Music Theory and Directed Progression', in *Music Theory Spectrum*, 28 (2006), 1–21.

Elizabeth Eva Leach, 'Nature's Forge and Mechanical Production: Writing, Reading and Performing Song', in Mary Carruthers, (ed.), *Rhetoric beyond Words: Delight and Persuasion in the Arts of the Middle Ages* (Cambridge: Cambridge University Press, 2010), 72–95.

Annemie Leemans, '*A Very Proper Treatise*: Specialist Knowledge for a Non-Specialist Public', in *British Art Studies*, 17 (2020).

Hester Lees-Jeffries, *Textile Shakespeare* (Oxford: Oxford University Press, forthcoming).

Peter le Huray, *Music and the Reformation in England, 1549–1600* (Cambridge: Cambridge University Press, 1978).

Peter le Huray, 'Some Thoughts about Cantus Firmus Composition, and a Plea for Byrd's *Christus Resurgens*', in Alan Brown and Richard Turbet (eds.), *Byrd Studies 48* (Cambridge: Cambridge University Press, 1992), 1–23.

Anne Leonard (ed.), *Arabesque without End: Across Music and the Arts, from Faust to Shahrazad* (London: Routledge, 2022).

Joan Linton, *The Romance of the New World: Gender and the Literary Formations of English Colonialism* (Cambridge: Cambridge University Press, 1998).

Megan Kaes Long, 'Cadential Syntax and Tonal Expectation in Late Sixteenth-Century Homophony', in *Musical Theory Spectrum*, 40 (1) (2018), 52–83.

Megan Kaes Long, *Hearing Homophony: Tonal expectation at the Turn of the Seventeenth Century* (Oxford: Oxford University Press, 2020).

Megan Kaes Long, 'What Do Signatures Signify? The Curious Case of 17th-Century English Key', in *Journal of Music Theory*, 64: 2 (2020), 147–201.

Edward Lowinsky, *Tonality and Atonality in Sixteenth Century Music* (Berkeley: University of California Press, 1961; repr. New York: Da Capo Press, 1990).

Scott Lucas and Samantha Arten, '"Delyght in the holy songes of veritie": Mid-Tudor Scriptural Verse—Words, Music, and Reception', in *Reformation*, 27: 1 (May 2022), 1–3.

Lien Luu, *Immigrants and the Industries of London 1500–1700* (Aldershot: Ashgate, 2005).

Raphael Lyne, *Shakespeare, Rhetoric and Cognition* (Cambridge: Cambridge University Press, 2011).

Raphael Lyne, *Memory and Intertextuality in Renaissance Literature* (Cambridge: Cambridge University Press, 2016).

Harriet Lyon, *Memory and the Dissolution of the Monasteries in Early Modern England* (Cambridge: Cambridge University Press, 2021).

Ita MacCarthy, *Renaissance Keywords* (London: Legenda, 2013).

Rab MacGibbon, 'The Most Ingenious Master and His Well-Profiting Scholar: Brief Lives of Nicholas Hilliard and Isaac Oliver', in Catherine Macleod (ed.), *Elizabethan Treasures: Miniatures by Hilliard and Oliver* (London: National Portrait Gallery, 2019), 30–39.

Peter Mack and Edward Chaney (eds.), *England and the Continental Renaissance* (Woodbridge: Boydell Press, 1990).

Catherine Macleod, 'Isaac Oliver and the Essex Circle', in *British Art Studies*, 17 (2020).

Catharine MacLeod and Alexander Marr (eds.), 'Special Issue: Elizabethan and Jacobean Miniature Paintings in Context', *British Art Studies*, Issue 17 (September 2020).

Laurie Maguire, *The Rhetoric of the Page* (Oxford: Oxford University Press, 2020).

A. H. Mamoojee, 'Suavis and Dulcis: A Study of Ciceronian Usage', *Phoenix*, 35: 3 (1981), 220–236.

John Man, *The Gutenberg Revolution: The Story of a Genius and an Invention that Changed the World* (London: Review, 2002).

Alexander Marr, Raphaele Garrod, Jose Ramon Marcaida, and Richard Oosterhoff, *Logodaedalus: Word Histories of Ingenuity in Early Modern Europe* (Pittsburgh: University of Pittsburgh Press, 2018).

Christopher Marsh, *Music and Society in Early Modern England* (Cambridge: Cambridge University Press, 2010).

Christopher Marsh, 'Pipers, Fiddlers and the Musical Lives of the Majority', in Michael Fleming and Christopher Page (eds.), *Music and Instruments of the Elizabethan Age: The Eglantine Table* (Suffolk: Boydell & Brewer, 2021), 205–218.

Lucía Martínez Valdivia, 'Audiation: Listening to Writing', in *Modern Philology*, 119: 4 (May 2022), 555–579.

Lucía Martínez Valdivia, 'Miles Coverdale and the Englishing of Luther's Geistliche Lieder', in *Reformation*, 27: 1 (May 2022), 4–26.

Jeffrey Masten, *Queer Philologies: Sex, Language, and Affect in Shakespeare's Time* (Philadelphia: University of Pennsylvania Press, 2016).

David Mateer, 'The Compilation of the Gyffard Partbooks', in *Royal Musical Association Research Chronicle*, 26: 1 (1993), 19–43.

Kerry McCarthy, 'Evidence of Things Past', in *Journal of the Royal Musical Association*, 135 (2010), 405–411.

Kerry McCarthy, *Byrd* (Oxford: Oxford University Press, 2013).

Kerry McCarthy, 'Josquin in England: An Unexpected Sighting', in *Early Music*, 43: 3 (August 2015), 449–454.

Kerry McCarthy, 'Tallis' Epitaph Revisited', in *Early Music*, 47: 1 (February 2019), 57–64.

Kerry McCarthy, *Tallis* (Oxford: Oxford University Press, 2020).

Susan McClary, *Modal Subjectivities: Self-fashioning in the Italian Madrigal* (Berkeley: University of California Press, 2004).

Peter McCullogh, 'Music Reconciled to Preaching: A Jacobean Moment?', in Natalie Mears and Alec Ryrie (eds.), *Worship and the Parish Church in Early Modern Britain* (Farnham: Ashgate, 2013), 109–129.

Stefano Mengozzi, '"Clefless" Notation, Counterpoint and the *fa*-degree', in *Early Music*, 36: 1 (2008), 51–64.

Stefano Mengozzi, *The Renaissance Reform of Medieval Music Theory: Guido of Arezzo between Myth and History* (Cambridge: Cambridge University Press, 2010).

J. Hillis Miller, 'Ariachne's Broken Woof', in *The Georgia Review*, 31 (1977), 44–60.

John Milsom, 'A Tallis Fantasia', in *The Musical Times*, 126: 1713 (November 1985), 658–662.

John Milsom, 'Tallis First and Second Thoughts', in *Journal of the Royal Musical Association*, 113: 2 (1988), 203–220.
John Milsom, 'The Music in Staff Notation', in Michael Fleming and Christopher Page (eds.), *Music and Instruments of the Elizabethan Age: The Eglantine Table* (Suffolk: Boydell & Brewer, 2021), 69–100.
John Milsom, 'Songs and Society in Early Tudor London', in *Early Music History*, 16 (1997), 235–293.
John Milsom, 'The Table and the Music of the 1560s', in Michael Fleming and Christopher Page (eds.), *Music and Instruments of the Elizabethan Age: The Eglantine Table* (Suffolk: Boydell & Brewer, 2021), 191–204.
Sidney W. Mintz, *Sweetness and Power: The Place of Sugar in Modern History* (New York: Viking, 1985).
Craig Monson, 'Reading between the Lines: Catholic and Protestant Polemic in Elizabethan and Jacobean Sacred Music', in Jessie Ann Owens (ed.), *Noyses, Sounds and Sweet Aires: Music in Early Modern England* (Washington, DC, and London: Folger Shakespeare Library, 2006), 78–89.
Fabio Morabito, 'Musicology without Heroes', in *Music & Letters*, 102: 2 (May 2021), 347–361.
John Morehen, 'The Southwell Minster Tenor Part-book in the Library of St Michael's College, Tenbury (MS. 1382)', in *Music & Letters*, 50: 3 (1969), 352–364.
Emilie K. Murphy, 'Making Memories in Post-Reformation English Catholic Musical Miscellanies', in Alexandra Walsham, Bronwyn Wallace, Ceri Law, and Brian Cummings (eds.), *Memory and the English Reformation* (Cambridge: Cambridge University Press, 2020), 403–421.
Tessa Murray, *Thomas Morley: Elizabethan Music Publisher* (Woodbridge: Boydell & Brewer, 2013).
Yelda Nasifoglu, 'Reading by Drawing: The Changing Nature of Mathematical Diagrams in Seventeenth-Century England', in Philip Beeley, Yelda Nasifoglu, and Benjamin Wardhaugh (eds.), *Reading Mathematics in Early Modern Europe: Studies in the Production, Collection and Use of Mathematical Books* (London: Routledge, 2021), 62–101.
Mellie Naydenova, 'Public and Private: The Late Medieval Wall Paintings of Haddon Hall Chapel, Derbyshire', in *The Antiquaries Journal*, 86 (2006), 179–205.
Noémie Ndiaye, 'Read It for Restoratives: *Pericles* and the Romance of Whiteness', in *Early Theatre*, 26: 1 (2023), 11–27.
Noémie Ndiaye, *Scripts of Blackness: Early Modern Performance Culture and the Making of Race* (Philadelphia: University of Pennsylvania Press, 2022).
Noémie Ndiaye and Lia Markey, *Seeing Race before Race: Visual Culture and the Racial Matrix in the Premodern World* (Tempe: Arizona State University Press, 2023).
David Nott, 'The Cross Relation in English Choral Music from Tallis through Purcell' (unpublished PhD diss., University of Cincinnati, 1976).
Onyeka Nubia, *England's Other Countrymen: Black Tudor Society* (London: Zed Books, 2019).
Rebecca Olson, *Arras Hanging: The Textile That Determined Early Modern Literature and Drama* (Newark: University of Delaware Press, 2013).
Joseph Ortiz, *Broken Harmony: Shakespeare and the Politics of Music* (Ithaca, NY: Cornell University Press, 2011).
Ceri Owen, 'Making an English Voice: Performing National Identity during the English Musical Renaissance', in *Twentieth-century Music*, 13: 1 (2016), 77–107.
Jessie Ann Owens, 'Concepts of Pitch in English Music Theory c. 1540–1640', in Cristle Collins Judd (ed.), *Tonal Structures in Early Music* (New York: Garland, 2000), 183–246.
Jessie Ann Owens (ed.), *Composers at Work: The Craft of Musical Composition 1450–1600* (Oxford: Oxford University Press, 1997).
Christopher Page, *The Guitar in Tudor England* (Cambridge: Cambridge University Press, 2016).

Tara E. Pedersen, *Mermaids and the Production of Knowledge in Early Modern England* (London: Routledge, 2015).
Lionel Pike, *Hexachords in Late-Renaissance Music* (Aldershot: Ashgate, 1998).
Lionel Pike, 'The Ferial Version of Purcell's *I was glad*', in *Royal Musical Association Research Chronicle*, 35 (2002), 41–59.
Lionel Pike, *Pills to Purge Melancholy: The Evolution of the English Ballett* (Farnham: Ashgate, 2004).
Lionel Pike, 'Howells and Counterpoint', in Philip A. Cooke and David Maw (eds.), *The Music of Herbert Howells* (Woodbridge: Boydell & Brewer, 2008), 22–36.
Harold Powers, 'From Psalmody to Tonality', in Cristle Collins Judd (ed.), *Tonal Structures in Early Music* (London: Routledge, 1998), 275–340.
Beth Quitslund, *The Reformation in Rhyme: Sternhold, Hopkins and the English Metrical Psalter, 1547–1603* (Farnham: Ashgate, 2008).
Beth Quitslund, 'The Psalm Book', in *The Elizabethan Top Ten: Defining Print Popularity in Early Modern England* (Farnham: Ashgate, 2013), 203–211.
Beth Quitslund and Nicholas Temperley, *The Whole Book of Psalms, Collected into English Metre by Thomas Sternhold, John Hopkins, and Others: A Critical Edition of the Texts and Tunes* (Tempe: Arizona Center for Medieval and Renaissance Studies, 2018).
Mary Rambaran-Olm, M. Breann Leake, and Micah James Goodrich, 'Medieval Studies: The Stakes of the Field', in *postmedieval*, 11 (2020), 356–370.
Mary Rambaran-Olm and Erik Wade, 'The Many Myths of the Term "Anglo-Saxon"', in *Smithsonian Magazine* (14 July 2021).
Jennifer M. Rampling, 'The Elizabethan Mathematics of everything: John Dee's "Mathematicall Praeface" to Euclid's *Elements*', in *Journal of the British Society for the History of Mathematics*, 26: 3 (2011), 135–146.
Matthias Range, *Music and Ceremonial at British Coronations: From James I to Elizabeth II* (Cambridge: Cambridge University Press, 2012).
Matthias Range and Julia Craig-McFeely, 'Forty Years in the Wilderness: John Sadler of the Sadler Partbooks', in *Music & Letters*, 101: 4 (November 2020), 657–689.
Susan Rankin, '*Terribilis est locus iste*: The Pantheon in 609', in Mary Carruthers (ed.), *Rhetoric beyond Words: Delight and Persuasion in the Arts of the Middle Ages* (Cambridge: Cambridge University Press, 2010), 281–310.
Richard Rastall, 'Spatial Effects in English Instrumental Consort Music, c. 1560–1605', in *Early Music*, 25: 2 (1997), 268–290.
Barbara Ravelhofer, *The Early Stuart Masque: Dance, Costume and Music* (Oxford: Oxford University Press, 2006).
Steven Reale, 'The Calculus of Finite (Metric) Dissonances', in *Music Theory Spectrum*, 41: 1 (2019), 146–171.
Lynneth Miller Renberg, *Women, Dance and Parish Religion in England, 1300–1640* (Woodbridge: Boydell & Brewer, 2022).
Neil Rhodes, 'Punctuation as Rhetorical Notation? From Colon to Semicolon', in *Huntington Library Quarterly*, 82: 1 (Spring 2019), 87–100.
Neil Rhodes and Jonathan Sawday (eds.), *The Renaissance Computer: Knowledge Technology in the First Age of Print* (London: Routledge, 2000).
Jennifer Richards, *Voices and Books in the English Renaissance* (Oxford: Oxford University Press, 2019).
Jennifer Richards, 'The Voice of Anne Askew', in *Journal of the Northern Renaissance*, 9 (2017).
Jennifer Richards and Richard Wistreich, 'Introduction: Voicing Text 1500–1700', in *Huntington Library Quarterly*, 82: 1 (Spring 2019), 3–16.
Richard Robinson, '"A perfect-full harmonie": Pitch, Tuning and Instruments in the Elizabethan and Jacobean Mixed Consort', in *Early Music*, 47: 2 (May 2019), 199–223.
Mary Beth Rose, 'Women in Men's Clothing: Apparel and Social Stability in *The Roaring Girl*', in *English Literary* Renaissance, 14 (1984), 367–391.
Nicholas Routley, 'A Practical Guide to *Musica Ficta*', in *Early Music*, 13: 1 (1985), 59–72.

Alec Ryrie, *Being Protestant in Reformation Britain* (Oxford: Oxford University Press, 2013).
Alec Ryrie, 'The Liturgical Commemoration of the English Reformation, 1534–1625', in Alexandra Walsham, Bronwyn Wallace, Ceri Law, and Brian Cummings (eds.), *Memory and the English Reformation* (Cambridge: Cambridge University Press, 2020), 422–438.
Andrew Sabol (ed.), *Four Hundred Songs and Dances from Early Stuart Masque* (Providence, RI: Brown University Press, 1978).
Katelijne Schiltz, *Music and Riddle Culture in the Renaissance* (Cambridge: Cambridge University Press, 2015).
Sarah Schmalenberger, 'Hearing the Other in the *Masque of Blackness*', in Naomi Andre, Karen M. Bryan, and Eric Sayler (eds.), *Blackness in Opera* (Urbana: University of Illinois Press, 2012), 32–54.
Paul Seli, Evan F. Risko, Daniel Smilek, and Daniel L. Schacter, 'Mind-Wandering with and without Intention', in *Trends in Cognitive Sciences*, 20 (2016), 605–617.
Gitanjali Shahani, *Tasting Difference: Food, Race, and Cultural Encounters in Early Modern Literature* (Ithaca, NY: Cornell Unviersity Press, 2020).
Kevin Sharpe, *Reading Revolutions: The Politics of Early Modern Reading* (New Haven, CT: Yale University Press, 2000).
Tim Shephard, *Echoing Helicon: Music, Art and Identity in the Este Studioli, 1440–1530* (Oxford: Oxford University Press, 2014).
Tim Shephard, 'Musical Classicisms in Italy before the Madrigal', in *Music & Letters*, 101: 4 (November 2020), 690–712.
John Shepherd, 'Thomas Weelkes: A Biographical Caution', in *The Musical Quarterly*, 66: 4 (1980), 505–521.
Bill Sherman, *Used Books: Marking Readers in the English Renaissance* (Philadelphia: University of Pennsylvania Press, 2008).
Bill Sherman, 'The Beginning of "The End": Terminal Paratext and the Birth of Print Culture', in Helen Smith and Louise Wilson (eds.), *Renaissance Paratexts* (Cambridge: Cambridge University Press, 2011), 65–88.
H. Colin Slim, *A Gift of Madrigals and Motets* (Chicago: University of Chicago Press, 1972).
Anne Smith, *The Performance of Sixteenth-Century Music: Learning from the Theorists* (Oxford: Oxford University Press, 2011).
Bruce Smith, *The Acoustic World of Early Modern England: Attending to the O-Factor* (Chicago: Chicago University Press, 1999).
Bruce Smith, *The Key of Green: Passion and Perception in Renaissance Culture* (Chicago: University of Chicago Press, 2009).
Ian Smith, *Black Shakespeare: Reading and Misreading Race* (Cambridge: Cambridge University Press, 2022).
Jeremy Smith, *Verse and Voice in Byrd's Song Collections of 1588 and 1589* (Suffolk: Boydell Press, 2016).
Simon Smith, *Musical Response in the Early Modern Playhouse, 1603–1625* (Cambridge: Cambridge University Press, 2017).
Paul Spicer, *Herbert Howells* (Bridgend: Seren, 1998).
Harry Spillane, '"A Matter Newly Seene": The Bishops' Bible, Matthew Parker, and Elizabethan Antiquarianism', in *Reformation*, 27: 2 (2022), 107–124.
Ellen Spolsky, 'Literacy after Iconoclasm in the English Reformation', in *Journal of Medieval and Early Modern Studies*, 39: 2 (2009), 305–330.
Rachel Stenner, *The Typographic Imaginary in Early Modern English Literature* (London: Routledge, 2018).
Tiffany Stern, *Documents of Performance in Early Modern England* (Cambridge: Cambridge University Press, 2009).
Alan Stewart, *The Cradle King: A Life of James VI and I* (London: Chatto & Windus, 2003).

Louise Stewart, 'Social Status and Classicism in the Visual and Material Culture of the Sweet Banquet in Early Modern England', in *The Historical Journal*, 61: 4 (2018), 913–942.
Roy Strong, 'A Unique and Compelling Image', in Katherine Ara (ed.), *Nicholas Lanier (1588–1666): A Portrait Revealed* (London: Weiss Gallery, 2010), 29–38.
Jeremy Summerly, 'The English cadence', in *Leading Notes*, 6: 1 (1996), 7–9.
David Summers, *The Judgment of Sense: Renaissance Naturalism and the Rise of Aesthetics* (Cambridge: Cambridge University Press, 1987).
Elizabeth L. Swann, '"To dream to eat Books": Bibliophagy, Bees and Literary Taste in Early Modern Commonplace Culture', in Jason Scott-Warren and Andrew Zurcher (eds.), *Text, Food and the Early Modern Reader: Eating Words* (London: Routledge, 2018), 69–88.
Elizabeth L. Swann, '"Sweet above compare"? Disputing about Taste in *Venus and Adonis*, *Love's Labours Lost*, *Othello* and *Troilus and Cressida*', in Simon Smith (ed.), *Shakespeare/Sense* (London: Bloomsbury, 2020), 85–109.
Elizabeth L. Swann, *Taste and Knowledge in Early Modern England* (Cambridge: Cambridge University Press, 2020).
Daniel Swift, *Shakespeare's Common Prayers: The Book of Common Prayer and the Elizabethan Age* (Oxford: Oxford University Press, 2012).
Kian-Seng Teo, *Chromaticism in the English Madrigal* (New York: Garland, 1989).
Ayanna Thompson, *Passing Strange: Shakespeare, Race and Contemporary America* (Oxford: Oxford University Press, 2011).
Vera Tobin, *Elements of Surprise: Our Mental Limits and the Satisfactions of Plot* (Cambridge, MA: Harvard University Press, 2018).
Robert Toft, *Aural Images of Lost Traditions: Flats and Sharps in the Sixteenth Century* (Toronto: University of Toronto Press, 1992).
Robert Toft, *With Passionate Voice: Re-Creative Singing in 16th Century England and Italy* (Oxford: Oxford University Press, 2015).
Michael Trend, *The Music Makers: Heirs and Rebels of the English Musical Renaissance, Edward Elgar to Benjamin Britten* (London: Weidenfeld & Nicholson, 1985).
Whitney Trettien, 'Isabella Whitney's Slips: Textile Labor, Gendered Authorship, and the Early Modern Miscellany', in *Journal of Medieval and Early Modern Studies*, 45: 3 (September 2015), 505–521.
Scott Trudell, *Unwritten Poetry: Song, Performance and Media in Early Modern England* (Oxford: Oxford University Press, 2019).
Richard Turbet, 'Two Invisible Songs by Byrd', in *The Musical Times*, 158: 1938 (Spring 2017), 57–62.
Henry S. Turner, *The English Renaissance Stage: Geometry, Poetics, and the Practical Spatial Arts* (Oxford: Oxford University Press, 2006).
Dimitri Tymockzo, *The Geometry of Music* (Oxford: Oxford University Press, 2011).
Peter Urquhart, 'Cross Relations by Franco-Flemish Composers after Josquin', in *Tijdschrift van de Vereniging voor Nederlandse Muziekgeschiedenis*, 43: 1 (1993), 3–41.
Peter Urquhart, *Sound and Sense in Franco-Flemish Music of the Renaissance: Sharps, Flats and the Problem of 'Musica Ficta'* (Leuven: Peeters, 2021).
Kate van Orden, *Music, Authority and the Book in the First Century of Print* (Berkeley: University of California Press, 2013).
Kate van Orden, *Materialities: Books, Readers and the Chanson in Sixteenth-Century Europe* (Oxford: Oxford University Press, 2015).
Kate van Orden, 'Domestic Music', in Iain Fenlon and Richard Wistreich (eds.), *The Cambridge History of Sixteenth Century Music* (Cambridge: Cambridge University Press, 2019), 335–378.
Susan Vincent, *Dressing the Elite: Clothes in Early Modern England* (Oxford: Berg, 2003).
Jennie Votava, '"The Voice that will Drown All the City": Un-Gendering Noise in *The Roaring Girl*', in *Renaissance Drama*, 39: 1 (2011), 69–95.

Wendy Wall, *Recipes for Thought: Taste and Knowledge in the Early Modern Kitchen* (Philadelphia: University of Pennsylvania Press, 2015).
Sarah Wall-Randell, *The Immaterial Book: Reading and Romance in Early Modern England* (Ann Arbor: University of Michigan Press, 2013).
Peter Walls, *Music in the English Courtly Masque 1604–1640* (Oxford: Clarendon Press, 1996).
Alexandra Walsham, *The Reformation of the Landscape: Religion, Identity and Memory in Early Modern Britain and Ireland* (Oxford: Oxford University Press, 2011).
Alexandra Walsham, Brian Cummings, and Ceri Law, 'Introduction: Memory and the English Reformation', in Alexandra Walsham, Bronwen Wallace, Ceri Law, and Brian Cummings (eds.), *Memory and the English Reformation* (Cambridge: Cambridge University Press, 2020), 1–46.
Alexandra Walsham, Bronwyn Wallace, Ceri Law, and Brian Cummings (eds.), *Memory and the English Reformation* (Cambridge: Cambridge University Press, 2020).
Tessa Watt, *Cheap Print and Popular Piety 1550–1640* (Cambridge: Cambridge University Press, 1991).
Rob Wegman, 'From Maker to Composer: Improvisation and Musical Authorship in the Low Countries, 1450–1500', in *Journal of the American Musicological Society*, 49: 3 (1996), 409–479.
Rob Wegman, *The Crisis of Music in Early Modern Europe, 1470–1530* (London: Routledge, 2005).
Heather Weibe, '"Now and England": Britten's *Gloriana* and the "New Elizabethans"', in *Cambridge Opera Journal*, 17: 2 (2005), 141–172.
Heather Weibe, *Britten's Unquiet Pasts: Sound and Memory in Postwar Reconstruction* (Cambridge: Cambridge University Press, 2012).
Tiffany Jo Werth, *The Fabulous Dark Cloister: Romance in England after the Reformation* (Baltimore: Johns Hopkins University Press, 2011).
J. A. Westrup, 'Music', in Ernest Baker (ed.), *The Character of England* (Oxford: Clarendon Press, 1947), 397–407.
Robert S. Wienpahl, 'Modality, Monality and Tonality in the Sixteenth and Seventeenth Centuries', in *Music & Letters*, 52: 4 (1971), 407–417.
Robert S. Wienpahl, 'Modality, Monality and Tonality in the Sixteenth and Seventeenth Centuries II', in *Music & Letters*, 53: 1 (1972), 59–73.
Frans Wiering, 'Internal and External Views of the Modes', in Cristle Collins Judd (ed.), *Tonal Structures in Early Music* (New York: Garland, 1998), 87–107.
Peter Williams, *The Chromatic Fourth during Four Centuries of Music* (Oxford: Clarendon Press, 1997).
Magnus Williamson, 'Queen Mary I, Tallis' *O Sacrum convivium* and a Latin Litany', in *Early Music*, 44: 2 (2016), 251–270.
Magnus Williamson, 'Musica Ficta', in Colin Lawson and Robin Stowell (eds.), *The Cambridge Encyclopedia of Historical Performance in Music* (Cambridge: Cambridge University Press, 2018), 424–425.
Jonathan Willis, *Church Music and Protestantism in Post-Reformation England: Discourses, Sites and Identities* (Farnham: Ashgate, 2010).
Edward Wilson-Lee, 'Tables of the Mind', in Michael Fleming and Christopher Page (eds.), *Music and Instruments of the Elizabethan Age: The Eglantine Table* (Suffolk: Boydell & Brewer, 2021), 219–230.
Amanda Eubanks Winkler, *Music, Dance and Drama in Early Modern English Schools* (Cambridge: Cambridge University Press, 2020).
Richard Wistreich, 'Vocal Performance in the Seventeenth Century', in Colin Lawson and Robin Stowell (eds.), *The Cambridge History of Musical Performance* (Cambridge: Cambridge University Press, 2012), 398–420.
Jeremy Wood, 'Peter Oliver at the Court of Charles I: New Drawings and Documents', in *Master Drawings*, 36: 2 (Summer 1998), 123–153.

Jeremy Wood, 'Nicholas Lanier (1588–1666) and the Origins of Drawing Collecting in Stuart England', in C. Baker, C. Elam, and G. Warwick (eds.), *Collecting Prints & Drawings in Europe c. 1500–1750* (Aldershot: Ashgate, 2003), 85–121.

Jonathan Woolfson and Deborah Lush, 'Lambert Barnard in Chichester Cathedral: Ecclesiastical Politics and the Tudor Royal Image', in *The Antiquities Journal*, 87 (2007), 259–280.

Emily Zazulia, *Where Sight Meets Sound: The Poetics of Late-Medieval Music Writing* (Oxford: Oxford University Press, 2022).

Amelia Zurcher, *Seventeenth-Century English Romance: Allegory, Ethics and Politics* (New York: Palgrave Macmillan, 2007).

Index

For the benefit of digital users, indexed terms that span two pages (e.g., 52–53) may, on occasion, appear on only one of those pages.

Figures and examples are indicated by an italic *f* and *e* following the para ID.

Acheson, Katherine, 165–67
Andrewes, Lancelot, 246–49
Anna of Denmark, 142–43
Anonymous (*Bel-Vedere*, 1600), 93–94
Anonymous (*The Life of Sir Henry Unton*, 1596), 28–30, 173, 174*f*, 199–200, 201*f*
Arten, Samantha, 126–30, 167–68
Audiation, 191, 205–8, 209–10

Bacon, Francis
    Sylva Sylvarum, 146–47
Bank, Katie, 205–6
Barley, William, 21, 60–61, 243–44
Bathe, William
    A Briefe Introduction to the Skill of Song, 21, 126–27, 219, 236–37
Baxandall, Michael
    cognitive style, 21–22, 25, 173
    English *disegno*, 25, 222–24
Bennet, John, 60–80, 105–6, 110–11
    All cre'tures now, 60–61
    O Sweete Griefe, 59–60, 63*e*, 62–79
    Rest now Amphion, 59–60, 69*e*, 68–79
Berger, Karol, xvi–xvii, 214–16, 237–38
Blackwork embroidery, 175–78, 177*f*, 227–28
Blow, John, 235–36, 250, 251–52, 258
A Booke of In nomines & other solfainge songes, 48, 185, 192–207, 198*f*, 203*f*
    educational purpose, 196–207
Butler, Charles
    The English Grammar, 217–18
    The Feminine Monarchie, 165–66, 216–18
    Principles of Musick, 56, 212–18, 215*f*
Butler, Katherine, 183–84
Byrd, William
    Ave Verum Corpus, 119–20, 193–95
    Cantiones Sacrae (1575), 4–6, 44, 188, 227–28, 238–41, 247–49, 252
    Cantiones Sacrae (1591), 193

Compell the Hawke, 106
Of Gold All Burnished/Her Breath is More Sweet, 107
O Salutaris Hostia a6, 192–96, 203*f*, 205–8

Camden, William
    Britannia, 44, 228–31, 258–59
Campion, Thomas
    A New Way of Making Foure Parts in Counterpoint, 8–9, 20–21, 24, 48, 95–97, 96*f*, 143–44, 148–49, 151–52, 156–57, 159–67, 213–16, 217–19, 222–24, 236–38
Case, John
    The Praise of Musicke, 95, 244
Cawdrey, Robert
    A Table Alphabeticall, 79
Chapel Royal, 60–61, 114–15, 193, 226–27, 251–53, 255–56
Chichester Cathedral, 197–99
    organ loft, 246–47
Choristers
    education of, 184–85, 196–200, 207–11
Church of England, 9, 39–40, 44, 123–26, 186–87
Cockeram, Henry
    English Dictionarie, 57–59, 83–84
Cognitive Style (see Baxandall, Michael)
Comma (see Hart, John)
Cotgrave, Randle
    A Dictionarie of the French and English Tongues, 57–59, 176n.105, 224–25
Crooke, Helkiah
    Mikrokosmographia, 154–56

Dahlhaus, Carl, 125–26, 135n.61, 175
Davies, John
    Nosce teipsum, 1n.1, 53
Discord, xiii–xiv, 3n.6, 6, 8–11, 49, 59–60, 97–99, 98*f*, 260–65

Dissonance, xiii–xiv, 42–44, 56, 59–60, 81, 84–85, 97–99, 109–10, 137, 193, 221–22, 243–44, 258, 260–61
Dow Partbooks, 209, 252–53
Dowland, John, 20–21, 165–66
  A Musicall Banquet, 104–5
  First Booke of Aires, 199–200
  Lachrimae, 199–200
Draft, draught, 25–27, 35–36
Ductus, 22, 125–26, 157–58

E. K. (see Edmund Spenser), 80–81, 92–93, 97
Elizabeth I, 41, 60–61, 139–41, 144, 158–59, 208–9, 224–27, 228–31, 238–41, 252
English cadence, 147–48, 214–16, 221e, 220–24, 250–53
Englishness
  the medius part, 117–18
  natural harmony, 36–39, 41–45
  the two-flat key signature, 222–24
Evett, David, 173–78

Fa above La, 212–16
  Pha, 213–16, 217–19, 220–22, 232–35, 236–37
Faculty Psychology, 86–87
False Relation
  as archaic, 39–44, 236–38, 257, 258–59
  definitions, 4–9, 14
  as impelled by canon, 125–26, 135, 193–96, 206–7
  as punctuation, 120–21, 131
  as spice, 91–94
  as strange, 45–46, 97–99, 224–25, 226–28, 232–35, 237–38, 257
Farmer, John
  First Set of English Madrigals, 103–5, 108–9
Ficta, 17–18, 22–23, 84–85, 193–96
Florio, John (see de Montaigne, Michel)
Fumerton, Patricia, 112–14, 145–46

Gyffard Partbooks, 193–95

Hamond Partbooks, 164–65, 183, 185, 207–11
Hardwick Hall, 32f, 34f
  Bess of Hardwick, 222–24, 237–41
  Eglantine Table, 199–200, 202f
Hart, John
  Orthographie, 133–34
Henry VIII, 39, 226–27
Herissone, Rebecca (see Hexachord), 17–21, 22–24

Hexachord, 14, 15, 55–57, 130–31, 144, 152, 167–70, 213–16, 253
Hilliard, Nicholas
  Man Against a Background of Flames, 145–46
  Portrait of Elizabeth I with lute, 139–41, 144
Hobbes, Thomas
  Concept of fairyland, 253–54
Howells, Herbert, 40, 41–44, 257–58

James I and VI
  project to establish Great Britain, 59–60, 228–31, 255–56
Josquin, 6, 226–27
Junius, Franciscus
  drawing, 25–26
  Painting of the Ancients, 25
  sourness, 139–41

Lanier, Nicholas, 142nn.9–10
Lanyer, Aemilia, 84–85, 91–92, 226–27
Lineall Pictures (see draft)
Logos, 11, 19, 154–56, 216–17

Master of the Countess of Warwick
  Four Children Making Music, 29f, 35, 173
McCarthy, Kerry, 35, 193, 226–27
Medius, 116–18
Mengozzi, Stefano (see Hexachord), 21–22, 27–28, 36
Miscellanies, 185–87, 196, 205–6, 207
Montaigne, Michel
  Essays, 110
Morley, Thomas
  O Griefe E'en in the Bud, 62–68, 63e
  A Plaine and Easie Introduction to Practicall Music, 6, 20–21, 97–100, 163–66, 219, 221e, 232
  Round around about a Wood, 237–38
  on the two-flat key signature, 224
  MS 31390 (alias *A Booke of In Nomines*), 196–207, 198f, 203f, 238–41
Mulcaster, Richard
  Elementarie, 133–34, 188–89
  Positions, 56–57, 190–91, 252–53

Norden, John
  Labyrinth of Mens Life, 258–61
  Speculum Britanniae, 258–59

Oliver, Isaac
  Female Figure Making Music (c.1610), 137, 138f
Oliver, Peter, 137, 139–42, 147–48

Oliver *née* Harding, Elizabeth, 147–48
Ornament, xvi, 13–14, 59–60, 82–83, 95, 145–46, 159–64, 178, 232–35, 236–37, 241–42
Owens, Jessie Ann (see Hexachord), 18–21

Parataxis (see Dahlhaus, Carl and Evett, David)
Parker, Matthew, 38n.86, 102
de la Primaudaye, Pierre
   The French Academie, 152–54
Peacham, Henry
   The Compleat Gentleman, 59–60
   Graphice, 149–50
   Minerva Britanna, 261–65, 263*f*
Peerson, Martin
   Laboravi in Gemitu, 39n.88, 226–27
   Private Music (1620), 205–6
Prat, Jos
   Order of Orthographie, 133–34
Prynne, William, 56, 119–20
Puttenham, George
   The Arte of English Poesy, 68–79, 154–56

Quill, quilling, 154–63, 179–80

Ravenscroft, Thomas
   A Briefe Discourse of the True (but Neglected) Charat'ring of the Degrees, 60–61, 79, 100–1, 236–38
Recorde, Robert
   Pathway to Knowledge, 168–70
Reformation, xiv–xv, 36–40, 60, 118–26, 186–87, 227–28, 232–35, 237–38, 244, 247–49, 257–58, 264–65

Shakespeare, William, 1–3, 9–11, 82, 93–94, 200–4, 256
Sidney Herbert, Mary (Countess of Pembroke) 142n.9
Sidney Psalter, 103
Simpson, Charles
   Compendium of Practical Musick, 8–9, 24, 152
Solmization
   diagrams, 25–28, 128*f*, 129*f*, 164–68
Sourness, 9, 83, 139–41, 188–89
Spenser, Edmund
   The Faerie Queene, 41, 44, 228–31, 253–54
   The Shepheardes Calendar, 80–81, 97
Strange, 95–99, 169–70, 175–78, 190–91, 224–27, 232, 236–37
Sweetness
   as artifice, 82–84, 94, 110
   as B-flat, 79, 84–86, 94, 108

   in relation to music, 36–38, 55–57, 79–82, 84–86
   as sugar, 82–85, 88–89, 109–10

Table Book, 199–207
Tallis, Thomas
   Cantiones Sacrae, 4*e*, 44, 188, 227–28, 238–42, 247–49, 252
   O Lord in Thee is All I Trust, 199–200, 203*f*
   O Nata Lux, 4*e*, 81, 119–20
   O Sacrum Convivium, 240*e*, 197–242
   Spem in Alium, 238–41
Teerlinc, Levina, 242
Thame wall painting, 28–30, 139–41, 140*f*, 170–73, 171*f*, 179–80
Tomkins, Thomas
   Add. MS 29996, 108–9
   Almighty God, the Fountain of All Wisdom, 114–15, 135
   Musica Deo Sacra, 112, 118–19
   O Sing Unto the Lord a New Song, 112–19, 135
Tomkis, Thomas
   Lingua, 86–90, 102

Urquhart, Peter, xvi–xvii, 4–6, 17–18, 195

Vaughan Williams, Ralph, 40, 41–42, 257–58
Verdelot, Philippe, 226–27
Visual Culture, 4–6, 14, 143–50, 159–64, 178–80, 222–24
Visual Rhetoric, 165–67

Weelkes, Thomas
   Balletts and Madrigals (1608), 105–6, 108
   Hark all ye lovely saints above, 45–46, 247–49
   Madrigals to 3, 4, 5 & 6 Voyces, 101–3, 105–6
   Ninth Service, 232–35, 246–49
   O Lord Grant the King a Long Life, 232, 235*e*
   Sweet Love, I will no more abuse thee, 108
Whitney, Geoffrey, 261
Whole Booke of Psalmes, 60, 126–31, 128*f*, 129*f*, 167–69, 190–92
Wilbye, John
   I Live and Yet Methinks I do not Breathe, 55n.4, 226–27
   Sweet Hony-Sucking Bees, 62–68
Woodcock, Clement, 197–200
Wright, Thomas
   Passions of the Minde in Generall, 150–52, 159–63